book was published in 1914. The ads pictured here are from that issue, and those of 1918, 1922, and 1926.

Historical
Persons & Places . . .

Historical Persons & Places . . . In San Ramon Valley

A personalized, pictorial, social history of Alamo,

Danville, Diablo and San Ramon

by

Virgie V. Jones

Volume Two

Morris-Burt Press, Alamo, California, 1977

Published By

MORRIS-BURT PRESS
10 Gary Way
Alamo, California 94507

Printed in the United States of America
Pioneer Publishing Co., Fresno, California

Dedication

With love and deep affection to my family members:

My mother, Bertha Morris Boggini, whom I call Moms; without her I would not be.

My husband, Alfred Bensen Jones, whom I call Fritz.

Our son, Alfred Garrett Jones, whom we call Gary — and his daughter,

Our granddaughter, Jennifer Jones, to whom I dedicated my first book.

All of these loved ones understand what I have been trying to do to help preserve in words on paper the heritage of the San Ramon Valley—rapidly changing due to growth. In this book, I am trying to relate how it began, how it was, and how it is— by its persons and places.

Table of Contents

Author's Foreword

As promised on May 1, 1975 in the Epilogue of my first California history book, *Remembering Alamo...and Other Things Along the Way*, here is Volume Two. When I began Volume One, I knew that my first book could not include all the history of the San Ramon Valley. It would be impossible even to condense all the available material into one book. And, I might add, it will *not* be possible to include *all* in this book either. But I had promised you, my readers, that when I decided to write another book of the area, I would go southward from the town of Alamo, to try to capture interesting persons and places—in the history of the San Ramon Valley—and as we know it today. I will update to the present, where possible.

The San Ramon Valley we know today encompasses Alamo, Danville, Diablo, and San Ramon, all part of Contra Costa County, to the east of the Bay Area cities. This includes areas of Alamo Oaks, Green Valley, Sycamore, Tassajara, all part of the town of Danville. All this area remains unincorporated by the vote of its residents. (For the fourth time in twelve years, the residents voted against incorporation on November 2, 1976.)

Many persons and places will not be found in this book, as they were covered in Volume One, my *Remembering Alamo...and Other Things Along the Way*. Several early settlers of Alamo, who pioneered the area, and whose descendants still reside in the Valley, will not appear in detail in this book, but in capsule form.

History is made every day, and every day should be an event for someone or something. I will endeavor here to pick up where I left off in 1975 and try to help you relive some history with me.

This book could not have been accomplished without research and personal interviews with the people involved—and through them, with their ancestors. There is no way that a writer can ever "get caught up" with writing history. It doesn't wait, but continues on and on. This Volume Two of the history of a rapidly growing community will not be complete, but as is my manner in writing, I will attempt to get the facts and bring them up-to-date where possible.

The bicentennial year of 1976 made all of us aware of history. For some while I have been trying to do what Alex Haley accomplished for his family through his best-selling book *Roots*, that is, to encourage people to trace their roots and origins and share them. Now, since the record-breaking twelve-hour televised dramatization of *Roots* in January 1977, on eight consecutive nights, interest in such activity has been stimulated. In this, my second California history book, I am the chronicler of many other people's recollections, as well as my own.

I once read an interesting article stating that the book may be mankind's noblest creation. Its form has remained unchanged for over 2,000 years. The book teaches and entertains. Without several early cultures we possibly would be without books. The Chinese discovered paper to hold the printed words. The Phoenicians gave us our alphabet. Germany was responsible for movable type to make possible the printing. The Romans set the format of style and the United States of America became proficient in book production. With this in mind I invite you to read this book and enjoy it, as much as I did in collecting and assembling its material for you.

For more detailed reading, I suggest you read *Remembering Alamo...and Other Things Along the Way*, Morris-Burt Press, 10 Gary Way, Alamo, California 94507. Copyright 1975, ISBN 0-900890-1-2, Library of Congress Number 75-22667. Printed in the United States of America, Pioneer Publishing Company, Fresno, California.

The symbol (RA) in this volume indicates that more information on that subject may be found in Volume One, *Remembering Alamo...and Other Things Along the Way*.

Acknowledgements
and Credits

My personal family of mother, husband, son and granddaughter, to whom I dedicated this book, for their encouragement, patience, tolerance and guidance.

Trent Evans, commercial artist, who designed the dust jackets for both books.

Lou-Ann Styles, Danville artist, for her pen and ink drawings done especially for this book.

William R. Hockins, Alamo photographer, who took the dust jacket photo of Mount Diablo in July 1977, two weeks before the second worst fire in the history of the mountain. He captured "the troubled sky" from San Damiano Retreat.

Special thanks to many people, those I interviewed in person, by telephone and correspondence, who shared their family genealogies where available, family diaries, logs and date books, incidents and anecdotes. They know who they are and the Table of Contents lists some of them, to whom I am grateful. And sincere appreciation to those readers of my first book, *Remembering Alamo . . . and Other Things Along the Way*, who urged me to write this follow-up book to include all the San Ramon Valley, as we know it today.

History of Contra Costa County, W. A. Slocum & Company, San Franciso, California, 1882.

History of the State of California and Biographical Record of Coast Counties, California, by Professor J. M. Guinn, A.M., The Chapman Publishing Company, Chicago, Illinois, 1904.

History of Contra County County, edited by F.

J. Hulanski, The Elms Publishing Company, Inc., Berkeley, California, 1917.

Walnut Kernel, Walnut Creek weekly newspaper, 25th Anniversary Historical and Progress edition, Thursday, August 22, 1957.

Contra Costa Gazette, Martinez, California, centennial edition, Thursday, July 31, 1958.

Valley Pioneer, weekly newspaper, Danville, California, centennial edition, Thursday, September 4, 1958. Also news stories from other editions and columns of "I Cover Alamo and Miscellany" by Virgie V. Jones, from 1963 to 1970.

Colorful California Names—Their History and Meaning, compiled by Thomas P. Brown for American Trust Company, 1955, and Wells Fargo Bank, 1957.

The World Book Encyclopedia, Field Enterprises Educational Corporation, Chicago, Illinois, 1958.

Walnut Kernel yearbooks from San Ramon Valley Union High School, 1914, 1918, 1922, 1926, 1927, 1928, and 1929.

San Ramon Valley Historical Society, historical photographs from their collection.

Photographs and memorabilia from the author's personal collection, copies of which will be donated to the San Ramon Valley Historical Society's file-safe at San Ramon Valley Library, Danville, California.

Prologue

Those of us who research history know that in some of the references we must use, the length of a biographical sketch was often determined by how much money the subject of the sketch had paid to be included. It was a common practice to be solicited and pay proportionately for the amount of information printed. This is why so often you will not find some of our famous early pioneers and settlers in some books and you will find others covered by quite a lot of space. I do not write my books in this fashion. However, the practice still prevails and perhaps it is a wise author who follows this method. You can at least be sure of some payment for your efforts.

—•—

More and more, as I delve into research I find errors. It is generally thought that all legal documents as found in county seats are flawless and accurate. Not necessarily so! I have found errors in dates and many mistakes in spelling. It stands to reason that an entry is only as good as the person who enters it. Some people, even if you stand over them and spell a name, will automatically write down one that is more customary to them. I have often found errors in spelling. Some early day maps of areas up and down the state of California show many towns misspelled, at least as compared with spellings used today. I have seen Alamo spelled without its second "A." I have found one good source of research material to be alert eyewitnesses who lived the scenes as they happened. These I have used whenever possible and am thankful for their cooperation.

—•—

Call me what you will but, among other things, I admit I'm a romanticist! There are those unidentified portrait photos I carry with me on my speaking engagements to admonish my audience to label theirs. What a help the name, date, and place would be for all of us, now and later. Actually I've "fallen in love" with some of the people in pictures. As I research certain persons for long periods I seem to, through my thoughts, end up in their time. I find myself living their lives. Why yes, I've crossed the plains many times—through my research. I've become a part of many pioneer families.

I'm the kind of person who, if exposed to any accent long enough will come away with that accent. I'm sure psychologists have a word for it! But do I care—not at all. It is exhilarating to relive others' lives and actions and feel their anguish, turmoil, and hardship, as well as their accomplishments and moments of glory. This I have done and I hope I'm a better person for it.

—•—

In my research and interviews I have never used a tape recorder, and I probably never will! I was pleasantly amused when I heard the *Christian Science Monitor* editor say on the radio that he has never used a tape recorder either and he never will. In a personal interview I like just that, the personal-ness of it. Very often I can detect where the thrust of the interview is, by voice, facial expression or body language.

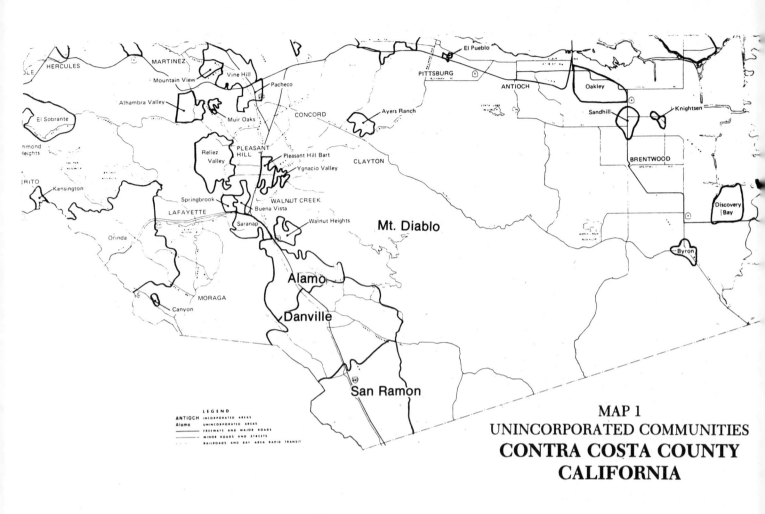

LEGEND
ANTIOCH INCORPORATED AREAS
Alamo UNINCORPORATED AREAS
FREEWAYS AND MAJOR ROADS
MINOR ROADS AND STREETS
RAILROADS AND BAY AREA RAPID TRANSIT

MAP 1
UNINCORPORATED COMMUNITIES
CONTRA COSTA COUNTY
CALIFORNIA

Majestic Mount Diablo oversees the San Ramon Valley. Left of center is Livorna Road, Alamo, going out to the valley. Photo taken in the 1930s from Las Trampas, looking due east. (Photo by Davies, courtesy of Margaret McCoy, Alamo)

Snowcapped Mount Diablo photographed from an unusual angle during the 1930s. (Photo by Davies, courtesy of Margaret McCoy, Alamo)

Chapter One
Geography and Topography —
Roads and Progress

In order to relive the history and go way back, you must remember there were no paved roads. Roads and their locations, as we now know them, are very different from the roads of the past, which in many cases were nonexistent.

Somewhere it is said that in the early days the road through the San Ramon Valley was known as Little El Camino Real. Many a Spanish padre and others traveled the route from Mission San Jose to Martinez.

The main street of Alamo, going right through town, Danville Boulevard, is now much as it was, in location. Stone Valley and Livorna Roads are the large arterial (off) streets going out into the developed valley.

The main street of Danville, however, was its very busy Front Street,[1] in the 1800s and (as many roads did then) it followed the natural flow of the San Ramon Creek to the east. Travel was arduous. Dirt roads were impassible during the rainy season with the slush and mud, and were crusty dry and dusty during the summer months. Travel time seemed endless, but because the area was undeveloped and virginal, it was tranquil and picturesque for miles upon miles.

Danville, from its beginning in 1858 to the turn of the century, had the following businesses. On Front Street were the Danville Hotel (1858-1873), a general store, Presbyterian Church and Danville Grammar school. What later became Hartz Avenue and the main street through town was a trail between the farms of Booth and Hartz. Prospect Avenue was called "Tiger Alley."[2] On Railroad Avenue were the Railroad Hotel, after 1891, and the Danville railroad station.

Between 1900 and 1930 Front Street progressed, as did Church Street. There was a Catholic Church; Olsson's Garage; a blacksmith shop; a plumbing shop; Close's general store with the IOOF Lodge on the second floor, adjoining the Close house and property and fronting what is now Diablo Road (then a county road); Clark's Harness Shop; the Presbyterian Church; and Grange Hall. On Hartz Avenue were the Danville Firehouse; a department store; San Ramon Valley Bank, Danville Branch; butcher shop; two houses; a dry goods store; and Medina's Shoe Shop. Across the street on Hartz Avenue were McDonald's drugstore; Danville Hotel (1927); Court House; Rose's Saloon (later Root's Restaurant); a house fronting Tiger Alley; and Groom's blacksmith shop. Going north from Tiger Alley (Prospect Avenue) were a lumberyard, a saloon, the telephone office, and a store on the corner. On Hartz Avenue were an express office, a poolroom and saloon, Elliott's Saloon Since 1907, a restaurant, a livery stable, Acree's Grocery, four houses, Root homes, a pear orchard, Danville Grammar school (now Community Center) and San Ramon Valley Union High School (1917). For more about many of these buildings and businesses, see Chapter Seven, *Places.*

In the next ten-year period, from 1930 to 1940, the additions were: the Howard Root house in the pear orchard, John Xavier's Shoes across Hartz Avenue from Austin Root's home, two houses, the Danville Firehouse next to Close's property on Hartz, a barber, a doctor, clothing shops, a grocery, the Bank of America, Monroe's barbershop, a butcher shop around the corner on Prospect, the Legion Hall, and two more houses. Rose's Saloon became a soda fountain and there were the harness shop, a gas station and garage, and McDonald's Drug Store had moved a block. There were Haskall's Hardware, Elliott's Saloon Since 1907, another saloon, Xavier's Shoes, the phone office, Acree's Grocery and the post office. Warehouses and a lumber yard were added to Railroad Avenue. "Progress" had begun!

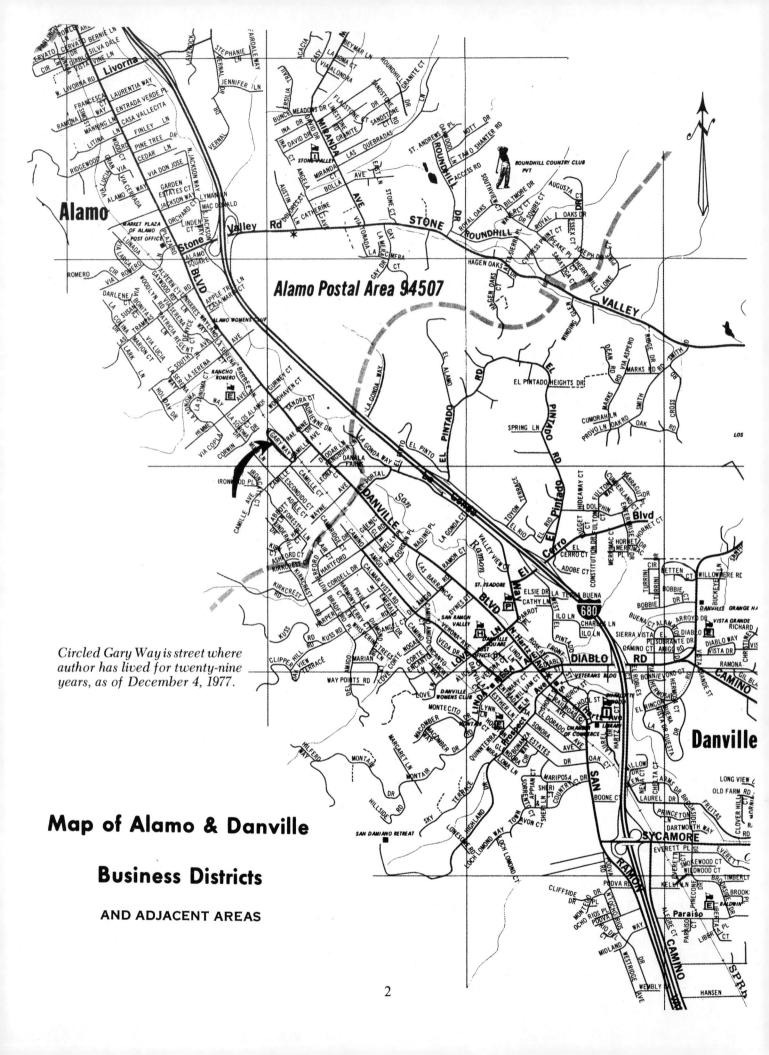

Map of Alamo & Danville

Business Districts

AND ADJACENT AREAS

Circled Gary Way is street where author has lived for twenty-nine years, as of December 4, 1977.

Alamo Postal Area 94507

2

On Front Street in Danville, left to right: Cohen's Store, Tiger Alley (now Prospect Avenue), Gibbons Harness Shop, Joe McCeil Barber Shop, Conway Store, Post Office with Library on second story, blacksmith shop, Close's Store, and IOOF Hall upstairs over store.

When I first visited Alamo and the San Ramon Valley, beginning in 1937, it was always enlightening to me, as we drove down "main street" (Highway 21, now Danville Boulevard, Hartz, etc.), to hear everyone call out, "Hi, Fritz!" (Fritz has been my husband's nickname since third grade.) It was refreshing and a bit startling to find that my Fritz was very popular—or that everyone knew everyone else in those days. How changed now, and how sad the change!

Roads: Old State Route 21

My thanks to Mark L. Kermit, Deputy Public Works Director, Transportation, who sent me the entire file concerning the naming of San Ramon Valley Boulevard—Hartz Avenue, etc., on August 7, 1975. His note to me said he hoped the information would serve as a basis for the research for my next book, and so it has!

The old road running from Martinez[3] to San Ramon[4] (approximately twenty miles) is apparently one of the oldest roads in Contra Costa[5] County. In Ordinance No. 56 passed by the Board of Supervisors on March 8, 1892, it was assigned Road Number 2 (in a list of 129 roads) and named "Contra Costa Highway." Its route was described as "Martinez to County line via Pacheco,[6] Walnut Creek[7] and San Ramon Valley."

A search of the records indicates that the Board of Supervisors, on December 13, 1948 passed a resolution which changed the names of various county roads and included "Danville Highway, Walnut Creek to Dublin to be changed to San Ramon Valley Highway."

These are the only two official actions of the Board pertaining to this road. It is now known by several names: *Pacheco Boulevard* from the south city limits of Martinez to State Sign Route 4 (Arnold Industrial Highway); *Contra Costa Highway* from State Sign Route 4 to Boyd Road; *North Main Street* from Boyd Road to the north city limits of Walnut Creek; *Danville Boulevard* from the south city limits of Walnut Creek to Linda Mesa; *Hartz Avenue*, both north and south, (named for John Hartz) from Linda Mesa to Railroad Avenue; *San Ramon Valley Boulevard* from Railroad Avenue to the Contra Costa-Alameda county line.

At the time of Ordinance No. 56, in 1892, the county was having "growing pains," and the document instructed unincorporated towns or villages to name their streets and to assign numbers with 100 numbers to the actual block or square. Designations were to be Alley, Avenue, Boulevard, Court, Park, Place, Plaza, Promenade,

Row, Square, Street or Terrace (no Way at that time). Numbers were to be the "Ten Block System of Numbering Country Houses." Odd numbers were to apply to the blocks on the left-hand side of the road, and even numbers to the right-hand side. Block numbers were to be displayed in figures not less than two inches or more than two-and-one-half inches in height, to be easily visible from the center of the road.

It is interesting to note the following at the end of the document: "Seal and Attest by F. L. Glass, Clerk; Chairman, J. M. Stow; The Ordinance was passed by the following vote, viz. Ayes: Supervisors Patrick Tormey, M. B. Ivory, J. C. Galindo and Chairman J. M. Stow; Noes: C. J. Clayton. Entered March 8, 1892, F. L. Glass, Clerk; By Elmer G. Cox, Deputy Clerk."

Also in the file which Mr. Kermit sent was a record of some discussion on September 25, 1969 to shorten San Ramon Valley Boulevard to San Ramon Road, which is the official name in Alameda[8] County. This of course was known as old State Route 21, which I often refer to as California Highway 21.

In another reference I noted that in January 1949 the San Ramon Valley Improvement Club, headed by President R. Biggs, objected to the widening of the Danville Highway because it would ruin its beauty. (As opponents, twenty-eight years later, still say today!)

BRIEFS

The following is from an old county history:

July 1873: Green Valley[9] and Mount Diablo[10] Summit road company incorporated for $5,000. Coach line for Diablo roads, one from Martinez through Pine Canyon, another from Hayward[11] through Green Valley. Will have the finest carriages and teams ever employed for coach passenger service on this coast. Fifty fine horses have been bought. Carriages to be built by the Kimball Company, especially designed for style, strength, lightness and elegance.

San Ramon Valley

As late as the early 1960s San Ramon Valley included Walnut Creek, which had been incorporated October 22, 1914, at a meeting in Justice Court in Walnut Creek. William J. Locke called the meeting to order. He was with the group of attorneys who conducted the legal proceedings.

Danville Shares Its Name

There are towns or cities called Danville in twenty-one states in the United States—Alabama, Arkansas, California, Florida, Georgia, Illinois, Indiana, Iowa, Kansas, Kentucky, Louisiana, Maine, Ohio, Missouri, New Hampshire, Pennsylvania, West Virginia, Tennessee, Virginia, Washington, and Vermont. To see how it happened, see the section about Daniel Inman in Chapter Two.

Businesses on Front Street, Danville, California, in early 1900s. This was original property purchased by Daniel Inman in 1858. Later purchased by James E. Close in 1875. This property is still owned by the Close descendants. Note Real Estate Business Agency - Money to Loan—this was Close's Grocery Store from 1910-1914. Upstairs was the IOOF Lodge until 1912. San Ramon Valley High School used the building from 1914-1917 for four classrooms until the new high school building was completed near Love Lane in 1917. (Photo courtesy of Dr. Wilson E. Close)

Subdivisions

When in downtown Danville a turnoff toward the mountain (east) on Diablo Road (some early history books refer to it as Mount Diablo Road) takes us out to more residential areas and directly into Diablo. Subdivisions really began in 1948. In Danville were Cameo Acres, Danville Estates, Montego, San Ramon Heights, Vista Grande and Montair, high on the hillside of Las Trampas range (west).

Tassajara Road

A drive out Diablo Road with a turn to the right on Camino Tassajara[12] eventually takes us out to open farm lands, rolling hills, and still virgin territory. Past Blackhawk Road on the left and Dougherty Road on the right (known as four corners) the drive becomes very peaceful, and after a time one begins to look for the next house. Lawrence Road goes through to Dublin. Further east we come to Finley Road to the left, which used to continue as a fire trail to Clayton, and Johnson Road to the right, which goes into Pleasanton directly or turns off into Livermore.

Some early settlers lived in very rustic homes of rough lumber. Often when they did rebuilding, the original lumber would be used from house to house. Other long-ago residents lived in two-story homes with high ceilings. Some of those early residents on Tassajara were: Flournoy, Chrisman, Isaac Russell (home now occupied by Andrew Anderson), Albert Sherburne, David Sherburne, and Charlie Wood (on "Woodside" site where George C. and Maevis Wood live). Others were the Eddy, Frank Matteson and Goold homes on Blackhawk, where an old road went to the Fairfield home (later a lake) and continued to where Bret Harte stayed. There was a tree named for him. Farther on were Munion, Felix G. Coats, Elliot, Zabel, McPherson, Alberg, Finley, Wilkes, and even farther were Thorup and Petersen. I recommend this drive. It is very peaceful and still rural.

San Ramon

After continuing through Danville along San Ramon Valley Boulevard (California Route 21—Highway 21) we come to large green pasture areas and we know we are approaching the town of San Ramon. The large open spaces are disappearing; in recent years the area has been developing rapidly.

Those Were The Days!

Talking with those over seventy years old who have made the San Ramon Valley their perma-

Mount Diablo with windmill. Taken in 1972 by Egon Pedersen.

nent home, and in some cases their only home, I found they experienced the following often with their parents, with fond memories:

Good food and good cooks and lots to eat. Dances were gala balls, going on all night, with a break for a midnight supper of fowl, ham, and beautiful baked foods, fruits, special preserves and many types of yummy pickles. Everything homemade. (No processed foods then!) During the Christmas holiday season, many balls would be held—masquerades among them—with lavish full costumes and removal of the masks at the strike of midnight—sometimes with surprises!

Ramona Park—Early Paladium

The following is from a newspaper clipping from *Contra Costa Standard*, dated April 19, 1906:

Posters are out for the opening of the beautiful, new Ramona Park at Danville, on April 26, [1906] Danville Lodge No. 378, Independent Order of Oddfellows and others have been invited from San Francisco, Alameda, and the rest of Contra Costa county and many have promised to attend. There will be speaking and an excellent entertainment.

A special train will leave San Francisco for Danville, at 8 o'clock on the morning of the 26th, stopping at intermediate points to take on board the merry picnickers, and returning the train will leave the grounds at 5 o'clock. A large crowd is assured, as the rate for the round trip will be one dollar!

Ramona Park has one of the finest dancing platforms in the State, which has just been put in. The managers, who are representative men of the San Ramon Valley, are about to dam the creek and place rowboats on the lake thus created. On the twelve acre tract a ballground is to be constructed and a tennis court. A cinder track for athletics and a shooting range are also planned.

5

Hartz Avenue, looking south from Prospect Avenue, Legion Hall corner, a tree-lined street with private residences. This photo was taken from a Beck postcard, postmarked November 16, 1911, to Miss Rose Wiedemann from Miss Mary Wiedemann.

No liquors are to be sold and it is always to be conducted on the temperance principles. This fact, together with the beautiful location of the park in a grove of maples and buckeye, is one to make it a popular resort and attract desirable people, thus advertising this beautiful part of the country.

Earthquake of 1906

The following is taken from the April 19, 1906, edition of the *Contra Costa Standard*, excerpted and edited.

April 19, 1906, at 5:15 A.M. a most severe earthquake hit the San Ramon Valley. Its duration was a full two minutes and was followed by aftershocks throughout the morning. Scarcely a chimney was left in the valley. There were no known serious injuries to persons. However, Miss Mollie McCauley broke a bone in her foot while getting downstairs.

The Danville Hotel on Railroad Avenue was seriously damaged and the Mountain View Hotel on Hartz Avenue lost its chimney. A schoolhouse and church lost their chimneys. The A. J. Young home had damage amounting to $500. C. G. Van Gorden's home had damage and Robert O. Baldwin and Charles Goold residences lost chimneys. J. P. Chrisman reported loss of a chimney, a water tank, much china, glasses and lamps. Mrs. J. Flournoy and Mrs. S. Flournoy also had similar breakage.

Mrs. George Wood of San Ramon had just arisen from her bed when the chimney crashed through the roof. Peter Thorup of San Ramon lost a chimney. Mrs. McCamly's house was damaged as well as others in the Valley.

Supervisor Districts

According to an old county history, five supervisor districts were named in April, 1873: 1. Martinez, Pinole, San Pablo, 400 votes; 2. Lafayette, Walnut Creek, Danville, 400 votes; 3. Pacheco, Concord, Bay Point and part of Black Diamond (Pittsburg), 300 votes; 4. Clayton, Nortonville, part of Black Diamond, 350 votes. 5. Antioch, Point of Timber, 390 votes.

In 1850 Nathaniel Jones, brother of Alamo's John M. Jones, was elected supervisor of Township 2. In 1865 Honorable David N. Sherburne was elected to the county Board of Supervisors and served many years, well into the late 1880s. He remained a bachelor and lived in Sycamore Valley, Danville. Sometime in the 1930s Oscar Olsson served the San Ramon Valley and we now have Eric Hasseltine of Danville in 1977.

Currently Contra Costa County Supervisors are: James Kenny, District One; Nancy Fahden, District Two; Robert Schroder, District Three; Warren Boggess, Chairman, District Four; and Eric Hasseltine, District Five which, among other areas, covers our San Ramon Valley. Eric and his wife Syma and their two children live on Camino Amigo in Danville. It is nice once again to have our supervisor living in San Ramon Valley.

Early Day Doctors Who Served The San Ramon Valley

Early day doctors, mostly general practitioners, serving the San Ramon Valley, as well as most of the county at the time, were Dr. Joseph Pearson[13] and Dr. Claude R. Leech[14] of Walnut Creek, who brought many babies into the world, several still Contra Costa residents. Dr. Raymond V. Burk practiced in Walnut Creek. Then came Dr. Arthur Huntington Beatty and Dr. Edward B. Radford, and they served the area well for many years. Dr. Ina Box was a practicing chiropractor in the Walnut Creek area.

In Danville there were Dr. Reimer, Dr. H. C. Gifford, Dr. A. V. Guntz, Dr. E. C. Love, Dr. W. D. Miner and Dr. Melvin Bolender. In 1934 Dr. John W. Blemer came to Danville. He still practices successfully in the area. (See Chapter Six) During his time Dr. Smith, Dr. Charles Woods and Dr. Muriel Boelter (all deceased) and Dr. Maurice J. Frost arrived. Dr. Frost moved to Castro Valley in 1951. In 1954 Dr. J. C. Forsyth arrived.

A 1977 San Ramon Valley telephone directory lists sixty-three physicians and surgeons, forty-two dentists, three optometrists, three chiropractors, and one podiatrist. In some of these categories there are probably more than the ones listed.

Back around the time of the San Francisco earthquake and fire (1906) a Dr. Victor John Vecki, a dentist, came to Danville. His office was at 169 Front Street (see Chapter Seven). I talked with some of his former patients and they said fillings Dr. Vecki had done still remain.

Dr. Fred Booth of Danville was an early-day veterinarian who traveled far and wide to administer to the needs of animals in the valley and the surrounding area as well. Sometimes house calls were a necessity in those days. Dr. Booth's wife, Teresa, was very talented. She sang and played the piano and I was told sometimes served as altar boy, as she knew her Latin well.

Another story told to me about Teresa Booth took place during World War I. The Catholic Church was raising money, so Rose (Bettencourt) Ferreira's mother made a quilt to be raffled. Teresa Booth won it. After Mrs. Bettencourt passed away, Mr. Bettencourt tried to buy it back, but Teresa would not sell it. However, she left instructions in her will that it be given to a sister, Mary Bettencourt, so it did return to the family.

Footnotes

1. I am told that many years ago Front Street was named Waterfront Street, later shortened to Front Street, as it has remained.

2. A few versions of how Tiger Alley got its name are: because it was narrow, like a tiger's stripe; that there was a "Blind Tiger Saloon" there; and that two men who owned property there were asked to give some land for a street and "fought like tigers!" as to which one gave the most land and how much. The identity of these two men has been long forgotten.

3. Martinez (Mahr-tee-nace). Named in honor of Ignacio Martinez, Mexican officer, commandant of the Presidio of San Francisco for several years.

4. San Ramon (Sahn Ray-mohn). The name was first given to the creek by a "Mayor domo" of Mission San Jose whose name was Ramon and "who had the care of some sheep there a long time ago."

5. Contra Costa (Cohn-tra Cohs-tah). Opposite coast. Originally applied to the entire shore of San Francisco opposite the Peninsula.

6. Pacheco (Pay-chay-coh). Named for Salvio Pacheco, a Mexican officer.

7. Walnut Creek. Taken from the creek which the Spanish, in 1810, named "El Arroyo de los Nogales," meaning "The Creek of the Walnuts."

8. Alameda. "Ah-lah-may-dah" is the old-time Spanish pronunciation but many now say "Al-a-me-da." An alameda is an avenue or boulevard shaded by trees. Derived from Alamo (Ah-lah-moh), poplar or cotton-wood. Alameda was first called Encinal (Ayn-see-nahl), oak grove.

9. Green Valley. Obvious. Named for its green belt appearance.

10. Mount Diablo (Dee-ah-bloh). Translates to Devil. The Spanish name was Monte del Diablo (Mountain of the Devil). Of the many legends about this mountain which resembles Vesuvius and which is used as "base and meridian" for surveys from Oregon to the Tehachapi and from the Pacific Ocean to the Nevada-Utah line, the most popular one, perhaps, is that recounted by General Mariano Guadalupe Vallejo. The theme of this legend is that an Indian tribe of Bolbones, fighting Spanish soldiers from San Francisco, had a medicine man called Puy or Pui (Evil Spirit) who appeared from the mountain caves to inspire them to victory.

11. Hayward. When Guillermo Castro, Grantee of Rancho San Lorenzo, laid out the town site in 1854, he named it for his friend, William Hayward, who had opened a hotel there in 1852.

12. Tassajara. (Tahs-sah-hah-rah) From Tasajera, a place where strings of beef or venison (jerky) are hung out in the sun to dry.

13. It is said that the oldest drug store in central California was located at Lafayette (Mount Diablo Boulevard) and Locust Avenue in Walnut Creek, opened by Dr. and Mrs. Joseph Pearson. Dr. Pearson died twenty-one years later, but his widow ran the establishment for over fifty years.

14. Mrs. C. R. Leech, an Oakland school teacher, heard the call of the Spanish-American War in 1898 when she was just a bride, and aroused enough interest to organize the Mount Diablo Chapter of the Red Cross in Walnut Creek. Volunteers from the San Ramon Valley and many parts of the county have given their time and effort over the years.

L. Stytes '75.

mt. Diablo

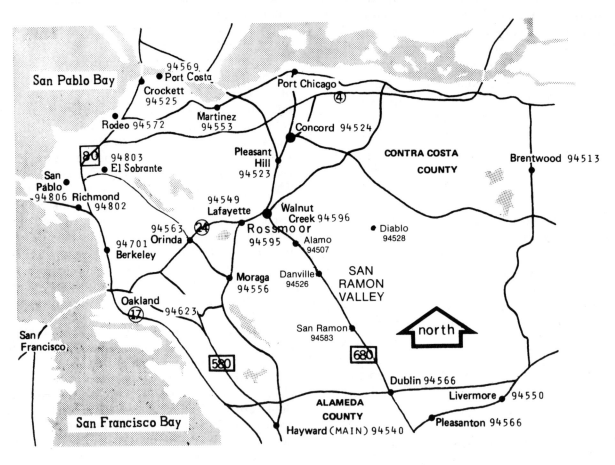

Map of Contra Costa County area with zip codes and road numbers, showing San Ramon Valley.   (Use of map by courtesy of Directory Sales Associates, Inc., Hayward, California)

POPULATION AND OTHER COMPARATIVE STATISTICS

The following information is excerpted from the Summary of 1975 Special Census Data for Unincorporated Communities.

Area	1970	1975	Percentage Change	Median Household Income 1970	1975	Median Years of Education 1970	1975	Average Household 1970	1975
Alamo	6,120	8,108*	32.5	$17,930	$24,123	13.5	16.0	3.5	3.3
Danville	16,218	18,885*	16.4	15,928	22,768	13.4	15.6	3.6	3.3
Diablo	794	1,036	30.5	16,905	25,690	13.5	16.0	3.8	3.6
San Ramon	4,884	12,749*	151.0	15,944	21,387	13.3	15.0	3.6	3.1

*More recent statistics showed population to be: Alamo 8,860, Danville 19,453, and San Ramon 12,782. No updated record shown for Diablo.

Chapter Two
Early Pioneers of San Ramon
Valley and Their Descendants

When I realized that I'd actually be doing another history book on the San Ramon Valley, I knew that part of it just had to be a chapter on those early settlers who had arrived in this lovely Valley before 1875. Their descendants still in the Valley qualify for having family status of at least 100 years here!

One history source lists those early pioneers of Contra Costa County who arrived October 10, 1846 as: James M. Allen, Elam Brown, S. W. Johnson, Leo Norris, J. D. Taber, John M. Jones, and his older brother Nathaniel Jones.

Among the early settlers to the town of Alamo were: John M. Jones,[1] 1851; David Glass, 1852; August Hemme, 1852; Silas Stone and his son Albert Ward Stone, 1853; Myron Ward Hall, 1857; Friederick Lorenz Humburg, 1863; John Baptiste Henry, 1868; and Vina (Bell) Cook, 1872. All of these and their family genealogies were included in my book, *Remembering Alamo . . . and Other Things Along the Way.* I will not repeat them here, but I do want you to remember them and some historical facts about them.

John M. Jones was Alamo's first postmaster and founded the only post office that served between Mission San Jose and Martinez for several years. That historic date was May 18, 1852. He served for nine years and the post office was in his two-story adobe home located on a knoll opposite the Alamo Market Plaza, now the site of the Alamo Safeway Store (1977).

August Hemme[2] was a philanthropist who was the owner of a large amount of land in the Alamo-Danville area. His large ranch in Alamo had a home of great splendor and was called Hemme Park (in part was where DanalaFarms area is now).

David Glass started and operated the first trading post in Alamo in 1852. He later bought large land holdings in San Ramon, where he built his home, which still remains and is in use.

Squire Silas Stone made the Overland trip to California in 1853 at the age of 61. His son, Colonel Albert Ward Stone, was captain of the wagon train and had also made the journey the year before. Stone Valley Road and Stone Valley School were named for the family. Many family members grew up in the area.

Myron Ward Hall in 1873 grafted, as an experiment, the first soft-shelled (English) walnuts in the area. The "Mother Tree" is still in Alamo and is identified with a plaque.

Friederick Lorenz Humburg[3] came from Kassell (Prussia)[4] Germany to Alamo, where he married Maria Kornmann of Zell-Romrod, Germany, on June 21, 1863.

John Baptiste Henry was born in France. He came to Alamo in 1868 and became the sixth postmaster.

Vina Cook, whose parents Henry and Emmrietta Latimer crossed the plains in 1846 and went to Oregon first, came to Alamo in 1872, when a child. She later married David Crockett Bell, who had a grocery store and was postmaster from 1905 to 1922. The Bell family was outstanding for its service as postmasters of Alamo for more than fifty-two years.

EARLY PIONEER WOMEN

In this day of women's liberation and the Equal Rights Amendment, when we research the history of those pioneers who crossed the plains, we can't accept that they were all men! No way.

You will note the photo of the early pioneers of San Ramon Valley—all are male, heads of their families. However, their wives played important roles, and in some cases had more duties and tasks than the men as they trekked across the country beside their husbands.

John M. Jones
(1822-1870)

Alamo Pioneers
1851

Mary Ann (Smith) Jones
"Grandma Jones"
(1825-1918)

On May 7, 1846, when at age twenty-four John M. Jones decided they would leave for California, his wife Mary Ann (Smith) Jones was just twenty-one years old. She had given birth to two daughters. Sarah Jane was just short of three years, and Candace was one year old, and Mary Ann was in early pregnancy with daughter Josephine, who was born January 24, 1847, In Chiles Valley, Napa County. It was Mary Ann Jones who drove the wagon much of the way across when her husband became ill.

Squire Silas Stone was sixty-one years old and his wife Susanna (Ward) Stone fifty-eight, when they trekked across the country in 1853, to Alamo, California. Their son, Colonel Albert Ward Stone, was thirty-two and his second wife Martha (Smith) Stone was twenty-four.

STONE—TWO JOHNS AND WILLIAM Z.

John Stone (RA) married Hannah Stratton, daughter of Elias and Millicent (Frost) Stratton, May 23, 1786. From their union they had twelve children: Millicent, Elizabeth, John, Hannah, Silas, Elias, Ebenezer, Abijah, Hannah, Sally, Amos, and Thirza.

John Stone, older brother of Silas Stone, married Matilda Bird (from an early Plymouth, Massachusetts family—her father John Bird was born in Berkshire county, Massachusetts in 1770 and he married Mary Kimball; their children were Matilda, Amanda, Almira, Lucinda, Sophia, John, Esther, Minerva, Joseph, and Mary). Children of John and Matilda Stone were Lucinda,

John B., Delia D., Almas E., Celestia Jenette, Esther A., Welcome G., Helen M., Bruce W., and George M.

William Z. Stone[5] was born March 4, 1829 at Fairview, Erie County, Pennsylvania, son of Silas and Susanna Ward Stone (RA) and younger brother of Albert Ward Stone (RA). When twenty years old he went westward, crossing the plains with his brother-in-law Reason Bell Willoughby (husband of Eleanor Thirza Stone) and John Keith. The threesome arrived in Sacramento on July 25, 1850. William Z. drove six yoke team of oxen. They settled in Sacramento and went into the cattle business, fattening stock for market.

William Z. and his younger brother Lysander, who had settled in Oregon in 1847, later came to the Valley with their brother-in-law, William Meek (husband of Sarah Stone). The three were engaged for a few months in trading with the miners.

In 1852, William Z. Stone became ill with the "chills and fever," which was common to the area, and returned east by the Isthmus on the steamer *Golden Gate* on her third voyage.

In Portage, Kalamazoo County, Michigan, January 11, 1853, William Z. married Esther Almira Stone, whose father, John Stone, was a brother of Silas Stone. That year they crossed the plains with ox teams and 100 head of cattle, stopping for a layover at Carson City, Nevada, as Esther was ill with mountain fever.

10

The William Z. Stone home in Danville. Built in 1885 it later became the home of the Spilker family. It is still standing and surrounded by condominiums, Danville Green.

They arrived in Green Valley, Contra Costa County in 1853 and purchased 410 acres on what later became Judge Cope's ranch. Stone immediately made improvements with buildings and an orchard of eighty acres. The remaining acreage was used for stock and grain.

In 1884 the Stones sold the property and bought 229 acres in the San Ramon Valley. They lived there until 1903, then sold out and went to San Jose to make a home for their son, Mark S., a nurseryman. Following the death of their son in 1904 they returned to Danville and bought a home. Their children were Sarah Jenette, Almas C., Esther M. (died in infancy), Mark S., Hugh B. (an engineer), and William E. Stone.

William Z. "Willie" Stone was a member of the Independent Order of Odd Fellows. He and his wife were both active in the Rebekah Lodge In San Ramon Valley.

This photograph of early pioneers of San Ramon Valley was taken at the Fourth of July picnic at Cox's Grove in 1890. Left to right are: Albert William Glass, John King, Milton Labaree, William Meese, Sr., Levi Alexander Maxcy, Edward McCauley, (head of unidentified man), Samuel Franklin Ramage, Lee Parker, Edward Shuey, Albert Ward Stone, Samuel Moore, Charles Gardner Goold, John P. Chrisman, Myron Ward Hall, David Glass, unidentified man and child, William Z. "Pap" Stone, Nathaniel Howard, Robert O. Baldwin, James O. Boone, William W. Cox, George McCamley, Elisha C. Harlan.

I never cease to marvel at research, and its differences of opinions, concerning this well-known photo. There are those who claim that this photo was taken at the Dedication of Danville Grange No. 85, on October 1, 1873, almost seventeen years' difference! However, to the best of my ability I have checked and rechecked and I accept the later date of 1890. Records show there were thirty charter members of Danville Grange, including some wives and daughters, but only five of them are included in the photo. My observation is that at the dedication ceremonies more of the members would have been photographed, as the Grange organization was a very popular one and its members were very active, as they still are today.

INMAN FAMILIES

The Inman family members are of English and Scotch origin and were identified with the South during the colonial period. Several participated in the Revolutionary War.

Shadrack Inman was born in 1800. A native of the south, he established his home on a plantation in Cocke County, in east Tennessee, where his two sons, Daniel and Andrew, and one daughter were born. In 1836 the family moved to Illinois, settling below Quincy on the Mississippi River. Shadrack Inman acquired 200 acres and engaged in farming and stock raising. He died at the age of seventy-eight; his wife Jane died at fifty-five. His mother, Peggy Wallace, a native of Scotland, lived to be 100 years old. She was a direct descendant of Sir William Wallace of Scotch fame.

Daniel Inman (RA) was born September 24, 1827, in Cocke County, Tennessee. When twenty-one, he went west to the call of gold, with his brother Andrew, two other young men, and four yoke of oxen to draw their wagon. On September 17, 1849 they arrived at Steep Hollow at Bear River. There they traded their cattle for mules and went with pack teams to the Yuba River to prospect with some success. That winter they went to Sacramento where Daniel built a canvas house and kept a hotel. High water washed out his property and caused him much illness. Following his recovery, he returned to the mines and headquartered at Hangtown. Then he went on to Georgetown and later, with his brother Andrew, to Nevada. He returned to California, spent the summer at Downieville, and struck a claim on Gold Hill at Grass Valley. From there he went to Middle Fork and then returned to Grass Valley to spend that winter.

In the fall of 1851 he located successful surface claims twelve miles below Auburn and remained there for two years, accumulating considerable wealth. In 1852 he arrived in Contra Costa County (Danville) and settled with his brother on a farm where they raised cattle and sheep. In 1854 he returned to the mines in Eldorado County and purchased a hydraulic mine.

He returned to the ranch in Danville in 1858. The 400 acres he owned formed the site of Danville. After the town began to grow from the small nucleus of businesses the townfolk wanted to call it Inmanville. At the time the town needed identity and postal service. The Inman brothers refused the honor, but in spite of their protest it was named Danville after Daniel Inman. (Another story says "Aunt Sallie" Young, Andrew's mother-in-law, named the town after her Kentucky home town. Descendants of the early pioneers favor the first story, and so do I!)

In 1863 Daniel and Andrew discontinued their partnership and divided their property. Aside from his farming and stock raising, Daniel operated a carriage house that he had taken in as settlement on a debt. Since he had learned the trade as a boy he had no problems.

On November 16, 1863 Daniel Inman married Josephine Jones (RA). She was born in Chiles Valley (Napa County) the third daughter of John M. and Mary Ann (Smith) Jones (RA) of Alamo. They had seven children: Jessie C., wife of H. P. Winniger, merchant, of Livermore (Alameda County); John L.; Mary L., wife of Charles M. Beck of Livermore; Anne, wife of Madison H. Beck, merchant, of Livermore; Daniel V., who died at seventeen; Josephine Linden, who went to San Francisco; and Edgar Percy.

In 1865 Daniel sold his land and shop and moved to Alameda County, where he bought 325 acres at $37.50 per acre. It had been used for raising wheat only, but he found that all other grains did well too. He purchased an additional 310 acres in 1869 in Livermore Valley, 90 acres in vineyards and the rest for farming and pastures.

For several years he was manager of the State Granger's Association with offices in San Francisco. When Livermore needed a hardware store in 1882, Daniel formed a corporation and put up $5,000 capital. Unfortunately the bookkeeper robbed the firm and the stockholders wanted to sell their shares. Inman met the large indebtedness. His generous disposition led him always to help those less fortunate—often they abused his kindness, but he never lost faith.

Politically Daniel Inman was a Democrat. In 1867-68 he served as a member of the Board of Supervisors. In the fall of 1868 he was elected to the State Legislature in spite of the fact that the district, at the time, was strongly Republican. His excellent record and integrity as supervisor swung many Republican votes his way. When the large railroad interests found him to be incorruptible they opposed his re-election (there were lobbyists then too!). He was defeated at the convention. In 1878-79 he was a member of the Constitutional Convention. He was a member of the blue lodge No. 218, F & AM at Livermore.

Daniel Inman died on October 29, 1908. He had celebrated his eighty-first birthday the month before. His large funeral was conducted by the Mason Lodge and was a Presbyterian service. He is buried in Livermore.

LEONARD EDDY

Leonard Eddy was born near Rochester, New York, January 15, 1828, the son of Daniel and Martha (Pellet) Eddy. In 1836 the family moved to Du Page County, Illinois. In young manhood Leonard located in Will County. In 1849 the call of the west beckoned and he crossed the plains and arrived at Coloma. That first winter he mined with some success near Dogtown. In 1850 he arrived in Contra Costa County. He acquired 160 acres of government land in the Sycamore Valley and later added a quarter section.

In 1854 he made a trip to Illinois, where on January 3, 1855, he married Mary A. Reed. She was born in Will County, Illinois, the daughter of Harvey and Cynthia (Kirkpatrick) Reed, who came to California with Eddy, by the Isthmus of Panama route. The Eddys settled in a little house he had built on the ranch at the foot of Mount Diablo. In 1860 he built a larger home and turned the first house into a granary. Improvements on his ranch included a family orchard. He continued his farming for many years. One large obstacle were the wild animals that came down from the mountain, but fortunately, Mr. Eddy was a good marksman.

Records at Martinez show that on February 15, 1871 Leonard Eddy homesteaded 160 acres, the southeast corner of section 25, on Blackhawk Road. In 1876 he purchased a ranch in the San Joaquin Valley. In 1885 he died near Martinez, while planting a vineyard of 100 acres. His widow remained in Danville. They had seven children, only four of whom grew to maturity, Mary C., Douglas, Harvey, and Lewis. Mary was the wife of William McCarley of Oakland; their two children were Lena and Lina. Douglas, a rancher of the area, married Emily Goold and had three children, Frank, Marcia, and Reed. At this writing Marcia is at a rest home near Sonora. Harvey, a rancher in Contra Costa County, married Addie Call. Lewis, also a county rancher, married Leonor Crow and had a daughter, Lola.

MENDENHALL FAMILIES

The name of Mendenhall is, according to family historians, a corruption of Mildenhall, derived from the residence of its first bearers at the Manor (as early as 1267 A.D.) or in the town, at Mildenhall in Wiltshire, England. In ancient records the name is also found to be Mendenhall, Mildhale, Mildenhale, and, in the contracted form, Minall. In America today the form of Mendenhall is used almost exclusively; the variant Mendinhall is found occasionally.

About the year 1683 three Mendenhall brothers, Benjamin, John and Moses, and one sister, Mary, came to America from England. Benjamin settled in Concord, Pennsylvania. (William M. "Philip" (RA) Mendenhall later of Danville, California, was a descendant from that line.) John also settled in Concord, Pennsylvania. Moses resided in Concord, Pennsylvania, where he secured a deed to 500 acres of land in Chester County, Pennsylvania from the William Penn Colonization Group. He later returned to England and remained there. In 1685 Mary Mendenhall married Nathaniel Newlin of Mountmelick, county of Tyrone, Ireland, who had emigrated with his father to America.

MARTIN, WILLIAM AND WILLIAM M.

Martin and Stephen Mendenhall were brothers. Martin laid out the town of Jamestown, Ohio, and had a large family. His second son William was born in 1794. William married Sarah Peterson and had nine children: William M., Elizabeth, Deliliah, Abigail, Martin, Absolom, Sardina, Martha, and Mary.

William M. Mendenahll (RA), often known as Philip, was born in Greene County, Ohio, April 22, 1823; married Mary Adelaide Allen, daughter of David and Elizabeth (Storey) Allen, April 18, 1847, and they had ten children: James Monroe born October 5, 1850, married Emma Shaw, 1874 in Pleasanton, California. Sarah Elizabeth, born March 18, 1852, married Curtis Lindley, 1872, in San Francisco, she died January 28, 1925. Emma Ann born January 1, 1854, married James M. Black 1876 in San Francisco. Luella Dora born April 5, 1855, married October 3, 1883 to George Washington Langan, in Oakland, Calif. David Archer born February 17, 1857 married June 24, 1903 to Edna Comstock, in Palo Alto, California. William Wallace born March 20, 1859, died January 7, 1925 and did not marry. Oswalt V. born August 9, 1862, married 1891 to Alma Jackson in San Francisco. He died in 1921. Effie born July 4, 1864, died about 1867. Asa V. born August 1, 1866, married 1904 to Florence Hatch in Oakland. He died in 1931. Etta born 1868, married 1895 to Fred Corrick in Oakland.

The following is a copy of a letter from Wm. M. "Philip" Mendenhall, written sometime in 1906, taken from the History Correspondence and Pedigrees of the Mendenhalls of England, the United States and Africa "relative to their common origin and ancestry methodically arranged and elucidated, after many years of diligent inquiry and research by Wm. Mendenhall, of Bath, England. Extended by the addition of authentic documents, and the compilation of tables of pedigrees of the American family by his son Edward Mendenhall of Cincinnati, Ohio. Until the year 1864 continued and revised by Thomas A. Mendenhall of Greenville, Ohio A.D. 1912."

I do not know to what part of Indiana my father's brothers moved to, and I do not know if any of the descendants are living. My grandfather's brother's name was Stephen, and he lived at Jamestown, O., with a large family when I was a small boy. Douglas Mendenhall's address is at Napa City, Cal.; Mrs. Dod Church at Oakland, Cal., and Earnest at Livermore, Cal.; these are my brother Absolom's children. My son James lives at Pleasanton, Cal. My brother Martin had three girls, Mrs. Clara Carey and Mrs. Julia Allen of Livermore, Cal., and Dora Brock, of Santa Clara, Cal.

John Mendenhall of the John line, moved to Indiana from North Carolina long before I was born; Rush Mendenhall, his son, died in Portland, Ore., about two years ago (1904). My grandfather laid out the town of Jamestown, O. I am satisfied we belong to the Benjamin line as I have heard my father and grandfather talk about it when I was a small boy. My grandfather moved to Ohio from Tennessee with his brother Stephen in 1803. My father moved from Ohio to Michigan in 1831, where I lived until 1845, when in July I started from there to California, leaving Independence, Mo., on Aug. 17th, with pack horse and saddle; there were ten in our party, and after many hardships and privations, we reached the American River in California on Christmas night of the same year. Was married to Mary Allen (RA) (who crossed the plains in 1846) on Apr. 18th 1847, by a justice of the peace in the Santa Clara Mission, Cal. I was the first Mendenhall to cross the Rocky Mountains; served under the Bear Flag; was volunteer while the Mexican war lasted. I have 9 children living: James, in the furniture business, Curtis H. Lindley, mining lawyer, James N. Block, insurance man, George W. Langan, attorney at law, David Archer, dry goods merchant, Palo Alto, Cal. William Wallace, business man, Big Pine, Cal., Oswald, county office at San Francisco, Cal., Asa V., attorney at law, Oakland, Cal. Mrs. Fred A. Carrick, manufacturer's agent.

I laid out the town of Livermore, Alameda Co., Cal., on the S.P. Railroad in 1869 and opened the Menden-hall Mineral Springs, ten miles east of Livermore in 1880. I think I am the oldest pioneer and the last one of the Bear Flag Party; as far as I know the rest are dead; brought father and mother and family here in 1853; all are dead now; father was 79 and mother 84 years when they died; have one great grandchild; my wife died Mar. 25th, 1903: she was 72 years old. I am making my home with my son-in-law, Geo. W. Langan.

Find out the name of the Mendenhall who made the first American flag and raised it on his man-of-war and which flag was adopted. Send me his name and the name of the ship. (See Capt. Thomas Mendenhall.) Very sincerely yours, Wm. M. Mendenhall, Oakland, Cal.

My thanks to Mayor William F. Mendenhall of Signal Hill, for his cooperation in supplying me with materials. Another known relative living in California is Captain Ferdinand Mendenhall, USN (Ret.) of Van Nuys, editor of the *Valley News*. Mendenhalls, all Quakers, are cross-connected with several other families, among them Mills, Milhous, Nixon and Hoover. Nixons are forebears of Richard Milhous Nixon, thirty-seventh president of the United States.

THE HOWARD FAMILY
AND MARY RIDGWAY LICHENS

Mary Ridgway Lichens is a direct living descendant of the sea-faring Howards. Her grandfather arrived in Contra Costa County in 1856. It seemed fitting that I interview her, and so I did, on two occasions. We chatted of many things.

The sea captain Nat Howard was her great-grandfather. Following the wars of 1812, a British gunboat fired at his merchant ship, and British sailors boarded it and tried to force him to pilot his boat where they wanted to go. He stood steadfast, but had quite an exciting experience, and almost lost his life. He was married to Sarah Elizabeth Jenne (later changed to Jenny). She was French.

His son, Nathaniel Samson Howard, was born January 19, 1819, in Wareham, Plymouth County, Massachusetts. He was the son of Nathaniel "Nat" and Mary (Briggs) Howard. He was educated at common school and when quite young followed in his father's footsteps and served at sea. After his schooling he apprenticed to the carpenter's trade at Fairhaven, Bristol County. On May 30, 1844 he married Elizabeth Sarah (Hitch) of Fairhaven, Massachusetts.

Nathaniel had a younger brother Charles who preceded him to California, lured by gold. August

1, 1849 Nathaniel and a company of men purchased the ship *Florida* for $40,000, including its cargo. They sailed around the Horn to San Francisco, arriving January 1, 1850, where they sold the cargo for $60,000 profit. Then they mined at Solomon's Gulch on the Merced River. Experiencing poor health, Nathaniel came to Contra Costa County and purchased 160 acres in the Alamo area known as White Gate. There he built his attractive two-story New England-style home, which is still standing and in use.

Nathaniel S. and Elizabeth Sarah (Hitch) Howard had three daughters: Lizzie Augusta, who was born August 1853 in San Francisco, became Mrs. William Quinn Smith; Amelia Stoddard, born February 24, 1855 in San Francisco, became Mrs. Frazer Ridgway; Kate Frances, born at White Gate eleven years later, became Mrs. Charles Joseph Wood.

Besides having a building business, Nathaniel S. Howard was appointed roadmaster and rode over to supervise construction of Fish Ranch Road on his champagne-colored mare.

Amelia and Kate Howard graduated from State Normal at San Jose and both were teachers. Amelia taught at two different times at Tassajara School, at Alamo School when there were eighty students, and also in Plumas County. Kate taught in Contra Costa County at several different schools.

Amelia married Frazer Ridgway, a graduate of the University of Kansas at Lawrence. He was an excellent accountant. His family was originally from Virginia and later Kentucky. They freed their slaves following the Civil War and moved to Kansas. The Frazer family in Scotland was knighted.

Frazer and Amelia Ridgway had two daughters. Mary Alexander (named for General Alexander, who was Lord Sterling of Scotland, for whom Alexandria was named) was born May 8, 1890 in Walnut Creek. She was almost born in the state of Oregon, but her mother returned to California in time. Her sister, Ruth Howard, was born in 1893 and died in June, 1970 at Sebastopol. The Ridgway family lived on the southwest corner of Mount Diablo Boulevard and Main Street in Walnut Creek (the present site of Great Western Savings). Their property was one-third of the entire block with a huge frontage and depth. (What a prize as business property today!) Mary Ridgway attended Walnut Grammar School, which was near where Simon Hardware is now.

Transportation from Walnut Creek to Concord was so bad she started high school in San Mateo and lived with relatives. Later she went to Mount Diablo High School in Concord and sometimes took the Southern Pacific train.

Mary Ridgway won a contest in 1911, becoming queen of the first festival in Walnut Creek. It was a harvest festival, and later became the popular Walnut Festival. She said it was a popularity contest, pure and simple—no bathing suits to pose in and no talent necessary! Other contestants were Gertrude Walker of Sulphur Spring Ranch, now Heather Farms, and Sybil Brown of the Elam Brown family of Lafayette. As runners-up, they were her maids of honor.

She first worked in the Danville Branch of the San Ramon Valley Bank for several months, and then worked for approximately thirty years for the Walnut Creek bank. When Joseph L. Silveira founded the San Ramon Valley Bank in Walnut Creek, the only other available "houses for money" were at Martinez or Oakland. She remembers the president and acting manager Alvinza Hayward Cope, and Numa S. Boone, James C. Jones, Robert O. Baldwin, Arthur Burton, and William K. Cole, who was with Anglo California Trust Company, Winfield S. Burpee, S. P. Borges and many others (see Chapter Seven). She drove herself to work every day by horse and buggy. It was a small bank and Mary grew up with it.

On February 6, 1944, at the Wood Ranch in Danville, Mary Ridgway ~~Howard~~ married Charles Edward Lichens, who was called Carl. He was a licensed building contractor and built homes and the Walnut Creek bridge. He had worked at American Bridge Company and for W. A. Bechtel Company, as supervisor of construction.

Mary was the first City Clerk of Walnut Creek and after she left the bank she also had her real estate broker's license. The newlywed Lichens moved to Sebastopol to live in 1944 and farmed and owned a dairy business until the early 1960s. They made many visits to the Danville-Walnut Creek area over the years, and of course to Woodside. She and her sister Ruth, who never married, began to sell their Walnut Creek properties about 1960. Ruth had moved to Sebastopol to live with Mary and Carl. Carl had passed away January 11, 1958, and Mary continued to manage the dairy ranch for three and one-half years. Between 1961 and 1973 she bought two other homes in Sebastopol, moving into the larger one first and then the smaller one. She continued to drive her own car until 1973.

She spoke of several people she remembered well. Among them was a Dr. Joseph Pearson, who was a Civil War doctor in Walnut Creek. He was married to Sarah J. from England. She studied under her husband and passed her state examination, and was a licensed pharmacist. For years Mary's sister Ruth had Mrs. Pearson's license among her memorabilia. Mary also remembered the two Isabelles of Walnut Creek, Isabelle Spencer Brubaker and Isabelle Crosby McGeehan.

Since 1973 Mary Ridgway Lichens has been a resident of Tamarack Manor in Danville, California.

"Woodside." The house was built for William M. "Phillip" Mendenhall in 1853. It became the residence of Charles Wood, Sr. in 1862 and a part of it is still standing on the property of George C. and Maevis Wood in Sycamore Valley, Danville. The cupola on the roof housed a water storage tank. (Courtesy of Vivian Coats Edmonston)

WOOD FAMILIES
"Woodside Farm"—Sycamore Valley

Charles Wood, Sr. (RA) (1830-1907) was born in Concord, Massachusetts, October 10, 1830. His great-grandfather, Ephriam Wood, was a judge before and during the Revolutionary War. His great-great-grandfather, Colonel Barrett, was in command of the American patriots at Concord in April of 1775, when the War of Independence broke out.

At the age of seventeen, Charles went to Michigan and worked four years as a clerk for the Michigan Central Railroad Company. In 1852 he traveled to California via the Nicaragua route, arriving in San Francisco in March of 1852.

Gold-fever-stricken, he went to Nevada and Sierra Counties, but failed to strike. That autumn, with his brother William, he went into the pack-train trade on the North Yuba River, then a lucrative business as no wagon roads had been built from Marysville to the mines. In 1855 he moved to Marysville and enlarged his merchant business. In April 1857 he married Miss Cynthia A. Rice, sister of Dr. D. W. Rice of Marysville and San Francisco, a leading physician and pioneer. The wedding was in Marysville.

They had four children, William Louis, Sarah Elizabeth, Charlotte and Charles. In 1862 the Wood family moved to Sycamore Valley where Charles acquired 700 acres and went into farming. Charles Wood was very active in public life. He served four years as Justice of the Peace, four years as Notary Public, appointed by Governor Booth, and was a member of the State Assembly for the term of 1875-76. He was a charter member

The Wood family. Left to right: David H. Wood, Maevis B. (Mrs. George C.) Wood, Donald C. Wood, Bernice (Mrs. Howard) Wood, George C. Wood, Charlotte E. "Lottie" Wood, Charles J. Wood, Howard C. Wood, May Batchelder (Maevis' mother), Merle (Mrs. Waldo E.) Wood, Bill Batchelder (Maevis' brother), and Leone Martin, family friend. Photo taken in September 1949 by Waldo E. Wood.

16

of Danville Grange No. 85. On a Monday morning, May 20, 1907, Charles Wood died at his Sycamore Valley home, "Woodside," which had been built in 1853 for William M. "Phillip" Mendenhall (RA), an early pioneer.

WILLIAM LOUIS WOOD

William Louis Wood was born March 8, 1858. He engaged in farming in Sycamore Valley, but soon moved to the vicinity of Davis, California, where he farmed on land now occupied by the University of California. June 15, 1900 he married Bertha Gaddis, daughter of William Henry Gaddis and Anna Campbell. They later moved to Berkeley, California. He died January 2, 1929 at age seventy. She died February 11, 1959 at age ninety-two. Their children were: Henry Charles, born May 10, 1901, married July 1, 1934; Everett Louis, born October 21, 1902, married November 9, 1940, died June 9, 1973; and Helen Bertha, born February 1, 1904, married September 5, 1925, died August 19, 1975.

SARAH ELIZABETH "LIBBY" WOOD

Sarah Elizabeth "Libby" Wood, was born November 10, 1859. She never married. She lived all her life at "Woodside Farm" in Sycamore

Miss Charlotte Elmire "Lottie" Wood
(1864-1961)

Valley. She studied painting and photography and assisted in many farm jobs, and died January 13, 1924, at the age of sixty-five.

CHARLOTTE ELMIRE "LOTTIE" WOOD

Charlotte Elmire "Lottie" Wood was born January 10, 1864. She never married. She earned her teaching credential in 1890 and taught for thirty-one years at the Sycamore Grammar School, which was about a half mile from her home. She retired in 1921 from public school teaching and did private tutoring for several years at the Blackhawk Ranch. She remained active until her death, April 12, 1961, at age 97. The Charlotte Wood School in Danville was named in her honor.

CHARLES JOSEPH WOOD

Charles Joseph Wood was born November 9, 1868 at the farm in Sycamore Valley. He attended the Sycamore School and lived on the home farm all of his life. In 1891 he and his sisters assumed the heavy debt owed on the farm and began operating the place under the name of Wood & Company. This continued until October 1, 1944, when his son George C. and wife Maevis began farming the place.

Charles was married October 24, 1897, to Kate Frances Howard, daughter of Nathaniel S. Howard and Elizabeth Sarah Hitch. She was born February 28, 1866, and died on April 28, 1945. Charles was a successful farmer, and took active part in community affairs. He was a member of Danville Grange, the Odd Fellows Lodge and Farm Bureau. He was one of those who helped organize the San Ramon Valley Union High School in 1910. He died November 10, 1949, at age eighty-one. He and his wife had three sons, all born on the farm in Sycamore Valley. They were Howard Charles, George Clifford, and Waldo Emerson.

HOWARD CHARLES WOOD

Howard Charles Wood was born February 10, 1900, attended Sycamore Grammar School, graduating in 1913, and graduated from San Ramon Valley Union High School in 1917. He worked on a county survey crew for the first concrete paved highway from Martinez to the county line near Dublin. In the fall of 1918, he entered the University of California, College of Civil Engineering, where he enlisted in the Student Army Training Corps. He received his B.S. degree in 1923 and was elected to Phi Beta Kappa. After graduation he worked for the American Bridge Company on the design and construction of the first Carquinez

Bridge at Crockett. About 1925 he went to work for the Great Western Power Company on the construction of the penstock pipeline from Bucks Lake and the powerhouse at Storrie on the Feather River. In 1928 he began work for the Bridge Department of the California State Highway Commission at Sacramento. In 1931 he was transferred to the San Francisco office, to assist in the design and construction of the San Francisco-Oakland Bay Bridge. Upon completion of that job, he returned to Sacramento and was appointed Superintendent of Bay Bridges. Later he moved to Berkeley and had charge of several bridges including Dumbarton, San Mateo, Carquinez and Antioch.

On July 20, 1929, Howard Wood married Bernice Donnelly, daughter of Daniel Webster Donnelly and Carrie Dell Terry. She was born September 27, 1900. Due to ill health, he took an early retirement in 1962, and moved to Rossmoor in Walnut Creek. The Woods traveled widely around the world. He died February 19, 1972 at Walnut Creek, California. They had no children.

GEORGE CLIFFORD WOOD

George Clifford Wood was born July 28, 1901, at Woodside Farm. He attended Sycamore Grammar School, graduating in June 1914. There were about fifteen students in the school, including the three graduates, George, Vivian Coats (now Mrs. Charles Edmonston) and Claude Andreasen. George entered San Ramon Valley Union High School in the fall of 1914. Most of the time he rode horseback the four miles to school, but occasionally rode in a horsedrawn buggy, when the weather was bad. There were thirteen in his class and four teachers in the school. In 1917 the family bought a new car and George then drove the 1911 Chalmers to school. The first three years the high school was at the old Odd Fellows Hall at the corner of Diablo Road and Front Street. He graduated in 1918 at the newly finished high school building at the present site, in a class of thirteen. He entered the University of California College of Agriculture that fall. He graduated in May, 1922 with a B.S. degree. His major was agronomy and he took courses in animal husbandry. He returned to the farm to help pay off the heavy debt. During the summer of 1926 he attended the Yosemite School of Field Natural History, conducted by Dr. H. C. Bryant and Carl P. Russell, Park Naturalist.

On August 13, 1930 George married Maevis Clare Batchelder, daughter of Courtney Carroll Batchelder and May Bates, at Danville, California. She was born October 3, 1900, in Aspen, Colorado. They built a small house on land he owned near the Wood home farm. During the depression years he took supplemental jobs, including collecting and preparing exhibits for the State Fair, job printing, and insurance. He passed the Civil Service Examination for land bank appraiser in 1935. During the late thirties he worked as a Range Examiner for the Agricultural Adjustment Administration.

In November 1944, George decided to return full time to the home farm, bought the livestock and equipment, rented a total of 1200 acres, and began operating the farm, raising cattle, sheep, hogs, poultry, hay and grain. He retired October 15, 1966, and his son Donald began operating the farm.

George and Maevis Wood continue to live at the Wood Ranch with its 114-year history. He has been a 4-H leader, for fifteen years served on the Contra Costa County Agricultural Stabilization and Conservation Committee (1955-71), has been a member of Danville Grange since February 1923, was active in establishing Mount Diablo as a state park in 1930, and was a charter member of the San Ramon Valley Historical Society for which he has served as treasurer since 1970. Children of the George Woods are David Howard and Donald Charles.

DAVID HOWARD WOOD

David Howard Wood was born August 4, 1931, in Berkeley, California. He attended Danville Grammar school and graduated from San Ramon Valley Union High School in 1949. He obtained his B.S. degree in Metallurgy in 1954 from the University of California. During vacations he worked at Bethlehem Steel, South San Francisco, and at General Metals in Oakland. He served two years in the Army in Maryland. Until August 1958 he was employed by the Battelle Memorial Institute in Columbus, Ohio.

David Howard Wood was married August 9, 1958, to Elizabeth Baker, daughter of Royal Frank Baker and Verna Nugen of Beckley, West Virginia. In the fall of 1958 they came to California, where David was employed by the Lawrence Livermore Laboratory, where he remains. They have two children, Charles Baker Wood, born November 22, 1959, and Thomas Clifford Wood, born February 4, 1963. The family makes its home in Livermore.

DONALD CHARLES WOOD

Donald Charles Wood was born August 14, 1935, in Berkeley, attended Danville Grammar School and graduated in 1953 from San Ramon Valley High School. Graduated from University of California at Davis, with a B.S. in Agricultural Production and a commission in the U.S. Army as a Second Lieutenant in 1957. While at Davis he was a member of the Sigma Alpha Epsilon Fraternity, Alpha Zeta (Honorary Agricultural Fraternity), Blue Key, and Sword & Sandals (honorary service organizations). Following graduation he worked on the home ranch. He later trained at Fort Benning, Georgia and completed active duty at Fort Ord, California. He spent a total of six and a half years in the active reserve, leaving with the rank of captain.

On October 12, 1958 Donald Wood married Marianne Weber, daughter of Ralph Lehman Weber and Orabel Turrentine Weber. She was born April 7, 1937 in Oakland, California. They lived in Danville until 1961 when they moved a house from Alamo and re-established it on the ranch property on Camino Tassajara. They have two children in local schools, James Donald, born September 3, 1961 and Cynthia Lynn, born September 26, 1963. Don worked on the family ranch except for 1960, when he sold real estate in Danville. In November 1966 he took over the entire ranching operation.

WALDO EMERSON WOOD

Waldo Emerson Wood (named for Ralph Waldo Emerson, friend of the Wood family while in Concord, Massachusetts) was born May 25, 1903. He attended Sycamore Valley Grammar School under tutorship of Charlotte Wood, his aunt, from 1911 to 1917. He graduated in 1918 with a class of two, and entered the then-new San Ramon Valley Union High School that fall. He graduated in 1921. There were only two in the graduating class, Waldo E. Wood and Evelyn Woodward. Total school enrollment was forty students. Waldo spent one year on the family ranch. He entered the University of California in the fall of 1922, and left it temporarily in June 1923. He took a leave of absence to make a three-month (August-October) voyage with his brother George to South America via the Panama Canal, Rio de Janeiro, Santos, Buenos Aires and across the pampas to Mendoza, Argentina, returning by the same route. (They were among twelve passengers on the Dollar Line's *S.S. President Harrison*. Space was available at the last minute due to the death of President Harding). He spent the remainder of the year on the family farm.

Waldo attended the University of California at Berkeley and Davis, majoring in Forestry, Range Management and Animal Husbandry, and graduating in the fall of 1928. During his college career he held several teaching Fellowships, joined the Alpha Gamma Rho Fraternity, and was awarded memberships in Alpha Zeta, Phi Sigma, Xi Sigma Pi and Sigma Xi honor societies.

He had temporary employment the summers of 1926 and 1927 with the U.S. Forest Service on Range Survey and Appraisal projects. Following Civil Service examinations, he took permanent employment September 1, 1928 on the Lassen Forest, Susanville, California. Other assignments have been: Assistant District Ranger, Hat Creek, Lassen Forest, 1929; Ranger Coppervale District, Westwood, Lassen Forest, 1930-35; Range and Wildlife Staff Supervisor's Office, Quincy, Plumas Forest 1935-41; Chief Range Analysis and Plans Section, California Region, San Francisco, 1941-64, including several details to the Washington, D.C. office of U.S.F.S.

Waldo Wood was married on June 14, 1941 to Merle Annabelle McLennan of Sacramento, California. In December 1941 they moved to Oakland and in 1948 to Piedmont. Merle was employed by the Oakland Public Schools as Supervisor of Child Welfare and Attendance, and was Attendance Area Administrator at her retirement. Waldo and Merle retired in January 1964 and make their home in Alamo, California. They had no children.

On February 4, 1956 they left on a trip around the world which lasted until September of that year. In January 1964, following their retirement, they made another European trip accompanied by Waldo's brother Howard and his wife Bernice. They were abroad thirteen months, bringing with them the first VW station wagon (Variant S) to California. Waldo has taken many photographs over the years.

Back in California, they purchased a house in Town and Country, Danville, for a short stay, then moved to Rossmoor for one and one-half years. They now live on Cervato Circle, Alamo, keeping busy with their household, garden, and community affairs.

CHARLES WOOD FAMILY HISTORY
by Charlotte "Lottie" Wood (1957)

Mr. Leonard Eddy was a first pioneer to locate

19

Charlotte "Lottie" Wood

they returned home that evening they found some of the neighbors at Woodside Farm with beds made up on the dining room floor. But no one slept!

Charlotte "Lottie" Wood passed away at the age of ninety-seven, April 12, 1961, in an Oakland Hospital. Services were held April 15 at San Ramon Valley Chapel with the Reverends Orville L. Shick and H. W. Van Delinder officiating. Internment was at Alamo Cemetery. She was born in the family home, "Woodside." She attended the old Sycamore School (1874-1882) and taught there for thirty-one years (1890-1921). Charlotte Wood Grammar School is named in her honor. She was an eighty-year member of Danville Grange. She authored several books of poetry, which she published herself. The following are examples of her talent.

EASTER GREETING
On Butterfly's Wing
Sweet Greetings
I bring
With the Birds and the Blossoms
That Herald the Spring
May sunshine and gladness
And Blessings galore
Bring Good Health and Happiness
To your Easter tide door.

OUR DANVILLE
By Charlotte Wood

To our olden-time Danville and the years long passed
  by,
We would turn in true reverence, with fond memory
  and tender sigh,
For those brave, sturdy builders of the pioneer days
Are with us no longer save in history's maze.

They came filled with vigor, with enthusiasm and
  cheer
Buoyed with hope, inspiration--never daunted by fear;
Through their wisdom, their courage, their labor and
  zeal
We, of today, have gained from their hard-earned
  weal.

Stalwart men, they, like the patriarchs of old,
Who had ventured far West in their long quest for
  gold,
Or to seek for new homes in contentment and peace
With their loved ones to dwell, where joys ne'er cease.

What spot more enchanting, more inviting, more fine,
Than this beautiful valley rich in verdure and vine?

in 1850 on the land now owned by the Wood family. He later moved up the valley. In 1853 Mr. and Mrs. William M. "Philip" Mendenhall, (RA) built the residence known as Woodside. The lumber was shipped "round-the-Horn." The marriage of Mr. and Mrs. Mendenhall was the first performed in San Jose. Mendenhall was one of an early party who crossed the plains from Michigan on horseback and accompanied General Fremont on his trip to Mexico City during the Mexican War.

In 1862 Charles and Cynthia Wood (RA) with son Louis, four years old and daughter Elizabeth, three moved by horse and wagon from Marysville to what was named "Woodside Farm." Mr. and Mrs. John McEwen had been living there for some time previous. Mr. McEwen was sheriff of Contra Costa County in 1863-64.

In 1864 Charlotte (Lottie) was born to Charles and Cynthia Wood. In 1868, son Charles was born, totaling four children. 1868 was a memorable year; October 28 was the big earthquake. Lottie's mother said the branches of the old oak swept the earth with its force; the stone milk house was wrecked, plaster ripped from the walls and ceilings, chimneys turned halfway around. The quake evidently came from east to west skimming the milk in the milk house of the then large dairy. Father (Charles J. Wood) and sister Libbie were in San Francisco that morning. When

20

Wild oats waving gently in the soft western breeze,
The brooks' winding course outlined by its myriad
    trees;

Gnarled oaks' spreading branches offering generous
    shade,
The vine-covered creek banks like deep everglades,
While anon in the distance, hid in snug leafy bower,
Peal the sweet warbling notes of the twilight hour.

The hill-slopes near by with golden poppies aglow--
Wild paint-brush, brodeia, baby-blue eyes, and so
To this primeval valley, Mt. Diablo its guard,
Came these pioneer people in Nature's garden, un-
    marred.

Daniel Inman came first, in the famed days of old,
And with his brother Andrew, built a smithy we're told-
A smithy not far from the one that now stands
On the western portion of the town's shifting sands.

From this same Daniel Inman the name "Danville's"
    derived
Early annals report, though other claims thrived;
Saying that to "Aunt Sally Young" that honor was due
A pioneer mother who to Danville, Kentucky, proved
    true.

Soon store-keepers many appeared on the scene,
And in our town, Danville, good business was keen;
The Cohens, the Conways, the Clarks and the Closes,
And doctors moved in with the queer bitter doses.
A school house near town in year '58
Was replaced by a new one,--'65 was the date--
But later as pupils more numerous grew
'Twas found best to locate for much better view,
Then a large one was built on a beautiful site
Where views of our mountain every heart could delight.
Wide-awake Danville said it never would do
To be out of date with school methods new,
So the town hired a High School,--not big or ornate,--
'Twas the house where the Handleys then held their
    estate,
From there the poor school moved to Odd Fellows'
    Hall,
But again 'twas too noisy, too awkward, too small.
Hence a change must be made to keep up with the
    times
And the one you now see had the proper designs.

A hall for the Grangers came in year '73,
And another where Odd Fellows met, happy and free,
Great improvements were made in each year passing
    by
But sad changes withal, borne with courageous sigh.

A stately white Church with its classical spire
Was the pride of the village until tragedy dire
Left naught but gray ashes of the landmark so dear,
Erected long since, in "Centennial Year".
In remembrance sweet it will live in each heart
For its loyal good works did rich blessings impart.

Many Churches and Clubs have come on apace bring-
    ing new interests, new shops, new duties to face.
Now we'll enjoy the new beauty with the colorful trees
    which add to the comfort and the fragrance of each
    wanton breeze.
Then All Hail to Our Danville on this "Centennial
    Year"!
May a wealth of rich blessings crown each twelve-
    month so dear
And Peace reign triumphant; Peace and Good Cheer!

In 1957 Miss Charlotte "Lottie" Wood jotted down the following list of "Visitors to Woodside:"

Dr. De Witt C. Rice (mother's brother) from New York state.

Mark Birmington (mother's brother-in-law) from New York state.

William Wood (father's brother) from Concord, Massachusetts.

In 1852, Charles Wood from Concord, Massachusetts. In 1854, Cynthia Avery Rice from Middlefield, New York, married in Marysville, California April 26, 1857.

In 1854, Lydia Kate Mitchell, from Canojoharie, N.Y. married De Witt Rice in N.Y. Mother came to California with this bridal couple in 1854.

In 1855 Charlotte (Rice) Birmingham (mother's sister from N.Y. and wife of Mark Birmingham.) Came to live with us in 1895. Died February 20, 1897.

In 1855 George Wood (father's brother) from Concord, Massachusetts. Came to live with us in 1902. Died March 25, 1915.

In 1855 Frank Rice (mother's cousin). Died 1873.

In 1855 Joseph Rice (mother's youngest brother) who married Louisa Kinney (who was born in the Sandwich Islands in 1848) in 1869. Joseph died two years later, 1871.

LEVI ALEXANDER MAXCY

Levi Alexander Maxcy was born January 12, 1827, on a farm at the edge of North Attleboro, Massachusetts. He was the sone of Henry and Ruth French Maxcy. Henry was the great-grandson of the first Maxcy to arrive in America, Alexander Maxcy, who came from Scotland about 1659. Alexander died in North Attleboro in 1721. Levi was the tenth child of a family of eleven. It is presumed he attended local schools and later learned the carpenter trade. (Some of his tools are still in the possession of his step-granddaughter Vivian Coats Edmonston of San Francisco.)

The first part of 1849, he with eighty-five other men formed a company, the Narragansett Trading & Mining Company, in Providence, Rhode Island. They purchased a ship, the *Velasco*, stocked it with provisions for two years and sailed around the Horn. The group sold the ship in Chile, to be turned over to the new owners in San Francisco. This no doubt was done, but all hands deserted and went to the mines and probably the ship rotted in the harbor as so many did at that time. Levi went to the mines but was not very successful. He then arrived in Tassajara Valley, Contra Costa County, and settled on a ranch on the Little Alamo Creek, six miles east of Danville. He was first married to Sarah McInturff, April 9, 1854, by George F. Worth, Justice of the Peace. Sarah probably came to California overland in 1852. She was born near Nashville, Tennessee, April 28, 1835. Record book at Martinez, California, book one page nine, gives her residence as Mount Diablo Township.

They had two sons, Asher Columbus, born October 12, 1855, and William Edward, born August 7, 1859. Both attended Sycamore School. Sarah Maxcy filed for divorce May 8, 1876, which was granted. She and the two sons lived in San Jose. William Edward graduated from Heald's Business College, March 1885. He died in Santa Cruz, November 12, 1910. Asher C. married Anna Frey of Purissima, San Mateo County. She was born 1871, the daughter of Henry Frey (1821-1898) and Anna Frey (1827-1896), both natives of Germany.

Coats-Maxcy family. Left to right: James L. Coats, Rhoda Hyde Williams Maxcy, Fanny Williams Coats, Levi A. Maxcy. The child is Vivian Coats. Photo taken in 1906 or 1907. (Courtesy Vivian Coats Edmonston)

Wilson Coats and his wife, "Polly" Mary (Phillips) Coats. (Courtesy Vivian Coats Edmonston)

Fanny W. Coats and her daughter, Vivian, in front of the Maxcy home. Photo taken in about 1910.
        (Courtesy Vivian Coats Edmonston)

Levi Alexander Maxcy home, built in 1890, is still standing and lived in. Photo taken about 1915. (Courtesy Vivian Coats Edmonston)

22

In 1880 or 1881 Levi A. Maxcy leased the ranch and went to Illinois to visit his sister, Mrs. Rebecca Messenger. While there he met Mrs. Rhoda H. Williams, widow of Solomon Williams, who died 1879. They had a daughter Fanny. Levi and Rhoda were married December 24, 1881. Rhoda was born August 31, 1835 in Petersborough, New York, the daughter of Elijah Clarke Hyde and Adeline Cornelia Lyman. The ancestors of both came to America just a few years after the *Mayflower* landing of 1620.

From their marriage in 1881 until 1888 Levi and Rhoda farmed near Warrenville, Illinois. They sold the farm and bought a hotel on Chicago's south side, on Prairie Avenue. They sold it in 1889, and returned in the fall to the ranch in Tassajara. That was an extremely wet winter. The rain seemed never to stop! In 1890 Levi built the house that is still standing off Camino Tassajara, six miles east of Danville. He planted grapes and a family fruit orchard on five or six acres. He made and sold wine. About a year before his death on May 17, 1913, the vines were removed and replaced with a walnut orchard. In 1918 the family of James L. Coats, his wife Fanny, their daughter Vivian, and Fanny's mother Rhoda Maxcy, leased the ranch and moved to Berkeley, where Mrs. Maxcy died December 20, 1918. She is buried beside her husband in the Alamo Cemetery.

Coats family photograph, taken in about 1902. Standing, left to right: unidentified man; Charles Worth; Ella Coats Worth; James L. Coats, son of Felix and father of Vivian; Vivian Coats, held by mother, Fanny W. Coats; Phoebe Coats, wife of Bethel; Lill Coats, wife of Nolen; May Coats, daughter of Felix; Jennie Coats, daughter of Felix; Alice Coats, daughter of Nolen; Wilson Coats, son of Nolen; Florence Coats, daughter of Nolen; Nolen Coats, son of Felix. Front row, left to right: Eunice Coats, daughter of Bethel; Bernice Coats, daughter of Bethel; Felix Coats; and Hazel Worth, daughter of Ella Coats Worth. (Courtesy Vivian Coats Edmonston)

COATS

The following was a talk given by Vivian Coats Edmonston of San Francisco, at the "Pioneer Night" sponsored by the San Ramon Valley Historical Society, Thursday, May 27, 1976. Her complete permission was given to me to edit and use it in this book.

One Contra Costa County history book says, "After a pleasant three months trip, Mr. Wilson Coats arrived in California." This was essentially true, as he was not scalped by Indians and only abandoned his wagon and most of his supplies before crossing the Rockies on his way from Missouri to California.

It was my great-grandfather, Wilson Coats, and his son, Felix, my grandfather, from Coats, Prairie, near Fulton, Missouri, who left from near Clinton, Missouri in May 1849 and walked while they cracked the bull whip over the rumps of the oxen most of the way to California. Their money, in gold coins, was buried in the axle-grease bucket which swung from the tail gate of the wagon.

At one rocky gorge they asked some Indians if they could get through. The Indians told them, "The Gee-Haws [meaning oxen] yes; the God-damn-yous [meaning wagons] no!" So they found another trail. There were icy rivers to cross and thirsty alkali deserts to conquer. They helped push the wagon up to the top of the mountains and often got back down on the other side by hitching the oxen to the back of the wagon facing uphill to act as a brake and prevent the wagon from running wild down the grade.

There was rain, hail and snow along the way. They crossed the Truckee River twenty-seven times in twenty-two miles and finally made it to the Placerville area, where they did not become golden millionaires.

In 1851, Wilson Coats returned to Missouri and brought out his wife, Mary "Polly" Phillips Coats, and the rest of the family, five more sons and a daughter, arriving in the summer of 1852. One married daughter remained in Missouri with her husband and family.

During the first year, Felix and two other men went into the freighting business with a ten-mule pack train. They took supplies to the miners who were working between Sacramento and Stony Bar. Everything went well until one of the partners gambled away all their money. At one time, Felix sold homemade pies for a woman, for a dollar each. It cost forty cents to send a letter back East. Felix and his brother Bill, who came to California by the Southern route, spent the first winter at Diamond Springs, near Placerville, but again the "pot of gold at the end of the rainbow" eluded them.

When Wilson returned in the spring of 1852 with the family, they all left the false romance with the gold fields and as they were farmers they "prospected" for land. They found a place six miles east of Danville on acreage which adjoined that of Levi Maxcy, on what is now Camino Tassajara.

Felix G. Coats home. Note snow on the ground. (Courtesy Vivian Coats Edmonston)

In 1856, Wilson cut trees in Redwood Canyon, near Moraga, and split them into lumber which he hauled to his place where he built a two-story house.[6] This house burned in 1917.

Felix built his second house in 1883. In 1860 he married Leona Peralee Doggett, who at eleven years of age rode a horse most of the way from Arkansas to Oregon with her family in 1853. Felix

and Leona had three sons, Nolen, James and Bethel, and three daughters, Ella, May and Jennie.

James Longstreet Coats was my father. He and my mother, Fanny Williams, were married in San Francisco in 1895. This was made possible because Levi Alexander Maxcy came to California from Massachusetts around the Horn in 1849. After a go at the gold fields, he too settled in the Tassajara area. In the late 1870s he rented his land and went to Illinois to visit a sister. It was there that he met Mrs. Rhoda (Hyde) Williams, a widow with one daughter, Fanny. Levi and Rhoda were married in Illinois in 1881. They came to California in 1889 and settled on his place, the one he had taken up in 1852. He built a house in 1890 which is still in use and in good condition.

On January, 9, 1901, I, Vivian Coats, was born in the Maxcy house. I rode horseback the two and a half miles to the Sycamore Grammar School and then the six miles to high school in Danville, before we moved to Berkeley in 1918.

Charles Ninian Edmonston and I were married in 1932. We had Charles Ninian Edmonston, Jr., who married Catherine Janet McTaggart, and they have Cristi Lynn, Celia Ann, Caryn Janet and twins Catherine Vivian and Charles Ninian the Third. They make their home on Springwood Way in Concord.

Our daughter, Frances Ann (Edmonston) Alcalay had twin sons, Aaron Brooke and Nolen David, going on three years old. They live in San Francisco. So for now, this ends the pioneer story of the Coats Family.

The Coats-Maxcy home is jointly owned by Charles N. Edmonston and his sister Dr. Frances Ann (Edmonston) Alcalay. Since 1918, when the James L. Coats family moved to Berkeley, there have been only two different families who have rented the home. The present tenant is Regner Hansen and the Hansen family has lived there since 1930.

WILSON COATS

The name Coats is erroneously spelled with an "e" in several history books.

Wilson Coats (1802-1886) was the first resident of Tassajara Valley. He arrived in 1852 and settled on 160 acres. He was born August 10, 1802, in Smith County, Tennessee. The Coats family moved to Callaway County, Missouri, when Wilson was fifteen years old. There they farmed. On Christmas day 1823 Wilson married Miss Mary "Polly" Philipps, a native of Tennessee. They were married in Callaway County and had ten children. His wife died November 27, 1875. Wilson died January 4, 1886, at the age of eighty-four.

FELIX COATS

Felix Coats (1828-1916), the eldest son of Wilson Coats, was born August 9, 1828 in Callaway County, Missouri. He traveled overland at the age of twenty-one and mined with his father in Placerville until the fall of 1851. Came to Tassajara Valley to try ranching. He later purchased 640 acres of his own near the 160 acres of his father. He added to his holdings until he owned about 1,200 acres, which he devoted to stock and grain.

He married Leona Doggett on February 23, 1860, at Tassajara. She was born in Arkansas. In 1852, when she was eleven years old, she road horseback from her native state to Oregon. Her family came from Oregon in 1855 and were the Coats' neighbors. Felix and Leona raised six children, three boys and three girls: Nolen, James L., Bethel S., Ella, Mary and Jennie. Leona died December 25, 1893, age fifty-two, and her husband died June 9, 1916 at eighty-seven.

DIARY KEPT BY J. F. BALDWIN WHILE CROSSING THE PLAINS IN 1850
(First printed in San Francisco by
The California Patron and Agriculturist, 1887)

On March 18th, 1850, eight of us formed a company to go to California, to work in the mines. The names are as follows: H. H. More, John Marshal, Wm. Baird, Wm. Meese, Wm. and John Payne, J. F. and R. O. Baldwin, (RA) all of whom were from Summit County, Ohio.

We first went to the county seat (Akron), where we were joined by one hundred and fifty more men, all of whom were bound for the same destination.

From Akron we went to Wellsville, on the Ohio River, and shipped from there to St. Louis. By this time the number of men had increased to about five hundred.

We sailed on the Steamer *Kansas* for St. Joseph; took a steerage passage. Some of the boys complained about the hardships and inconvenience of the trip. If they could not stand a trip like that they certainly were not calculated to make a trip to California. We all had good health and were thankful for this blessing.

The Missouri river was one of the worst streams to navigate that I have ever seen. The water being low made navigation all the more dangerous.

April 3, 1850.—We are at Independence landing. The town is situated about six miles from the landing.

April 11, 1850.—We arrived at St. Joseph one week ago today and saw a great many familiar faces congregated there. At St. Joseph we first heard of fatal cases of cholera, the victims being from the vicinity of Akron, Ohio.

We are at present located at a farmer's home, by the name of Compton, and will remain for a few days.

Henry More and Wm. Meese have gone down to Fort Leavenworth to buy some mules at a public government sale. They succeeded in buying nine Spanish mules.

We started for Fort Kearney and had to travel slowly on account of scarcity of food. We next came to Savanah, where we laid in necessary supplies.

April 22, 1850.—Today Mr. James Griffin died from Erysipelas and was buried near by.

We traveled twenty miles on toward Fort Kearney and laid by for one week. Found corn one dollar per bushel and very scarce at that price.

We left Fort Kearney for the Frontier Fort, but concluded to cross eight miles below, which we did on the 5th of May.

May 6, 1850.—On above date, the weather very cold and the season backward. No grass yet. Bought twenty bushels of corn.

May 7, 1850.—On this date we came to the Missouri river and crossed eight miles below Fort Kearney. Camped on the opposite side, this being the first Indian ground we camped on.

May 8, 1850.— We started this morning at eight o'clock; traveled twenty miles on the open prairie. No wood. Found good water.

May 9, 1850.—Traveled twenty miles and camped. No wood. Used dry weed for fuel.

May 10, 1850.—We came on to Salt Creek and

Robert O. Baldwin home, built in 1888, burned down in 1953. It was between Danville and San Ramon. (Courtesy Vivian Coats Edmonston)

found some short grass. Still no rain and very cold for the season.

May 11, 1850.—Left Salt Creek and came to Cottonwoods, a distance of eighteen miles. Found very little grass and some water.

Sunday, May 12, 1850.—Left Cottonwood Creek, and traveled twenty miles. Came to Oak Grove and camped. No grass and some water.

May 13, 1850.—Started from camp and next came to the Platte bottom. Found some grass and camped without water.

May 14, 1850.—Started at eight o'clock and traveled sixteen miles and camped without water or wood. Good grass.

May 15, 1850.—Rolled out early this morning and traveled fifteen miles. Passed an Indian village — no inhabitants — and camped about four o'clock. Found grass. Got water out of the Platte river, which was very muddy.

May 16, 1850.—Started at 7:30 o'clock, and traveled slowly, finding very little grass. The water still muddy.

May 17, 1850.—We got an early start. Found grass, poor water and no wood. No rain for two weeks. Roads quite dusty.

May 18, 1850.—Rolled out this morning at 6:30 o'clock and came to New Fort Kearney. We camped two miles to the west of the Fort, having traveled sixteen miles that day. Grass very short and still no rain.

Sunday, May 19, 1850.—Started at nine o'clock and traveled twelve miles. Found a little poor grass. Rain for the first time to do any good for two weeks.

May 20, 1850.—Left this morning at seven o'clock; after traveling twenty miles we camped. Good water and grass. Wood very scarce.

May 21, 1850.—Made an early move, traveling along the Platte bottom. Found grass very scarce and some places none at all. Not much wood. Traveled twenty-five miles that day and camped without grass or water.

May 22, 1850.—Started early and camped at sundown. Grass scarce, also wood. Traveled twenty-five miles that day. Wagons in sight all the time.

May 23, 1850.—Made an early start. Water and grass very scarce. Saw some buffalo. Great many killed by emigrants. Twenty-five miles today.

May 24, 1850.—Made start this morning. Traveled slowly finding grass scarce. Got some buffalo steak which one of the boys killed. Sky cloudy; looks like rain.

May 25, 1850.—Traveled this day sixteen miles. Grass scarce; water good. We had quite a wind this evening; so much so that it was necessary to take down the tent. No rain.

May 26, 1850.—Started about nine o'clock and traveled three or four miles, where we found good grass and camped for the day.

May 27, 1850.—Left camp early and came to the fords. Found many wagons at the crossing. We passed over without any accident and drove on to the north fork of the Platte. Made thirty miles this day and camped at sundown.

May 28, 1850.—Made an early move this morning. Road sandy and rough. Saw a great many Indians, which was quite a curiosity to us. They were very friendly to emigrants. Made twenty miles today.

May 29, 1850.—Left camp in good season this morning. Came in sight of Chimney Rock near night and camped. Grass scarce; no water. Twenty miles today. Very dry.

May 30, 1850.—Started early this morning. Passed Chimney Rock about noon. Camped at night in sight of it still. Made twenty-five miles today. Good grass.

May 31, 1850.—Started at five o'clock this morning. Passed Scott's Bluff. We are now six hundred miles from the Missouri River and forty from Fort Laramie. Twenty-five miles today.

June 1, 1850.—Made an early move this morning. Came thirty miles today. Saw some French traders.

Sunday, June 2, 1850.—We lay by today. Grass rather scarce. Some rain.

June 3, 1850.—Rolled out early and came to Fort Laramie about noon. Stopped some time there. Started again and had heavy rain. Found plenty wood and grass. Twenty miles today.

June 4, 1850.—We made a good start and traveled twenty-five miles over a rough road. Came to a good spring of water. Could see Laramie mountains which were covered with snow. Foggy on the summit. Good grass.

June 5, 1850.—Started in good season this morning and came thirty miles. Found wood and good water.

June 6, 1850.—Rolled out early this morning. Came twenty-five miles. Found no water. Still in sight of mountains spoken of above. At present we are crossing the Black Hills.

June 7, 1850.—Left early this morning and camped nine miles west of Deer Creek. Twenty-five miles today.

June 8, 1850.—Made an early move this morning, in order that we could cross the Platte, which we did a little after two o'clock. Camped a little above the ferry.

June 9, 1850.—We remained in camp today, as we sold our wagon. We were kept busy making pack saddles. We dispensed with all unnecessary articles.

June 10, 1850.—Moved off this morning, but with some difficulty and vexation.

June 11, 1850.—Left our encampment at Willow Springs about nine o'clock; came on to Independence Rock and camped near it. Grass very short.

June 12, 1850.—We crossed the Sweet Water river early; came twenty miles and camped. The face of the valley had a very singular appearance. Mountains and valley. Very desolate looking.

June 13, 1850.—Early start this morning. Twenty-five miles today over very sandy roads. No grass or vegetables except wild sage, which nothing will eat or subsist on. Our packing goes on somewhat better than it did when we started.

June 14, 1850.—Moved out this morning in good season. After dinner we commenced to ascend the Rocky Mountains. We find it extremely cold owing to high altitude. Snowing occasionally. Eighteen miles today.

June 15, 1850.—Moved out today rather late. Came to the south pass of the mountains. Camped at Pacific Springs. So called I suppose from the fact that they pass into the Pacific Ocean. Very cold today and windy. Twenty-five miles today. Not much grass, owing to a large emigration. Behind us are thousands of wagons.

June 16, 1850.—Moved out in good season this morning. Thirty miles today. Found wood and grass.

June 17, 1850.—Left camp about ten o'clock. Winter weather on the mountains.

June 18, 1850.—Early start. Came to Green river, and will have to lay by a day or two before we can get over the river.

June 19, 1850.—Left Green river early this morning and came twenty-five miles. Camped after crossing a very deep and rapid stream. Found good grass and plenty of wood.

June 20, 1850.—Left our camp early and traveled thirty miles. Grass good.

June 21, 1850.—Made thirty-seven miles today. Road not good. Plenty good grass and water.

June 22, 1850.—Made a hard day's drive over the mountains, valleys and streams. Found plenty wood and water then camped.

June 23, 1850.—Traveled twenty-five miles today. Road very bad.

June 24, 1850.—Started early this morning; traveled most of the day through a canyon, crossing a stream many times. The evening brought us in view of Salt Lake City.

June 25, 1850.—We moved out early this morning, all in good spirits and reached the Celestial City at ten o'clock a.m. We found here a beautiful city, on a sloping plain. The city was laid out in squares. Beautiful snow water from the mountains was running down on all sides of the streets, for the purpose of irrigation, etc. At this place we expected to lay in a new supply of provisions, but were disappointed. There were none to be had. Many of the inhabitants there had been living on meat for two weeks without any flour. Brigham Young had given orders to his people not to supply the Gentiles with provisions as they were short themselves. We however succeeded in trading tea, coffee and sugar for seventy-five or eighty pounds of flour. Money being no object, you couldn't buy any-thing of them. This was about three weeks before harvest time. By waiting two or three weeks we could then get plenty of flour. We couldn't think of stopping that long. After having a consultation we concluded to move on and take our chances. We took the precaution however, to limit each man on so much food per day, in order that it might last as long as possible.

June 26, 1850.—We started and came out of town. Met two spring wagons on the way. We stopped and arranged so that each man could have a riding animal.

June 27, 1850.—Left this morning early and came to Weber river, twenty-eight miles. Found a ferry-boat. Unloaded our packs and put them aboard. We were obliged to swim our mules however.

June 28, 1850.—Moved out this morning in good season. Traveled thirty miles to Box Elder Creek. Found plenty grass, wood and water.

June 29, 1850.—Left our last encampment and came in to Bear river, which we crossed, having to swim our mules again. We had to pay $1 for each pack, which we considered cheap in these early California times and prices.

June 30, 1850.—We traveled today, as we could not get any grass or water.

July 1, 1850.—Started in good season, and traveled thirty miles. Good grass and water.

July 2, 1850.—Started early; found plenty of water; grass not plentiful. We camped on the road-side leading to Fort Hale.

July 3, 1850.—Made an early start this morning, passing many wagons of all kinds. Came thirty miles, and found good grass and water.

July 4, 1850.—This being the morning of Independence, it was ushered in by the discharge of fire-arms in the bands of the emigrants. Came thirty-five miles today and camped. Very poor water.

July 5, 1850.—Left at sunrise today; twenty-five miles today. Good grass and water.

July 6, 1850.—Came up to St. Mary's river today. Traveled thirty miles. Had bad crossing.

July 7, 1850.—Started early this morning. Passed by the grave of a man who had been killed by an Indian and buried this morning.

July 8, 1850.—Left our last encampment late this morning. Found the roads very rough and hilly. Grass not very good.

July 9, 1850.—Came thirty miles today. Roads very dusty. Grass difficult to get, as the river is very much swollen, and sloughs full of water.

July 10, 1850.—Started before the sun was up this morning. Had no grass for the stock during the night.

July 11, 1850.—Laid by today getting grass, as we had been informed that we were within eight miles of the desert. This did not prove true, as we were still one hundred miles away yet.

July 12, 1850.—Started early this morning and came thirty miles. Found good grass.

July 13, 1850.—Left early, expecting to reach the Sink, but did not.

July 14, l850.—Again we stopped half a day getting grass, as we were informed that the desert was only six miles away. This also proved not to be the case.

July 15, 1850.—Left early, and understood the sink was not within sixty miles. Grass good, but hard to get.

[Here the author of the diary changes from J. F. Baldwin to R. O. Baldwin.]

From some cause J. F. Baldwin failed to keep his diary from the 15th to the 28th of July 1850. The probable cause was owing to great fatigue which we all had to undergo during our journey.

After thirty-six years, I will try and recall past recollections and complete the past few days of our journey.

On the last date mentioned above, we were probably fifty or sixty miles from the desert. It probably took two days to reach the Humboldt Sink.

After taking a good rest and securing what water and grass we could conveniently carry, we started about four o'clock in the afternoon, on the 18th of July, to cross the forty mile desert. We traveled slowly until about twelve o'clock at night, when we halted to rest. We were about one-half way across then. We found dead animals and wagons all along the road. After resting for one hour we moved on again, in order to get water before the heat of the day came on. We passed several persons who were without any water and we divided with them. As we approached the Carson river, we found dead horses, cattle and abandoned wagons.

At the time we halted in the desert, we ate the last of our provisions, not knowing when or where we could get any more. We arrived at the Carson river about nine o'clock a.m., with the loss of one mule. We were all glad to find grass and water.

On the 19th of July, we rested part of the day, and then moved on again. We had traveled only a few miles when we met a team from California, loaded with provisions. Everything we bought cost $2 per pound, flour included. We bought enough for our immediate wants and moved on again. Grass was plentiful along the Carson river.

As we traveled on everything was cheaper in the way of provisions, etc. A day or two before we began to ascend the Sierra Nevada mountains, we met Andrew More with several mules packed with provisions coming to meet us and his brother, Henry More, who was one of our party.

The More brothers stopped to buy stock of the emigrants, and the rest of the party moved on, passing over the old emigrant road leading to Placerville. We arrived in Placerville on the 28th day of July, 1850, all

Our Congressman and his Area Chairmen
Photo taken on August 16, 1956 shows, left to right: Howard Wiedemann, San Ramon; Mary
Baldwin; Alfred Jones, Alamo; Congressman John F. Baldwin, Danville (deceased); Joseph
F. Smith, Alamo; and Mac D. Osborn, Danville.

well; we camped on a hill overlooking the town. We camped together that night, as a company, the last time, after traveling seventy-five days from the Missouri River, and then parted all good friends.

During the latter part of our journey, we stood guard over our stock, each man taking half the night; our turn came every fourth night. On our arrival at Placerville we found a thriving camp. Wm. Meese, my brother and I remained and mined near Placerville that winter with varied success. In February 1851, we broke camp and went north into Feather River Rich Bar, and mined in that locality for eighteen months with good success. In October 1852, left the mines and located in San Ramon Valley, Contra Costa County.

In November, 1852, J. F. Baldwin returned to his old home, Summit County, Ohio. After remaining there a short time, he moved west to Iowa, it then being a new country and land cheap. Wm. Meese and R. O. Baldwin remained in Contra Costa County and engaged in stock raising and farming. At the time of locating here the country was new, and wild cattle were roaming over the valleys at will. During a residence of thirty-five years here, I have noticed the wonderful progress of the county and State.

Of the original eight men who started for California in 1850 to better their situations, four have died within the lapse of thirty-six years; three of us are living in California, and the other in Ohio.

(Signed with the signature of R. O. Baldwin)

WIEDEMANN

The following was copied April 22, 1969 from letters from Uncle Henry Wiedemann, written September 22, 1956, while he was at the Odd Fellow's home in Saratoga and sent to Roxanne Wiedemann (Mrs. Randolph) Lindsay who lives in the original Christian Weidemann home in San Ramon. I have edited and taken excerpts to share with you, with her permission.

My Dear Roxanne: The time passes so quickly that I can hardly realize that this month will soon be gone. I always regretted that I did not get more first hand information from some of the pioneer settlers, who have all passed away, that took part in that history making era. In my young life I did not fully realize the importance as a native Californian to know more of the environment in which I was raised. I am glad to know you are taking an active interest, at an early age, so I will to the best of my knowledge describe conditions as I know them. There is always something of interest that is left unmentioned. I will try to take note of it for future reference.

Christian Wiedemann, my father, was a native of Germany. He worked in the shipyards of Kiel, as a shipwright, and was in contact with seafaring people. At the age of 18 he shipped out bound for San Fran-

cisco. Around Cape Horn they encountered terrible storms which nearly wrecked the ship. He arrived in San Francisco fall of 1853, at the height of the gold rush. Nearly all ships in the harbor were deserted. Father and some of his shipmates decided not to go to the mines and remained in San Francisco for several years. He took a job in a dairy operated by Henry Schwerin, who owned the property where the Cow Palace now stands. Being city-raised and never in contact with livestock, he worked at the dairy for seven or eight years. With his acquired knowledge of livestock he decided to take up ranching on his own.

In 1865 a brother of Henry Schwerin went across the bay to acquire some property, the choicest having been taken up by earlier settlers. The brothers Schwerin formed a partnership and acquired a tract of land which included the old Wiedemann residence, which was built by Schwerin when he married about 1865. They engaged in cattle business but father (Christian) also ran a butcher business in San Francisco. After a few years the partnership was dissolved and Fred Behm (Belm), a distant relative of Schwerin, had a place adjoining, which was also added to the Wiedemann ranch.

By 1865 there were roads between San Ramon and Hayward for horsedrawn vehicles. They were very narrow, and like all unpaved roads, muddy in winter and dusty in summer. Before the roads, travel was by horseback and pack horses. For many years the old trails were visible. The higher elevations were safest.

During the gold rush people from the Atlantic seaboard came around the Horn or crossed the Isthmus of Panama. Those from the interior came in groups or caravans to prevent possible attacks from the Indians. The wagons were drawn by oxen or horses. Most of the ranchers slaughtered their hogs and cured for ham, bacon and sausage. Some slaughtered beef and made corned beef. There were a number of flour mills in the vicinity where a rancher could take his wheat to be ground into flour. Nearly everyone raised an abundance of vegetables. Game of rabbits and quail was plentiful. Ground squirrels were eaten and also good sport for hunters. There were but few deer in comparison to what there is now. Since the coyote has been nearly exterminated there is a deer increase. The coyote would destroy many fawns, sheep and poultry. Hunting them with hounds was great sport.

San Ramon, as I first remember it as a youngster going to school, was like most country towns of that time. Chief occupations were farming and cattle raising. There were two blacksmith shops, a shoemaker shop, two stores, three hotels, four bars, a Chinese laundry and schoolhouse and livery stable.

The name San Ramon was derived from the Spanish word Saint Raymond. It was once known as Limerick, which clung quite a few years. The remaining hotel is now owned by Jerome Thorup [see Thorup Family later in this chapter], and one of the few remaining landmarks. The Chinese laundry also burned down. The creek known as San Ramon Creek flowed through the town and has as its main source Bollinger Canyon. It also carried the water from Norris Canyon which it originally did not, enlarging the channel by volume. I was told by one of the early roadmasters that there was only a 25 foot span across the creek at San Ramon, where now it is about 125 feet across. This creek was called something like Catano. Water from Norris Canyon diverted below George Norris' residence and straight to the San Ramon Creek above the old Lynch home. Originally the water from Norris Canyon flowed toward the Bishop Ranch and spread out. Some places there were springs along the creek bed. Some of the school boys, including myself, rode our horses in those water holes and when real muddy the fish would come to the surface. They were called suckers.

San Ramon was in existence quite a while when father arrived in 1865. There was a railroad that ran between Oakland and Hayward before the Transcontinental came through in 1868. Those who wished to go to San Francisco usually drove to Hayward, took the train, and then ferry boat. There were ferry boats for general freight business and passengers. After the Wiedemanns settled in San Ramon they did not go to San Francisco too much. Father also did wood cutting as a source of added income. Wood was always needed. There were some ox-teams, but horses were more satisfactory for ranch work.

Fred Wiedemann was born in 1872 about three miles southwest of San Ramon near the county line of Contra Costa-Alameda on the ranch which our father acquired in 1865. There were a number of early pioneer settlers in California before the discovery of gold, while California was under Mexican rule. Spanish grants were large land holdings, such as the noted Amador Grant of which Norris and Harlan ranches are a part. Cattle ran at large. It was the chief occupation. The cattle were slaughtered for their hide and tallow which was taken in sailing vessels around the Horn to the east coast. Everybody's cattle would run together. They would have a round-up, or rodeo, to use the Spanish term, and different owners would know their cattle by brand and earmark. After the work, they would pick out a maverick and have a barbecue.

San Ramon, the town, has been known by several names. Among the first was Brevensville, named after Breven, the first blacksmith. Then Lynchville, after William Lynch, one of the earliest settlers who conducted a store there. There was a large immigration from the Emerald Isles (Ireland), and not to be outdone by neighboring Dublin, they honored it by calling it Limerick. San Ramon still had some of the glamour of a typical frontier town as far as law and order, but to a lesser degree. There were three hotels and four bars.

At about 1880 the first Post Office was in a store run by Doran and Demont and owned by William Lynch. The store building was later moved to his ranch near town. When property on the east side of Limerick (San Ramon) was purchased by George McCamley, all the buildings were moved off. One, a tavern, was moved across the way and is still occupied by a Mrs. Fry. When Doran and Demont discontinued business the post office was moved across the San Ramon creek to a store operated by James Barrett, Sr. which stood opposite a huge white oak tree, a noted landmark of the Valley. It stood in the middle of the road, its large limbs spread across the street on both sides. Low branches could be reached from the balcony of the Barrett Hotel. It became a traffic hazard and was cleared away. The other hotel was named San Ramon Hotel, operated by Pat Horan, brother of Mrs. James Barrett, Sr., who conducted it until he passed away about 1881. The hotel was renovated and James Coaster of San Francisco ran it, followed by Gus Belmont, Bowman, Claus Tiedemann, Frank Tinnon and Harry Strange, when it burned down. The other hotel, owned by A. C. Tervelling, was sold to Pete Thorup, the shoemaker. With all the fires and the big oak tree removed, Limerick looked deserted.

The hotel and livery stable were necessities for the traveling public, as were the stages. Jerry Philps, a colorful old stage driver, carried mail and passengers between San Ramon and Martinez. He was followed by Frank Childs. The last stage driver was George Jones. With the railroad the stageline folded. The railroad was hailed as quite an event about 1890. San Ramon was the end of the line until 1907 when it was extended to Livermore.

Farming required many ranch hands. With poor transportation few left town and there was lots of activity, especially on Sundays when big crowds would gather. San Ramon still retained that western atmosphere. San Ramon was a sporting town, there were the Sunday afternoon fights at Dublin, racing tracks at Lynch and Meese and tug-of-war games.

There was the Chinese laundry, nearly every town had them and San Ramon was no exception—it had two at one time! Many ranchers employed the Chinese as cooks and they worked during harvest time to bind the grain, as the self-binding machines were not yet in general use. There was a certain element throughout California arousing the people to the detriment of the cheap coolie labor. Their slogans were, "The Chinese must go!" and "Boycott the Heathen Chinese!" There were anti-Chinese Leagues organized statewide. There was one in San Ramon, which caused some heated arguments, but since the area was equally divided, things soon got back to normal.

The old San Ramon School brings back fond memories. If those walls could speak! The school building served many purposes besides dispensing the three R's. It was a meeting hall until the San Ramon Hall was built later. San Ramon was known for its high-class entertainment, with lots of local talent. Margaret McMahon (Mrs. Walter) Bartlett, a brilliant educator who taught for eight years at San Ramon, led the entertainment. The schoolhouse could be converted into a sizeable ballroom by taking out the partitions. Its fame as a dance hall, including many masquerades, was county wide in the 1880s.

Horseback was the main mode of travel to get to school and with it, racing went on and there was a keen rivalry over who had the fastest horse. There were two training tracks in the Valley, used mostly for harness racing. Some of the students walked and hiking was fun.

One San Ramon boy who won fame as a brilliant scholar graduated from San Ramon school in 1889. He was a noted educator and attorney and once a candidate for governor of California—Judge William H. Langdon, who became an outstanding jurist of our state. One of his greatest pleasures was to pay a visit to his former home with its humble surroundings, now owned by Fred Wiedemann.

Politics: One gala event in San Ramon was when old-time Demos celebrated Grover Cleveland's presidential election. He was the first Democratic president to be elected in twenty years. A huge barbecue at the San Ramon Schoolyard was held. A speaker's platform was erected in front of the schoolhouse. The event began by firing off anvils. Many noted Demos occupied the speakers' stand. The principle speaker of the day was John P. Irish, a noted political figure of the era. After the feast, a grand parade through town was led by John Camp and a prominent lady of San Ramon.

Peter Thorup was San Ramon's shoemaker for 65 years. His reputation as a boot and shoe maker was known far and wide, especially by the old cow pokes. They feared something might happen to Pete and would order an extra pair of boots made. This caused Pete to chuckle, "I fooled them all."

One story was of a young chap who started a barn fire, making an unwilling old hen get off her nest. After the fire, she had disappeared, but the apple trees close by held baked apples on the trees, from the intense heat of the barn fire.

Bollinger Canyon was settled in the early 1850s by Joshua Bollinger, a native of Missouri. He acquired a large tract of land in the canyon and was joined by more of his people, who were a pioneering class, very generous and hospitable. Their favorite pastime was whittling. At one time Bollinger Canyon had quite a large population and about twenty children from the Canyon attended school.

Blacksmithing was a popular business. There were two in San Ramon, run at different times by Breven, Jay Dutchee, George McPhuters, Jake Buttner, among the early ones. Later there was Erickson and Albertsen, Webster, Olsson and Fry.

San Ramon had a resident doctor for a number of years, Dr. G. E. Alexander, a G.A.R. veteran and son-in-law of William Lynch, an early pioneer settler. He later moved to Hayward. There were two other early doctors, Dr. Larabee and Dr. Dragoo.

Every town has its men-about-town—here I mention a few: Timothy McMahon Howard, George Gray, J. Bowman, A. Brigaw, Nicolas Obrien, Jud Williams, Gus Belmont, D. Perkins, Jim Sievers, Harry Oden, James Norris, Pete Madsen, Cooper, Julius Cathcart, Greer, James McPhuters, John Camp, James Barrett, Sr., Jeff Crow, John Oswill, George Starkey, King Tinnin, Jake Dragoo, Hargrave, Brown (horse shoer), E. Hayes, Frank Dragoo, Dave Caldwell, Phurst Williams, A. Griffin, Bill Perkins, Sam Uybark, Tom Corneal, Vincent, William Howard, John Woodhouse and Ed Drew.

WIEDEMANN GENEALOGY

Christian Wiedemann married Catherine Dittmer. Their children were Mary, Henry, Rose and Fred. Mary and Rose Wiedemann did not marry and remained in the original Wiedemann home until their deaths. Henry married Alvina Skow of Hayward. They had one daughter, Alberta, who married Sam Smoot, and they have one daughter, Patricia (Pat), who is Mrs. Walker and lives with her son Graham in San Jose. Alberta Smoot makes her home at Petaluma, California.

Fred Wiedemann married Mattie Jorgenson and they had two children, Howard and Ann M. Howard Wiedemann married Doris Chapman of Albany, California, and they have three children, Roxanne, Sandra and Jeffrey. Roxanne (Roxie) is married to Randolph Lindsay. They have one baby daughter, born January 29, 1977. She is named Mattie Alice for her two great-grandmothers. The Lindsays make their home in the original Christian Wiedemann house. Sandy is world-traveled. (She graduated in the same class as our son Gary Jones from San Ramon Valley High School, June 1963.) She presently is making her home in one of the houses on the Wiedemann ranch. Jeff lives in the home that was built for Uncle Henry, which has been redecorated for his needs.

Ann M. Wiedemann married Al Kaplan of Redding, California, now a Danville realtor. They have three daughters, Christine, Hazel and Freda (named for her maternal grandfather). Christine graduated after two years at Cal Poly and now attends California State College at Bakersfield.

31

Hazel graduated from San Ramon Valley High School in June 1977 and will go to Cal Poly starting in the summer session. Freda is a freshman at the local high school.

The entire Wiedemann family, over the years, has been active in community, civic, and political affairs.

Found in newspaper—December 1931, Fred Wiedemann of San Ramon was elected director of the Chamber of Commerce with Arthur Beede, Phil Bancroft, Edward Rowland, Edgar Lion, W. L. White, Ray Spencer, G. M. Parsons, O. W. Fletter, Carl Karling, Horace Breed, Harvey Rotherman, and William Mayhes.

Fred and Henry Wiedemann continued the farming and expanding, then Howard Wiedemann took over and now his son Jeff, the fourth generation of Wiedemanns, is working to keep the land productive.

It is interesting to note that all the Wiedmanns have attended local schools and graduated from San Ramon Valley High School. They also all still live on original Wiedemann property and have Norris Canyon Road for their addresses though they live in different houses. Baby Mattie makes the fifth generation of Wiedemanns living on original Wiedemann ranch property dating back to 1865, well over one hundred years. That is truly remarkable, and staying close to one's heritage and "roots!"

HARLAN FAMILIES
GEORGE - JOEL - GELDERMANN

The following information is from *History of Contra Costa County*, Slocum and Company, 1882, and *History of the State of California* by Professor J. M. Guinn, A.M.

George Harlan, the head of the Harlan family, brought his wife and children across the plains in 1846. In 1845 he had left Indiana and gone to St. Joseph, Missouri. He outfitted ox teams and came to California via the Hastings' Cut-off. First settled in Santa Clara. Later Mission San Jose and Napa Valley and Calistoga. Until the discovery of gold this remained their home. The family then went to the American River territory for mining. At her death Mrs. Harlan left the following children: Rebecca, Joel, Mary, Nancy and Elisha. A son Jacob had died while in Napa Valley. George Harlan took a second wife, Mrs. Catherine Hargrave, daughter of William and Catherine (Speed) Fowler who had crossed the plains in 1846. They had two children, Sarah and George.

Joel Harlan (1828-1875) arrived in California in 1846 and the San Ramon Valley in 1852. He was born in Wayne County, Indiana September 27, 1828. When he was seventeen the family moved west to St. Joseph, Missouri. The following spring he migrated to California. He was living in San Francisco when gold was discovered in 1849. His uncle was supposedly in the mill enterprise with John W. Marshall when Marshall made his great gold discovery.

Harlan took a fling at gold mining and on his return on April 2, 1849 married Minerva J. Fowler, a native of Illinois. She was another of the daughters of William and Catherine Fowler. The ceremony was performed at Sonoma Mission by Ex-Governor Boggs. (RA) After a stay in Napa the couple moved to Sacramento and later to San Francisco, where their eldest child was born in 1851. During 1851 they moved to San Jose and became the first settlers in what is now the San Lorenzo area. In 1852 they purchased land and erected a house in Amador Valley, a part of the San Ramon grant of Jose Amador. When Alameda County (RA) was created, mainly from the original territory of Contra Costa County, one of the defining boundary line points was the "house of Joel Harlan." He, however, always considered his home on the side of Contra Costa County. The house was demolished in 1857. In later years, when another survey of the boundary line was made, it was necessary to find the location of the original Harlan house. This was done by locating the well and a native oak tree which had marked the original point of survey. The bark of the old tree was cut to find the original marker made in 1853, which read: "A. C. & C. C."—Alameda County and Contra Costa.

The Wiedemann Ranch in the fall of 1888.

In 1856 Harlan purchased 2,000-plus acres of the Norris tract, which had been a part of the San Ramon rancho of Jose Maria Amador. Two years later Joel Harlan built a large home for his family, calling it "El Nido," which means "the nest." This home still stands, remodeled and well maintained, and is occupied by his great-grandson Harlan Geldermann. The Joel Harlans had nine children: Elisha C., who married Elmina Plamondon; Anna, who died at six years; Laura M. (deceased); Mary, who married W. A. Llewellyn and had a son Loren Llewellyn; Horace (deceased); Helene, wife of Fred Osborn of San Francisco; Henry Leo (deceased), who married Minnie Hicks and had a daughter Helene Hazel; Fred; and Addie Elmina who married Fred A. Stolp and had one child, Carmen Minerva.

Joel Harlan was a very respected member of the San Ramon and Danville areas. When he died March 28, 1875, the Danville Grange, (RA) of which he was a charter member, adopted the following memorial resolution: "Whereas, it has pleased the Divine Master to remove from our midst our Beloved Brother, Joe Harlan; Resolved, That, in the death of Brother Harlan, we have lost an esteemed member of our Order; the commu-

nity, a worthy and upright citizen; and his family a devoted husband and father." He had risen to prominence and affluence entirely through his own efforts. But he never failed to remember the less fortunate. His interests were in education and he established a private school in his neighborhood.

The remainder of this section about the Harlan family was excerpted from *Harlan, the Great Trek and the Golden Opportunity* by William K. Harlan. This book was researched in twelve reputable books, making an impressive selected bibliography.

The first Harlan, a Quaker, was George, who arrived in America in 1687. For the next 100 years four generations of Harlans lived around the Quaker settlements of Chester County, Pennsylvania.

After the Revolutionary War, one George Harlan(4), who had served as a "wagon boy" in the conflict, moved his family to central Kentucky (now Lincoln County) on the Barren River. Among his children were four sons: Elijah(6), William(5), Samuel(8), and George(7). It is with George Harlan(7) that the course of nineteenth century frontier expansion is most evident in the Harlan family.

The original Christian Wiedemann home was built in 1865 on what had been government land. In those days, veterans were given land grants. The hill land was purchased by three partners, Wiedemann, Henry Schwerin, and Schwerin's brother. In this picture are Christian Wiedemann and his children, Fred, Henry, Mary and Rose. Note the turkeys eating. Little has been changed over the years except for the vegetation. All the original outbuildings are still standing. The charming old home was redecorated for use by Mr. and Mrs. Randolph "Randy" Dale and Roxanne "Roxie" (Wiedemann) Lindsay, who moved in in time for Christmas 1974. This photo was taken in 1888.

In 1806, when George Harlan(7) was four, the family moved north to Ohio, near what is now Dayton. His father died in 1815 and the family moved west to Wayne County, eastern Indiana. Jacob Harlan(12) recounts how he grew up "like an Indian" and was ten before the first school was built.

In 1823 George(7) married Elizabeth Duncan of Pennsylvania. Eight years later they moved to Barrien County, extreme southwest corner of Michigan, near Niles (perhaps how Niles, California got its name). Their six children were Rebecca, Mary, Joel, Nancy, Elisha, and Jacob. In 1845 the two older girls married two Van Gordon brothers, John and Ira.

In 1845 it was Langsford Hastings' book on Oregon and California that led George Harlan to leave Michigan and go west, with eleven wagons and the following people: himself, his wife Elizabeth and their six children; his mother-in-law Mrs. Duncan, near ninety; his two sons-in-law, the Van Gordons; the children of his brother Samuel (deceased), Sarah, Jacob W. and Malinda; George W. Harlan, his deceased brother William's son, also Sarah's first cousin and husband (married in 1845); William Harlan's widow and son William Jr. As the train moved south through Illinois and Missouri, they picked up more followers. Around St. Claire, Illinois it was joined by the Fowler Party of six. Henry Fowler was an architect or master carpenter in Albany, New York, moved to Illinois, and to Oregon in 1843, with his two sons. In California they built for General Vallejo, and obtained property on the present site of Calistoga. He sent his son William back to bring the rest of the family, his wife, two unmarried daughters, and Catherine Fowler Hargrave and her husband William; it was this group that joned the Harlan party.

They traveled with the Donner Party part of the way. Three major parties went through Fort Bridger in 1846 following Hastings' new trail: a pack train led by Bryant and guided by Hastings' partner Hudspeth; the Harlan-Young train with 66 wagons, which left Bridger July 23 with Hastings; and the Donner Party which started around July 31. The Harlan-Young train, the first wagons over this trail, reached the head of Weber Canyon in the Wasatch Mountains of Utah and literally ran into a stone wall! It was a miracle the wagons got through at all. Everything was bad! For miles the canyon was so narrow there was hardly room for a team between the river and the cliffs. Once the party made only a mile and a half distance in one week. One wagon fell into the river. William Hargrave died, William Fowler lost seven yoke of oxen, and most of the livestock of the train perished. The Harlan-Young wagons reached Johnson's Rancho over the Sierras on October 25, 1846, the day of the first snow. They were the last train to cross the mountains that winter.

The harshness of the overland journey and of social conditions of pre-Gold Rush California took its toll. Young John Van Gordon and Elizabeth Harlan died soon after they reached San Jose; Elizabeth's daughter Rebecca died the next year, and her little son Jacob in 1848. Mrs. Duncan died at ninety-three in 1849 near Coloma, and George died the summer of 1850. The younger generation carried on with the new life and most of the girls who had made the overland trip were soon maried. In 1847 George married the widow Catherine Fowler Hargrave and his nephew Jacob married her sister, Ann Fowler. At their marriage Governor Boggs (RA) "enjoined upon us to act as good citizens, and to have a big family to help people in the country which was in need of American population." Two years later Joel Harlan completed the interesting marital pattern by wedding the third Fowler girl, Minerva, thus making his sister-in-law and stepmother the same, and his stepbrother and sister, nieces and nephews. Apparently the scarcity of suitable brides precluded any stigma in this union. "Joel made much fun about it, calculating what the relationship would be; that he would be his father's brother-in-law. He said it would take a Philadelphia lawyer to determine what the relationship of their children might be!"

From 1847 to 1852 Joel, George W., Jacob and until his death, the patriarch George(7) operated as a family unit in a variety of enterprises. First they cut redwood shingles and fence posts in the Oakland hills for the village of Yerba Buena (San Francisco). Then there was the Fremont, a hotel opened in the wilds of Santa Clara by George W. and his wife Sarah. Jacob and Joel operated a livery stable in San Francisco until 1848, which was a big success financially and enabled them to obtain supplies and open the first general store in Coloma in March of 1848. The Harlans really began to strike it rich selling food and supplies to miners at what Jacob confessed were very high prices but far lower than would later be charged: $25 for a pair of boots, $16 for a pick, $8 for a bottle of whiskey. Their biggest killing, $1,200 in

Family get-together at El Nido, Harlan Rancho.

a few hours, came from selling serapes made of carpeting and coarse cloth to gold-laden Indians. In 1849 they sold their store and few remaining goods to Lansford Hastings.

Their brief experience with gold mining was also phenomenal. Joel got $1,450 in dust on the American River in one day, but lost his claim to jumpers. The next year George W.(9) and Jacob made a strike near Sonora but left because of Indian hostility. Despite their successes in the diggings, land and farming remained the Harlans' chief goal. Returning to San Francisco, Joel and Jacob started a dairy with George's eight milk cows which had survived the trek. Their price for fresh milk was $4 a gallon. Jacob also, in the speculative spirit of the time, made an easy $2,500 selling a "worthless" lot on Bush Street, so-called because it was simply sand hills and greasewood bushes, to Dr. Coit and two partners.

After an unsuccessful farming attempt near Niles, Jacob, Joel, and their families led a group of squatters onto a piece of rich land at the mouth

El Nido (the nest), Harlan Rancho, San Ramon, was built for Joel Harlan in 1854. This photo was taken in 1900.

35

of San Lorenzo Creek, being disputed by the Castros and Estudillos. He accepted a contract to plow 200 acres on the Estudillo rancho. He and Joel completed this by January of 1852, made more money and put in their own crops. From a mere acre of potatoes, which Jacob first thought the frost had killed, he made over $1,250, selling his crop at twenty-five cents per pound. With this money Jacob paid Castro, the rightful owner, and then departed for his Indiana home.

With his money, Joel Harlan purchased a 1,000-acre ranch in the Amador Valley around 1852. When the new county line was drawn for Alameda, the Harlan house was used as a boundary marker. In 1856 the family moved to the Norris Tract at Danville. He added to a total of 1,800 acres, built his two-story house, "El Nido," and became one of Contra Costa County's earliest cattlemen. On his death in 1875, the control of the property, which was never divided among his seven children, passed to his widow and eldest son, Elisha C. Harlan. Elisha added more acreage and enlarged the house before his death in 1938. The land then passed to Mrs. A. J. Geldermann of Danville.

Elisha Harlan(19) grew to maturity and married Lucy Hobaugh in 1871 in San Luis Obispo. By 1875 he had established the Harlan Ranch, twenty-five miles south of Fresno, at Riverdale. Later it was divided between Jerome and Leroy. Dairying and beef cattle were their main occupations.

—•—

GEORGE HARLAN FAMILY
GELDERMANN

George Harlan was the great-grandfather of Mrs. A. J. (Carmen) Geldermann (deceased), whose husband was a pioneer realtor of the San Ramon Valley. Their son, Harlan S. Geldermann, (RA) named for his mother's family, is a prominent realtor. Late 1976—James H. "Jim" Geldermann and his wife Wendy (Fowler) have also gone into the Geldermann Realty business.

The following story was written by Mrs. Carmen Geldermann and concerns the overland trek which the Harlan family made to California in 1845. The story was written in 1956-57 and printed in the August 1957, Twenty-fifth Anniversary Historical & Progress edition of the *Walnut Kernel* (newspaper).

In 1845 great-grandfather George Harlan was living at Niles, Michigan, when a Mr. Hastings came lecturing about California. George Harlan determined to head a party to that faraway land of opportunity and hired Hastings to meet them at Fort Bridger, Wyoming, and lead them over the Hastings cutoff, which Hastings claimed to have discovered. The lure which drew the Harlans west was land and opportunity. The discovery of gold was still a couple of years off.

The Harlans sold their ranch in Niles, Michigan. They joined with the Young family and the group wintered in Independence, Missouri, in order to be able to start for California in April 1846. It was here that they teamed up with the ill-fated Donner Party.

At Fort Bridger, Hastings met them and all went well for three weeks until they came to a spot called Weber Canyon in Utah. The narrow canyon appeared almost impenetrable. The Donners, due to their heavy wagons and equipment, were forced to turn back and retrace their route to Fort Bridger.

George Harlan had eighty wagons under his command and many of the party wanted to turn back at the foreboding canyon and return to Fort Bridger with the Donner Party. However, Harlan consulted with his 103-year old grandmother, who was a member of the party and she advised them to go ahead. This Mrs. Daugherty was 103 and had been blind for years. She had been carried across the plains on a litter. She urged her grandson to go forward and so the party did!

Meanwhile, the Donners returned to Fort Bridger and took the well-known Ft. Hall route, the established overland "highway" to California.

Weber Canyon was only a mile long, but it was such an obstacle that it took the Harlan-Young party seven days to go the mile. The wagons literally had to be lifted over and around the huge rocks.

When the group finally emerged from this ordeal they were immediately faced with a giant cane brake, the cane twelve feet high and so thick that it seemed impossible to get through. That night a storm came which soaked all their provisions and made them pretty miserable. The storm, though, had stretched the cane flat and the party rode right over it.

That brought them to the head of the great Salt Lake desert where Hastings told them it would take from sunup to sundown to cross. Instead, it was three days and three nights! They finally had to loose the oxen from the wagons and let them run to water. Many of the animals died and three members of the party also died, including a man named Hargraves. George Harlan lost a whole herd of English cattle.

When the party did reach water, it was bitter springs and the water was all but impossible to drink. It took the group three weeks to go back and gather up their supplies and cattle.

As they started up the eastern slopes of the Sierra, they realized that the lack of oxen and also provisions was perilous and that they needed new supplies. So George Harlan sent Jacob Harlan (author of "California from '46 to '88") and Tom Smith to ride ahead to Sutters Fort for provisions and cattle. The two did and met the Harlan-Young party again at the crest of the Sierra with additional cattle.

When the party came down into the Sacramento Valley, it was October. It was raining very hard. The same rain was the one which brought the snowstorm that trapped the Donners at Donner Lake. Only a few members of that expedition escaped alive.

First campsite for the Harlan-Young group was at Johnson's ranch above the town, which was known as New Helvetia and is now Sacramento. The following night they camped in the heart of New Helvetia and that night Grandmother Daugherty died. She was buried with only a little wooden cross to mark her grave.

Thirty years later, when the capitol was built, her grave was found to be in the exact center of where the capitol dome rose. Officials wrote to Joel Harlan, her great-grandson, asking if he wanted the remains moved. There was really nothing to move, so Mrs. Daugherty's final resting place is beneath the capitol dome.

The Harlan family settled first in Mission San Jose, then went to San Francisco where George Harlan bought a tract of forty Vera lots which extended from the back of the Palace Hotel in a straight line to the Bay. Also, he built the family home on what is known as Harlan Place today in San Francisco.

Joel Harlan, his son, was whipsawing lumber in Redwood Canyon at the time gold was discovered. Not trusting his luck in mining he went to Leidesdorf, the big merchant of the time in San Francisco, and had him outfit him with a complete line of merchandise to take to the mines. Outside of once finding a $600 nugget, Joel didn't do much mining, but made a great deal of money from his merchandise.

He and his wife slept many times on bags of gold. His wife (my grandmother, Minerva Harlan) never believed gold would be the legal tender because it was too plentiful.

In 1850 they returned from the mines and bought part of the old Amador grant, at which time Amador, who was not a good businessman, sold them land which had already been sold to the Norris family. So, in order to straighten out the mistake, the Joel Harlans were given the site of the present Harlan ranch known as El Nido. They built a home which took four years to complete. The home is still in the family today. (Author's note: and also today, 1977.)

When Mrs. Joel Harlan died, Mrs. Geldermann received a letter from Patsy Reed, who was one of the children of the Donner party who was saved. She and Minerva had played together while crossing the plains. Neither had known what had happened to the other until Mrs. Joel Harlan's death which Mrs. Reed had read about. She then wrote to the Harlan family.

In *Remembering Alamo... and Other Things*

Along the Way, reference is made in Chapter 6 "The Story of My Life" by Mary Ann (Smith) Jones to "the Donner party, the best equipped on the road."

Still owned by Mr. and Mrs. A. J. Geldermann and maintained as their permanent residence is the famous and beautiful Harlanton, between San Ramon and Dublin. Mrs. Geldermann is a direct descendant of the Harlan family which founded Harlanton. It has been in the Harlan family since the early 1850s. The Harlans came to California at the same time as the ill-fated Donner party. In fact, the Harlans traveled with the Donners for a time on the way west.

The name of the Harlan home at Harlanton is still El Nido. It has been modernized without destroying any of the original buildings. The name, "el nido", by the way, means "nest" in Spanish. (The above also from *Walnut Kernel*, August 1957.)

—•—

RECALLS MANY HAPPY VISITS TO HARLAN HOME
by Bessie Hargrave Drury
(Wrote article in 1957, when she was 63 years old)

Every summer, as a little girl, my mother and I visited my great aunt, Mrs. Minerva Harlan, whose home was El Nido, at San Ramon.

Such happy times as we had! Evenings of music and entertainment with neighbors dropping in.

Once the Ladies Aid of the Methodist Church in San Ramon came for a garden party. The garden was hung with Chinese lanterns, while music from two beautiful harps filled the air. My cousin, Hazel Harlan, and I had "Rebecca at the Well," dispensing lemonade. Business was not so good, so we wandered in the garden. When we returned Lorin Llewellyn, Clifford and Claude Glass, George and Will Meese had finished the lemonade, and the glasses were hid in the shrubbery.

We always went calling "down the valley." My parents, Fred and Julia Hargrave, came to Walnut Creek as bride and groom in 1875. My father farmed the Harlan Ranch, which was most of the Castle Hill area, so there were many old friends to contact.

We had early lunch at Aunt Minerva's and in the "surrey with fringe around the top," drawn by two lovely horses, away we went.

We stopped at the Cox home. My mother knew Mrs. Cox as a girl in the Silver Days in Nevada in 1863. Then over to the Baldwins' and to gentle Mrs. Meese's who kissed me and said, "How you've grown, dear!" A stop at Captain and Mrs. Harrison's where the captain, true to his calling, remarked if it were a fair or blustering day.

At the lovely old Hemme home, where I sat prim and proper on a hassock bobbing my blonde curls, listening to grownup chatter, children were seen, not heard!

At the big hospitable home of the Stowes we often stayed overnight. Pearl° was just my age. What fun! We rode the old white horse, who would carry four. Her back was broad, and she was gentle. We rode into Walnut Creek to play with Zita Ford°° on the hill. Want to see Ruby Burpee°°° and marvel at her wonderful laughter. One Sunday night the grownups went to church, and the boys prepared supper.

Such a jolly time! Such good old days! The memory lingers.....

°Mrs. Joseph Lawrence, Walnut Creek.
°°Sister of Ada and Tom Ford.
°°°Mrs. Charles Guy, Concord.

Bessie Hargrave Drury was born September 6, 1884 and died December 16, 1976 at age ninety-two. She was married to Harry Lloyd Drury. In 1933 they moved to Walnut Creek. Their home was called "Casa Cristina." Mrs. Drury was born on the Harlan Ranch in San Ramon. Henry Clay Smith, her grandfather, came to California on horseback in 1844. He was called the father of Alameda County as he helped put a bill through the legislature creating the county. Mrs. Drury has a daughter, Elizabeth Drury French, of Walnut Creek.

GELDERMANN REALTORS

The following was an advertisement in a 1957 newspaper:

"Oldest established real estate office in Danville. Staff: Al Geldermann, Harlan Geldermann, Juanita Legg, secretary; Roberta McMillen, stenographer.

Insurance Division - William Hockins, broker and manager; Mildred Glock, secretary,

Sales Department: Nita Pasquale, sales manager; Ray McCoy, Frank Wallace, Glen Givva, William Heider, Eldora Elder, Helen Glines, Ruberta Pearce and Bea Gibbs.

Developing the SAN RAMON VALLEY specializing in: lots, homes, subdivisions, industrial developments, general brokerage. A complete line of insurance.

People who think of the SAN RAMON VALLEY think of — GELDERMANN REALTORS, Hartz Avenue, Danville, California, tel: VErnon 7-4242. (Author's note: with the dial system the phone number was slightly changed: 837-4242.)

The following was noted during some research:

The Harlan Ranch once had a gardener called a "remittance man." It is said that he once was a physician to a Scandinavian king.

—•—

HARLAN - GELDERMANN GENEALOGY

George Harlan to America in 1687, James Harlan born 1692, James Harlan born 1721, George Harlan born 1750, George Harlan (1802-1850), Joel Harlan (1828-1875), Addie Elmina (Harlan) Stolp, Carmen Minerva (Stolp) Geldermann (May 2, 1901-1967), Harlan S. Geldermann born November 15, 1923, Jim, Joel and Tracy (deceased) Geldermann.

—•—

Carmen Minerva Stolp married Al J. Geldermann (August 21, 1890-1969) December 1, 1928. "A. J.," as he was affectionately known, was in the real estate business in Oakland from 1913. He worked as a salesman for Fred Reed (deceased), realtor in Oakland. In 1930 the family moved out to El Nido in San Ramon from Piedmont where "A. J." worked out of the home selling real estate. In 1947 after World War II the son, Harlan S. Geldermann, became actively engaged in the real estate profession in partnership with his father. Their small real estate brokerage office was on Hartz Avenue between Acree's Grocery Store and the old telephone office. "A. J." Geldermann retired from active real estate business in 1953.

—•—

HARLAN S. GELDERMANN

Harlan S. Geldermann was born in Oakland, California. He is a descendant of the Harlan family, pioneers of 1846. He was educated in public schools in Alameda and Contra Costa Counties and graduated from San Ramon Valley Union High School in Danville in 1941. Entered Stanford University in the fall of 1941 where he participated in a number of campus activities, including varsity football.

Subsequent to Pearl Harbor he enlisted in the United States Navy and attended Colorado College where he was a member of the V-12 Unit. He played on the Rocky Mountain championship football team of Colorado College. Geldermann graduated from Midshipman School at Plattsburg, New York, in June of 1944 and volunteered for submarine duty. After attending a number of submarine training schools, he graduated as a submarine officer from the United States submarine training base at New London, Connecticut. He served aboard the *USS Spikefish* which had a rather illustrious career in Pacific waters. He was honorably discharged as a Lieutenant J. G. at the end of World War II. He returned to Stanford University where he graduated with a B.A. degree in Economics in 1947.

While completing his college education, Geldermann obtained a real estate broker's license. Upon graduation he joined his father A. J. Geldermann in the Danville, California real estate business. Since 1947 he has been actively engaged in the business, serving as president of the Contra Costa Real Estate Board in 1952 and participating in other California Real Estate Association activities as a regional vice-president and chairman of the Land Development Committee on numerous occasions.

For a number of years he has been a member of the B.P.O.E., the American Legion, and Sonoma County Trail Blazers. In more recent years he has participated in several important real estate transactions, both as a principal and as a broker. He was responsible for a substantial number of Bay Area subdivisions, approximately forty. He directed the land acquisition for the San Ramon Village development which extends into both Alameda and Contra Costa Counties.

He has two children. Jim, age thirty-two, a graduate of Stanford University, and his wife Wendy make their home in a house in San Ramon on Geldermann Ranch property. Joel is twenty.

Harlan Geldermann is owner/operator of the well-known brokerage firm of Geldermann Inc. dba Geldermann Realtors, the oldest real estate company in the San Ramon Valley. He is owner and developer of Round Hill Golf and Country Club and is developing the residential properties surrounding it. In addition to other development and brokerage activities, Geldermann was a 50% joint venture partner with the Hawaiian corporation, Castle & Cooke, Inc., in the development of an 11,500-acre new community in San Jose. His interest in that venture was merged with Castle & Cooke. He is a director of Oceanic Properties, Inc., the real estate arm of Castle & Cooke. Due to this association with projects of this magnitude and importance, he has on several occasions been asked by HUD to give testimony before Congressional sub-committees on matters in the housing industry and urban problems. He was appointed to the California State Real Estate Commission by Governor Ronald Reagan in 1968 and served for nine years.

BOONE FAMILIES

The first account of the Boone Family was written by John, uncle of Daniel Boone. Transcribed by John's nephew James in 1788. First published in *Pennsylvania Historical Magazine* in 1897, Vol. XXI, page 112. The original manuscript is in the archives of the Wisconsin Historical Society, Madison, Wisc. Mrs. Flora Vivian Witherspoon of Los Angeles has records of Boone and Vivian Families, compiled by Mrs. Ida Meechan (genealogist).

From the Records of James O. Boone and Transcripts from the "The Ancestry of Abraham Lincoln" by Lea & Hutchinson, Published 1909 by Houghton Mifflin Company.

The Boone family record was made by Cora May Boone, Jan. 1932. She made a copy for Travis Boone Jan. 1937. Typed by Travis Boone Jan. 1968. (Three of Daniel Boone's cousins married Lincoln ancestors, and four married Lees.)

George Boone I was born and died in England. George Boone II was born and died in Exeter County, Devon, England. He married Sarah Uppey. George Boone III, a weaver, was born at Stoke, near Exeter county, England in 1666. He married Margaret Milton Mauridge, born 1669 at Bradnich, England, eight miles from Exeter. Came to America, Philadelphia, Pa. 1717, (Quakers) brought certificates from Collumption meeting.

1. George Boone (uncle of Daniel) born in 1690 Devonshire, England, went to Pennsylvania 1712 (five years before his parents). Trustee to will of Mordacai Lincoln II. He married Deborah Howell. They had six children. Had a grant of 400 acres in 1718 now known as Exeter County, Berks, Pa. Son William married Sarah Lincoln in 1724 (daughter of Mordacai Lincoln II). Moved to Maryland, died 1771. Had eight children. Daughter Abagail married Pancoast; Mary married Isaac Lee (Maryland).

2. Sarah Boone, born 1692 Devon, England, came to Pa. 1712, married Jacob Stover of Oley, Pa. 3. Squire Boone, born 1696, came to Pa. 1712, married Sarah Morgan, appraised estate of Mordacai Lincoln (1736). Moved to Davie County, No. Carolina 1750. 4. Mary married John Webb 1720. 5. John (uncle of Daniel) unmarried, born Oley, Pa. first genealogist of Boone family 6 Joseph. 7. Benjamin born 1706, married Ann Farmar, five children baptised in Episcopal Church in Douglasville, Pa. Later married Susanna and had six children. Daughter Dinah (1749) married Benj. Taliman, son of Wm. and Ann (Lincoln) Taliman. 8. James born 1709, Pa.,

—•—

Forest Home Farms, San Ramon. This home, built in 1900, was pictured on a postcard which was postmarked November 1, 1907 and addressed to Mrs. B. F. Chaboya, sent to her by Minnie Thorn Boone. The home was painted French grey with green pillars.

The same home, picture taken in August 1958. The house had been painted white, as it still is. It has twenty-two rooms.

married Mary Foulke, had twelve children: Ann born 1757 married Abraham Lincoln III, son of Mordacai Lincoln II. He was Representative in Pennsylvania Assembly, State Convention, Constitutional Convention. Martha married a Lee, Judah married Hannah Lee, a mathematician and writer of Boone Genealogy in 1788, using his uncle John's accounts. 9. Samuel, his widow married an uncle of Mary Yarnell, daughter of Mordacai Lincoln.

Children of Squire Boone and Sarah (Morgan) Boone were: 1. Sarah born 1724; 2. Israel born 1726; 3. Samuel born 1728 married Sarah Day, had a son Samuel; 4. Jonathan born 1730; 5. Elizabeth born 1732; 6. Daniel Born Oct. 22, 1734; 7. Edward born 1741; 8. Squire; 9. Hannah mar-

ried Pennington; 10. Mary; and 11. George.

*6. Daniel (1734-1820) born Oley, Pa. moved to No. Carolina 1750. Married Rebecca Bryan (died 1813). She was an ancestor of Wm. J. Bryan. Daniel and Rebecca (Bryan) Boone children: 1. James born 1757, killed by the Indians on the road to Kentucky; 2. Israel, born 1759; 3. Susanna born 1760; 4. Jemima, born 1762, married Flanders Callaway and went to Adrian County, Mo.; 5. Lavinia; 6. Rebecca born 1768; 7. Daniel Morgan born 1769, went to Kansas 1827; 8. John Bryan, born 1773; 9. Nathan born 1790, married a Van Biber.

Daniel's granddaughter Emeline Roberta Callaway (daughter of Jemima and Flanders Callaway) married his great-grandnephew Haden Boone, born 1805 in Missouri. He crossed the plains in 1865. Their children: 1. Elizabeth married Andrew Marshall; 2. James Orval Boone* born Feb. 28, 1825 in Mo.; 3. Martha; 4. Wellington T. born 1829 in Mo.; married Miss J. E. Carter, had a daughter Edith; 5. Joel, daughter Ina; 6. Lemuel, son Curtis; 7. William died at sea returning from California; 8. John Callaway, a lawyer, son John C. Jr., who had no children.

*James Orval Boone in 1852 came to California with his brothers. Returned to Missouri and married Nov. 12, 1861 to Sara "Sally" Elizabeth Sims, born Nov. 7, 1841, daughter of Elias Sims (fought in Mexican War) and Cynthia Pemberton (whose mother was a Vivian.) They came to California in 1865, settled in Contra Costa County, Danville (now Sycamore Road.) Their children: 1. Cynthia Emiline "Lina" (named for her grandmother Cynthia and for Daniel Boone's granddaughter Emeline) born 1861 in Mo., died in Sacramento, California; 2. Cora May Boone born in 1864 in Mo. died in Oakland, Calif.; 3. Numa Sims Boone born 1867 on Sycamore Rd., Danville, Calif. died at the family home "Forest Home" in 1941.

1. "Lina" Boone married William Alexander Moore, D.D.S. (Baltimore University) son of Jno. Samuel Moore, D.D.S. (Baltimore University), cousin of Sydney Lanier (poet and musician of So. Carolina.) Their children were: Helen Ruth, married Herbert Alton Waterman and had a daughter Patricia, who married Frank Durkee, Sacramento, Calif.; William Vivian married Lila Rodgers and their son William was accidentally shot.

3. Numa Sims Boone married Minnie Thorn born 1863 in Santa Clara, died at Merritt Hospital

in Oakland, 1951. They had a son Travis Moore Boone, known as "Bud," born Aug. 10, 1901 at "Forest Home," San Ramon, Calif. He was married Oct. 5, 1929 to Ruth Berry Quayle, born March 12, 1904, daughter of William Foote and Fannie (Edwards) Quayle of Hollywood. A daughter, Eleanor Sims Boone, unmarried, born Aug. 17, 1905, at "Forest Home". She was a graduate of Mills College and a professor. She died 1954 following a stroke.

—•—

(Author's note: Permission was given to me to use the Boone Families Genealogy by Travis M. and Ruth Boone of San Ramon.)

Further research and update: Numa Sims and Minnie (Thorn) Boone, when first married pooled their funds and purchased 200 acres, later added to it, in San Ramon, seven miles from Danville. The location on the creek was origianlly an Indian encampment. On the property were several large trees, among them four large Mission fig, and an olive, planted by the Indians. It is said that Mission San Jose gave away the trees for home planting and the Indians got some. Three of these old trees still remain, two huge fig and a mammoth olive in front of the home.

In 1900 the Boones built the two-story 22-room house and named it "Forest Home." When I visited in March 1977, I was given a tour of the handsome garden areas with camellias, azaleas, roses and huge old trees. Two roses have quite a history of their own. They are at their fifth location in over 100 years of life! Leland Stanford bought some roses from New York, which came around the Horn by ship. When Grandfather Thorn was delivering them to him he asked if he could purchase some. One was the White Lamark and the other a climber, Yellow Bankshire. Captain Thorn always took these roses with him when he moved. They have been planted in Santa Clara County, San Francisco, and Alameda.

When Captain Thorn passed away his widow sold the Alameda property, had the roses dug up and brought them with her when she came to live at "Forest Home" in San Ramon. And they remain there today. Ruth Boone related she paid 15¢ for the interesting twisting wisteria in the dime store in Hayward in 1939, the same year she planted more redwoods. Twenty years ago the 22-room house was remodeled into five apartments, three above and two on the first floor. The Boones live on the south end lower section. Travis and Ruth

Boone had no children. The home site consists of thirteen acres and the lovely home is all that is left of "Forest Home Farms."

—•—

DANIEL BOONE

Daniel Boone was born in a log cabin beside the Schuylkil River in Pennsylvania, near the site of what is now Reading, Pennsylvania. When sixteen he moved with his family to wild country on the forks of the Yadkin River along the North Carolina frontier. The forest was Daniel's only school. He loved to travel. He led a hunting party across the Alleghenies. In 1765 he went to Florida. Two years later he made his first expedition into Kentucky. The Indians called his "Wilderness Road"[7] Quasioto (mountains with much deer). He guided a party of settlers over it in 1775. They built Fort Boonesboro on the Kentucky River. Boone's wife and their daughter Jemima were the first white women to stand on the banks of the river. Indians captured Boone several times. The Shawnees took him to Detroit where their chief adopted him. He escaped when he learned they planned to attack Boonesboro. When land grabbers came to Kentucky, Boone left of North Carolina.

In 1780 he returned to Kentucky, to a wilder section. In 1790 he moved to Virginia. In 1795 he left for Spanish territory near St. Louis, Missouri. He was given a grant of land and named commander of the district called Femme Osage. In his position he judged law cases, though no lawyer, but he was a very fair man. He lost his land again when the U.S. took the territory via the Louisiana Purchase. In 1810 Congress gave it back as a reward for opening the wilderness for mankind.

Boone was a born leader. He loved peace. He was a quiet man of medium height, usually dressed in buckskins with coonskin cap. While in Kentucky he was a surveyor and served in the Kentucky Legislature and was Lieutenant of Fayette County. It is said he went as far as what later became Yellowstone National Park. At the age of eighty-two he was hunting alone in Nebraska. He died September 20, 1820 at the home of his son Nathan in St. Louis, Missouri. His and his wife's remains were disinterred and moved to Frankfort, Kentucky in 1845. A monument was placed in his honor. The Boone Trail was marked in 1915. It shows America's memorial to one of the country's greatest pioneers.

Peter Thorup Shoe Shop, San Ramon, was a building to the right of the family home. All buildings are now gone and there is a gas station on one corner of the busy intersection.

The Thorup residence in San Ramon was a hotel and stagecoach stop. It was at the intersection of Crow Canyon Road and the main county road (California Highway 21). The sale of the building and five acres was transacted with a down payment of one cow. In the photo are Louis Hansen, left, and unidentified man on upstairs porch; Jacob Henry Thorup on step; Edna Christine Thorup (later Smith) in highchair; and unidentified man and woman.

Residence of Jacob Thorup and Anton Petersen, built in 1888 and burned in 1898. It was at the end of Finley Road in Tassajara Valley, Danville.

THORUP FAMILIES

The following material on the Thorup Family genealogy was excerpted from over thirty typed pages of research compiled by Dorothy (Smith) Peyret, Grass Valley, California, October 28, 1976. She is the daughter of Edna Christine (Thorup) Smith, and niece of Christine (Thorup) Wardrip, who kept records of her parents and their descendants and inspired the very complete results. I have been given full permission from family members to use the material in this book. Here's a family that *has* found its roots!

JACOB JOHANSEN THORUP

Jacob Johansen Thorup (1820-1892) was married twice. No records of first wife, but there was one son, Hans Johansen Thorup, born October 8, 1847. Hans married and had two sons, Jake and Chris (both deceased). Their mother remarried and became Mrs. Miltersen. She died Feb. 23, 1923. There is a great-grandson of Jacob, John Thorup, living in Arizona.

Hanne Marie Andersen (1827-1892) was Jacob's second wife. They had ten children, all born in Denmark. They were: 1. Peder Andersen born June 27, 1850, married Jan. 8, 1884, to Ane Marie Rasmussen, born Sept. 28, 1863. He died June 16, 1939, she July 4, 1938. 2. Ane Margrathe, born Feb. 8, 1852, married Anton Petersen. Ane died in 1939. 3. Ane born March 15, 1853, married a Mr. Alberg, no further dates. 4. Peter Christian, born Feb. 23, 1855, married Maria Boree. 5. Eline Marie, born June 12, 1857, no further record. 6. Ane Kathrine, born Aug. 5, 1859, married Jan. 25, 1888 to Iver Sorensen Jacobsen, born Nov. 26, 1860.[8] She died Dec. 5, 1959, he died Sept. 12, 1897. 7. Andrea born Aug. 23, 1861, married Christopher Ericksen, born March 17, 1865. She died Nov. 9, 1943. 8. Kjerstine born Sept. 28, 1863, married Louis Hansen. No further records. 9. Johan Henrik born Sept. 3, 1865, died Aug. 18, 1867. 10. Jacob Harold Benedickt (always known as Harry) born March 3, 1870, married Emma Elvena Prowse born Oct. 16, 1881, died Feb. 5, 1911. His second wife was Marguerite Scoville. He died May 5, 1955, she Aug. 28, 1944.

Jacob Johansen Thorup and Hanne Marie (Andersen) Thorup came to the United States and lived with their son Peder A. and his wife Ane Marie Thorup in San Ramon.[9] Jacob and Hanne both died in 1892, she four days following him. They were buried the same day in the family plot at Pleasanton, California. Jacob J. was born Sept. 16, 1820, Hanne Marie (Andersen) April 28, 1827.

—•—

PEDER/PETER ANDERSEN THORUP

Peder/Peter Andersen Thorup, was born in Slesvig (Schleswig) Medolden, Denmark. Peder/Peter came to America in 1868 to avoid being drafted in the war. Slesvig was taken over by the Germans, but he remained loyal to the Danes. He went to Peoria, Illinois and learned the shoemaker trade. In 1872 he crossed the plains to Hayward, California, but did not like it. He settled in San Ramon. Ane/Anne Marie Rasmussen came to the U.S.A. with her brother Hans in April 1882. Hans left Denmark to avoid compulsory military service. They went to Petaluma, stayed three months. Hans went to the Peter Rasmussen family in Livermore. Ane/Anne went to work in San Ramon for the Moore family, of Moore Canyon (now Crow Canyon Road).

Peder/Peter A. Thorup and Ane/Anne Marie Rasmussen met and they were married Jan. 8, 1884 (on her parents' twenty-fifth wedding anniversary). The wedding was at the Peter Rasmussens' home in Livermore. Ane/Anne Marie was born in Rudenkoben, Langeland Island, Denmark. Her parents were Hans, a bookkeeper, and Anne Christine (Hansen) Rasmussen, both born at Trykalo, Northern Bro., Denmark. They lived to celebrate their fiftieth wedding anniversary Jan. 8, 1909.

The newlyweds settled in San Ramon, which at that time (1884) had a store, school, church, blacksmith shop and saloon. Later, when their second child was small, they bought a hotel with five acres of land. Developed it by planting fruit and walnut trees and raised their own produce and livestock of horses, cows, pigs, and chickens. Peder/Peter had his own P. A. Thorup Boot & Shoe Manufacturing Shop in San Ramon. He specialized in custom-made shoes for everyone in the Valley. Peder/Peter Andersen and Ane/Anne Marie (Rasmussen) Thorup had seven children, all born in San Ramon, California. 1. Jacob Henry (always known as Henry,) born Dec. 5, 1884, married Dec. 17, 1905, to May Baum Colberg, born Sept. 18, 1883. He died May 29, 1964 and she June 22, 1959. 2. Edna Christine born Feb. 15, 1887, married Aug. 15, 1909 to Johannes Sorensen Smith born Oct. 7, 1886. He died Jan. 12, 1953. She celebrated her 90th birthday in San Francisco, February 1977.[10] 3. Helene Marie born Oct. 31, 1888, married Oct. 16, 1912 to Nis Jorgen Jorgensen, born Feb. 22, 1883. She died July 4, 1921 and he Jan. 23, 1923. 4. Jerome R. born Apr. 27, 1890, married Aug. 8, 1938 to Alma Holmes born June 23, 1887. He died May 13, 1962, she April 1, 1976. 5. Julia Anita Thorup (always known as Anita) born Jan. 23, 1893, married May 27, 1917 to Louis Hans Kamp born Feb. 11, 1893, celebrated their sixtieth wedding anniversary May 1977. 6. Christine Alvera, born Oct. 2, 1895, married Dec. 14, 1920, to Guy Emerson Wardrip born Jan. 28, 1891. He died Dec. 11, 1959. She makes her home in Danville. 7. Petrea Arnoldin was born Oct. 3, 1906, married May 5, 1925 to Beryl Wille, (RA) born Dec. 8, 1900. They make their home in Danville. Thorup Lane in San Ramon was named for Peder/Peter A. Thorup.

—•—

Thorup family. Standing, left to right: Andrea Thorup Ericksen, Ane Thorup Alberg, Peter A. Thorup, Peter Christian Thorup, Ane Margrethe Thorup Petersen, Ane Kathrine Thorup Jacobsen. Seated, left to right: Jacob Harold Benedickt (Harry) Thorup, Hanne Marie (Andersen) Thorup, Jacob Johansen Thorup, Kjerstine Thorup Hansen.

THORUP DESCENDANTS
CHILDREN, GRANDCHILDREN
AND GREAT-GRANDCHILDREN

1. Jacob Henry, called Henry Thorup, adopted Marie, who was the daughter of May Baum Colbert. Marie died very young, no dates.

2. Edna (Thorup) and Johannes S. Smith had one daughter, Dorothy Edna Smith, born July 20, 1911, married Nov. 7, 1931 to Joseph Gene Peyret II, born Jan. 31, 1904. They had one son, Joseph Gene Peyret III, born Sept. 15, 1936, married Sept. 17, 1955 to Olive May Hugi, born Sept. 19, 1935. They had three children: Douglas Gene born Aug. 18, 1956, Roger Lee born Aug. 3, 1957 and Melinda Sue born Oct. 8, 1958. They divorced and he was married Dec. 28, 1974 to Betty Joan Peterson Lawton with two children by a previous marriage, Carolyn Sue born Sept. 16, 1959 and Michael James born March 3, 1966. They all live in Grass Valley.

3. Helene (Thorup) and Nis Jorgensen had two daughters, Anita Christine born May 30, 1915, married June 6, 1936 to Joseph Hutton, born March 21, 1907. She died May 13, 1976. Marjorie Jorgensen was born Nov. 21, 1920 and died June 9, 1922. Anita (Jorgensen) and Joseph Hutton had a daughter Jo-Ann born Sept. 15, 1939, married Nov. 24, 1964 to James Martin Whitty, born Sept. 22, 1939. They had Anne Whitty born March 24, 1964 and Christine born Nov. 9, 1970. They divorced. Jerome Joseph Hutton born Aug. 26, 1941, married March 9, 1968 to Kathy Kauffman born May 22, 1948. Their children are Jodi Ann born Sept. 30, 1971 and Jennifer Lynn born April 18, 1974. Jo-Ann (Hutton) Whitty lives in Concord, California. Jerome and Kathy Hutton are in Miami, Florida where Jerome is with Western Air Lines.

4. Jerome R. and Alma (Holmes) Thorup had no children together. Her daughter was Clara Holmes, who became Jerome's step-daughter. Clara was born June 24, 1916, married Nov. 10, 1939 to Philip Harris born Oct. 7, 1899. They live in Danville. They had one daughter, Karen (Harris) born Jan. 20, 1944, married Feb. 7, 1965 to Alvin Eckert born Aug. 13, 1939. They have one son Steven Eckert born Dec. 4, 1969.

5. Anita (Thorup) and Louis Kamp had four children. Lois Ann was born June 11, 1918, married May 5, 1940 to Malcolm Albert Gompertz born June 17, 1914. Their children are: Thomas Malcolm born Feb. 12, 1941, died Feb. 8, 1968, in Viet Nam while working for the U.S. Government as a civilian. Michael Albert born March 22, 1944, a bachelor tennis court contractor, lives in Sausalito, California. Lois Ann born June 6, 1947 married April 8, 1967 to Ronald Simmons, they had Mathew Simmons born Nov. 13, 1968. They divorced and Lois Ann remarried to Eugene Pons and his children are David Pons born Aug. 30, 1967 and Jennifer born Jan. 22, 1964. Robert Hayden Kamp born Sept. 2, 1920, married April 29, 1946 to Regina Kelly born Sept. 20, 1924. He died Feb. 22, 1964, as a result of an automobile accident. Their children are Robert Jr. born Aug. 6, 1948 and Paul born Jan. 12, 1950. Doris Margaret Kamp born April 6, 1924, married Feb. 24, 1946 to Albert G. Morgan born Aug. 3, 1922, and their three children are: Russell Louis Morgan born Jan. 25, 1947, married Sept. 21, 1974 to Cheryl Marie Sullivan born Nov. 12, 1948. They have one daughter, Kathleen Anita, born Sept. 5, 1976, and live in Pleasanton. Sharon Lee Morgan born Nov. 1, 1949, married June 12, 1971 to Terrance Charles Clore born Jan. 29, 1947. Their son Greg Morgan[11] was born Oct. 5, 1975. They make their home in Carson City, Nevada. Timothy Albert Morgan born Feb. 23, 1954. Shirley Kamp born Jan. 17, 1929 married April 22, 1949 to Floyd Charles Fairchild, they adopted Sarah Fairchild born Dec. 29, 1956. Shirley divorced Fairchild 1960, on Aug. 15, 1962 was married to Frederick Gillette Brear born March 1, 1916. He had previously been married July 25, 1942 to Mary Frances Lax born November 5, 1918. They had one daughter Barbara Patricia who married Kerry Germann and had two daughters, Aimee and Emily. Shirley and Fred have two children, Linda Marie, born April 9, 1964 and James Frederick, born Aug. 15, 1965. They make their home on Blackhawk Rd., Danville.

6. Christine (Thorup) and Guy Wardrip had no children.

7. Petrea (Thorup) and Beryl Wille had four children. Betty Jean born April 25, 1926, married Carlos Reed. Had a daughter Patricia Ellen born June 18, 1947. She is in a home for the retarded. Reeds divorced May 10, 1950. Betty Jean married May 26, 1963 to Jack Creighton, had twins who died at birth. Creighton died Sept. 21, 1972. Betty Jean now lives in Montana. 2. Lambert P. Wille born July 13, 1930 is an architect and a bachelor, lives in the family home in Danville. 3. Beverly Fay born March 22, 1932, married April 21, 1951 to Richard E. McNeil, born April 14, 1925. Their children are Dennis McNeil born April 12, 1954,

married Aug. 2, 1975 to Marilyn Virginia Royce. Dennis McNeil has two step-children, Michael and Douglas. Coleen Judith McNeil, born May 8, 1952, died Feb. 15, 1958 of leukemia. Richard Kevin McNeil born April 23, 1953 and Bridget Ann McNeil born April 3, 1960. Rich McNeil was killed in an airplane accident Aug. 25, 1964. Beverly married to Roy Buckley Dec. 21, 1968; the marriage was annulled. She lives in Alamo. Anne Marie Wille born Aug. 23, 1933, married Feb. 13, 1952 to William Kenneth Kendall born Dec. 29, 1932. They have three daughters, Kay Marie born Dec. 4, 1958, Katheryn born Sept. 16, 1960 and Karleen Louise born April 18, 1964. Bill and Anne Marie Kendall live in Walnut Creek. He is a broker/realtor. Doris and Albert G. Morgan make their home in Danville. He is owner-manager of Du-Mor Milk Depot Inc. in Walnut Creek.

—•—

A family reunion was held June 27, 1937 for Peter A. Thorup's 87th birthday. His children (with the exception of Helene who died in 1921), his grandchildren and first great-grandchild were present.

Author's note—I don't know of any pioneer family that settled in the San Ramon Valley over 100 years ago, that has as many descendants still in the area.

KAMP

The following excerpts are from the Family Tree titled "All in the Family," by Linda Brear, age twelve, daughter of Frederick G. and Shirley (Kamp) Brear, dated February 7, 1977. It was an assignment by Mrs. Garay at Los Cerros School, Danville. Researched by Linda from her maternal grandfather Louis Kamp, who is eighty-four years old. I have been given permission by the family to use the information.

Mrs. Karl (Kamp) Grayson (-1902) was married in Denmark to a Mr. Kamp, who died in Denmark. They had a son and only child Hans Nicholsen Kamp (1855-1938). He was born in Slesvig, Denmark and came to the U.S.A. in 1872 when he was sixteen. He traveled across country by train to Hayward where he worked on a ranch. In 1880 he married Honsina Lausten (1827-1929). Her parents were born in Langeland, Denmark. They came to America because of the war. They had four daughters: Margret, Minnie, Maria and Honsina. The father was a shoemaker. Honsina Lausten and Hans Nicholsen Kamp had twelve children: Hans (1881-1957), Carl (1886-1960), twins Ed (1888-1971), Bill (1888-1948?), Louis died in infancy, Andrew (1894-1932), Carolyn (1890-1970), Mame

(1892-1974), Louis Hansen Kamp born 1893, Ida (1895-1972?) and two who died at birth. Their father Hans owned "Yar-Yar Stables" on Tassajara Road, Livermore.

Louis and Anita (Thorup) Kamp were married in 1917 and have lived in the San Ramon Valley area. They bought a dairy farm on Blackhawk Road, Danville. Their four children were all born in the Danville area. They make their home at Rossmoor, a retirement community in Walnut Creek. Two of their daughters with their families live on a part of the dairy farm.

Linda Brear also did her paternal family:

BREAR

Frederick Brear married Sarah Herbert. He was born in Bradford, England, and was a cloth designer. His father was a pipe organ builder. Sarah was born in Hawick, Wales. They came to America and settled in Philadelphia, Pennsylvania. They had four children: Albert Edward (RA) (1885-1955), Nellie, Maud and William, no records. Albert graduated from Julliard School of Music in New York and sang as a baritone with the Metropolitan Opera Company. He moved to Berkeley in 1914 and established an Academy of Music. He married Grace Marie Gillette (RA) (1890-1945?), daughter of Samuel and Elsie (Tyron) Gillette. Her father was a carpenter who was born in Vermont and served in the Civil War. Her grandparents were from France. Her mother was born in Winser, Vermont. Samual and Elsie Gillette moved to Lawrence, Kansas,

This picture of the Fred Humburg home, off Stone Valley Road in Alamo, was taken from a postcard. Postmarked December 21, 1907, it was addressed to Miss Alice Stone, Thornton, Whitman County, Washington, from Aunt Annie Alice (Stone) Humburg. In 1924 purchased by Albert E. Brear family and named "Brear-Brae" (later the site of Jim-Yve Stables, east of Dorris-Eaton Schools).

where their only child, Grace Marie, was born. Albert E. and Grace M. Brear moved to a ranch in Alamo in 1924. They named their property "Brear-Brae." (RA) By this marriage they had three children: Jean Isabelle born 1914, Frederick Gillette born 1916 and Samual Scott born 1921.

Albert E. Brear worked for the American Trust Co. for twenty-nine years. He was a charter member of Francis K. Shattuck Lodge 571, F. and A.M., member of the Berkeley Kiwanis Club, and music director at St. John's Presbyterian Church. In later years he was remarried, and lived in El Cerrito at the time of his death in 1955.

— • —

NORRIS FAMILIES

Leo Norris, the son of John and Barbara (Moore) Norris, was born March 3, 1804, in Nelson County, Kentucky. He received his education and later farmed. He worked for five years in a distillery. Married July 21, 1829 to Mary Jane Kizzie, in Nelson County, Kentucky. They had five children: William H., Mary (Mrs. Wm. Lynch), Annie (Mrs. Perkins), James, and Emily (Mrs. Lewelling).

When twenty-six years old Leo moved the family to Morgan County, Illinois, where they lived for seven years. They then moved to St. Louis and up the Missouri River to what is now Weston, and farmed. In 1840 they went to Atchison County, Missouri, and farmed until they left for California in May 1846.

They joined the fifty-wagon train which included the Donner family. When the wagons reached the Green River, they were met by several men coming from California. One was Caleb Greenwood, an old mountain man, who had successfully led other pioneers through the mountains to California. The Norris family decided to follow his route rather than take the "short cut" through which Hastings led the ill-fated Donner Party.

Their route took them to Fort Hall and south to the Sierras where they crossed in the early fall near what is now Emigrant Gap. They crossed before the snow fell. Their first stop in California was at Sutters Fort, which they reached on October 4, 1846. Then they went to Santa Clara and in June 1847 moved to Mission San Jose, where they lived until the fall of 1850, when they settled in the San Ramon Valley and bought one league of land from Senor Jose Maria Amador.

— • —

WILLIAM H. NORRIS

William H. Norris, son of Leo and Mary J. Norris, was born in Morgan County, Illinois on July 6, 1832. When he was seven years old his family moved to Platte County, Missouri, where they lived for three years. Then they moved to Atchison County, Missouri. May 10, 1846 he crossed the plains with his parents in five weary months. Arrived at Johnson's ranch on Bear River October 13, 1846. William H. Norris was married January 8, 1860 to Margaret Nash, daughter of Thomas Nash, a native of Lower Canada. They were married in San Francisco. They had four children: Leo, born November 29, 1860; Thomas, born December 30, 1862, Henry, born September 14, 1864 (died August 19, 1881); George born February 3, 1867; and Mary, born November 21, 1869. They were large landowners in the San Ramon Valley; their holdings included land in Bollinger Canyon. They did ranching and raised cattle. William H. Norris was the grandfather of Leo and Noel Norris, longtime residents of San Ramon. Norris Canyon was named for the family.

LYNCH FAMILIES
WILLIAM LYNCH

William Lynch (1827-1910), in whose honor San Ramon was first named Lynchville, was one of the first American settlers in San Ramon, arriving the winter of 1850-51. He was born in Flushing, Long Island, New York, on July 12, 1828, the son of Michael and Elizabeth (Smith) Lynch. When fifteen years old he apprenticed as a carpenter. At the end of five years he was considered a skilled journeyman. He followed his trade in New York City for two years.

In December 1848 he took passage on the pilot boat *William G. Hackstaff* for California via the Straits of Magellan, up the Pacific to Yerba Buena (San Francisco) where he arrived on June 28, 1849. He went immediately to the mines on the Tuolumne River, but did not like it and returned to San Francisco in the spring of 1850. He took a $2,000 contract to repair an adobe house at the Mission of San Jose for Don C. Vallejo. While in Santa Clara County he preempted a quarter section of land and planted potatoes. Due to the grasshoppers the venture was not a success.

In his travels he met the Norris family and in partnership with William Norris he bought a league of land in Contra Costa County. After dividing it, he came into possession of 333 1/3 acres, in the area of Crow Canyon Road and

Highway 21. He went to San Antonio (now Redwood Canyon) with his ox team and cut and hauled timber for his house. This trip took him one week. He built the first wood frame house in San Ramon. It was a two-story house with an upstairs veranda. The home was occupied until it burned in 1950, when it was 100 years old. In 1852 the first schoolhouse in San Ramon was built on the Norris property.

William Lynch increased his land to 400 acres, which he first devoted to grain and raising of sheep. Later he sold the sheep and stocked the ranch with cattle.

On April 5, 1852, in California, William Lynch married Mary Elizabeth Norris, daughter of Leo Norris, who was born in Illinois. They built their home in 1855, again from redwood logs hauled from Moraga, over the hills and through Bollinger Canyon to San Ramon. This home was torn down when Lynch Lane became the county road we now know as Crow Canyon Road.

Children by their union were: Leo, who married Minnie Coxhead and had nine children; Mary, who married Dr. George Alexander of Hayward and had two children; Naomi, the wife of John Toopley, had one son; William, who died in youth; Jennie, who married George Woodard and had one child; James, who died at age seven; and Almina, who married Robert Campbell.

William Lynch was a member of Alamo Lodge No. 122 F. & A.M., joining in 1863. He once experienced some excitement with a mountain lion, while he was cutting brush. The man working with him shot the lion, but it was not killed. While the lion was on its back, William ran up and killed it with one stroke of his ax on its breast. The lion measured nine feet from tip to tip.

William Lynch became well known in San Ramon as a landowner and community leader. He was also sought for medical and veterinarian advice. He finally decided to give up the medical responsibilities and deeded a small piece of land to a doctor who could care for the residents of the Valley. He died at eighty-two. His wife, a county resident for sixty years, died at her San Ramon home December 26, 1916 at the age of seventy-eight.

LEO LYNCH

Leo Lynch (1853-1935) was said to be the San Ramon Valley's first native son, born December 23, 1853 in San Ramon. His parents were William and Mary Lynch, who settled in 1850. Leo attended local schools and St. Mary's College when it was located in San Francisco, and was at Santa Clara, before attending the University of California. He graduated with an engineering degree in the class of 1870. Following college, he opened one of the first stores in San Ramon and was appointed postmaster in 1877. He sold the business to B. W. Dunn & Co. in 1879, and went into farming with his father on 350 acres south of town, where remained until his death in 1935 at age eighty-one.

Leo Lynch married Mary Coxhead (one source said Minnie), daughter of Oakland physician, T. C. Coxhead, in Oakland November 28, 1878. They had nine children: Ramona, Leota, Mervyn, Everett, Ralph, Laura, Roberta, Viola and Leo. Leo was better known to the San Ramon residents as "Pete," as he shadowed Peter Thorup so much as a child.

The name Leo Lynch has been carried on for four generations, starting with the grandfather of Marilyn (Lynch) Morrison who was Leo Lynch, then her father Leo Grey Lynch, who first farmed and then was in construction work throughout the world, then her brother Leo Watson Lynch, who farms in Stanislaus County, and his son, Leo Timothy Lynch, who is a student in Waterford, California.

Viola (Lynch) Jones, who lives at Rossmoor, Walnut Creek, was in the first graduating class from San Ramon Valley Union High School in 1914. Also graduating from that high school were: Leo Grey Lynch, 1918; Edna Lynch Scott, 1947; Marilyn Lynch Morrison, 1950; Leo Watson Lynch, 1951; Kurt Randolph Morrison, 1975 and Wendy Louise Morrison, 1976.

Roberta Lynch Reed makes her home in Oakland, California.

THE NORRIS FAMILY GENEALOGY

The following genealogical information was supplied by many sources obtained by Viola (Lynch) Jones of Walnut Creek via her niece, Marilyn (Lynch) Morrison, of Danville. I have been granted permission to use any or all of the material.

First Generation: Leo Norris born 1804, died 1893, married in 1829 to Mary Jane Kizzie (- 1855). Second Generation: Their children: 1. Mary Norris* (Mrs. Lynch); 2. Annie Norris (Mrs. Perkins); 3. James Norris; 4. Emily Norris (Mrs. Lewelling); 5. William H. Norris,* born 1832, married in 1860 to Margaret Nash.

Third Generation: Their children: 1. Leo Norris, born Nov. 1860; 2. Thomas Norris, born Dec.

1862; 3. Henry Norris, born 1864; 4. Mary Norris, born 1869, 5. George Norris,* born Feb. 3, 1867, died May 8, 1954, married Grace E. Morgan, born Jan. 26, 1870, died April 8, 1955.

Fourth Generation: Their Children: 1. Georgia A. Norris, born Aug. 5, 1888, died July 28, 1970, married Fred Reed, born April 6, 1886, died Aug. 15, 1968. 2. Leo J. Norris, born July 23, 1890, died April 8, 1972, never married. 3. Noel D. Norris, born June 23, 1893, died June 28, 1975, never married.

*Refers to the families with information for the family genealogy.

THE LYNCH FAMILY

First Generation: William Owen Lynch (1827-1910) married 1852 to Mary Norris (1834-1915). They had seven children: Leo, Mary E., William H., Naomi J., Jane, James and Elmina.

1. Leo Lynch, born Dec. 1852, died Oct. 1935, married in Nov. 1878 to Minnie Gray Coxhead, born Sept. 1858, died Nov. 1923. They had nine children: Ramona, Leila Leota, Mervyn, Everett Thomas, Ralph C., Laura Louise, Roberta, Viola and Leo Gray Lynch. The following will be their line of descendancy: 1. Ramona Lynch, (1881-1959) married in 1900 to Egbert Read (-1942). Born and lived in San Ramon. Their children: Ramona Read, born March 8, 1903, married June 17, 1922 to Andy Lloyd Abrott, born Nov. 9, 1898. They live in Rossmoor, Walnut Creek, Calif. Their son Robert Abrott, born 12-27-24, married 7-17-48 to Mary Foster born 8-11-25, no children. Their daughter Ramona Lee Abrott, born 8-22-27, married 12-29-45 to Curtis Ash, divorced, married 4-26-50 to Louis Frank, born May 1, 1917. They have 1. Steven Frank born 10-12-46 (adopted by Louis Frank), married 3-8-72 to Susan Nichols, born 8-15-45, they have Bonnie Frank born 5-19-74. 2. Andrew Frank, born 1-26-51. A second daughter Sally Abrott, born 11-8-30, married 3-17-51 to Charles Houston, born 8-28-30. They have Charles Houston, born 12-15-51, Robert Houston, born 7-9-53, married in 1974 to to Pauline Reif, born 8-13-54, they have Amy Houston, born 10-2-76. John Houston, born 5-4-55, Susan Houston, born 6-24-58 and Danny Houston, born 9-16-62. Helen Read (deceased) married in 1928 to Howard Groom (deceased), they lived in Hawaii. Their son Howard Groom, Jr., born 8-2-36, daughter Sharon Groom born 9-24-38, married in 1958 to Thomas Gilham. Their children Sandra Gilham, born 11-17-59, Thomas Gilham, Jr., born 7-19-61, Ramona Gilham, born 5-17-65. Sheila Groom was born 10-11-49.

2. Leila Leota Lynch, born July 1882 in San Ramon, lived in Oakland, died Aug. 1956, married in 1903 to Roy R. Read, born Aug. 1876, died 1972 (married to both Leila Leota and then Roberta Lynch).

3. Mervyn Lynch, born April 1884, in San Ramon, died 1963, married in 1903 to Clara Culver. Their children: Geraldine Lynch, married a Mr. Brink who died, then married William Chess. They had a daughter, Pat, who married Gerald Kane, and a son, Leigh Mervyn Brink, who is married to Lucille. Their children are Timothy and Thomas Brink.

Dorothy Lynch married Malcolm McGown, no children. Mervyn Lynch married Bea.

Elizabeth Lynch married Harold Wheaton and their son is Warren Wheaton.

Hazel Lynch married Robert Dietz. Their son, Roger Dietz, married Lesley Quast; their son, Ronald Dietz is married to Lucille. They had Kelley and Rachel Dietz.

Helen Lynch married George Dressel. Their son, Melvin Dressel, married Kathy

Stanley Lynch married Phyllis; they have Erick Lynch, who married Susan Stevens; they have Andrea Lynch.

Viola Lynch married Elmer Hendrickson.

4. Everett Thomas Lynch, born Jan. 1887, in San Ramon, died May 1970, lived in San Ramon area and Danville, never married.

5. Ralph C. Lynch, (1889-1923), born in San Ramon, California., married Lurabelle Howell, born 4-19-89, died 1-19-63. Their children: Lurabelle Leota Lynch, born 4-5-12, married 1-28-35 to Albert B. O'Donnell. They had Nicholas Albert O'Donnell, born 12-13-40, married 3-26-60 to Elizabeth Tellefsen. Their children: Elizabeth Anne O'Donnell, born 6-6-68 and Nicholas Christian O'Donnell, born 4-26-74. Jeffry Richard O'-Donnell, born 10-3-43, married 10-3-64 to Paula Joann Spencer. Their children are Lura Pauline born 1-28-66, Erin born 11-1-68 and Quinn born 11-26-69. Ralph Francis Lynch born 12-27-14, married 7-23-76 to Margaret Guthrie Ewing. James Jackson Lynch born 11-30-16, married 7-20-41 to Audrey Walford, born 10-20-19. Their children: Judith Ellen Lynch born 7-30-45, married 5-10-66 to Spencer Ellis. And they have: Scott McIntruff Ellis, born 9-20-68; Christopher Lynch Ellis, born 2-10-71 and Shanna Malia Ellis,

48

born 11-14-74. William Clinton Lynch born 7-31-47, married 7-10-76 to Patricia Henderson. Barbara McClung Lynch born 7-17-23, married 9-22-42 to Wayne Gordon Schlosser, born 4-6-23, have lived in Alamo. Their children: Wayne Gordon Schlosser II born 10-8-43, married 10-29-66 to Carolyn Goddard, born 6-24-46, their children: Amy born 12-26-67 and Wayne Schlosser III. Loxi Schlosser born 7-28-46, married 7-25-66 to Louis V. Sneeringer, divorced, married 2-14-74 to Edward Looney, born 3-16-49. Their children: Seanne Nicole Sneeringer born 11-25-68 and Britt Amber Looney born 7-25-75. James Rad Schlosser, born 5-4-48, married 6-1-74 to Kay McLaren born 4-23-52, no children.

6. Laura Louise Lynch, born 1-30-1882, died May 1957, born in San Ramon, lived in Concord, Calif., married 6-4-11 to Elwood William Glazier, born 12-14-1880, died 5-19-49. Their children: Elsie Glazier, born 6-10-16, married 2-5-44 to Melvin Garcia, born 8-12-15, they have Michael Garcia born 9-18-45. Robert Earl Glazier, born 1-3-21, married 2-4-44 to Bonnie Jean McCormick, born 10-22-26, divorced 2-20-67, married 2-25-68 to Dorothy E. Garrison, born 1-16-19. Their children: Stuart Elwood Glazier born 6-12-45, married 2-5-66 to Jeanne LaVera Florin, born 7-12-48, their child Eric Stuart Glazier born 7-4-66. Sandra Paulette Glazier, born 3-4-47, married 11-14-69 to Daniel Wayne Dube, born 3-24-44. Their children: Deanne Arlene, born 2-7-72, Angela Danielle, born 3-4-75 and Christina Valarie Dube, born 2-14-77. Roberta Jean Glazier, born 11-8-48, married 9-19-70 to Charles Richard Fisher, born 1-1-44. Their child Tara Laura Fisher, born 4-9-76. Randy Earle Glazier, born 3-13-50, not married. Armand Glazier, born 12-16-21, married 2-1-48 to Marie Belleci, born 5-18-25, no children. Clinton Glazier, born 12-11-22, married Jean Tesch. Their children Robert, born October 1945 and David, born 1947.

7. Roberta Lynch, born July 1894 in San Ramon and lives in Oakland, married in 1957 to Roy R. Read, born August 1876, died 1972. She is a retired registered nurse.

8. Viola Lynch, born March 1896 in San Ramon, lives in Rossmoor, has lived all over the world, was a teacher. Graduated from San Ramon Valley High School in its first graduating class. In 1926 married William Petersen born 1890, died 1933, in 1935 married Dudley Bates, born 1896, died 1939, married in 1947 to John R. Jones, born 1896. No children.

9. Leo Gray Lynch, born 9-12-99, died 8-18-50, born in San Ramon, died in Afghanistan, lived mostly in Danville, but traveled all over the world. Graduate of San Ramon Valley High School. Married 2-11-28 to Mildred Louise Watson, born 11-17-02. Their children: Edna Roberta Lynch, born 11-30-29, born in Oakland, graduated from San Ramon Valley High School, married 2-3-52 to Jess L. Scott, Jr. born 10-13-28. Their children: Dana Adele Scott, born 1-25-55 in Berkeley, Michele Leone Scott, born 11-8-56 in Davis and Eric Martin Scott, born 1-27-58 in San Luis Obispo. Marilyn Louise Lynch, born 8-1-32 in Berkeley, graduated from SRVHS, married 2-28-54 to Donald William Morrison, born 6-19-26. Their children: Kurt Randolph Morrison born 8-23-57 in Berkeley, Wendy Louise Morrison, born 10-17-58 in Berkeley, both graduates of San Ramon Valley High School in Danville. Leo Watson Lynch, born 2-27-34 in Phoenix, Arizona, married 6-13-54 to Barbara Eleanor Andreasen, born 4-24-34, their children: Melinda Irene Lynch born 4-5-57 and Coreen Louise Lynch, born 5-21-59, both in Walnut Creek. Nancy Lorraine born 12-4-60 and Leo Timothy Lynch born 3-23-63, both in Modesto.

2. Mary E. Lynch, born July 1856, died August 1932, married Oct. 1877 to Dr. George Alexander. Their children: Dr. Archibald Alexander, born 1880, died 1942, married Veronica M. Hoey (-1949), no children. Adele Alexander, born 1887, married in 1911 to John E. Bowersmith, their son John A. Bowersmith born 1914, married in 1936 to Jane V. Tuttle.

3. William H. Lynch - (1858-1860).

4. Naomi J. Lynch, born 1861, died 1905, married in 1890 to John Tarpley. Their children: William Tarpley (1889-1973), married to Lilas Podva born 5-16-99. Their children: Dolores Tarpley born 2-20-25, not married. Phyllis Tarpley, born 2-18-31, married 2-3-51 to John Mozingo born 3-18-32. Their children: Cheryl Ann Mozingo born 6-23-52, married 12-12-75 to Rick Dryer born 9-3-53. William Ernest Mozingo, born 10-1-54, married 11-76 to Bonnie R. Stanton born 12-55. Their child Casie Stanton Mozingo born 12-72. Michael Raymond Mozingo born 2-19-56, married 10-27-75 to Denise Francis born 4-14-56, their child Mikell Mozingo born 1-21-77.

5. Jane Lynch, born July 1864 (deceased) married in 1890 to George Woodward (- 1908), later married to George Shurtcliff.

6. James Lynch, (1868-1875).

7. Elmina Lynch, (1877-1963) married in 1899 to Robert Campbell (-1962). Their son, Burns A. Campbell, born 1916.

LAURENCE

Mr. and Mrs. Manuel Laurence were the first Portuguese settlers on Dougherty property on Lawrence Road, five miles out of Danville. They settled in the early 1800s and bought 160 acres from the Dougherty Ranch.

Manuel Laurence was a grain farmer. He took his grain by wagon to sell in Pacheco, an inland seaport at that time.

Manuel and Mary Laurence had twelve children. The girls were Mary, Louisa, Annie, Rose, Isabel, Josie, Marian and Nellie. The boys were Bill, who had a general store in Dublin, which also housed the library; Jessie, who ran the library; George, who drove the creamery wagon for Spreckels and took the cream in to Oakland; and Joe. All the children remained in the area.

In 1886, at the age of forty-three, Manuel Laurence passed away from a ruptured appendix. This left his widow Mary to raise her large family alone. All the children attended Sycamore School. Mary Laurence died in 1919.

A Joseph Bettencourt came from the Azore Islands on a sailboat when he was twelve years old. He landed in New York and was met by relatives. He later came west and worked as a farm hand and met and married Louisa Laurence. They had eleven children.

In 1922 Joseph Bettencourt bought the original Laurence ranch of 160 acres, the same ranch Louisa was born and raised on. Joseph and Louisa Bettencourt lived there until their deaths.

JOHN C. PETERSON

John C. Peterson, was born in Denmark, March 30, 1822. He received common school education and then served an apprenticeship as a blacksmith. In 1843 he went to the island of St. Thomas, a Danish possession in the West Indies, where he lived for almost five years. He landed in Tuckapo, Louisiana, where he was hired as cook on board ship to pay his passage to New York City.

He toured Boston, New York, Maine, Nova Scotia, Savannah and Charleston. In January 1849 he sailed for California by way of New York around the Horn, landing in San Francisco July 17, 1849. From that fall to the following spring he was cook for McCann & Parker in the sawmill in Sausalito, Marin County. He mined in Marysville, Yuba County, and at the Wyandotte Diggings and Rich Bar on the Feather River. He then moved to Yreka in Siskiyou County, and later to Shasta County. In the fall of 1851 he mined on Clear Creek with good results. At Weaverville, Trinity County, he mined at Big Prospect for five years.

In the spring of 1858 he came to Contra Costa County. The following spring he settled on Tassajara Road, in Sycamore Valley, five miles east of Danville on a 235-acre farm. On April 29, 1865 he married Eliza P. Shaw of Ohio. They had five children: Jessie, Elizabeth "Lizzie", Ella, Emma and Chancey. John C. Peterson died at the age of seventy-one in 1893. His wife Eliza died in 1898 at fifty-six. One of their daughters, Elizabeth "Lizzie," married and was the mother of Homer Hunt, who, with his family, lived in Alamo for many years.

HALVERSON

John E. Halverson (1855-1929) sailed out of Skein, Norway when in his teens with an uncle who was captain of a lumber schooner out of Norway. They sailed the seven seas and around the Horn for nearly twenty years before he left the sea to become a rancher and raise horses. John met Jessie Fremont Peterson, daughter of John C. and Eliza P. (Shaw) Peterson, and they were married in the 1870s. To them were born a son Roy (1885-1969) and daughter May (1888).

In 1891 they moved from their ranch on Tassajara to a new home on Hartz Avenue in Danville. John built and opened the Danville Livery Stable (present site of Dan McGrew's Restaurant). He rented horses and surreys and heavy wagons for the transporting of milk and cream to Hayward milk dealers. It was hauled either through Norris Canyon or Crow Canyon. The large wagons hauled hay and grain to Pacheco where it was loaded on the river barges and towed up or down the river to the ranches or to various businesses along the water.

The Livery Stable was on a fairly large piece of property which had access to Front Street on one side and Hartz Avenue on another. The business fronted on School Street. At the turn of the century Roy Halverson, the son, was operating the rigs to Hayward and Pacheco. At that time his mother worked for Charles and Ella (Elliott) Gust at the Mountain View Hotel, just across the street. (See Chapter Seven, *Places*.) Visitors and traveling salesmen passing through the Valley stopped at the hotel, lunched and had their horses cared for at the stables. The family all worked in the business.

Roy Halverson married Phoebe "Phyllis" Hoover (1886-1961) from the Woodland area. His sister May married Carrol Wilson (1878-1948), the brother of Josephine (Wilson) Close. The Roy Halversons lived in the family residence (site of Dan McGrew's Restaurant) until the early 1960s. Roy was with California Water Service for many years.

Phoebe opened the first beauty shop in Danville at her home. Her second salon was in the Colonial Inn[12] in Walnut Creek. She was known professionally as Phyllis. She was a feminist at heart. She felt if the men of the town could have a service club, so could the women. She wanted it to be a Soroptimist Club, as one of her customers living in Lafayette was a leader in that Bay Area club. Their dues at $20.00 per year were too high for the depression years, 1932-33, and Walnut Creek.

There was much pressuring going on in Walnut Creek at that time, with a big drive on for the Broadway Tunnel. On September 14, 1933, a group met and organized. Mrs. Mildred Barry (later Mrs. Clyde Laird) was town clerk and was elected the first president; Phoebe Halverson was secretary-treasurer, Alda Stoddard parliamentarian, and Freda Brown luncheon chairman. Dues were $1.00 a year! This was the beginning of the Walnut Creek Professional & Business Women's Club, second oldest service group, and very civic-minded. (Walnut Creek Lions was the first service club and Walnut Creek Rotary was the third to organize.) Mrs. Halverson was also active in the East Bay Beautician group.

A direct descendant still living in Danville is Le Roy H. Halverson, son of Roy H. and Phoebe "Phyllis" (Hoover) Halverson. He makes his home on Gil Blas Road with his wife Ricky (Hanell), who was born in San Jose and grew up in Patterson. Their five children are: Harold Halverson, born July 14, 1941, married to Nancy Bigelow, they had a son Todd born 3-30-63. They divorced and he married Aned Martin. Presently living in Danville. Ellen Halverson born 3-1-44, married 3-30-63 to David Spetch. They have two daughters, Edie born 7-31-64 and Erica born 3-

Halverson's Livery Stable in Danville was built by John Halverson in 1891. This large piece of property was parklike, with many trees, especially redwoods. Each generation of Halversons planted more redwoods on the property. Some are still there, but many have been removed over the years. This is the present site of Dan McGrew's Restaurant.

20-68. Lee Halverson, born 6-7-47, USMC GY. SGT. SOMS Weather Operation, Beaufort, South Carolina married Marge and have two sons Lee, Jr. born 4-2-68 and Chris born 8-5-72. Linda Halverson born 5-5-49 (died November 1972). Jon Halverson, born 10-9-51, resides on Tassajara Road, Danville. All attended local schools and graduated from San Ramon Valley High School.

Le Roy said he was really named after his father, Roy Harold Halverson, but there were four men with the name of Roy in the immediate neighborhood—Roy Wells lived at the corner of Hartz and School (present home of La May and Cecile Podva), Roy Wilcox lived where the Dan McGrew parking lot is now, and there were the father and son Roy Halverson. When the mother called "Roy!" it was confusing, so the son's name was changed to Le Roy.

Le Roy related to me some of his memories of those early days of bobbed hair. The women would come into his mother's shop with very long thick hair, to the waist or longer. After it was bobbed, they almost all went into a crying jag for a time. Small wonder!

My husband and I knew Ricky and Le Roy when we all worked at State Farm Mutual Automobile Insurance Company in its Berkeley branch office, before we were married, and we all double-dated.

—•—

GEORGE McCAMLEY

George McCamley was born in New York, Ontario County, in 1826. He came west in 1849 and mined in Nevada for a time. Then came to Contra Costa County and in 1860 bought a ranch of 375 acres in San Ramon. He married Ann Jenkinson, built a home on the ranch and settled there, ranching and raising cattle. He was a school trustee. He passed away in 1898, and his wife in 1913. They are buried in Sacramento, California.

DANIEL ROBERT McPHERSON

Daniel Robert McPherson (1835-1904) was of Scotch ancestry. He was born in Logan County, Kentucky, December 26, 1835, the son of Murdock and Elizabeth (Fitzhugh) McPherson. They moved to Kansas City, Missouri, where he lived during his youth. While quite young he accompanied Mr. Major and Mr. Russel across the plains on freighting expeditions. In 1857 he came to Contra Costa County, California to grant land in Ignacio Valley.

In February 1856 he married Rhoda Harris (1841-1896) born August 25, 1841, a native of Blue Springs, Missouri, daughter of William Harris. In 1859 they arrived in Sycamore Valley where they lived until 1862. He then purchased some land in Tassajara Valley where he did farming and stock raising, later specializing in grain raising. He continued to purchase land until he owned 724 acres.

In 1897 he rented his land and moved to Oakland where he remained for four years. He returned to Contra Costa County after a bout with asthma. He purchased the 100 acres of Wells ranch in Walnut Creek, and the Hammett ranch, where he made his home.

His wife Rhoda died in California at the age of fifty-five in 1896. Their children were: Martha Jane, the wife of William Barnett; Mary, the wife of Adolph Podva; William L.; Emma V., the wife of James Kerr; Effie M., the wife of W. Goold, married October 9, 1889; Robert E.; Nina, the wife of Edward R. Williams, married September 9, 1897; Ernest F.; Clarence L.; Elsie, wife of W. S. Clyman; and Tessie A., who married a Mr. Dart.

Daniel Robert McPherson was a first cousin to Robert E. Lee.

HACK

George W. Hack, married Mary Ann Jenkinson, who was born in England. They had seven children, all born in Freeport near Sacramento, California. The home is still standing. 1. George W., 2. John T., 3. Annie E., became Mrs. Carrington, 4. Nathan D., known as "Dock," 5. Mary Ann, became Mrs. John Oswill, 6. Emma, became Mrs. George Landis, and 7. Charles J.

Nathan D. Hack was born September 23, 1856, married January 3, 1881 to Miss Lavina Kirtland. Her father, Thomas Kirtland, came from England to Salem, Ohio. He married Narcissis Tucker; they had nine children.

OSWILL

John Oswill was born in Philadelphia, Pennsylvania, in 1851. He came west and settled in Freeport, California near Sacramento and worked in a brickyard. He met Mary Ann Hack, born in Freeport, and they were married. They came to work for George McCamley at San Ramon. They had seven children born and raised in San Ramon. John Oswill died in 1922.

Their seven children were: 1. George McCamley Oswill born January 1880. He married Edna Mathison of San Francisco and they had two children, Thelma and Virginia. Thelma (Oswill) married Alfred Ghiradelli of San Francisco; they had two children, David and Diane. Virginia (deceased) married Lawrence Victor and had a daughter Janice, and later married a Mr. Rice and had another daughter.

2. Charles Emmett Oswill, born April 20, 1881, married Marie Borba. They had two children, Donald (deceased), whose daughter Toni (Oswill) Crowley lives in Reiliz Valley, and Dorothy (deceased). Charles Oswill was known as "Tunne" because he liked to play the piano. He died August 15, 1970 at Boyce Springs, California.

3. William Daniel Oswill, born June 9, 1882, married Ethel Oakes and had three children. A daughter Chandler married Harold Markle and lives in Santa Rosa. They have three children, Jean, John and Judy. Wilda married Elmore Hoff and had one daughter, Suzanne, who is married and lives in New Jersey. William Daniel, Jr. married Fern and had two sons, Kenneth and William.

4. Richard Cathcart Oswill, born 1884(?), married Minnie Lafranz of Livermore. They had two children, Gurdon, who lives in Oakland, and Evelyn, who lives in Los Angeles.

5. Addie Pauline Oswill, born June 4, 1886, who used to celebrate her birthday June 9 with her brother William, married Claude Leslie Glass (RA). They had a daughter Claudina Lucille born September 12, 1911. She married Elliott Lewis Mauzy, September 20, 1930. They have two daughters, Claudia Diane and Sylvia Kathleen. Claudia was married December 5, 1960 to Howard F. Nemir. They have one daughter, Allison Kathleen Nemir, born October 1, 1962, and make their home in Alamo. Kay married Earl P. Wightman December 21, 1956. They have two daughters, Lori Diane, born September 11, 1963 and Kimberly Ann, born June 15, 1966. They live in Walnut Creek, California.

6. Ruby May Oswill, known as "Tokie" because she enjoyed Tokay grapes, was born October 12, 1892. She married Roger La May Podva, born October 15, 1884, died February 24, 1967 at Walnut Creek. They have two sons, Adolphus La May Podva, known as La May, born March 27, 1912, and Roger Oswill Podva, known as "Boo," born July 31, 1916. Both were born in the family home on Danville Boulevard, Danville. La May Podva is married to Cecile Bradley, daughter of Edward and Hilda Bradley[13] of Walnut Creek. They were married in September, 1933 in Reno, Nevada. They have two children. Their daughter Marilyn, born June 16, 1934, is married to David Kristick of Concord. They have three children: David, Paula and Kevin. David Michael Kristick graduated from the Military Academy at West Point in 1976. He is attending the University of Kentucky, stationed at Fort Campbell, Kentucky. His great-great-great-grandfather's cousin was the noted southern general, Robert E. Lee, the longest serving Commander at West Point. Kevin Randolph Kristick attends Northern Illinois State College. The family home is in Illinois. The son of La May and Cecile Podva, David Podva, was born May 23, 1939 and is married to Diane Cottrell of Alamo. They have two children, David and Holly, and make their home in Pleasant Hill, California. In 1977 David received a medical disability retirement from the Danville Fire Department. Roger Oswill Podva married Margaret Neilsen (deceased). She was born January 16, 1917 in Tuolumne. She died June 21, 1971 in Berkeley. They had four children, Deneice (died 1959), Dorenne, Dolf and Jonie Lee. Dolf married Janice Timmons. They had two children, Jessleen and Roger of Danville. Jonie Lee married Gordon Talaska, has a son Chad, and lives in Concord, California.

7. Donald Cameron Oswill (deceased) was known as "Gint" from the oldtime song. He married Eva Turk (deceased) and they had two children, Mary Barbara and Warren W. Oswill. Mary Barbara married Dave Sonnickson of Danville and they have two children, Linda and Mary Ann. Warren married Margaret Sorum of Piedmont and they have three daughters, Georgeann, Claudeen and Donnalee.

PODVA

Adolphus Godfrey Podva was born in Montreal, Canada (French Canadian). He married Mary Alma McPherson. They had three sons, Roger L., Robert Randolph and Alfred McPherson Podva.

Adolphus G. Podva's brother, Roger, was a pioneer rancher in San Benito County in Hollister, California. They had three daughters, Norma Podva Wilson, Mina Podva and Mabel McPhail. All are deceased and at rest in the family plot in Hollister, California.

LOVE FAMILIES

Robert O. Love married Amelia Harvey and their children were William Golder, Charles Oliver, Ida, Sophia and Mary Drussila. William Golder Love came to Contra Costa County, California when he was about eleven years old, in 1860. He came around the Horn from Quincy, Illinois. He married Ella Irene True of Lafayette and they had three children, Chester Arthur, Earl and Nita Irene.

William Golder Love was ordained an Elder of the Presbyterian Church on September 20, 1908. He was a teacher of the Adult Sunday School Class for many years. He was also Assistant Superintendent of the Sunday School.

Charles Oliver Love had two sons, Ira and Ray. They lived in Parlier, California in Fresno County. William Golder and Charles Oliver Love lived in the Danville area. Charles had lived about where the Montair School is now in Danville. The Love home at the end of Love Lane, Danville, named for the family, was built well before 1900 and is still standing.

Chester Love married Lyda Love; they had no children. Earl Love never married and passed away in 1914 while still a young man. Nita Irene Love, born November 24, 1891, was married in Oakland, California, August 20, 1915, to Harvey Thorpe Wing (died March 7, 1977). He was named for the Dr. Thorpe who delivered him. They had ten children: Margaret Ella 1915; Robert Murry 1917; Paul Eugene 1918; Ruth Mae 1921; Dorothy 1922; Helen (deceased) 1924; Leslie 1925; Harvey Thorpe Wing, Jr. 1928; Beth 1930; Fredrick Eugene 1931. All were born locally except Robert, who was born in the town of San Quentin and delivered by Dr. Stanley. All attended local schools and graduated from San Ramon Valley High School.

1. Margaret Wing married Howard Riley of Danville. They had no children and make their home in Grants Pass, Oregon.

2. Robert Wing married Laurine Frederickson of Dublin. They have two children, Carolyn Laurine who lives at Tahoe with two children Glen and Tami; and Ronald Robert, who lives in Byron and has three children, Jami, Jessica and Justin. They do ranching. Robert was divorced and later married Mrs. Betty Neese. They have no children and live in Livermore.

3. Paul Wing married Mildred Freitas, was divorced and married to Audrey Danielson. They had no children. Paul owns and operates Alamo Hay & Grain.

4. Ruth Wing, unmarried, lives in North Highlands, California, retired March 1, 1977, from government employment.

5. Dorothy Wing married Heber James Beckemeyer and lives in Pleasant Hill. They have five children: Nancy Elaine Beckemeyer married Douglas McCool from a pioneer family of Redding, California. They have two children, Kendra Page and Geoffery Douglas and live in Tracy.

This photograph of the Love family was taken in about 1918. Standing, left to right, are: Mrs. Ina Boone Root, Miss Spencer, Mrs. Sophie Boone, Nellie Love, Mr. Campbell, Charles Oliver Love, Mrs. Campbell, Nita (Love) Wing, Herb Daley, Elizabeth (Hansen) Root, and Cora (Root) Daley. The baby held by Elizabeth Root is Aileen Root. In the front row, left to right, are: William Golder Love, Robert Murry Wing, Miss Spencer, Miss Ida Love, Margaret Ella Wing, Drucilla Love, and June James Root.

Love Ranch, view toward Mount Diablo to the east, pre-1900.

54

Barry James Beckemeyer married Diana Gomes of Turlock, May 7, 1977. Beverly Jane Beckemeyer married Vincent Crifrasi of New York and lives in Concord. Nadine Lynn Beckemeyer graduates from Sacramento State in 1977 with a major in Social Welfare. David Scott Beckemeyer attends high school in Pleasant Hill, California.

6. Helen Wing (died August 1975) married Elmer W. Carey of Lafayette and had three children: Daniel Thorpe, in U.S.A.F.; Victor William who resides in Willets and has two children, Jessica and Nathan; and Laura Jean, who resides in Concord.

7. Leslie Wing is married to Doris Cahill of Martinez and they have two children. Denise Jay married Gary Brown of Walnut Creek and Dennis Leslie resides at home and is employed in Concord, California.

8. Harvey Thorpe Wing, Jr., unmarried, lives in Pleasanton.

9. Beth, unmarried, lives at the family home on El Alamo and is employed by Blue Cross in Oakland.

10. Fredrick Eugene Wing married to Constance Rodricks of Oakland (died in 1972). They had two children, Fredrick Jr. and Julie.

—•—

I visited the Wings at their El Alamo home in the spring of 1977 and interviewed Nita (Love) Wing about her family. On March 7, 1977, a few days after a second trip there, Harvey Thorpe Wing passed away with a stroke. He was eighty-five years old. Surviving him are his widow, Nita Wing, nine children, fourteen grandchildren and nine great-grandchildren. He was a native of Provo, Utah. Interment was at Alamo Cemetery.

The former Love ranch home at 357 Love Lane was the home of the Woodburn family for many years, and prior to 1965 was the home of the son, Ridgway, and his wife, Azella Woodburn. In 1965 they sold the house to Louis A. Jr. and Barbara Dore, who over the years have remodeled and restored it. When redoing the dormer windows upstairs to make them functional, the Dore family found some late 1850 newspapers between the walls and boards. Louis Augustus Dore, Sr. was born in Nortonville, California and then the family moved to a ranch on Springhill Road in Lafayette. Uncle Pete Carpenter, who married Dore's daughter, lived in a pear orchard in the center of Lafayette before development took over. Part of the Dore family still lives in the

Robert Love residence on Love Lane, Danville, was built in about 1860. What appears to be sleeping equipment and a privacy screen on the upper porch is just that. The family often slept outside on warm nights, according to Nita (Love) Wing. This home is still standing. It is the property of Louis A., Jr. and Barbara Dore, who have remodelled and restored it.

general environs of the former family ranch in Lafayette.

CLOSE

The following was told to me by Dr. Wilson E. Close of Danville, in April 1977, with permission to use. As he told it:

My paternal grandfather, James E. Close, came to Danville in 1875 from Toronto, Canada. He was one of fourteen children. His trade was blacksmith, so he purchased a blacksmith shop near the corner of Front Street (the main street then) and Diablo Road, as we now know it. This was the first building built in Danville in 1858 by Daniel and Andrew Inman, who gave Danville its name. Close paid $1,100 in gold coin for the property and it is still owned by the Close family to this day. He operated the shop until 1904.

In 1877 he married Lillian Ramage, who had come to Danville also in 1875 from Illinois. From this union a daughter was born who died at an early age. A son, Clarence Close, was born in 1879.

Lillian (Ramage) Close (1858-1935)

James E. Close I (1848-1904)

My grandfather John Wilson and grandmother Mary Jane Wilson came to Walnut Creek in 1875 from Humansville, Missouri, a town named after my great-great-grandfather. They had a family of seven children. Clarence Close married Josephine Wilson in

Clarence W. Close (1879-1933) was married in 1900. He opened Close's General Store on Front Street in Danville in 1907. Both he and his wife were active in community affairs.

1900 and they had four children, Dorothy, James, Kathryn and Wilson E. Close.

Clarence and Josephine Close were active in community affairs and members of the Danville Grange, Eastern Star, Presbyterian Church and others. Clarence Close was a trustee of the church and served as trustee for the Danville Grammar School and also the San Ramon Valley Union High School. Both he and my grandfather were members of Alamo Masonic Lodge, as am I.

In 1907 Clarence Close opened Close's General Store on Front Street. Danville's first Telephone Exchange was located in the store and Viola (Scott) Root was the operator. Each subscriber had to put up their own poles and wires, buy the telephone instrument and make repairs as needed. For this the charge was twenty-five cents per month, and then you were part owner of the telephone system.

My grandmother Lillian Close, on November 9, 1913, opened the Danville Branch of the County Library, established that year. There were 104 books in the Improvement Club room over the Post Office in the Close Building.

In 1914 Clarence Close moved his store to the northwest corner of Hartz Avenue and Prospect Street; in later years it became Acree's Store.

56

The upstairs of the old Close Building on Front Street served as a location for the Oddfellows Lodge, Alamo Masonic Lodge, and from 1914 to 1917 as a temporary location for the San Ramon Valley High School, until it opened at its present site.

In 1918 Clarence Close started the first mail route in the San Ramon Valley, serving San Ramon, Danville, Diablo and Alamo. The mail was picked up twice daily. It was the beginning of the R.F.D. route. He also did all the hauling for Diablo Country Club, delivering canned foods and staples from the Southern Pacific Depot in Danville and delivering vegetables, fruit and meat from wholesalers in San Francisco, that came to the Walnut Creek depot of the Sacramento Northern Railroad.

Clarence Close passed away in 1933. His wife Josephine died in 1959. At the present time Kathryn Close Kantrowitz and Dr. Wilson E. Close reside in Danville. James Close lives in Concord and Dorothy Close resides in San Francisco.

Close Family update: James E. Close II married Vera M. Whitmore June 28, 1923 and they had one son, James E. Close III, born May 8, 1924. James E. Close III married Vivian Vanucci February 26, 1949 and they had two daughters, Justine R. Close, born 1950, and Denise Close, born 1954. Justine is now married.

Kathryn A. Close was married June 14, 1930 to Samuel B. Kantrowitz and they had one son, David N. Kantrowitz, born February 9, 1940. David N. Kantrowitz married Laurel Elaine Matteson November 17, 1962 and they have three children, Richard Lance Kantrowitz, born May 4, 1963, Elaine, March 15, 1965, and Samantha, September 24, 1966.

Neither Dorothy or Wilson Close have ever married.

FOOTNOTES

1. 1851, John M. and Mary Ann Jones, with two daughters, passed through Alamo in 1847. Returned to settle November 10, 1851.

2. I have always held the opinion that Rancho-Romero School in Alamo, on Hemme Avenue, should have been named August Hemme School, in honor of this early pioneer, especially since he was a strong advocate of education. At one time, there was a Hemme Station for the train route. A granddaughter and great-granddaughter of August Hemme have resided in Danville for the past thirteen years, since they returned from Berkeley. They are Marian Johnson, who was ninety years old December 28, 1976, and her daughter, Jean Y. Carroll. They make their home on Lomitas Drive, Danville. I paid a visit on February 14, 1977, St. Valentine's Day.

Josephine (Wilson) Close (1882-1959)

3. Judge Thomas I. Coakley told me of his early childhood days spent at the home of his uncle Michael Coakley and his wife Elizabeth, who lived in Oakland. They had a summer home next to the Humburg family in Alamo and drove out on the old walnut-lined highway to visit. As a youth, Tom would visit during early summer, before the one-room Alamo School recessed for vacation, and attend classes with his eight cousins. Tom Coakley is remembered as a well-known band leader of the mid-thirties. His band started at the Athens Athletic Club in Oakland (razed spring 1977). There Tony Martin (Al Morris then) sang with the band for two years. The band later played the Palace and St. Francis Hotels in San Francisco.

4. My maternal grandmother, Mary Zesmant (Jesmant, Jeszmant) was born of nobility near the East Prussian border (Kiebartas, Suvalcoa Gubernia County) in Lithuania. For diversion she worked in an office where she met my grandfather, John Morris, a German and a commoner. They fell in love and were married. Realizing he would never be accepted by her family, she gave up her inheritance of much property. The newlyweds decided to make their fortune across the sea, in America. They took her younger sister Veronica with them and ended in Pittston, Pennsylvania. Veronica, also a natural beauty, married the town's most eligible bachelor two months after arrival in the new country. My mother, Bertha Morris Boggini, is the third youngest in a good Catholic family of nine

(actually ten, as my Aunt Mary, the eldest, had a twin at birth). My grandmother was superstitious and always believed if one twin died the other would soon follow. My Aunt Mary lived to a normal old age. My mother and her older sister, Anna Chape, who makes her home in Florida and Michigan, depending on the season, remain of the "Morris Girls." A cousin, Veronica's daughter, Helen Savage Le Bel D.C., lives in Lake Worth, Florida, and we continue to correspond.

5. William Z. Stone was known to his neices and nephews as "Uncle Pap." On February 22, 1977, I received a letter from the Washington state branch of the Stone family, the family of Edward Albert Stone (RA)...The family portrait on page 17 of *Remembering Alamo...and Other Things Along the Way* was taken in 1898. Five neices and one nephew still live in Washington. They are: Alice Pauline (Stone) Hanson, who was ninety-eight years old February 1977 and lives in Auburn; Lucia May Stone who was ninety-six years old December 25, 1976 and is in Seattle; Martha Elizabeth Stone, eighty-eight years, Seattle; Ethel Viola (Stone) Oakes, eighty-six years, Seattle; Albert Edward Stone, eighty-one years, Spokane; and Myrtle M. Stone, seventy-nine years, Seattle.

6. This was very often the manner of the day for acquiring lumber for a home.

7. The "Wildnerness Road" is one of the most important pioneer roads. It was operated by Daniel Boone in 1775 and was sometimes called the Kentucky Road. It began at the Block House in Virginia, crossed the dark Powell Mountains and entered Powell Valley. It continued up the Cumberland Mountains through the Cumberland Gap out to the plateau of central Kentucky. It was rocky and mountainous and populated by unfriendly Indians. The road ran almost 300 miles through the most dangerous and bloody country in pioneer history. By 1800 more than 200,000 settlers had crossed westward into Kentucky over this dangerous route.

8. November 26—the author's birthday.

9. When Peter came to the U.S. he worked and earned and saved. When he had enough he sent for his sister. Then the two worked and saved and eventually sent for the entire family, one at a time, to come to America. Last to arrive was the youngest brother with the grandparents.

10. Edna (Thorup) Smith celebrated her 90th birthday with a luncheon in her honor given by her daughter Dorothy (Smith) Peyret of Grass Valley. Also a church banquet with many guests was held in her honor.

11. By coincidence, cousins Kathleen Anita Morgan and Greg Morgan Clore were both born on Sundays on the fifth day of the month, eleven months apart, and both weighed six pounds and three ounces at birth.

12. In previous years the Colonial Inn was the Rogers Hotel at Main and Walker Streets in Walnut Creek. In its early days it had trees on both sides. It was later called Ala Costa Inn, Colonial Inn, El Curtola, and Las Palmas. It was torn down in 1958.

13. Edward Bradley is a former mayor of Walnut Creek and Hilda Bradley is a past president of the Walnut Creek Women's Club. They have lived in Walnut Creek since 1913.

Three generations were together at the new residence of Ruby Podva, on April 18, 1977, when I interviewed them. They were Ruby "Aunt Tokie" Podva, our hostess, Lucille (Glass) Mauzy and her daughter Claudia (Mauzy) Nemir of Alamo. Thelma (Mrs. Henry J.) Smith, a former longtime San Ramon resident, came down to visit from Manteca, her present home. I was told by Lucille that her parents, Claude Leslie and Addie Pauline (Oswill) Glass, were the last couple to be married in the San Ramon Methodist Church. It was later removed for lack of attendance. Coincidentally, Lucille and her husband, Elliott "Buck" Mauzy, were the last couple to be married in the old Danville Presbyterian Church before it burned down.

The Podva home on Danville Boulevard is said to have been purchased by Adolph Podva from a Mr. Burgess in 1884. Roger and Ruby Podva bought it from Mary Podva in 1911. It is said to be 125 years old and is still standing near Sycamore Valley Road. After living in the home for sixty-five years and having her two sons born there, Ruby Podva moved to the Regency Apartments on Podva Lane in April 1977. The 125-year age of the Podva home is doubtful, as it would mean it had to have been built in 1852. History and research tell us the first homes built by white men were the two Garcia adobes built in 1848 in Alamo, and the Leonard Eddy cabin in Sycamore Valley. The first building in downtown Danville (Front Street) was Daniel Inman's blacksmith building, built in 1858, when Danville was born and named. The Glass home (still standing) was built in 1859. White Gate is said to have been built in 1856 by the Howard brothers, since we now know the Howards arrived in September of 1856. In my research over the years, I have found that one big problem in determining the ages of homes and buildings is the "stretching of time!"

Most of the people mentioned in the above story attended local schools in the Danville area and graduated from San Ramon Valley High School.

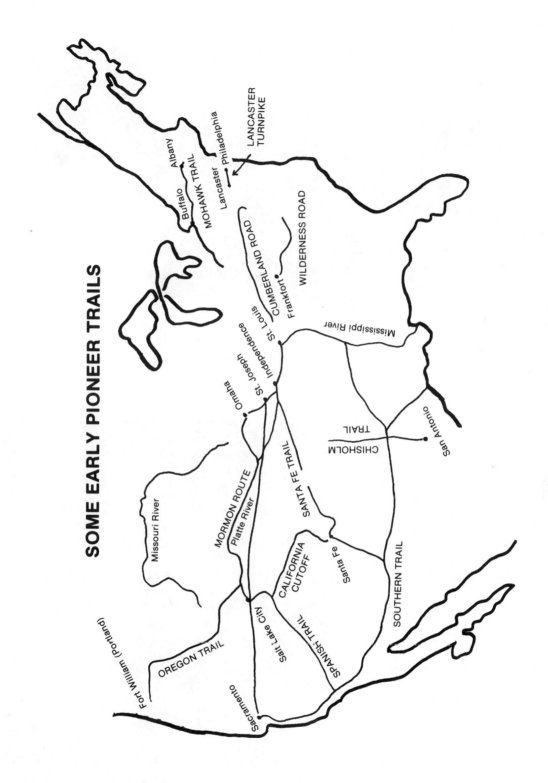

SOME EARLY PIONEER TRAILS

59

Above, this Yager family portrait was taken before 1900. Standing, left to right: Daisy, Maude, Elfleda, Frances, and Birdie. Seated, left to right: Alda, Susan, Bessie (child), the father, Francis Marion Yager, the mother, Alice (Foster) Yager, Marguerite (child), Mary, Belle, and Ruth (in front). Note handmade lace on the dresses.

Right, all thirteen Yager girls. Standing, left to right: Maude, Elfleda, Frances, Susan, Daisy, and Belle. Second row, seated, left to right: Bessie, Birdie, Marguerite, Norma (the youngest, born in 1900), and Mary. Seated in front: Alda and Ruth.

Chapter Three
Other Pioneers and
Longtime Residents

CORNELIUS YAGER

Cornelius Yager and his wife lived in Kentucky and they had five children. The youngest was Francis Marion, who was born in 1851, when the mother died in childbirth. Cornelius Yager, with the five children—the oldest a daughter about nine years old and the youngest, Francis Marion Yager, only three months old—accompanied by their Negro "mammy," crossed the plains in the spring of 1852. They arrived in Alamo, California that fall.

The Reverend Cornelius Yager was appointed by the Presbytery as Supply Pastor at Alamo on March 21, 1856. He was one of the strongest men of the Cumberland Presbyterian Church in California. He served the Synod of the Pacific as its third moderator in 1862, and again as its sixth moderator in 1886.

One of the first things he did was organize a Camp Meeting in Alamo, held in September 1856. He was the minister in Alamo for several years. When he left Alamo he was called to Fresno to organize that church. In his honor there is a bust of him there. He continued his service in the Cumberland Church for almost fifty years. He was over six feet in height and always stood very erect and tall. He preached his last sermon a few days before he died at the age of eighty. A eulogy to his memory was found on page thirty of the Minutes of the Synod of the Pacific for 1895.

FRANCIS MARION YAGER

Francis Marion Yager grew to manhood in Alamo and married Alice Foster when he was twenty-four years old. He attended the University at Berkeley. He and his wife had fourteen children, thirteen daughters and one son who died at birth, the only child of this family to die. Yager was an inventor of several things including an agitator-type washing machine, which unfortu-nately he never had patented. All thirteen girls took their turns operating it over the years.

Daughter 1. Birdie married John Hitchcock and they had five children, Percy, John, Alice, and twins who died at birth. Birdie also died at their birth. 2. Frances married Ray Hogue and they had five sons, Raymond, Ronald, Robert, Roland and Russell. 3. Susan married Charles Burgess. They had two children, Frances and Cecil. 4. Elfleda married Lew Sellars and they had three daughters, Gertrude, Myrtle, and Doro-thy, and one son. 5. Mary married Frank Hartley. Their children were Nora, Raymond, Lois and Robert. 6. Maude married a Mr. Huber. They had no children. 7. Bessie married a Mr. Wallace and they did much missionary work in the Phillipines. They had three children, Homer, who was also a missionary, Elton and Patricia. 8. Ruth married Elmer Smith, son of Josiha "Si" Smith (RA) and had a daughter, Bernice, and a son, Rodney. Later Ruth remarried and had a son, Paul Cornelius Palermo, who was named for his great-grandfather. 9. Belle married Frank Hen-derson and had four children, two daughters, Jerry and Jean, and two sons, Norman "Mickey," and Ernest. 10. Daisy married Allen Herrick and had four children, Thelma, Allen, Gordon and Shirley. 11. Alda married a Mr. Ryan and had three children, "Timer," Patricia and Mildred. 12. Marguerite married Elmer Stevens and they had two daughters, Bertha and Audrey. 13. Norma married Jack Fenno. Their children were Dennis, Jackie, and Gary.

Most of the Cornelius Yager descendants, via son Frank Yager, remained in Contra Costa County and raised their families there. Some still remain.

DAVID P. SMITH

David P. Smith came to Contra Costa County and settled in Tice Valley in 1847. He moved to

Alamo in 1850 and farmed on property where now are Ramona and Francesa Ways. He married and had five children. A son was Josiha "Si" Smith, and two of his daughters were Marie and "Bracky," who was born as they were crossing the state of Nebraska.

JOSIHA "SI" SMITH

Josiha "Si" Smith married Mary Cook and after her passing married Alice Foster Yager, widow of Frank Yager. They had no children. They remained in Alamo until their deaths and are buried in the Alamo Cemetery.

Bernice (Smith) married William Harmon Strutton (died May 8, 1977). Their children are Michael, Patrick and Kathleen Ruth, who has a five-year-old, Candace Harr. Bernice has many happy memories of times in her early childhood spent with her grandfather "Si" Smith in Alamo. Rodney Smith married Winona Siebert. They live in Napa and have a daughter Susan.

Bernice (Smith) Strutton of Antioch, granddaughter of two Contra Costa pioneers, apparently inherits her inventive mind from her maternal grandfather, Francis Marion Yager. She has designed an arm sling and more recently what she calls the Natural Childbirth Positioner, a contoured obstetrical chair attached to a base table which forms a full-length bed. It was very interesting to interview her and learn of her family ancestors as well as her upcoming inventions.

She spoke of many reunions over the years with her many aunts (the thirteen Yager girls). Only two are still living. She told several stories not unlike those of "The Walton Family" on TV, of the growing-up period of this large family of girls.

Paul Cornelius Palermo married Darlene Page. They had two daughters, Paula and Darla, and a son, Perry, and live in Sacramento.

DR. JOHN LYMAN LABAREE

John Lyman Labaree was born in 1822 in Lafayette, Indiana, son of Joseph Labaree. He married Sarah Minerva Cox, also born in Indiana. They crossed the plains together in 1850 and settled in the San Ramon Valley. There they had a ranch of 500 acres. Their first home was a small house, which they replaced in 1872. Dr. Labaree practiced medicine throughout the Valley, traveling on horseback. He also farmed and raised grain and stock.

They had the following children: 1. Olivia, who married David Edwards; 2. Hubbard, a miner,

who married Minnie Hemme and had two daughters, Isabella and Marion; 3. Milton S.; 4. John, who married Alice Linekin and had three children, John Lyman, Anna and Eugene; 5. William, a dentist, also a member of California Assembly in 1902, who married Amy Balch, and had three children, Margaret, Olivia, and Adel; 6. Jennie; and 7. Minerva, wife of Jack Campbell. They had two children, Gladys and Isla.

Dr. Labaree was a Mason. He died in 1871 at his Danville home, and his wife died in 1897.

MILTON S. LABAREE

Milton S. Labaree was a native Californian, born January 16, 1858, at the family ranch in Danville. He was the son of Dr. John Lyman and Sarah Minerva (Cox) Labaree.

Milton was educated at a military academy in Oakland. Following his studies he returned to the Danville ranch, bought 120 acres of the Stevens estate, and farmed, raising hay, grain and stock. He married Annette Stevens, from an old colonial family which had settled in Andover, Massachusetts. Her father was Charles O. Stevens of Massachusetts. Their children were Alma, twins Elsie and Edna, and Sarah. Mr. Labaree was an active member of Woodmen of the World and held office in that organization.

MARCO B. IVORY

The family of Marco B. Ivory (1831-1925) dates back to 1638, when they left England, settled in Erie County, Pennsylvania, and helped in the colonial development. There on November 29, 1831, Marco B. Ivory was born to Thomas and Clarissa (Durkee) Ivory. After receiving his schooling, he ventured to the northern part of Wisconsin and worked in the lumber business for five years. He returned to his home in Pennsylvania, and in September 1858 started for California by way of New York and the land journey across the Isthmus of Panama. He arrived in San Francisco on October 16, 1858.

The following month he arrived in Green Valley (Danville), Contra Costa County, became associated with Urial Huntington, and took over the management fo 480 acres in stock-raising. On this ranch many of the finest horses of the day were raised. He remained on the "Cook Ranch" and farmed until the fall of 1871, when he was elected sheriff of Contra Costa County, chosen by the Republican party. He served two terms, commencing March 1872, as he was re-elected in 1874. He sold his Green Valley farm in 1873 and moved to Martinez, California, the county seat. There in 1877 he became manager and superintendent of the Los Meganos Rancho (John Marsh Ranch) and was appointed to superintend the original "Marsh Grant" by the Clay Street Bank of San Francisco. He served in this capacity for over twenty years. The ranch of over 13,000 acres was mostly in open pasture land when he took over his duties. He put one-fourth in wheat, with good returns. He and his family lived in the famed "Stone House,"[1] built by John Marsh but never occupied by him. The only member of the Marsh family ever to live in the home was John Marsh's son Charles by his first wife.

Marco B. Ivory married Sarah Bunker, born in 1833 in Massachusetts. She was a teacher when she arrived in California and gained a good reputation for her literary ability. Mr. Ivory, a Republican, also served his party as county tax collector and supervisor. He was active in the Masons and the Independent Order of Odd Fellows. He died at the age of ninety-four in 1925.

FRANCIS E. MATTESON

Francis E. Matteson was born March 20, 1819, in Shaftsbury, Bennington County, Vermont, to Isaac and Phoebe (Olin) Matteson. When sixteen years old he left his home and went to Will County, Illinois where he farmed until 1852. He married Elizabeth Eddy in Illinois in 1849. They set out for California via ox teams and settled in Contra Costa County, Sycamore Valley, on the south slope of Mount Diablo. They had 160 acres beside a creek. In 1858 Frank set out one of the first orchards and vineyards in the area. It consisted of 4,500 peach trees, 300 apple trees, 300 cherry trees, other fruit trees, and 1,600 grapevines. His wife Elizabeth (Eliza) died when she was thirty-three years old. They had the following children: George Leonard, who died in Illinois, Martha, Charles, Dwight and Fred.

Matteson took a second wife, Mrs. Mary Reynolds, born in Ohio, daughter of Daniel Gardner. She died at the age of sixty-two years. His third wife was Mary (Mrs. Peter) Hunter, born in Indiana, daughter of John Hughes. They had the following children: Belle, William, Jesse, James, Millie and Cora.

When he first settled in Sycamore Valley there was only a small trail to his house, and many animals—deer, bear, elk and antelope—roamed in the area, but he was a good marksman. In later years he became interested in bee culture and had one hundred hives and a good market for his quality honey.

His ranch on Blackhawk Road later became known as part of Blackhawk Ranch and for many years was the property of R. C. Force.

WILLIAM W. COX

William W. Cox (1833-1910) arrived in Danville in 1853, a native of Rush County, Indiana. He was born August 19, 1833. When he was nineteen, he went to Daviess County, Missouri by ox team with a brother and five sisters. Starting on May 2, 1853, they continued westward on a five-month trek and arrived in Amador County. They remained a short while in Stockton and then traveled on to Contra Costa County. Cox purchased 200 acres south of Danville and only about a half mile north of San Ramon. His neighbors were Robert O. Baldwin and William Meese, who had arrived the year before. Baldwin and Meese later married two of William Cox's sisters.

William Cox married Mary E. Grist of Illinois in San Ramon, November 20, 1865. Their children were Livia M., Elmer G., Jessie, Mary R., Delia, and Mabel F. Cox was a charter member of the Danville Grange. (RA) He died in 1910 at the age of seventy-seven.

THOMAS FLOURNOY

Thomas Flournoy was born June 24, 1824, in Estill County, Kentucky, the son of Hay B. and Mary (Brinegar) Flournoy. The family moved to Linn County, Missouri, where they lived until 1850. On October 21, 1847 Thomas married Elizabeth Neal, a native of Kentucky. In 1850 they started to cross the plains to California. On August 30, 1850, at Big Meadows on the Humboldt, his wife died. She was buried there. They had one son, William H., who in later life settled in Sonoma County.

The widower Flournoy and his son arrived in California in September 1850 and for the next five years farmed in Santa Clara County. In 1855 he came to Contra Costa County and settled in the town of Danville, where he bought 450 acres on which he farmed and raised stock. On August 31, 1854 he was married to Laurentie Kifer. They had the following children, raised in Danville: Lillian who became Mrs. Rice; John T., a professor of mathematics at the University of the Pacific; Roland F.; Ada E.; Laura; Dora; Shelby H.; and Lucy.

SAMUEL FRANKLIN RAMAGE

Samuel Franklin Ramage was born July 1, 1836, in Butler County, Ohio. When he was quite young his family moved to Pike County and later Adams County, both in Illinois. On September 8, 1856 he sailed from New York via Panama for California and settled in Contra Costa County in Danville. He drove cattle from Oregon to Contra Costa County and also worked the mines in Antioch. In 1860 he married Sarah J. Flippen, who died in 1873. They had the following children: John A., Joseph C., James W., and Clara E. On October 2, 1879 he married Mrs. Lizzie Boswell and they had one son, Robert C. Ramage.

In 1881 Samuel F. Ramage was appointed Justice of the Peace. He was also a school trustee for Green Valley School District.

DAVID N. SHERBURNE

David N. Sherburne (1822-1897) was born in Bennington, Wyoming County, New York, October 14, 1822. His uncle took him to Kendall County, Illinois in 1841. In the spring of 1850, when he was a young man, with four companions he went down the Mississippi River to St. Louis to purchase ponies. Later they started on horseback to California via Independence and the old emigrant route. The journey had many hardships, but they arrived in Placerville August 26, 1850 and struck out in mining.

Sherburne arrived in Sycamore Valley, Danville, California in 1856, where he farmed. After a short while he sold out and moved to Alameda County. In 1859 he returned to Sycamore Valley, three miles southeast of Danville, and purchased 647 acres.

He was among Contra Costa County's first politicians. In 1865 he was elected to the Board of Supervisors representing Township Two. In 1879 he was elected to the state legislature, defeating Josiah Wills of Lone Tree Valley. In 1880 he was elected again and served for four successive terms as county supervisor. He remained a bachelor, and died in his Sycamore Valley home, August 19, 1897 at the age of seventy-five.

ALBERT SHERBURNE

Albert Sherburne was born September 4, 1823, in Bennington, then Genesee County, later a part of Wyoming County, New York, twenty-five miles east of Buffalo. When he was four years old his mother died, leaving him in the care of people who used him and gave him only his board and clothes. His education was limited. At the age of seventeen he visited his uncle, Lewis Flanders, in Maine, where his brother and sister had been given a home.

In 1847 he took a bride, Caroline Louise Craig, native of Kennebec County, Maine. They had a son, George Alfred. Albert was adventurous and wanted to strike out westward to make his fortune. He booked passage in New York on the steamer *Ohio*, via Panama, and crossed the Isthmus, but could not get to San Francisco, as all boats were engaged well in advance. With a group of companions he took passage on the brig *Phelena*. After thirty-four days they had to make port at Point Arena for equipment and supplies. Later they had to land in Acapulco. They finally arrived in San Francisco via the steamer *Winfield Scott* on April 28, 1852.

Albert went to the mines in Eldorado County, but became ill. In 1853, in partnership with Hiram Little and later Joseph Berry, he built a bowling alley and saloon at Kelsey's "dry diggins." It burned and they lost all they had in it, including the expensive furnishings. In 1855 he sent for his wife and child and joined his brother David in Contra Costa County. He built an addition to his brother's cabin and worked on adjoining farms. He rented land from his brother in Sycamore Valley, and later bought a quarter section which he farmed until 1869 and later sold at a profit.

He purchased a Walnut Creek merchandise store from L. G. Peal, where he spent twelve years, only to have it burn. In 1880 he rebuilt the store and took his son to run it. When he was fifty-six years old he returned east and brought his sister to share his home. His wife died in October 1903, almost seventy-eight years old. They had eight children. Among them were Mary, who married W. S. Burpee of Walnut Creek; Lewis F., a farmer in Sycamore Valley; and John O., a merchant in Danville. Albert Sherburne joined the Masons Lodge No. 41 of Readfield, Maine in 1851, and later demitted to Alamo Lodge No. 122.

JOHN JOHNSTON

John Johnston arrived in the San Ramon Valley in 1855. He was born in November 1811 in Scotland, where he learned the stone mason trade. When twenty years old he migrated to Toronto, Canada and continued his trade. In 1834 he arrived in the United States and spent fifteen years in Mississippi. The gold rush of 1849 called, and he arrived in San Francisco on July 9, 1849 and went to the mines. Later he settled in San Diego County and raised stock. After about three years he returned to Tassajara Valley in northern California. In May 1855 he purchased land from Abner Pearson and the Gillette brothers. He increased his properties to 1,560 acres in the valley and 1,400 acres of hill land for pasture. He engaged in general farming and stock raising, having made two importations of Clydesdale horses from Scotland. (In later years the site of his farm was owned by Harrison Finley.)

JAMES FOSTER

James Foster was born October 31, 1824, in Waterville, Kennebec County, Maine. He attended public school until he was fifteen years old. He moved with his parents to Clinton, Penobscot County, Maine and worked with his father at the millwright trade until he was twenty-one. He continued his trade in Carmel, Penobscot County, Maine and went into the lumber business. On March 7, 1852, he married Nancy A. Prescott of Dixmont, Maine.

In August 1856 he started for California, leaving his family. He sailed from New York via Panama and arrived in San Francisco in September 1856. In the San Mateo redwood forests he followed his trade until February 1857. He then completed the building of a grist mill on Bear River near Auburn, California, in Placer County. In the fall of 1857 he sent east for his family—his wife and two children—and they located in Contra Costa County, in the then thriving town of Alamo. There he opened a wheelwright shop. He was appointed Alamo postmaster (RA) from October 2, 1866 to April 3, 1879, and was elected Justice of the Peace in 1860 and served eight years. He was elected County Assessor in 1869, an office he held for ten years. He studied law and had a natural flair for it and was admitted to the Bar in the Fifteenth Judicial Court in 1872. He served it well. He was often called upon as a referee in Spanish grants subdivisions and was the sole referee for dividing lots in Martinez. He replanned many divisions and streets to the benefit of all, and was considered one of the best judges of real estate in Contra Costa County.

In March 1881 he sold his Alamo holdings and purchased a block of land in Walnut Creek, where he built a beautiful home and improved upon it until it was one of the nicest in the county. He was a senior member of the real estate firm of Foster & Stow. He and his wife had three children, James Everett, who died at age four April 21, 1864; Florence, who died at the age of twenty November 14, 1872; and Fred Lewis, who was part owner and associate editor of the *Contra Costa Gazette*.

THOMAS E. WILKES

From a newspaper clipping with dateline of March 5, 1921 and headline, "Pioneer Dies at Linn's Valley Home; Wilkes Came to this State in 1856; Lived in Kern since 1870":

The death of Thomas Wilkes, 77, of Linn's Valley, Friday evening, marks the passing of another pioneer figure in Kern County history. He had been confined to his room for two weeks and the end was not unexpected.

The deceased, a native of Missouri, was one of the most widely known and highly respected citizens of Kern County, having lived here since October 1870, where he was engaged in the stock raising business.

In the year 1856 he came to this state with his father, mother and other members of the family, who were on a gold-seeking tour. They crossed the plains with ox-teams and endured many hardships, encountering Indians and enduring short rations and severe exposure.

In his early manhood he was married to Miss Lizzie Gilman, and in 1870 moved with his little family to Linn's Valley, where he had resided ever since. Surviving him are his widow, two daughters, Mrs. Lulu Pascoe and Mrs. Emma Carver, and three sons, Morris, Elmer and Will, all of Kern County. Interment will be in the Linn's Valley Cemetery Sunday afternoon at 1 o'clock.

LULU (WILKES) PASCOE

Taken from a newspaper clipping dated February 1961 with heading "Last Rites Saturday for Mrs. Lulu Pascoe":

Last rites will be held Saturday at 11 a.m. in the Glennville Presbyterian Church for Mrs. Lulu (Wilkes) Pascoe, 92, one of Kern County's earliest pioneers. She died Tuesday at a Bakersfield hospital after a short illness. Mrs. Pascoe was born Feb. 4, 1868, in Contra Costa County (Danville, Calif.), the daughter of the late Mr. and Mrs. Thomas E. Wilkes, who came to Kern County in a covered wagon in 1870.

As a young woman before her marriage, Mrs. Pasco joined her brothers in homesteading other ranch land adjacent to the original parental home.

She became the wife of Lee Pascoe in 1891. He was the son of the late Jeptha Pascoe who was one of the survivors of the Donner Party. The couple settled on the old Pascoe ranch of Glennville where she continued to live for the remainder of her life. She was held in high regard by friends and neighbors. Her keen memory of early events made her a source of interesting history. She is survived by two daughters, Mrs. Eva Petersen of Glennville and Mrs. Florence Lawson of Oakland, and by two sons, Lester Pascoe of Glennville and Clark Pascoe of Dinuba, by nine grandchildren, 18 great-grandchildren and eight great-great-grandchildren. She is also survived by a brother, Elmer Wilkes, of North Bakersfield. The funeral services coincide with the date of the 93rd birthday anniversary of Mrs. Pascoe. She died Feb. 1 in a Bakersfield hospital.

ALBERT GALATIN WILKES

Albert Galatin Wilkes was born in 1820 in Murray County, Tennessee. He came to California October 1, 1849, to Georgetown. He was a miner, baker and storekeeper from 1849-52. He left California, to return later from Missouri with his family. He bought 100 head of dairy cows, including sixteen thoroughbred Durhams, the first in California.

He established a dairy ranch in Tassajara Valley, Danville, and raised cattle and grain on a 1,000-acre farm. He moved to Stockton in 1873. He had two sons, Thomas E., born at Wilkes' home, and Joseph.

The Wilkes home on Finley Lane, Tassajara Valley, Danville, was later lived in by the Albergs and a Johnston family, was owned by the Reinsteins at one time and also by Anton Petersen, who, it is said, bought it from Johnston.

WILKES

I was working from a copy of a letter dated January 20, 1967, from John and Patricia McKenna of Manhattan Beach, California, given to me by Vivian Coats Edmonston, regarding the Wilkes Family. After some researching, several letters and phone calls, I have a current letter from the McKennas dated April 5, 1977, with a corrected line of descendency on Wilkes:

Judge Edmund Wilkes and wife Cynthia Houston; Albert Galatin Wilkes born 1820, Murray County, Tennessee; Thomas E. Wilkes, born in the Wilkes' home in Tassajara Valley, Danville; Lucy Ann Wilkes, one of many children of Thomas, born in house in Tassajara; Florence E. Pascoe, daughter of Lucy Wilkes and Henry Lee Pascoe, born in Glennville, Kern County (other children were Lester, Clark, Eva, Clara); Patricia Williams, daughter of Florence Pascoe and Desmond A. Williams of Woody, Kern County, born in Oakland, California. (There are other descendants but not known to me.)

Cynthia Houston was the granddaughter of Christopher Houston, who came to Pennsylvania from England and later founded the town of Statesville, North Carolina. He took part in the Revolutionary War.

One of the granddaughters of Thomas E. Wilkes is Mrs. Helen Carver Bowen of the Carver-Bowen Ranch, Glennville, Kern County.

Patricia Williams is now the wife of John S. McKenna and the mother of three sons, John Stephen, Jr., Keven Patrick and Timothy Desmond. I have her permission to use the above information.

Old Harrison Finley house on Finley Road. (Courtesy of Vivian Coats Edmonston)

HARRISON FINLEY

Part of the following is from an 1882 research history reference.

Harrison Finley (1837-1918) was born in Callaway County, Missouri, December 26, 1837. When he was fifteen years old his family moved to Morgan County and in 1853 to Bates County, where he remained until coming to California.

On May 12, 1860 he joined a company with five wagons and ox teams and arrived in Calaveras County, from where he moved to Amador County. On April 3, 1862 he married Lavina J. Ray, a native of Missouri. Her parents were William Ray and Matilda Phillips.

In 1863 he arrived in Contra Costa County and leased land in the Tassajara Valley. In October 1875 he purchased a home with 1,080 acres and farmed and raised stock. They had eight children, one son and seven daughters, all of them born in Contra Costa County: Mattie L. born August 29,

The Harrison Finley family. Standing, left to right: Belle, Abbie, Mary, Wilson, and Lucy. Seated, left to right: Tillie, Harrison Finley, Livonia (Ray) Finley, and Mattie. Seated in front: "Lulu" Louise. (Courtesy Vivian Coats Edmonston)

1864, Matilda N., Eliza B., Wilson E., Mary F., Abbie J., Lucy R. and Livonia L. Finley Road, off Tassajara Road ten miles east of Danville, was named for the Finley family. It used to go through to Morgan Territory on the north side of Mount Diablo near Cowell. Where Finley Road now ends is where the road used to branch and go along the creek past two old coal mines, neither of which was ever productive.

In 1888 the Finley family moved from Tassajara Valley to the Santa Rosa area. Harrison Finley died in 1918 at the age of eighty-one years.

The following information was taken from a Finley Family Bible which was in the possession of Abbie Josephine Finley (Mrs. Grant Laughlin). Note some discrepancies from above—the name Lavina is Livonia, there are ten children listed in the family Bible instead of eight, and some of the names are slightly different.

Harrison Finley born Dec. 26, 1836, married April 3, 1862 to Livonia Josephine Ray. He died July 5, 1917 in Sonoma County, California. Livonia Josephine (Ray) Finley, born Morgan County, Mo. June 9, 1849, died Dec. 14, 1945 in Sonoma County. Their children were: Missouri E. born Feb. 10, 1863 in Amador County, Calif., died May 1863, Amador County. Mattie Lee (Zoe) born Aug. 29, 1864, Contra Costa County, first married Mr. M. F. Babb, June 27, 1902, later Mr. Claude Davis Coats, Jan. 1909* in Tulare

County. Died Dec. 1945. Elizzy Belle, born Oct. 20, 1868, Contra Costa County, married Nov. 29, 1917 to Mr. H. Blanck, later married a Mr. Simcoe. Wilson E. born Feb. 3, 1871, Contra Costa County, married Nov. 28, 1895 (wife not named). He died Nov. 1952. Mary Frances born Jan. 23, 1873, Contra Costa County, died April 8, 1893. Abbie Josephine, born Jan. 31, 1876, married April 25, 1912 to Grant Alexander Laughlin. Lucy R. born April 11, 1879, married June 1, 1911 (husband not named), died Feb. 6, 1936. Livonia Louise, born July 21, 1881, married January 21, 1908 to Leslie Cox (lived in Napa, Calif. with a daughter and son-in-law, Dayton and Ray Coffey). Alicia V. born September 26, 1885, Contra Costa County, died March 17, 1889.

Tombstone inscriptions in the cemetery at Santa Rosa show: Harrison Finley died July 5, 1917, 80 years 6 mos. 9 days; Algis (Alicia) Finley, daughter of H. and L. J. Finley, born Sept. 26, 1885 died March 17, 1889; Mary, daughter of H. and L. J. Finley, born Jan. 23, 1873 died April 8, 1892; Matilda Finley Blanck, wife of H. Blanck, daughter of H. and L. J. Finley, born Nov. 10, 1866 died May 13, 1913—known as "Tillie"; Matilda Phillips, daughter of John Phillips, sister of Mary Phillips Coats, married William Ray of Holland. They were the parents of Livonia Josephine (Ray) Finley, who married Harrison Finley.

My thanks to Charles N. and Vivian Coats Edmonston of San Francisco for some of the above information and clarification.

ROOT FAMILIES

Genealogy of one branch of the Root family:

John Root came from Badly Parish, Northamptonshire, England, and settled in Farmington, Connecticut about the year 1600. Thomas Root, son of John, was born in 1605. Most of the Root family lived in Connecticut. James Root, son of Lloyd Root, was born May 7, 1825 and died October 15, 1877. He left his home in Connecticut and went to Harrisburg, Pennsylvania, in 1847, and also lived in many different states. He left Camden, South Carolina, for California with $120 and a bowie knife, pistol, two rifles and

*Tulare County records show that C. D. Coats, native of Nevada, age 38, resident of Hanford, Kings County, California and Mrs. M. F. Babb, native of California, age 32, resident of Santa Rosa, Sonoma County, were married June 27, 1902 in Visalia. (Signed Claude D. Coats and Mrs. M. F. Babb.) Witnesses: Mrs. W. J. Carter and Frederick V. Fisher. Recorded September 25, 1902 at request of C. D. Coats.

clothing, for a trip to Fort Smith, Arkansas.

In August 1849 he left with the Mac Louis Company of 100 men to seek their fortunes. Travel was very difficult, though they used mules mostly for transportation. They lost many of the men from illness or trouble with the Indians. Finally arrived in San Francisco in 1851. He married Sarah Maria Parker, June 11, 1857 in San Francisco. His son June James Root was born December 25, 1867. For a time they lived in Oakland. When June James was sixteen years old he came to Danville and worked on the Baldwin Ranch. He married Ina Boone, who was born October 3, 1873. They were married in Danville, November 5, 1891. They went to Martinez for their marriage license on the first Southern Pacific train out of Danville in November 1891.

Their children were: James Pearley Root, born November 24, 1892; Elmer Austin Root, born January 11, 1894; Cora Amelia Root, born May 17, 1896; Sara Adeline Root, born August 3, 1897, died in infancy; Harold Boone Root, born December 12, 1901.

June James Root died January 28, 1948. His wife Ina Boone Root died October 24, 1963.

James Pearley Root married Viola Scott (RA)[2], June 9, 1920. They had no children.

Elmer Austin Root married Elizabeth Hansen in 1917. They had three children, Eileen, Jean and Elmer Austin, Jr., known as "Bud." Elmer Austin Root died February 11, 1965.

Cora Amelia Root married Herbert H. Daley. They had five children, James Herbert, Elwood, Evelyn, and twins Harold and Harvey.

Harold Boone Root married Pearl Hansen of Livermore. They had three children, Marilyn, Phyllis and Janice.

Ina Boone Root was the daughter of Joel Haden Boone, who built a house in 1860 in the north end of Danville, between what is now Front Street and Hartz Avenue. Joel Haden Boone married Sophie Love, daughter of Robert B. Love. They had five girls and one boy. All except Ina died of tuberculosis. In 1860 Robert B. Love built the house at the west end of Love Lane which is still standing. The Love and Boone families owned most of the land in northern Danville from Prospect Avenue to Del Amigo for many years.

June James Root and family lived in the house on Front Street for a number of years and four children were born there. They moved to Oakland and lived there for a time, then moved to

Sacramento and back to Danville about 1910. Mr. Root did farming and raised bees on the Love Ranch. Later they moved to a home where the Shell Oil Station is on Hartz Avenue and Linda Mesa in Danville. The house, which is now used as an antique shop, was moved in later years to the street in back of the Shell station.

Austin Root and Steve Johnson built houses in the late twenties, until 1931. June James and Austin Root started the Mount Diablo Diary business in 1931 and delivered milk to many people until 1945. Austin then purchased the property on the corner of Hartz and Prospect Avenues and opened a bar and restaurant in 1943. It closed in 1968. (It was a very nice family restaurant and we were patrons at times.)

Eileen Root was married in Reno, Nevada on June 28, 1949, to Robert "Mac" McCauley, son of Mr. and Mrs. Hugh McCauley of Philadelphia, Pennsylvania. He died January 25, 1968. They had no children. She lives on Laurel Drive, Danville, and works for the San Ramon Valley School District.

Jean Root was married in Reno, Nevada, May 4, 1946, to Kenneth H. Witte, son of Mr. and Mrs. Emil Witte of Racine, Wisconsin. They make their home on Danville Boulevard, Danville. He is package store manager at Oak Knoll Hospital. They have three children, Joan, Nancy and James Kenneth "Jimmy."

Joan was married April 27, 1968 to Louis Mahoe, son of Mr. and Mrs. L. Mahoe of Kailua, Hawaii. They make their home in the Hawaiian Islands with their two children, Louis and Dana.

Nancy has lived with her maternal grandmother, Elizabeth "Libby" Root, on Westridge Avenue, Danville. She recently took her own apartment. She is senior secretary for E.G. & G. in San Ramon.

Jimmy married Terry Ann Goodhew, January 15, 1977, in southern California. She is the daughter of Mr. and Mrs. William Goodhew of Palos Verdes Estates. He is employed by Goodhew Inc., at Redondo Beach, California.

Elmer Austin Root, Jr., known as "Bud," was married in September 1945 to Dorothy "Dottie" Hardiman, daughter of Mr. and Mrs. Charles Hardiman of Livermore. They had four children, Marvin, Debra, Joyce and Charles. They divorced and she married Joseph B. Ramos of Danville. He is owner of Danville Feed & Garden Supply on Railroad Avenue, Danville Depot (see Chapter Seven, *Places*.) "Bud" was remarried and lives in

Marysville, California. He and his two sons operate North Valley Respiratory and Wheelchair Equipment and Home Patient Care in Yuba City.

From *Oakland Tribune*, dateline Tuesday, April 12, 1977:

RITES FOR J. P. ROOT, NATIVE OF DANVILLE

Memorial services for James Pearley Root, 84, held at 7 p.m. Wednesday in the Danville Presbyterian Church. Mr. Root, reputed to be the oldest living native of Danville at the time of his death Sunday (Easter) April 10, died at his Danville home.

He was a veteran of World War I and worked for Shell Oil Co. for 25 years and served Danville Fire Department for 17 years. He was a member of the Community Presbyterian Church, Mount Diablo Post No. 246, American Legion; past-commander of the Ninth District of American Legion, a member of 40 et 8 voiture No. 573, Walnut Creek; World War I Barracks No. 3346, the Last Man's Club of Contra Costa County, Pittsburg Elks Lodge No. 1474, Concord Redmen and a charter member of the San Ramon Valley Historical Society.

He is survived by his widow, Viola, a sister, Cora R. Daley of Concord; and a brother Harold B. Root of Auburn.

FEREIRA FAMILIES

Manuel Jose Fereira was born in 1862 in the village of Faitoda Foyal, Azores Islands, Portugal. In 1878, at the age of 16, he left his homeland and came to California. He came across the continent alone, not able to speak a word of English. His brother John, who had come a few years earlier, had sent for him. Manuel worked on a farm in San Leandro. With his first wages, he walked to town to buy a new pair of shoes, his first American shoes. On his way back to the farm, he dropped the bundle with his old worn out shoes on the roadside. When he arrived back at the farm, his old shoes had arrived ahead of him. A neighbor had seen him in town and picked up the worn shoes on the roadside, thinking he had lost them. He told the story often and enjoyed it, as did others.

Manuel repaid his brother John for his fare (passage) from the old country. Together these young men worked and sent money to their parents for fares so they too could join them in America. The parents and three youngest children arrived in about 1883 and settled in Pleasanton, where some of the older married daughters lived. The parents were Joao and Isabella Fereira. He was born in 1816 and died in 1891. She was born in 1829 and died in 1913.

In 1885 Manuel and his sister and brother-in-law, Miguel and Isabella Silva, started farming at the Dougherty Ranch. The property was later owned by Fred Wiedemann. In 1890, when Manuel was twenty-eight years old, he married Leonora Aurora Silva (born 1872), who was eighteen years old. She was born at 1775 B Street, Hayward, Alameda County. The old home still stands. Her father, Joao Silva, came from San Jorge, Azores Islands. He was a carpenter and helped to build the first school building in Hayward, on First Street. In 1918 a great-granddaughter, Marjorie Martin, attended school in this old building.

When Joao Silva's sister and her husband spoke of coming to America, Joao asked them to bring him a bride. She was Maria Josephine Maio, sixteen years old, the only child of her family. After Maria arrived in 1861, she and Joao were maried by the local Justice of the Peace in Hayward. In 1862, a year later, they went to San Francisco and had their marriage blessed by the Catholic priest at old Mission Delores.

Leonora and Manuel lived on the Dougherty Ranch. Two couples and their children lived in a very small farm house. There was no running water. They bailed water by hand with a bucket from a well. She told of driving a buckboard wagon with a team of balky mules to Pleasanton to trade eggs and homemade butter for groceries at the old Cobb's Store. She talked of churning butter and molding it, putting it in a bucket and lowering it by rope into the well, to keep it firm. One day the rope broke and her butter ended at the bottom of the well. Her week's supply of butter—a total loss.

Manuel hauled baled hay by wagon drawn by six horses out of the Dougherty hills to Elmhurst (near Oakland). He would leave home at two in the morning, then return to the ranch to load the wagon for the next day's trip to Elmhurst. He spoke of hauling sacked threshed grain to Pacheco and loading it on barges to be shipped to the East Bay.

Manuel and Leonora had three children while living on the Dougherty Ranch: Mary, born in 1891, Nora, born in 1893 and William Carlos, born in 1894. In 1901 they bought a half section of farm land in Bollinger Canyon. It was called the Simpson Ranch. Their fourth child, Elsie, was born there in 1902. All four children attended elementary school in San Ramon. Their first teacher was Miss Blanche Wilson, an aunt of Dr.

Wilson Close of Danville. The San Ramon School had two rooms and two teachers. The rooms were known as "the big room and the little room." Miss Wilson taught the first four grades in the "little room."

Mary, the oldest daughter, married Joe Martin, a farmer, in 1911. They were the first couple to be married in the new Catholic Church in Danville, St. Isidore's. (See Chapter Seven, *Places*.) They lived on a farm in Crow Canyon. Their daughter was Marjorie Mary, born in 1912 at Bollinger Canyon.

Nora, the second daughter, married Frank A. Marshall in 1913, also at St. Isidore's Church in Danville. They built a house in Danville. It is now the Shoe Stable on Diablo Road (See Chapter Six). Frank was assistant cashier at the San Ramon Valley Bank (See Chapter Seven, *Places*). They had a daughter, Ellamae, born in 1914 in Bollinger Canyon.

William Carlos, the only son, married Lena Caldeira of Castro Valley in 1918, at all Saints Church in Hayward. Manuel and Leonora retired in 1918 and moved to Hayward to live. William C. and his wife farmed on the family farm for a number of years. Later they bought the Harry C. Hurst store in San Ramon and left the farm. They had three sons, William J., born in 1920, the first full time Fire Chief of San Ramon; Clifford C., born in 1922; and Howard P., born in 1927.

Elsie, the youngest daughter, married Elmer Valentine in 1942 and lives in Walnut Creek. She was in the first confirmation class at St. Isidore's Church. The Church was dedicated by Archbishop Edward Hannah in 1912, the same day as the confirmation.

William C. Fereira was postmaster at the San Ramon Post Office for thirty-four years, until he retired in 1963. (See Chapter Four, *Post Office*.) William J. Fereira married Violet Krga of Chicago, Illinois, in 1946. They have two children, a daughter Virginia, born in 1948, and son William M., born in 1949. They live in Danville, California. Clifford C. Fereira married Kathryn Johansen Ward (deceased) of Oakland in 1951. They have four children: Leslie K. Ward Brown, born in 1946; Eve E., born in 1957, Ruth A., born in 1959, and James C., born in 1966. They live in Tahoe City, California. Howard P. Fereira married Doris Burrowes of Alameda in 1960. They have no children and make their home in Pleasanton.

All three Fereira sons attended local schools and graduated from San Ramon Valley High

School in Danville. They also all were in the navy during World War II. William Carlos Fereira passed away July 28, 1964.

My thanks to Elsie (Fereira) Valentine of Walnut Creek, for supplying the above material. Permission to use was given me by the family members. The following are interesting recollections as given to me by Elsie in March 1977:

In 1913 Manuel and Leonora Fereira bought their first automobile, a seven-passenger Stoddard-Dayton. Mr. Abrott, the Danville blacksmith, had a sideline of selling used automobiles. Manuel was one of the first customers in San Ramon. The car cost $600 second hand. In 1938 the receipt for the car was still in the family.

Virginia, William, Eve, Ruth and James Fereira are fifth generation of Fereiras. They have two sets of great-grandparents and three sets of great-great-grandparents buried in St. Joseph's cemetery in Hayward. These graves all have markers with names and dates. The grave marker of Joao Silva, the father of Leonora Silva Fereira, is dated 1883.

William J. Fereira, five years old, and Clifford C. Fereira, age three, in front of the San Ramon Store in 1925.

During the 1890s there was a Chinese Laundry and saloon in San Ramon (present site of a produce market). There were many large ranches with many laborers. They patronized the Chinese laundry. There was also a store, blacksmith shop, a shoe repair shop, jail, school and a church.

Whenever there was a wedding or a birth, all the relatives, friends and neighbors gathered at the honoree's home to celebrate. Food was always plentiful, attractive and delicious. Some of the men played string instruments and sang *fados* for dancing the Chamarita, a Portuguese circle dance. A *fado* was a song made up by a musician about one of the pretty girls who was dancing with the group, in the manner of the minstrels of medieval days and throughout history.

Kathryn J. Fereira passed away in Reno, Nevada, April 13, 1977, a resident of Tahoe City. She is survived by her husband, Clifford Fereira, daughters Mrs. Leslie Brown of Fresno, Eve E. and Ruth A., and son James C. Fereira, all of Tahoe City, a sister Mrs. William Lynch of Sebastopol, and granddaughter Jennifer Brown. A native of Oakland, she was fifty-four years old. Services were at Hull's Walnut Creek Chapel on April 18, 1977. Interment in Oakmont Memorial Park, Lafayette, California.

MUELLER

(The following are edited portions of a talk by Carola (Kuss) Cordell, given to the Alamo Women's Club, and of personal interviews with her in March 1977.)

Ernest Mueller (Carola's grandfather) was born in 1824 and married in 1848 to Amelia Isfeldt. Their children were Wilamena, August and Carola Rose. Ernest Mueller, having lost his wife, left family ties and his jewelry business in Illinois, and sailed to California by way of Panama, arriving in Oakland in 1862. Oakland was at that time quite undeveloped. The streets were muddy and unpaved and the business area consisted of one-story shops along Broadway from the waterfront to about Ninth Street. The hills around the town were studded with oak trees. Not many years before Indians had inhabited the area. Mueller set himself up in business and when the first three-story brick building was erected on Ninth Street, in 1867, he occupied part of it for his jewelry store. He bought a long strip of land along a muddy slough, an arm of the San Antonio Slough, a mosquito-infested bog he thought would never amount to much, and so resold for very little. Later Edson Adams and Dr. Samuel Merritt saw great possibilities and it eventually became Adam's Point and Lake Merritt.

KUSS RANCH

Peter Nicholas Kuss, at twenty-two a handsome Dane of strong character, was a man of great potential and had a colorful future. He was born in 1852. His father wished him a maritime career, and he was educated in navigation and went to sea. After a harrowing experience in a Chinese harbor where most of the men developed

Peter Nicholas Kuss
(1852-1909)

cholera, scurvy, and goodness knows what else, the ship eventually came to a port in California. After his first look, he was through with a life at sea forever! He was well-educated and spoke three languages. Kuss was a good organizer, so began employing men into a work crew. In 1876, when he was twenty-four and had enough substance, he asked Carola Rose Mueller, nineteen, to marry him. They had four children, Edward, Amelia, Mabel and Carola.

In the years that followed Peter developed two stores, with merchandise of paint and decorating supplies of wallpapers, glass, etc., and employed over fifty people. The main store was on Mission Street in San Francisco, behind the Palace Hotel. The branch store was on San Pablo Avenue, Oakland.

When Peter saw the San Ramon Valley, he fell in love with it. In 1886 he began buying land in Danville, 117 acres. The first acreage was purchased from William H. Hemme, whose original home had burned down and been replaced with a six-room one-story ranch style house. Kuss enlarged it and surrounded it with porches large enough for dances. He also acquired 600 acres in Kings County, but the ranch in Danville was his pride and joy. The family all loved spring and summer vacations there over the years.

The boundaries of the Kuss Ranch were from Harrison Lane (named for Ralph Harrison who

The William H. Hemme home was purchased in 1886 by Peter Nicholas Kuss, who made additions and built porches all around large enough for dancing.

owned the cherry orchard, presently Del Amigo Road) to what is now Rutherford, west to the O'Neill property (Tao House) north across the Alamo line to the Stoddard place (end of Camille Avenue) and east to the Van Gordon place. There were horses, cows, pigs, chickens, etc.

Kuss loved entertaining large groups. Oakland business friends, several Shriners among them, would come out and take two-day trips up Mount Diablo. Often after the large groups left, Peter's wife would give a sigh of relief to be able to return to her Oakland home with its conveniences.

Peter Kuss was a man who dared social change. During the early years of his business, at about the turn of the century, he was greatly concerned over the rights and well-being of the working man. He was the first employer on the Pacific Coast to try a plan of profit sharing with his employees. He felt if, through their efforts and loyalty, his employees helped to produce and increase profits, they should be able to share in a percentage of those profits. He also believed that an employee who was an efficient worker should be paid more than an inefficient one. The unions were beginning to gain strength, making it impossible to make choices based on merits of employees.

When the big earthquake and fire of 1906 hit, Kuss was completely wiped out, and survived only by enlarging the Oakland store. Three years later, in 1909, he died; his wife followed in 1915. Soon after, the Danville property was divided among the surviving heirs: Amelia "Amy" (Mrs. Jack) Harper, Mabel Kuss and Carola (Mrs. Russell) Cordell. "Amy" had married in 1905 and Carola in 1921. Carola's husband was a newspaper man, in commercial art and advertising, on

the *Examiner*. Mabel Kuss was unmarried.

Carola remembers those "precious years" before the first World War which they called the "innocent years." Their more sophisticated life was in Oakland, but on the ranch they were more informal, with outdoor sleeping, picnics, barbecues and week-end visits. There were many dance parties and midnight suppers, the large porches decorated with Chinese lanterns and greens from the hills. Often a group, including Oakland friends, would attend other dances in the San Ramon Valley, at large private homes or at the Grange Hall. Then, as today, the women enjoyed the fun and excitement of purchasing that ball gown.

Now, of course, many homes cover what was a peaceful countryside of orchards and hay fields. Only two members of the Kuss family survive and live on the old ranch property, Miss Mabel Kuss on Kuss Road and Carola (Kuss) Cordell on Cordell Drive, both in Danville.

CORDELL DRIVE

Cordell Drive was developed through "blood, sweat, love and tears!" it was laid out parallel to Harper Lane. Carola and Russell Cordell built their first home at the west end of Cordell Drive, now Kirkcrest Road. After he died of cancer in 1948, Carola found it necessary to sell the home to J. Graham and Ellen Sullivan. They still reside there. She then began her second home at the opposite end of Cordell Drive. It started as one large room and garage and grew into a complete and comfortable home. It has been owned since 1952 by Bruce L. and Bernice Schremp. In 1953 Carola's present home was started; she still resides there. All three homes were designed by Carola and built by Hans Rodde of Alamo. The two old apple trees on her present property were probably planted by Will Hemme as part of the orginal fruit orchard. They must be 100 years old or older. The Cordells placed all power poles at the rear of the properties, not on the street and in view. Carola feels she has three different "roots," all her former and present homes on the old Kuss Ranch property.

JOHN HARTZ

John Hartz (1847-1920) was born in Holstein, Germany, January 6, 1847. He was the son of Vieth and Metta (Plauschau) Hartz. He was raised and educated in his native land. In young manhood he engaged in farming. He came to California in 1865, working as a farmhand first, in Alameda County. He was a "stranger in a strange land," not knowing the language or the customs, and with only ten dollars to his name! He worked hard and often against heavy odds. In 1876 he rented land in Dublin, Alameda County, which he farmed until 1888. That year he purchased 220 acres from James Stone on the westside of Danville (present site of Danville Estates).

He sold part of this land to the railroad company. About twenty acres he divided into town lots, reserving 200 acres of his own ranch at the end of Prospect Avenue. He erected a handsome two-story house and commodious barns, which added to the value of his ranch. He had his own fresh water stream which flowed out of the Las Trampas range onto his property. He had a vast orchard, fine corn and other crops, as well as grain and stock.

On September 17, 1877, John Hartz married Catherine Johnson, who was also born in Holstein,

Germany. She was the daughter of Nicholas Johnson. They had three children: Henry, who married Alice Hampton; Hannah, who married Neil Harrison; and Matilda "Tillie," who married Hiram N. Elliott. John Hartz was a member and past noble grand of IOOF and the Rebekahs lodge. He was treasurer of the Odd Fellows lodge of Danville for twenty years. His wife and daughters also were members of Rebekahs. Mrs. Hartz was treasurer of the lodge for ten years and Tillie was a past noble grand.

In his honor, Hartz Avenue in downtown Danville was named for John Hartz. He was seventy-three years of age when he died in 1920.

The Hartz family home was built about 1890, in the general vicinity of Prospect Avenue, Danville. It later became the home and ranch of Fred and Ernestine Houston, for whom Houston Court

Above, remains of the old home following a three-hour fire which took place on June 29, 1957. Palm tree at left is still part of Schwartz's front garden.

Left, Hannah, Henry, Matilda "Tillie," and their father, John Hartz, for whom Hartz Avenue was named, in front of the Hartz family home. It was built in about 1890 in the general vicinity of the end of Prospect Avenue, present site of Dr. and Mrs. Stanton Schwartz's home.

was named. Still later, owners were Richard and Peggy Quinn, who restored the house and for whom Quinterra Lane was named. They divorced and are both remarried, Richard living in New York and Peggy in southern California. Next owners were Jack and Kay Parsons. Parsons Lane was developed while they lived there. On June 29, 1957, the house was destroyed by a three-hour fire.

The site is now the location of the home of Dr. and Mrs. Stanton Schwartz, and Parsons Lane is their private circular drive.

HOUSTON

The Kelly Ranch, which raised coach horses for the Palace Hotel in San Francisco, was purchased by Frederick King Houston, father of Frederick William Houston, about 1927. It consisted of 198½ acres then, going up into the hillside. The property was bounded on the south by Wilford Harrison and beyond was the Otto property. On the north was Charley Love's pear orchard.

The father passed away about 1929 and Fred Houston took it over. There was no electricity or gas. With advice from Frank Rutherford of the Bishop Ranch (see Chapter Twelve), Houston planted several varieties of walnut trees on the sixty-two acres on flat land. It became one of the finest walnut groves in the area (now the vicinity of part of Danville Estates). He also had horses and sheep, and raised grain for the animals.

When Fred Houston was twenty-one years old he entered military service and served four years in France and Germany during World War I. He was a graduate of Berkeley High School, as was his wife Ernestine Porter, who came to the Danville area in about 1937.

Later, during the war years of World War II, there was much controversy about using sprays on trees, and there were petitions pro and con. Finally, on the day before Thanksgiving 1946, Fred and Ernestine Houston moved back to Berkeley. They had sold out to the Quinns. Fred Houston passed away February 21, 1959. His widow still makes her home in Berkeley. They had no children.

ELLIOTT FAMILIES

The family name Elliott, known to be the Scotch spelling, can also be spelled Eliot and Elliot. A study in 1964 of the Social Security files found the name Elliott to be the 145th most common name in this country. There are approx-imately 136,000 adult Elliotts in the country today.

Records show that Richard Elliott was born in Kentucky in 1806. He died in California on April 20, 1878 and is buried in College City, California. His son Newton married Susan Barham. She was born August 18, 1839 and died March 30, 1909. The Barham family settled in Sonoma County near Santa Rosa, from where one of the family served as Representative to the U.S. Congress.

Newton and Susan (Barham) Elliott's children were: Wesley, born November 8, 1860, died 1935; Ivory B., born May 22, 1869; Ella V., born February 14, 1872; Hiram N., born November 8, 1873; Birdie F., born December 31, 1878. Newton was a cheese maker. The family lived five miles south of Knights Landing in Yolo County, at the bend of the Sacramento River. The children attended school in Knights Landing.

Hiram left home at the age of twelve to make his living as a jockey. He was so small he had to be tied in the saddle. His exploits took him as far east as Chicago. He returned to California and rode for several seasons at the Emeryville Track. With a promise to his mother not to diet and stay small, for the sake of his health, he left the jockey business.

Prior to the turn of the century, he came to Contra Costa County, by the kindness of free food and lodging for the down and outers of the race track, from the Curry family (Irish hospitality). Curry served as Postmaster of El Cerrito and Coroner of Contra Costa County for many years. Hiram "Hi" found a job at a hotel in Crockett, California, owned by the Patric Lucey family, then in Walnut Creek at the Rogers Hotel, and later at a bar in Walnut Creek, where he learned the business thoroughly and expertly from a Mr. Burpee, who ran a very clean and orderly bar and would not tolerate any foolishness. He later went to Concord, and went into a partnership with his sister Ella (Elliott) Gust.

About 1905-06 Hi came to Danville to operate the bar at the corner of Front Street and Diablo Road for his brother-in-law, Charles Gust. This bar had formerly been owned and operated by an Irish family named Lawless. At about this time Ella (Elliott) Gust operated the Mountain View Hotel at the corner of School and Hartz Avenue, where some of the victims of the 1906 San Francisco earthquake were housed. One of them was Dr. V. Vecki, a dentist for many years in Danville. About this time Hiram Elliott met and married

Tillie Hartz. Of all the places he had seen and worked in, he said many times, Danville looked like the best place for growth and success and he wanted a part in the building of the town. In 1907 he purchased the bar from Charles Gust.

Hi and Tillie rented the old James Close home across from the bar, for $6 a month, and it was there that a son, Duane "Hi" was born to them on June 19, 1909. The news of the birth was delivered to the grandparents, John and Catherine Hartz, by Raymond Clark, oldest son of Judge Clark, who ran the distance to the Hartz Ranch without a stop! On Thanksgiving Day 1909 the family of three moved to their new home at the corner of Diablo and Rose Street (present site of Grubb & Ellis Co.). Hiram lived in this home for thirty-four years and his wife Matilda for fifty-nine.

In 1911 Hi Elliott built a building on Hartz Avenue (Walnut Street), which he rented out as a drug store, and later an ice cream store, barber shop, then hardware store. Next door, in 1912, the present building of Elliott's Since 1907 was built and occupied by Hi Elliott. It was known as The Eagle Bar.

On May 19, 1911, a second son, Walter, was born in the family home. On March 19, 1915, a third son, Gordon, was born there, attended by Mrs. Pynn.

About 1917 Hi Elliott had a garage built on the corner lot of Hartz and Diablo, next to the home place. It was rented to and later sold to Oscar F. Olsson. About 1921 Hi Elliott leased the Old School grounds next to the Odd Fellows Hall (present site of Village Theatre) to preserve the large beautiful black walnut trees. He made a park and campgrounds for people to enjoy.

For the next thirteen years of prohibition Elliott's survived without bootlegging, by changing businesses to ice cream store, grocery, and snooker parlor. A short while after the repeal of prohibition, Hi Elliott suffered a slight stroke and was forced to retire. He passed away December 3, 1943. He was truly a pioneer of many businesses and improvements in downtown Danville.

After the repeal the place was reborn, supervised by Matilda Elliott. For the next thirty-five years "Elliott's Since 1907" found Duane and his brother Gordon seven days a week behind the bar, taking time out only for World War II. Duane was in the Army and served in Europe under General George S. Patton, and Gordon was in the Coast Guard.

Duane Elliott attended Danville Grammar School from 1915 to 1923, and San Ramon Valley Union High School, 1923-27. He worked in the Danville Post Office, 1933-35; was a member of the Danville Volunteer Fire Department 1928 to 1961 (took C. W. Close's place); was a member of the Contra Costa County Grand Jury in 1942; and worked in the family liquor business from 1930 to 1976. Duane, known as "the Chief," married Tillie Hammrich of Ipswich, South Dakota, June 26, 1940. They had a daughter, Duana, born April 21, 1951. Duana was married on June 19, 1971 to Mike Cabral of Oakland. He is a dispatcher for the Danville Fire District. She is operations manager for the Bank of California in Danville. Tillie (Hammrich) Elliott died of cancer on September 25, 1976.

Walter Elliott attended Danville schools and graduated from the local high school. He married Barbra Koperski on March 21, 1952. They had two daughters, Janet, born October 17, 1955, and Beverly, born August 2, 1953.

Gordon Elliott also attended local schools and graduated from the local high school. He married Dorothy Benzing of Walnut Creek on September 26, 1939. They had a daughter, Donna Lee, born May 15, 1943. She married Steve Van Cleve of Walnut Creek. They had one son, Gregory, born December 13, 1967, and live in Riverside, California. While Gordon Elliott still lived in Danville, his telephone number ended with "1907" (the year the bar was established).

Duane Elliott resides on Prospect Avenue, and Walter Elliott lives on West Prospect Avenue, both in Danville. In April 1977, Gordon Elliott moved to Hemet West, in the city of Hemet, eighty-five miles east of Los Angeles and eighty-three miles north of San Diego, in the heart of Riverside County. Hemet West is a mobile home park and recreation center, including a chain of crystal cool lakes, a sporty three-par golf course, and a sparkling waterfall droppinjg from seven-and-a-half-acre Rock Mountain, in the midst of Hemet Valley at the base of Mount San Jacinto.

For many years the Elliotts sponsored a popular golf tournament in San Ramon Valley. All proceeds were for the Youth Boosters League. New owners of "Elliott's Bar Since 1907" since the first part of 1977 are Vera Hutchison and Tony Cline, former Oakland Raider. They both live in the San Ramon Valley.

RUTHERFORD FAMILY

Frank Rutherford (1865-1953), born in Edinburgh, Scotland, arrived at Santa Barbara, California, in 1872. There he was later employed by the pioneer agriculturalist, Elwood Cooper, and acquired acreage of his own. His ability came to the attention of another large California landowner, Thomas B. Bishop, of San Francisco, and he was offered the superintendency of Bishop's San Ramon Rancho (2800 acres). He and his wife, Susan Grant (1872-1952), also a native of Scotland, and their four daughters arrived at San Ramon on October 30, 1904.

During his tenure of forty years, Rutherford altered the productive capacity of the ranch from hay and grain to pears and walnuts. At one time this was the largest single pear orchard in the world. The Bishop Ranch (see Chapter Twelve, *San Ramon*) was also noted for its award-winning sheep. Rutherford was one of the organizers of the Contra Costa Walnut Growers Association in Walnut Creek in 1920, and served over the years as director, vice-president, and president. He was also a director of the San Ramon Valley Bank.

In 1919 the Rutherfords acquired the fifty-two-acre Stelling property north of Danville. Cherries and prunes were the chief crops, later replaced by walnuts and a dehydrator built for their processing. The property was sold following Mr. Rutherford's death in 1953, and later the two-story home was demolished. The area is now the Glenwood subdivision, and Rutherford Drive perpetuates the name of this pioneer agriculturalist.

Mr. and Mrs. Rutherford became the parents of two more daughters at San Ramon, where they continued to live until his retirement in 1944. At that time his son-in-law, Verner T. Andreasen, who had resided on and maintained the Danville property, became the ranch superintendent. The Rutherfords celebrated their fifty-ninth wedding anniversary on April 30, 1951 at their Danville home.

Their six daughters: 1. Daisy (1893-1970) married Henry H. Steinmetz (1896-1967), they had three children: George E. Benicia, a teacher at Hogan Senior High School in Vallejo, Henry H., Jr. "Hank," of Sacramento, executive vice-president and manager of Cache Creek Bank, and Florence Susan (Mrs. R. W. Breidenbach) of Davis. She is an elementary teacher and her husband is a professor at UC, Davis. Their children are Wendy Lynn and Lauren Ann.

The Rutherford home at Rutherford Drive and Danville Boulevard, Danville.

Henry Trevitts home, which was at the intersection of Livorna Road and Freeway 680, Alamo.

Henry H. Steinmetz was the grandson of an early San Ramon Valley resident, Henry Trevitts (1819-1897), whose home stood at the intersection of Livorna Road and the freeway (Alamo). Trevitts was a native of Pennsylvania, a veteran of the Civil War, and a resident of Livermore, where he purchased the fifty-eight-acre site in 1875 and moved with his wife Jemina Dorn (1826-1888) and children, all of whom were residents of the San Ramon Valley until their deaths: Alice; Florence (Mrs. August Steinmetz); Carrie (the mother of Braddick Peterson, still a resident); Frank; and George E., who married Susie Stone and whose daughter is Susan (Mrs. Whitney M. "Tut" Dunford) of Fremont, California.

August (1853-1935) and Florence (1859-1932) Steinmetz moved to Alamo from San Francisco after the earthquake and fire of April 18, 1906 and acquired property north of Danville from Mrs. Lillian Close in 1907. Pears, apples, prunes, nuts and chickens provided a livelihood. They, and later their son Henry and his family, resided there until the property was sold in 1970.

2. Florence (1895-1969) married Frank E. Roy. They had a daughter Jean (Mrs. Herbert Baldwin Elworthy). The Elworthys have a 700-acre cattle ranch in Crow Canyon. Their children are Sandra Ayesa, Cathy, Mark and Bert.

Frank Roy came to the San Ramon Valley to work on the Danville-to-Diablo roadbed of the Oakland, Antioch and Eastern Electric Railway, founded in 1909. After this job was completed, he worked for Robert N. Burgess, owner of the property which was to become the Diablo Coun-

try Club, breaking wild mules, some of which had been used in the building of the rail bed. When this job was completed, he was employed by a pioneer San Ramon Valley resident, Charles G. Goold. After serving in France in World War I, Mr. Roy returned to Danville and with Mr. Goold's aid opened the Service Garage on Hartz Avenue in 1919. He continued the business until 1939. During World War II he worked for the Moore Shipbuilding Company in Richmond, and then for the Danville Fire Department until his retirement. Many students of the San Ramon Valley Union High School during the 1920s remember Frank, for he operated the school bus facility, providing daily transportation from the ends of the District. At one time he also provided U.S. Mail service from Danville to Diablo. He now resides on Estates Drive in Danville.

3. Christina "Chrissie" (1897-1956) (Mrs. Jesse Robbins) is remembered by many as a teller for the San Ramon Valley Bank, the Bank of Italy, and later the Bank of America in Danville. She and her husband resided in San Martin at the time of their deaths. They had no children.

4. Frances, born in 1903, was the wife of Verner T. Andreasen who died in 1975. They had three children: Lloyd E. of Alameda, is with the education department. Barbara "Honey Bear" (nickname from San Ramon Valley High School, where she was very active in school affairs) is married to Leo Watson Lynch. They make their home in Waterford, California, where Leo is a rancher, primarily almonds, and Barbara runs a catering service. Their children are Melinda, Coreen, Nancy and Tim. James G. Andreason of Sacramento is Personnel Director for beauticians in the western states. Frances (Rutherford) Andreasen now makes her home in Oakdale.

Edith, born in 1910, married Malcolm Russell. They returned to the Valley after a long residence in Yreka, where Mac was manager of Litrell Parts Company. He is now retired from Amico in Oakland and they live in Walnut Creek. They had no children.

6. Helen "Blinky," born in 1915, married Merle Johnson and they live in Little River, Mendocino County, after being residents of Danville and Walnut Creek for many years. Merle followed in his father Stephen Johnson's footsteps as a building contractor. They built many homes in the San Ramon Valley area as well as elsewhere. His mother, Pearl Johnson, was a well-known Valley

civic leader. Helen and Merle have five children. Douglas is in the U.S. Navy. Gary is married to Lynelle McLennan of Danville, and is an officer of the Walnut Creek Police Department. Their children are Erik and Mindi. The family resides on Green Valley Road, Danville. Bonnie is Mrs. Jim Pointer and lives in Vacaville. They have two children, Rob and Jennifer. Craig Johnson is a student at Diablo Valley College. Carol (Johnson) is married to Larry Salo and they have a daughter, Michelle.

WIESTER

John Calvin and Sarah J. (Mercer) Wiester were born in Pennsylvania and were married August 2, 1882. (Their family home carried a deed signed by William Penn.) J. Calvin died February 12, 1909 and Sarah on June 30, 1917. Their sons Edward (1883-1963) and Alfred (1884-1949) were born in Westertown, Pennsylvania. They came to San Francisco in 1890 and later formed an association with their father and uncle in Wiester and Company, a wholesale household hardware business, near the Palace Hotel. The San Francisco fire and earthquake of 1906 burned them out. Mr. Wiester, with the aid of his sons, took over the Warehouse on Prospect Avenue, which extended along the railroad track. It was

the Danville Warehouse and Lumber Co. They lived in a house which faced Hartz Avenue. (Still standing, it is now Stitch and Time Yardage Shop.)

Alfred Wiester was married on September 16, 1908 to Cora Billings of San Francisco.

Edward Wiester was married June 1, 1906 to Violet Verdolyack. They had a daughter, Eleanor Bertha, born March 9, 1907. She married Frank Byrnes Jantzen Neel on February 19, 1927 and they had a son, Edward Mercer Jantzen Neel, born June 27, 1930. Violet Wiester died June 18, 1908. Ed Wiester was married November 13, 1912 to Hazel Arthur, born April 20, 1890, the daughter of John C. and Eliza Jane Arthur of San Jose.

Eleanor married Rodney Langlais of San Francisco in 1933. She experienced a stroke in 1973 and is in a rest home in San Francisco.

Before trucking days! A team of warehouse horses coming down Prospect Avenue from Hartz. The building on the left is the back of Close's Store. On the right is Groom's Blacksmith Shop.

Gondolas loaded and ready to leave the Danville Warehouse and Lumber Company. The warehouse and buildings burned in the early 1940s.

Edward Mercer Neel spent part of his growing up years with Ed and Hazel Wiester in Danville and attended local schools. He was married August 27, 1955, to Dolores Agnes Karlo of San Francisco, daughter of Mr. and Mrs. Leo H. Karlo. She attended San Francisco State College, where they met. They have five children: Kathryn Marie, born June 20, 1956; Edward Leon, June 28, 1958; James Bernard, April 16, 1960; Virginia Ann, October 16, 1962; and Dolores Eleanor, February 14, 1967. They make their home in Chadds Ford, Pennsylvania. Edward is president of Analytical Instrument Developments, Inc. in Avondale, Pennsylvania, which he founded. He is a graduate chemist.

Hazel A. Wiester lives on Esther Lane in Danville, California.

The following is excerpted from the March 22, 1950 *Oakland Tribune*. The article was headlined "Veteran Fire Commissioner Recalls Old Bucket Brigade," and included a photograph of E. C. Wiester.

Ed C. Wiester, 67, secretary of the first Volunteer Fire Dept. Danville, and commissioner since 1924, looked back on the progress of local fire fighting during the past 38 years.

The Danville Fire District currently has five fire trucks, one of which is being converted from a former Army crash truck to a 1000-gallon hose and pump equipped tanker. Today's radio-equipped trucks and fire station, and mechanized fire equipment are a far cry from the original bucket brigade, formed early in 1912.

Sometime prior to March 1912, the local fire department's old minute book shows that the organization of a Volunteer Fire Brigade was discussed at a meeting called by the Danville Improvement Club. The organization is to be known as the Danville Volunteer Fire Dept. and is being formed to preserve and protect property in the village of Danville.

Officers elected at the first meeting were: J. A. Freitas, fire chief; G. W. Groom, first assistant chief; Harvey Eddy, second assistant chief; C. W. Close, treasurer; and E. C. Wiester, secretary. Wiester is the last surviving officer of the original group.

In the early days, fire fighting was carried on by bucket brigade. A. W. Fichtenmueller, who subsequently became fire chief and retired about two years ago, soldered cone-shaped bottoms on the fire fighting buckets which had the dual purpose of preventing them from being "swiped" for flower pots, and made it impossible to set down during actual fire fighting.

On September 6, 1921, the County Board of Supervisors appointed James Cass Jones, W. A. Ward and Frank Rutherford on the first board of commissioners to set up a fire district as a political subdivision.

March 22, 1921 saw passage of a measure for taxing district property to purchase and maintain fire equipment and Danville Fire District was on its way. Other commissioners of Danville Fire District who have served on the board for many years are Roger L. Podva and S. H. Johnson. Duane Elliott is current chief of the fire district.

OSBORN FAMILIES
928 Diablo Road, Danville

I. Melvin Osborn was born and raised on a ranch in Montpelier, Idaho, on April 7, 1880. He was a Mormon. He came to Oakland, California in 1908 and met Myrtle McNally in San Francisco. They were married January 1, 1912 in San Francisco.

In the spring of 1926, Mr. Osborn purchased forty-seven acres on Diablo Road, Danville. On the property was a two-story home built in 1856 by the Howard brothers, a large barn, and a garage, but no inside plumbing! Mrs. Osborn, city bred, said she would move out to the "wild, bleak countryside" if he would correct the plumbing situation. He did, and the family arrived in Danville on April 26, 1926. The children were: Mac D. Osborn, born in Oakland (12-11-13); Fern, born in San Francisco (8-14-16); Melva (1-12-18); Grant (12-8-19); Ardith (12-8-21); and James (11-23-23). The four youngest Osborn children were born in Utah. They all attended Danville schools and graduated from San Ramon Valley Union High School in Danville.

On the property they raised livestock—horses, cows, hogs, chickens, and rabbits—and their own hay for feed. Mr. Osborn raised and bred fine horses and participated in rodeos. He was supervisor of roads for the county for ten years in the San Ramon Valley area, before his retirement. He passed away in Danville in June 1966.

Myrtle Osborn was the Danville librarian for twenty-eight years, from 1945 to 1973, when she retired. The Danville Library was established in 1913 by Lillian (Mrs. James E.) Close, and was upstairs in the building on Front Street. When Mrs. Osborn was librarian it was in one room in the Veteran's Hall. In 1962, due to community growth, a new building was built at Hartz Avenue and Willow Drive.

It is said that before Diablo Road was in its present location there was a road which ran along the creek at the base of the hillside (common practice for roads, see Chapter One) and that a group of Cambellites used the creek for their baptisms. Prior to 1861 two Boone brothers, possibly Joel and James as bachelors, lived in the house.

1. Mac D. Osborn served in the Philippines during the war years. He was married June 18, 1950 to Patricia Anderson of Oakland and they live at 934 Diablo Road. They have three children, Charles, David and Marcy. David was married February 14, 1976 to Sherry Gessel of Danville. They live in the upstairs apartment of the Osborn family home. Marcy lives in Salt Lake City, Utah.

2. Fern married John C. Craig and they have two sons, Dennis and Carl. They divorced, she married George Pike and they have two sons, George, Jr. and Ross. George is married and has two children. Ross is unmarried.

3. Melva married Irvin Magill and they adopted two children, Janice and Kevin. Janice is married to Ron Saieva and they have two children, Toni and Tara. Kevin is married to Sandy and they have two sons. Melva was widowed and later married Willard Woods. They make their home on Diablo Road.

Grant graduated from Brigham Young University and married Marge Cottam of Provo, Utah. They have six children: Jefferey married to Chris and they have three children, Michelle, Cindy and Ruth. Their other children are Steven, David, Becky, Mark and Jennifer, who attend college. The family lives in Massachusetts. Grant is a college professor at Amherst College.

5. Ardith graduated from Brigham Young University and was married December 1, 1950 to Jack Steger of Danville. They have three children. Jack is a local realtor. Jane was married February 1977 to Paul Osborn of Salt Lake City in that city and had a wedding reception in Danville. John, Jr. "Jay" lives in Logan, Utah and Cynthia lives at the family home on Roan Drive, Danville. Ardith teaches at San Ramon Valley High School.

6. James also graduated from Brigham Young University and served in Europe during WW II. He is married to Shirley Newell of Provo, Utah, and they have five children and live in Walnut Creek. Their children are twins Nancy and Kathleen, who attend college in Rexburg, Idaho, Russell, Michael and Mary Ellen, who attend schools in Walnut Creek.

I first met Mr. Osborn and his daughter Melva in the late thirties, when we all worked for State Farm Mutual Auto Insurance Co. in Berkeley. For a time Mr. Osborn was a sales representative while Melva and I worked in the office. Mrs. Osborn told me she too had her insurance license for a while.

Mac D. and James Osborn have operated Osborn Spraying Service since 1938.

OLSSON

Andrew Olsson came to San Ramon in the late 1880s and opened his blacksmith shop on the site of the former Villa San Ramon, now Franco's. It took him three years to earn enough money to be able to send for his wife, Amanda. His son, Oscar, did his apprenticeship in San Francisco and then worked with his father. He left San Francisco at 9:00 P.M. the night of the earthquake and fire of 1906 and was in San Ramon when it happened.

Other members of the family were: Reuben, Ella, Astrid (Humburg), and Edwin, all born in San Ramon. Oscar Olsson opened an electric store and the first garage and service station at Hartz Avenue and Diablo Road. He acquired dealerships for Buicks, Fords and Durants. He was elected constable and in 1924 was appointed Second District Supervisor by Governor Richardson. He married Ella Boucher, who was principal and taught at the San Ramon School.

Their four sons, David Edwin, Robert Frederick, John Wesley and James Russell, were raised in Danville until 1932 when they moved to Martinez, where Oscar Olsson became Superintendent of the County Hospital until 1946, when he retired. James R. Olsson is County Clerk and makes his home with his family in Martinez.

1. Construction on Stone House was begun in 1852 by John Marsh, the building to be the most beautiful home in all of California. He was building it for his wife, Abigail Tuck, and their daughter, Alice, who was born in 1852 in an adobe home close by. Abigail selected the site in a large grove of oak trees on Marsh Creek about two and one-half miles south of Brentwood. The bricks were made on the site and the stone quarried from the nearby hills. Abby died in 1855 and John was murdered September 24, 1856, a few weeks after the house was completed. The home still stands and is listed on the National Register of Historic Places.

2. Viola Scott (Root) worked for the Pacific Telephone Co. for thirty-five years. She went to work in 1917 at the age of seventeen right out of high school, and worked until 1952 when the Agency Office turned to the dial system. She was the best telephone operator I ever knew, and served the San Ramon Valley patrons with free "answering service."

Chapter Four

Post Offices

ALAMO POST OFFICE

The Alamo Post Office (RA) was established May 18, 1852. John M. Jones, an early pioneer, was appointed its first postmaster and served for nine years. The first site was his two-story adobe home located on a knoll opposite the Alamo Market Plaza. The current postmaster, appointed January 3, 1976, is Joseph J. Coppa. He has lived in San Leandro for twenty-two years and serves as vice-mayor. The Alamo Post Office is first class and has over 700 boxes. There are five delivery routes. The population of Alamo was 8,018 in 1975 and 8,825 in March of 1977.

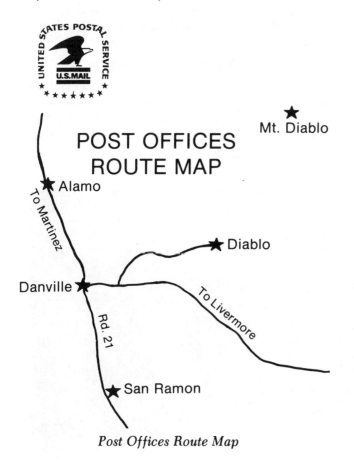

Post Offices Route Map

DANVILLE POST OFFICE

The Danville Post Office was established August 31, 1860.

POSTMASTERS	DATE OF APPOINTMENT
Henry W. Harris	August 31, 1860
Michael Cohen	July 3, 1865
Henry Hurst	November 23, 1877
Michael Cohen	August 23, 1878
John Conway	May 15, 1886
John A. Shuey	August 21, 1889
John Conway	October 9, 1893
Teresa Conway	September 22, 1896
Albert E. Clark	February 24, 1898
Emma Dodge, served until October 31, 1933	February 11, 1913
Ruby Podva, served until October 31, 1963	January 20, 1940
Henry Neidenbach	???
La Vern Morris, current postmaster	June 30, 1973

Danville Post Office has been first class for over twenty years. It has been at its present location in Danville Square since December 15, 1966, when it moved from 151 East Prospect Street. There are 668 boxes and would be more if space allowed. Danville serves sixteen delivery routes and will start another soon. There are 6,831 home resident deliveries and 483 business deliveries, a total of 7,314, with an estimated population as of March 25, 1977 of 24,933.

Vern Morris transferred to the Danville Post Office October 1956 from Hayward. He has thirty-one years with the postal department. He and his wife Grace have three children, all of whom attended local schools and graduated from Monte Vista High School. Daughter Yvette is now Mrs. Supriano of Walnut Creek and has a son James, born on Mother's Day, May 13, 1973. Daughter Vernette attends California State University at Hayward, and son Steven is a student at

Diablo Valley College and works part time. The family home has been on Turrini Drive, Danville, since June 1965.

*Ruby Podva served the Danville Post Office for thirty years. She was appointed acting postmaster October 31, 1933, when the Post Office was in the Acree Building on Front Street, following Emma Dodge's retirement. Duane Elliott was her clerk. The Postmaster General was James Farley and Franklin D. Roosevelt was President of the United States. On January 20, 1940 Mrs. Podva was appointed postmaster. She retired October 31, 1963.

SAN RAMON POST OFFICE

The first San Ramon Post Office was established on November 20, 1852. Samuel Russel was its first postmaster, appointed on that date. Seven years later, on November 16, 1859, this post office was discontinued. For fourteen years San Ramon did not have its own post office. It was re-established as "San Ramoon" on December 4, 1873. The name was changed back to San Ramon on December 31, 1883.

POSTMASTER	DATE OF APPOINTMENT
Samuel Russel, served until November 16, 1859	November 20, 1852
Emery T. Mills	December 4, 1873
Leo Lynch	July 10, 1876
Henry C. Hurst	February 6, 1884
Harry C. Hurst	August 18, 1915
Mrs. Annie L. Fry	October 8, 1924
William C. Fereira, served until December 31, 1963	November 13, 1929
Crawford F. Smith, current postmaster	June 20, 1968

After Mr. Fereira's retirement a Clerk-in-Charge, Byron Cochrane, was the manager until June 20, 1968.

Mr. Fereira had a thirty-four-year tenure, the longest service in San Ramon. The post office was then fourth class.

Mr. Smith had about twenty-two years as a Railway Mail Clerk on the SF & LA Line, where his father had spent over forty-six years. Crawford Smith began his postal career on May 9, 1936, two months before his nineteenth birthday. He served more than five years as a letter carrier. He spent three years and eight months in the service in World War II as a radio operator-gunner on a B-24 bomber.

In 1968 the post office was second class and there were only three full routes. In 1977 it is first class and serves eleven routes. The San Ramon area, which for so long was rural, with a population of less then 500 farming families to support the post office, is now a "bedroom community" with little heavy industry to support it but many more families. There are ten different subdivision builders at work building or planning to build right now.

At one time the San Ramon Post Office was in H. C. Hurst General Merchandise Store. Later it was on San Ramon Valley Boulevard and now is at 270 Old Crow Canyon Road. To date, there has been only one postmistress.

TASSAJARA POST OFFICE

The following information on the Tassajara Post Office is from the National Archives in Washington, D.C. The Tassajara Post Office was established October 24, 1896 and discontinued October 31, 1922, in service for twenty-six years

One-time location of the San Ramon post office. When this was Fry's Place, it was also used in part as the post office. Annie L. Fry was postmistress from October 8, 1924 to November 13, 1929.

with the following postmasters and their appointments:

DATE OF

POSTMASTERS	APPOINTMENT
George M. Cole	October 24, 1896
Clara M. Cole	June 22, 1897
Herbert L. Dalton	October 1, 1898
Alton Petersen	July 17, 1899
Annie C. Petersen	February 25, 1903
Addie Souza	September 9, 1910
Margaret Souza	December 1, 1913
Peter A. Peterson	August 22, 1917
Elmer A. Reinstein	January 15, 1920
Clifford Hutchinson	March 3, 1921
Elmer A. Reinstein	December 15, 1921

George M. Cole was known as Captain Cole, as he was a retired sea captain. He lived in the Wilkes-Reinstein house. One of his daughters married Frank Dalton. Their son was Herbert L. Dalton, who married Meta Alberg. Her mother was a Thorup of San Ramon. Mrs. Alton Petersen was also a Thorup. Clara M. Cole was a daughter of George M. Cole. Annie Catherine Petersen was Anton Petersen's daughter. Addie Souza was the older sister of Margaret Souza who had a twin

First Tassajara Post Office. Note mail slot just above corner of superimposed stamp. (Courtesy of Vivian Coats Edmonston)

Anton Petersen home in Tassajara, built in 1899, housed the post office until rural delivery came on October 31, 1922. (Courtesy of Vivian Coats Edmonston)

sister. Peter A. Peterson was not related to the other Petersens. Elmer A. Reinstein was the son of Fred Reinstein.

My thanks to Vivian (Coats) and Charles Edmonston for the use of the above.

The first post office was a little building. In 1899 when Alton Petersen built their home across the road, a room was made in it for the post office. Their carriage house was used as a dance hall and many fine dances were held there. Paintings of the Petersen homes were on the walls.

San Ramon Post Office circa 1900.

DIABLO POST OFFICE

Diablo is the only community in the San Ramon Valley without home delivery service. All mail must be picked up at the small but friendly post office building. Diablo Post Office was a part of the old three-story Cook barn for forty-one years, from 1907 to 1948. The barn was torn down about 1948 by developer Lawrence Curtola. The post office then moved to the Chalet near Apartment #1 for about five years. When it outgrew that location it moved to the original milkhouse and was there from approximately 1953 to 1974.

Its current location is the remodeled pro shop, which held its dedication ceremonies August 1974, climaxed with an "Ice Cream Social" evening held in the Diablo Country Clubhouse.

Diablo's population currently is 1,150. They are served from 492 boxes. The post office is now second class.

Historical records of postmasters over the years seem sketchy, but there was a postmaster for a short time who was followed by a Mr. Cooper, whose wife Helen Cooper followed him. They are both now deceased. From 1955 to 1969 Mrs. Ethel Stott was postmistress. She now makes her home in Sun City, Arizona. Since 1969 the postmistress has been Mrs. Bettye B. Johanson, who now makes her home on Calle Arroyo, Diablo.

The Diablo post office was in this old milkhouse from 1953 to 1974.

JOHANSON

Waldo and Bettye (Brown) Johanson moved to Diablo in August 1949 from Oakland. They had no children but worked during the 1950s with young people of Diablo as advisors to Danville Junior Horsemen. Waldo and his brother, Hobert Johanson, converted the Old Red Horse Tavern, which had been used as a stagecoach stop, into the Red Horse Apartments in 1950, and so it remains to this day. The Johansons lived in Diablo and for an eleven year period lived on Smith Road in Alamo Oaks, Danville. Mr. Johanson died in 1972.

Osborn Home

84

Chapter Five

Clubs and Organizations

DANVILLE ODD FELLOWS LODGE NO. 378, I.O.O.F.

Danville Odd Fellows Lodge No. 378, I.O.O.F. was organized July 26, 1892. Officers and charter members were B. W. Bennett, Noble Grand; J. M. Huckins, vice-grand; B. W. Stone, recording secretary; E. A. Bunce, treasurer; Willie Z. Stone, Edward Griffith, Charles G. Goold and M. L. Simpson, members.

DANVILLE REBEKAH LODGE NO. 123, D. of R.

Danville Rebekah Lodge, No. 123, D. of R., was instituted September 22, 1894, with the following charter members: B. W. Bennett, Ennetta Botts, Margaret Boydston, Wilson N. and Lillian Coats, William Hayden, William and Lucy Stark, B. W. and Lydia Stone. The Lodge was given the number of Banner Lodge No. 123, which surrendered its charter January 1893. The Danville Rebekah Lodge, due to lack of member participation, consolidated with the Concord Lodge in 1958. You will note as you read *Early Pioneers* and *Longtime Residents* how many had been members for many years. At one time in its history it had a very large membership and many came long distances to attend meeting and club functions.

NATIVE SONS OF THE GOLDEN WEST

San Ramon Parlor No. 249 of the Native Sons of the Golden West was organized in Danville, April 10, 1919, with twenty-three members. Charles Goold was its first president and S. H. Flournoy its first secretary. The parlor was later dissolved.

GOOD TEMPLAR

In 1882 Good Templar (temperance) lodges were organized at Antioch, Danville, Lafayette and Martinez.

The following Lodge Directory is taken from page fifty-three of the June 1918 issue of the San Ramon Valley Union High School Year Book. Twelve lodges were listed.

Danville Grange No. 85. P. of H. Regular meetings second and fourth Weds. at 8 p.m. Fraternal Hall, Danville. Chas. W. Stillwell, master; Margaret B. Martinelli, lecturer; Lou L. Stillwell, secretary.

Danville Lodge No. 378 - I.O.O.F. Regular meetings first and third Saturdays at 8 p.m. Fraternal Hall, Danville. Oscar F. Olsson, Noble Grand; J. Hartz, Treas.; Leonard Grass, Secretary.

Danville Lodge No. 123 Daughters of Rebekah. Regular meetings second Saturday at 8 p.m. Fraternal Hall, Danville. Elizabeth Wood, Noble Grand; Fannie W. Coats, Secretary.

Alamo Lodge No. 122, F. & A.M. Regular meetings first Saturday on or after the full of the moon at 8 p.m. Masonic Temple, Walnut Creek. H. H. Daley, Master; Frank Straight, Secretary.

Ramona Camp No. 159, Woodmen of the World. Regular meetings last Monday at 8 p.m. Fraternal Hall, Danville. James P. Root, Council Commander; J. S. McCeil, Banker; Oscar F. Olsson, Clerk.

Laurel Camp No. 7275 R.N. of A. Regular meetings third Thursday at 2:30 p.m. Fraternal Hall, Danville. Oracle, Alice Swartz; Recorder, Phoebe A. Halverson; Receiver, Carrie F. Wing.

Danville Camp No. 13231 Modern Woodmen of America. Regular meetings first Thurs. 8:30 p.m. Fraternal Hall, Danville, Frank A. Nola, Council Commander; Matt Lawrence, Secretary.

Court Mount Diablo No. 118 Foresters of America. Regular meetings first and third Weds. at 8 p.m. Matt Lawrence, Chief Ranger; C. R. Gibbons, Financial Sec.; George Lawrence, Recording Sec.; H. Daley, Sub. C.R.,; F. A. Marshall, Treasurer.

Conselho Danville No. 33 U.P.E.C. Regular meetings third Sunday at 1 p.m. Fraternal Hall, Danville. M. J. Lawrence, President; Joseph S. McCeil, Secretary.

Conselho Verdade No. 70 I.D.E.S. Regular meetings first Sunday at 1:30 p.m. M. J. Lawrence, Pres.; M. B. Nevis, Secretary.

Senhoura de Lourdes No. 60 S.P.R.S.I. Regular meetings last Thurs. 2 p.m. Fraternal Hall, Danville. Mrs. Isabelle S. Macedo, Secretary; Emma G. Maderos, Mary V. Peters, Treasurer.

Almona Chapter No. 214 Order of Eastern Star. Regular meetings last Sat. before the full moon at 8 p.m. Masonic Temple, Walnut Creek. Ruby Harlan, Worthy Matron; Stephen Johnson, Worthy Patron; Florence Foster, Assoc. Matron; and May Spencer, Secretary.

I will attempt to update, where possible, those Clubs and Organizations that were included in *Remembering Alamo . . . and Other Things Along the Way* in 1975.

SAN RAMON VALLEY LODGE NO. 724, F. & A.M. Master for 1976 was Roger Morse and for 1977 is Walter Ebbett, Jr.

SAN RAMON VALLEY CHAPTER ORDER OF EASTERN STAR NO. 588. Matron for 1976 was Rose Nell "Boots" Kauder and for 1977 is Marilyn Freese. Patrons for 1976 were Ernie Mitchell, until he moved to Oklahoma, then Marvin Freese, who also serves for 1977.

DANVILLE GRANGE NO. 85. Master 1975-77 is Leo Bergeron of Tracy, California. Current membership is over 130 members. Dixie Fremerey of Danville is Master of Contra Costa County Pomona Grange No. 45, which assists all county Granges.

NEIGHBORS OF WOODCRAFT, DIABLO CIRCLE NO. 655. Guardian Neighbor 1976-77, Bertha L. Linhares.

ALAMO WOMEN'S CLUB FEDERATED. President 1975-76 was Dottie (Mrs. Ted) Low. Elected March 9, 1977 to serve in 1977-78 was Alma (Mrs. John A.) Brown. Both reside in Alamo. Installation was May 26, 1977 with Dorothy (Mrs. J. Vaughn) Shahbazian the installation officer.

ALAMO MOTHER'S CLUB. I unintentionally omitted Barbara Schlosser, president in 1962. To update: Alamo School, 1975-76, Shirley Bennett; 1976-77, Linda Gieda. Rancho-Romero School, 1975-76, Linda Best; 1976-77, Alice Scott. Stone Valley School, 1975-76, Sue Paul; 1976-77, Susan Paul.

Other San Ramon Valley P-TAs and Parent's Club Presidents: Neil Armstrong, 1975-76, Robert Buckner, 1976-77; Mildred Enke. John Baldwin, 1975-76, Honey Pettigrew; 1976-77, Janet C. Leonard. California High, 1975-76, Sue Cramer; 1976-77, Sue Cramer. Charlotte Wood, 1975-76, Shirley Hart; 1976-77, Ginger Allen, until she moved to Southern California, then Shirley Whee-

Dress Rehearsal for "Fathers' Follies of '54," the Alamo Dads' Club Benefit Show of April 23 and 24 and May 1, 1954. Standing, left to right: Bert Conlin, Fred Dull, Ange Muzzini (all past presidents of the club), Emil "Gus" Gustafson (deceased), and Bill Cottrell (deceased). Front row, left to right: Paul Bohr, Howard Menges, Dorothy Powell (deceased), Lorene Bohr, and Ken Davis. The photo was taken by Don Smith.

ler. Country Club, 1975-76, Sandy Taylor; 1976-77, Dorothy Rivers. Walt Disney, 1975-76, Gay Wyne; 1976-77, Peni Pooler. Green Valley, 1975-76, Jean Blackmur; 1976-77, Connie Wadsworth. Greenbrook, 1976-77, Honey Pettigrew. Los Cerros, 1975-76, Dorothy Chase; 1976-77, Barbara Simmons; Montair, 1975-76, Claudia Edwards; 1976-77, Joan Kaufmann. Monte Vista High, 1975-76, Joan Brandes; 1976-77, Joan Brandes. San Ramon Valley High, 1975-76, Sharon Ritchey; 1976-77, Bethany H. Hall. Twin Creeks, 1975-76, Rusty Mellor; 1976-77, Carol Neach. Vista Grande, 1975-76, Joan Sussman; 1976-77, Cherie McAfee.

ALAMO DADS' CLUB. (RA) I unintentionally omitted Spencer Arnold of Ardith Lane, who was president 1958-59 and Ange Muzzini (RA) of Laverock Lane, 1959-60. Spencer Arnold sold his home in the spring of 1977 and moved up country. When moving he found the long lost Alamo Dads' Club Scrap Book. In it I found the following programs for the Alamo Dads' Club annual Variety Shows: "The Bartender's Daughter," May 16 and 17, 1952; "Green Grass," April 17, 18 and 25, 1953; "The Lost Penny," April 29 and 30, 1955; "Father's Fearless Follies," May 4-5, 1956; and "The Merry Minstrels," May 3-4, 1957. Those members of cast, production staff and committee not mentioned in *Remembering Alamo...and Other Things Along the Way* are the following: Carol and Louise Awalt, Andy (dec.) and Bernie Barbeau, Paul Baron, Pamela and Rose Beck, Nancy Bogue, Elsa Bollaert, Patricia Brown, Libby Bushman (dec.), Gina Capers, Helen Carroll, Dave Comstock, Janet Coop, Andrea Cory, Bradford Craig, Joe Crouch (dec.), Cloyce and Michael Davis, Bonnie De Roco, Pat Dieterich, Richard Faulkner, Jade Fon, the artist who did the 1955 set design, Les and May Fox, Vickie Hardie, Carol Heinemann, Floyd Hicks, Ed and Jean Hofrichter, Bob and Roger Husted, Arline Kelley, Merry Kyle, another artist who did sets, Olive Langridge, Helen (dec.) and Jules Loeb, Eleanor MacDonald, Jim Marsh, Howard and Miriam Menges, Bill and Junene Mivelaz, Harry Monell, Ed Moore, Dorothy Morcum, Patricia Myrick, Howard Nelson, Verne Nerden, Gordon Norby, Elaine Parkhurst, Frank and Vera Plum, Byrne, Dorothy (dec.) and Mike Powell, Dave Pye, Bud and Peg Richardson, Jim Riley, Bill Robertson, Nancy Rutherford, Betty and Vern Sanderson, Bill Sawyer, John Silvera, Ted Smith, Bob Sneeringer (dec.), Adrienne Sowers, George Spelvin, Bud Stephens, Evelyn and Paul Stieger,

Marge Swedberg, Ed Thomas, Bill and Lila Ward, Beverley Watson, Lloyd West, Jon Welty, Taylor White, Gladys, Har, Harold and Mason Williams, and Woody Woodman. The organization was disbanded in 1964.

SAN RAMON VALLEY CHAMBER OF COMMERCE. President for 1976 was Nik Kelly and in 1977 is Al Huovinen.

DIABLO GARDEN CLUB. President for 1976-77 is Mollie Szybolski (Mrs. Steven).

MARY DOYLE UNIT, MDRC (Mount Diablo Rehabilitation Center). President for 1975 was Virginia (Mrs. Samuel K.) McHenry, who served to December. Marion (Mrs. A. H.)Bushey was president to June 1976, when Suzanne (Mrs. Samuel) Abbott of Bolla Place, Alamo, took the reins.

SAN RAMON VALLEY REPUBLICAN WOMEN'S CLUB. President for 1976 was Rosemary Ramsey and for 1977 is Jean Schwafel.

ALAMO ROTARY. President for 1975-76 was Chris Burford, for 1976-77, Bill Garrison, and 1977-78 Fred Moore. Club calendar year is June to June.

ALAMO IMPROVEMENT ASSOCIATION. President for 1975-76 was Bob Bush, for 1976-77 is Eve Auch. 1977-78 Wm. E. Gore.

HISTORY OF DANVILLE WOMEN'S CLUB
1911 - 1977

The history of the Danville Women's Club was prepared by Hazel Arthur (Mrs. Edward) Wiester of Danville, and Merle (Mrs. Waldo E.) Wood of Alamo. Permission to use it, or portions of it, was granted me, for which I thank them.

In 1911, a new teacher, Miss Hazel Arthur, later to become Mrs. Edward Wiester, came to the one-room Danville Grammar School on Front Street. She saw a need for closer relations between parents, teachers and school, and invited the mothers to meet for that purpose. From that meeting a Mothers Club was organized with Leona Abrott president. It became the nucleus of the Danville Women's Club of today, following the same course of development as the Alamo Women's Club (RA).

As community interests developed, the club later became the San Ramon Valley Welfare Club. At the instigation of Mrs. Claude Leech of Walnut Creek, Alameda District President of the California Federation of Women's Clubs, the Welfare Club united with the State Federation in 1919 and the General Federal in 1939, as the Danville Women's Club.

Meetings were held in the Grammar School building (present site of San Ramon Valley Mortuary). Over the years the club has met in various places, including the new Grammar School (present site of the Community Center on Hartz Avenue), in private homes, Grange Hall, Odd Fellows Building, (present site of Village Theater), Sunday School unit of the Presbyterian Church (present site of Lynn School), Fire House on Hartz Avenue (present site of the Cuisinary), and eventually the present clubhouse on Linda Mesa Avenue, Danville.

When club interests enlarged, covering many departments of state and national interests of the Federated Clubs, it was decided that the group would become the Danville Women's Club. Activities centered around local community needs: Red Cross, Boy and Girl Scouts, the Detention Home in Martinez, Crippled Children's Society, history and landmarks, music, art, drama, conservation, health, and better homes and gardens.

Efforts were concentrated on a tuberculosis preventorium called "Sunshine Camp" on Marsh Creek Road, beyond Clayton, where underweight children could go for general build up; Saving the Redwoods; and providing the school with milk or orange juice. This was discontinued in 1928 when a pre-school examination by the local doctors found that underweight children needed rest more than milk.

For many years a decorated Christmas tree and gifts were taken to the women's ward at the County Hospital in Martinez. The Club cooperated with the county health nurse in every way possible. In those early days there was just one nurse, Miss Rachel Miller.

Information and control of narcotics was a club interest as far back as the 1920s. In the department of conservation, they joined the State Federation and the Save-The-Redwoods League, to buy forests of virgin redwoods in Humboldt County to be set aside as a State Park. They also helped preserve the sugar pines in Yosemite Valley, saved walnut trees on the Danville Highway, protested the cutting of trees on the Grammar School grounds, and opposed billboards on the highway. Arbor Day was observed for many years by the planting of trees. Five Monterey Jack pines were planted on the San Ramon Valley High School grounds at the corner of Love Lane and Hartz Avenue, to honor the five local servicemen who lost their lives in World War I. One by one, these trees have died from disease, but the marker still stands. On March 6, 1931, two redwood trees were planted in front of the Danville Grammar School, one dedicated to Hazel Wiester and one to Kate Wood. On that same day a cedar was named for Herman Sandkuhle of Sunset Nursery, Danville, who had donated the trees. Later, one maple and one European plane tree at the school were dedicated to George and Martha Washington, one maple to Calvin Coolidge, and a spruce at Grange Hall, Diablo Road to Pearl Johnson in 1934.

Other trees were dedicated to Leona Abrott in 1940, and to Edna Watson, Phoebe Halverson, and John Muir, on Mount Diablo. The Club endorsed the Easter sunrise service on Mount Diablo, and the saving of Bret Harte Park at the junction of Diablo Road and Camino Tassajara (Vista Grande area). In June 1940, a plaque to mark the site of Union Academy on Danville Boulevard was dedicated. War activities in 1941 kept members busy serving two days a week for the Red Cross.

Maintaining the status of a service club, the club has sponsored scholarships for high school seniors, and other local and worthwhile causes. All of these projects have meant raising money. In the early years, with transportation and communication limitations, card parties were favored. Other popular sources were food sales, flower shows, musical teas, and dances. In recent years, house and garden tours, garage sales, bake sales, and arts and crafts shows have been held.

Membership has fluctuated during the years. In 1938 the idea of owning its own clubhouse started and funds were needed for that. The funds were invested in government bonds. In 1945 a committee was appointed to look for a lot to purchase, but it was unsuccessful until 1947. In 1948 the Club incorporated. In 1949, with Gertrude Haskell as president, the deed for one-half acre on Linda Mesa was received, at a cost of $1,650. Payments were $50 per month, plus interest.

In 1955, the present building was dedicated. At a cost of $9,936.89, added to the cost of the lot, the total cost was $11,586.89. William Diehl was the architect and Shiviley Construction Co. built the clubhouse. Donations of many hours of work and materials helped lower the cost.

The Fiftieth Anniversary of the Club was celebrated in 1969 with many events. The Danville Women's Club has encouraged the preservation and restoration of historical sites and buildings. The latest is "Tao House" (see Chapter Seven, *Places*). An award-winning picture of the John Muir home, painted by past president Carolyn (Mrs. George) McMullen, was donated by the club and hangs in the Ranger Station at the John Muir Historical site.

White Gate (see Chapter Seven, *Places*), the lifetime home of Ray Donahue, was made an historical site of San Ramon Valley in 1976. Mrs. Ruth Donahue, Ray's mother, was an active member of the Club, as were members of the family of the original builder and previous occupant of the home, Nathaniel Howard. His daughter, Kate Howard Wood, was active, and her daughters-in-law, Mrs. Waldo Wood and Mrs. George Wood, are current and past presidents.

The Club meets the first and third Thursdays of the month at 12:30 P.M. All meetings open with an Inspirational, flag salute and patriotic song. Executive Board officers are president; first and second vice-presidents; recording, corresponding, and financial secretaries; treasurer; auditor; parliamentarian; and three directors. Committee chairmen are appointed by the president. The catagories vary from year to year, depending on interests and needs. Basically standard ones are California heritage, amenities, ways and means, membership, health, family living, publicity, conservation, rentals, and spiritual values.

The 1977 roster shows seventy-five members, three of whom are honorary. Mrs. Hazel Wiester, organizer of the first mother's club in 1911 is still an active member. The Club has had two County presidents, Mrs. Wiester in 1928-29 and Mrs. Pearl Johnson in 1933-34. The Danville Women's Club is a member of Mount Diablo District No. 8, which includes clubs in Contra Costa, Calaveras, Tuolumne, and San Joaquin Counties.

The significance of the club emblem is: the band encircling the center—eternity; the shield emerging from the field of blue—enlightenment; red—courage; white—purity; blue—constancy; the letters G.F.W.C.—General Federation of Women's Clubs. The motto, "Strength United Is Stronger," is demonstrated in Club accomplishments. Never underestimate the power of women!

Past-presidents are: 1920-21 Mrs. A. J. Abrott*, 1922-23 Mrs. Charles Goold*, 1924-25 Mrs. G. S. Spilker*, 1926-28 Mrs. G. W. Groom*, 1928-29 Mrs. Roy Halverson*, 1929-32 Mrs. Stephen John-son*, 1932-33 Mrs. Oscar Olsson, 1933-34 Mrs. Melvin Bolender, 1934-35 Mrs. Carl Dauth*, 1935-36 Mrs. Clinton Mullaly, 1936-38 Mrs. Frank Watson*, 1938-40 Mrs. Albert Harris*, 1940-41 Mrs. Fred Egbert*, 1941-42 Mrs. Frank Watson*, 1942-44 Mrs. John Butter, 1944-45 Mrs. Henry Smith, 1945-46 Alice Luchetti, 1946-47 Mrs. Stephen Johnson*, 1947-48 ten members served a month each, 1948-49 Mrs. Curtis Haskell, 1949-51 Mrs. Richard Quinn, 1951-53 Mrs. Frank Lonergan, 1953-55 Mrs. Herbert Polk, 1955-56 Mrs. Lee Decker, 1956-57 Mrs. Fred Wiedemann, 1957-58 Gladys Fager, 1958-59 Mrs. Maurice Marotte, 1959-60 Mrs. Max Selzer, 1960-61 Mrs. Guy Albright, 1961-62 Mrs. Joseph Roberts, 1962-63 Mrs. Helen Haun, 1963-64 Mrs. William Hume, 1964-66 Mrs. Julian Ramelli, 1966-67 Mrs. E. M. McCarthy, 1967-68 Mrs. George McMullin*, 1968-70 Mrs. Lloyd Mosier, 1970-72 Mrs. Forrest Cain, 1972-74 Mrs. George C. Wood, 1974-75 Mrs. Jules Jacquin, 1975-76 Mrs. Foster Daoust, 1976-78 Mrs. Waldo Wood.

The following material is excerpted from a mimeographed pamphlet titled "A Brief Sketch of the History of our Valley," by the Danville Women's Club, no date given. Through research I have determined its date to be 1958. It was signed by Gertrude Haskell and Flora Egbert. Mr. and Mrs. Travis M. Boone have given me permission to use it.

"A Brief Sketch of the History of Our Valley"

The history of our community goes back years before the signing of the Declaration of Independence. We do not know when the Indians first came here but mounds have been uncovered to show that they were here thousands of years ago.

What is now Highway 21 was called "Little El Camino Real" (Author's note: this information, taken from another source, also appears in Chapter One.) from Mission San Jose to Martinez. The towns in the valley were started along this route in early pioneer times, as this was the main route. It was the main road from Monterey and other localities in the south to Martinez and the gold areas of the north.

In 1833, Rafael Soto de Pacheco received a grant to Rancho San Ramon, which included our Valley and from whence came its name. In 1850,

*Known to be deceased.

the section east of San Francisco Bay was named "la tierra de la Contra Costa," land of the opposite coast. Thus Contra Costa County received its name. (RA)

The town of Danville is supposed to have received its name from Daniel Inman, who with his brother opened a blacksmith shop here in 1858. It was later purchased by Dr. Wilson Close's grandfather. This smithy was on Front Street, almost the spot where "The Village Dime and Dollar Store" is now located [1958]. Most of these early day homes have been destroyed by fire or the ravages of time, but in the last twenty-five years, the "Parade of Progress" has really made inroads on the homes, gardens, shade trees and orchards which made our Valley known all over the United States for its quiet charm and beauty.

Trail blazers in the valley, among others, were: John Jones (RA), Wm. Lynch, Leo Norris, Joel Harlan, R. O. Baldwin (RA), David Glass (RA), Samuel More, Wm. Meese (RA), Leonard Eddy, Felix Grundy Coats, Phillip Mendenhall (RA), Charles and Nathaniel Howard, Wade Hays, W. W. Cox and Mark Elliott. These settlers came between 1846 and 1852. (Author's note: not all came that early.) In the ten years following more settlers arrived, including Charles Wood (RA), Wm. Love, Joel Boone, Albert Young, Thos. Flournoy, John Chrisman, George McCamly, Messrs. Hemme (RA), Bollinger, Sherburne and others.

In 1849 Mr. Lynch built a home for himself— the first in the valley built and owned by a white man. This home burned after World War I.

In 1910 San Ramon Valley had thirty-eight students and two teachers, a $4,261 budget and a twenty-three cent tax rate.

In 1860 there were wagon roads to the top of Mount Diablo (RA), where bears, lions, wild cats and wild horses roamed. The Diablo Country Club was a stock ranch where race horses were raised and trained.

The Valley Pioneer's newspaper quarters [when it was on Prospect Avenue] were once occupied by the Lawrence Meat Market, which was established in Danville in 1897. This market is now in Walnut Creek.

Christian Wiedemann, father of Fred Wiedemann, homesteaded land in Norris Canyon about 1850. He was a ship's carpenter and built his home when he was nineteen years old. His daughter still lives on the land. (Auther's note: remember this was written in about 1958.)

Woodburn Home—this attractive home was built for Robert Love, grandfather of Mrs. Ina Boone Root, about eighty-two years ago [1876?]. It was occupied by the Love family for many years. The interior of the home has been redone.

On the south side of Diablo Road was the Frank Rose home. John Chrisman formerly owned this property, but it was purchased by Thos. Flournoy and the home built in 1870. The Flournoy field was the scene of many picnics, political gatherings, Fourth of July celebrations, etc., and as recently as twenty-five years ago [1933?] boys of Danville were swimming in the Chrisman pool in the field now owned by Mr. Kantrowitz (deceased).

In conclusion it was stated in the pamphlet: "Our tour today included many historic spots. There are too many to include all of them. If any are left out, it was not done intentionally. They were just not brought to their attention. The following notes have been obtained from many sources and we are not responsible for the accuracy of any of them. Please let us know if there are any glaring mistakes so that they may be corrected if any later publications are made." An Epilog on the last page states, "The Danville Women's Club hopes you have enjoyed this little excursion into the past of our Community and if it aroused your interest, we may do other parts in the future."

The following are portions of a talk by Hazel Wiester to the Danville Women's Club and information from her personal notes and interviews.

CHINA CLUB

The China Club (the country, not dishes!) was organized April 9, 1919, and had its beginning as a two table card playing group. When Mrs. Sam Prather observed Lent by giving up cards, the group studied the book *Ancient Peoples at New Tasks* by Willard Price. When they came to Chapter Three, called "Trees and Men," they became fascinated with the mysteries of the country of China, and decided to study about it.

The object of the study group was to seek knowledge and to try to understand the people of the world by studying their country, government, characteristics, religion, manner of living, history, etc., ever bearing in mind the great proverb, "Get knowledge, get wisdom, but with all its getting, get understanding, which we believe means understanding of the ways through which God manifests himself."

Photo taken in the early 1920s of the "China Class," a cultural organization. Seated are Olivia Chaboya and Hazel Wiester. Standing, left to right, are: Emily Eddy, Bertha Mariana, Kate Wood, Edith Clark, Annie Van Gorden, Margaret Van Gorden, Nellie Baldwin, and Charlotte Wood.

When formally organized, the Wednesday Club changed to China Class, as Mrs. Louise Easton always referred to it as the "China Class." The group met in each other's homes (alphabetically) on the third Wednesday, and every Wednesday during Lent. Membership was limited to twelve, thought to be the best number for study. The program was assigned at the previous meeting, and might be current events, articles from magazines such as *Atlantic Monthly, National Geographic, Asia,* or from newspapers, sometimes chapters from chosen books, other times a book review or an art exhibit. In 1929 they decided to take a one-half hour period to study current events.

Members were: 1. Mrs. Sam (Myra) Prather. She lived in the present Spilker home, former William Z. Stone residence, and came from Oakland. Her husband built the Yosemite railroad. 2. Mrs. Edward (Hazel) Wiester. She lived where Westridge condominiums are now. Her husband had Danville Warehouse and Lumber Company. 3. Mrs. Ben (Olivia) Chaboya. She lived at "La Cueva" (means the cave), former Otto home, now Lawrie Development, 643 San Ramon Valley Boulevard, Danville. Mr. Chaboya was a horse trainer at Diablo. His mother was a Bernal. 4. Mrs. Charles (Kate) Wood of "Woodside," Sycamore Valley, teacher and mother of Howard, George and Waldo Wood. (See Chapter Two, *Early Pioneers*) 5. Miss Elizabeth "Libby" Wood, aunt of the Wood brothers. Her home was also "Woodside." She often entertained in the

guest cottage called "Rest a Bit." 6. Mrs. George (Annie) Van Gorden, affectionately called "Monnie." She lived in a large Victorian home just beyond Las Barancas on Danville Boulevard. She was a flower lover.

7. Mrs. Alfred (Cora) Wiester. She lived in what is now The French Colonial Kitchen, former home of Mrs. Edward and Mrs. Alfred Wiester's mother-in-law. 8. The eighth member of the card club, Mrs. Rollin (Florence) Foster, did not choose to join the study group. 9. Mrs. Ansel (Louise)★Easton became president and leader after Mrs. Prather dropped out due to the illness of her husband. Mrs. Easton was the aunt of the famous photographer, Ansel Adams. The Eastons came to the Blackhawk Ranch from Easton, near Millbrae, and raised thoroughbred horses and shorthorn cattle. A Spanish-type home was completed in 1918. It was U-shaped and had formal gardens with fountains, etc. (See Chapter Seven, *Places*) A garden house was called the "Godown," a Chinese term meaning "warehouse." The arcade around the U was glass-enclosed and filled with large brass urns and art objects—twenty tons of brass! They were a much-traveled family. Later Mr. and Mrs. Raymond Force lived in the house, and still later it was the site of the home of Peterson Ranch, of Peterson Tractors. In the summer of 1977 it became Renaissance West, a health and beauty spa. ✶✶

10. Mrs. William (Mary Bates) McLellan*, renowned national interior decorator, formerly of San Francisco. She was chosen to decorate the California Building at the World's Columbia Exposition in Chicago in 1893. She was the first

Louise Easton

★~~Mary Bates McLellan~~ was presented at Court in England prior to 1919 and her move to San Ramon Valley. She had a standing order at Holmes Book Company of San Francisco for all books on China. Miss Bates was born in Honolulu in 1852, the daughter of Asher Bates, superior court judge, and came to California when twelve years old. She began her colorful career as a decorator for the most prominent gatherings of the nation's society during the "gay nineties." Her first job as a professional decorator was the arrangement of the Hotel Del Monte in Monterey on June 18, 1885. She was a member of a famous family of long-lived pioneers, the Judd family. Miss Bates was married in 1898 to Wm. S. McLellan of Beresford, San Mateo County. He died in La Honda in 1915. She died on a Saturday morning in 1933 shortly before her eight-second birthday.

on record to ship flowers on ice. She wanted to use California poppies in her display, so dropped a melted piece of wax in the centers of the blooms so they wouldn't "go to sleep!" She brought forget-me-not seeds from Belgium, which she planted in "Old Maids Paradise" in Corte Madera Canyon near Mill Valley, some of which she later transplanted in Blythedale and Cascade Canyons on Tamalpais. They probably grow wild to this day, thanks to her. 11. Mrs. Doug (Emily Goold) Eddy. She was from a pioneer family on El Camino Tassajara and lived in a neat white cottage at Church and Hartz which is still standing. The Eddys were former neighbors of Hazel Wiester on San Ramon Boulevard. 12. Mrs. A. E. (Edith) Clark. She was the wife of Judge Clark and a librarian for many years. They lived on Diablo Road, corner of Hartz and Linda Mesa (present site of Contra Costa Bank).

Replacement members joined the club later. They were: 1. Mrs. John (Nellie) Baldwin, mother of Margaret Wildenradt and John Jr., our former late Congressman. The Baldwin Ranch was called "Osage" for the Osage trees that lined the highway. A train whistle stop called "Osage" was on their property. The home was a very large two-story house built in 1888. They had a lovely collection of named iris. 2. Mrs. Gilbert (Margaret, called "Peggy") Van Gorden. Her home was on Danville Boulevard just south of Alamo (still standing). 3. Miss Evelyn Van Gorden, her daughter. 4. Mrs. Harold (Dorothea Torrey) Kelley. Her father was a member of the firm Vickery Atkins & Torrey of San Francisco, a contemporary of Gumps. 5. Miss Charlotte "Lottie" Wood, retired teacher and the club's secretary for many years.

The China Club continued until 1940, and then disbanded, and was no more.

SAN RAMON VALLEY
FARM BUREAU WOMEN

The following is taken from an article by Barbara Kerns in the *Walnut Kernel* of August 1957:

January 27, 1922 saw the birth of this Center, called then Home Department; it has met continuously from that day. Miss Helen Burling was the Home Advisor from the day of organization until 1949 when she retired. Since 1950 Mary Williams has ably filled the post.

Miss Rose Wiedemann [deceased] is our charter member with Hazel Wiester, then Ruth Donahue [deceased] joining shortly after her. All of them are members today with Mrs. Donahue extremely active in our program.

In those early days their objectives were the same as ours today; to make ourselves better informed homemakers with the help of the University of California Extension Service.

In the library room of the Town Hall, above a store on Front Street, their first project was clothing, with the making of dress forms and later food evaporators in which to dry beans, corn, etc. They set about making each home a better one.

We still study clothing and nutrition as well as other phases of a well-adjusted home. We also further the work of the 4-H clubs in our area. Our aim for the future is still better homes, and to set up a fund for 4-H youngsters desiring to raise Guide Dogs for the Blind. To raise funds for this program we hold card parties, all proceeds going into this effort.

Other early members of Farm Bureau Women were Mrs. Lillian Close, Olivia Chaboya, Veda Wayne, Ramona Read, Nellie Baldwin, Maevis Wood and Thelma Smith.

No record is shown when the club name changed to Danville Farm Bureau Women, as it is known today. It was originally organized through the University of California extension, and each month a Home Demonstration Agent from the county would come to the meetings and give lessons or demonstrations on various homemaking arts. The San Ramon Valley club was made up of members from Alamo, Danville, Diablo and San Ramon (as we know it today) and each area had its own "leader" who would go to the county meetings several times each year.

One of the first Home Demonstration Agents was Helen Burling, who is a resident of Concord. Another was Britta Cascio, who resides on Veda Drive in Danville.

Over the years the agricultural nature of the Valley changed and so did the Danville Farm Bureau Women. At the present time meetings are held in members' homes on the second Wednesday of each month, September through June. Present chairman is Peggy Cronen. Speakers at meetings share information on nutrition, sewing, interior decorating, gardening, crafts, etc. The main function, however, is fund raising for Guide Dogs in San Rafael and for the 4-H Guide Dog Program.

This fifty-five year old organization has between twenty-five and thirty members and raises a substantial amount each year for these two main groups, through various fund raising activities. It also supports the Heather Farm Garden Club, Children's Hospital and Mental Health.

Recent chairmen have been Ruth Donahue, charter member (deceased), Betty Johanson, Laura Macedo, Florence Weisend, Helen Tefft, Martha Kovatch, Leona Hoffman, Laura Tennis, and currently Peggy Cronen.

DANVILLE LIONS CLUB

Danville Lions Club, the oldest men's service club in this area, became a part of the International Service Organization when it was chartered in 1940. On June 10, 1940 charter officers were: M. R. Marotte, president, G. P. Williamson, first vice-president; Edwin Olsson, second vice-president; E. H. Rodger, third vice-president; E. A. Anderson, secretary-treasurer; William Schramm, Lion Tamer; and George S. McMullin, Tail Twister. Two-year directors were Louis Schoener and E. A. Bloomquist. Ray Faveto and C. H. Sonnichsen were one-year directors. Other charter members were Floyd Benn, A. B. Cabral, George V. Cooley, Duane Elliott, Roy Halverson, Francis T. Harris, George Matthiesen, I. C. Nelson, M. E. Pereira, Jr., Joe Ramos, Lee Van Patten and John C. Wayne.

Lions Club history goes back to Chicago, Illinois, on June 7, 1917, when a young Chicago insurance man named Melvin Jones founded the association. Service to the community and assistance to the less fortunate were established as the objectives of Lions International, which differed from other men's groups of the day devoted primarily to promoting the business interests of the membership.

Civic-minded men across the United States concurred, and Lions Clubs multiplied rapidly. The service movement spread to Canada in 1920 and to China and Mexico in 1927, when the membership stood at 60,000 with 1,183 active Clubs. Panama became the first Central American nation to have a Lions Club, and the following year the first South American Club was organized in Colombia. Lionism reached Europe in 1948 when Clubs were organized in Sweden, Switzerland and France. Today, Lions International is truly global in scope with nearly 150 nations and geographic areas hosting Lions Clubs. As of January 31, 1977, Lions International had 1,181,337 members in 30,352 clubs in 149 countries and geographical areas.

Lions Clubs participate in a broad scope of humanitarian services with ten major activities.

They are: sight conservation and work for the blind*; hearing conservation and work for the deaf; services to citizenship, education, environment, health, international understanding, cooperation and youth exchange; public; recreational; and social.

Past presidents of the Danville Lions Club are: 1940-41 M. R. Marotte, 1941-42 G. P. Williamson, 1942-43 G. S. McMullin, 1943-44 E. A. Bloomquist, 1944-45 Harold B. Root, 1945-46 George V. Cooley, 1946-47 Albert T. Handley, 1947-48 Harry C. Stewart, 1948-49 James R. Ulrich, 1949-50 Dr. Ben C. Dykes, 1950-51 Dr. Roger Schulte, 1951-52 George A. Hill, Jr., 1952-53 Homer B. Blincow, 1953-54 Robert C. Cook, 1955-56 Reuben D. Tuttle, 1956-57 Francis T. Harris, 1957-58 Wayne L. Hawkins, 1958-59 Dr. Allen F. Faber, 1959-60 Ivan D. Chappell, 1960-61 Charles G. Rathburn, 1961-62 Le Roy Ashworth, 1962-63 Richard Keefe, 1963-64 William Roberts, 1964-65 Carsten O. Fossan, 1965-66 Charles W. Lowell, 1966-67 Fenton E. Chaon, 1967-68 William A. Ghirardelli, 1968-69 Roy V. Whitten, 1969-70 Joseph W. F. Parrish, 1970-71 Richard W. Morgan, 1971-72 Ben A. Singer, 1972-73 Dr. Robert Arbeau, 1973-74 Brian D. Thiessen, 1974-75 William Henderlong, 1975-76 John C. Steger and 1976-77 Herbert E. Oas. There are forty-one active members, and three inactive.

Lion Lines is the official weekly publication of the Danville Lions Club. The Danville Lions Club meets first and third Wednesdays at The Brass Door Restaurant in San Ramon, at 6:45 P.M. Among the local club's 1976-77 activities were: three $200 high school scholarships; $300 to Community Center; other money donations to Hope, Care, Eye Foundation, Oakland Blind Center, and Pittsburg Blind Center; and participation in Pet Parade, July Fourth, Christmas Aid to Needy, glasses to locals, student speakers contest, and Flag Day. The club sponsored the visit of the Lions Mobile Sight Unit to San Ramon Valley.

Newly elected officers to serve from July 1, 1977 to June 30, 1978 are: President, Harold R. Nelson; First vice-president, Arthur F. Lawton; Second vice-president, Jack D. Vinding; third vice-president Royce E. Lewis; secretary, Francis T. Harris; treasurer, Richard W. Morgan; Tail Twister, Randolph D. Lindsay; Lion Tamer, Edward J. Heuertz; one-year directors, George A. Case and Ernest B. Yoakum; and two-year directors, Dr. Stuart Heller and Michael Rupprecht.

MOUNT DIABLO BUSINESS AND PROFESSIONAL WOMEN'S CLUB OF DANVILLE

Mount Diablo Business and Professional Women's Club of Danville received its charter in 1951, although some meetings were held as early as November 1950. It has celebrated twenty-six years as an organization in the San Ramon Valley, and is a part of Bay Valley District in which there are thirty-six clubs. The Grand Lake Club was the mother club that sponsored the Danville Club.

The Charter was presented by Lillie M. Budde, President of Bay District B.P.W.C. Installation of Officers was by Margaret Gunderson, President of Grand Lake Club. The Charter Dinner and Program took place at Diablo Country Club on April 25, 1951, with 115 attending.

Charter Officers were Mary Leanora Silva, president; Mildred E. Wing, first vice-president; T. Elizabeth Wolters, second vice-president; Claire B. O'Neal, recording secretary; Thelma Y. Rodman, corresponding secretary; Ruth M. Joseph, treasurer; Isabel E. Gans, education and vocations; Ruth M. Joseph, finance; Lorine R. Kihlken, historian; Mildred E. Wing, health and safety; Margaret Haney, international relations; T. Elizabeth Wolters, legislation; Greta E. Hoffman, membership; Genieveve M. Cirincione, program coordinator; Paula F. Vierra and Claire B. O'Neal, public affairs; Edith E. Thomas, radio and television; Greta E. Hoffman, bulletin editor; June O. Morris, name of bulletin; T. Elizabeth Wolters, parliamentarian; Hazel J. Daley, news service. Other members were Mary P. Bolte, Mary B. Gertsen, Harriett B. Olsson, Lavina Rarey, Maud Wagner, Margaret Risse, Mabel Rodricks, Alice M. Stevick, and Dellrose I. Phinney.

*My step-father, John K. "Chappie" "Buddy" Chaplik, was Albany Lions Club president in 1950-51. I still have his desk pen set with the large impressive roaring lion attached to it. He and my mother were both very active in the Oakland Blind Center and put in many volunteer hours there.

*Frank Harris remains as the only active charter member. He was helpful in getting the necessary information for me to share with you.

National Federation Aims and Objectives are: to elevate the standards for women in business and professions; to promote the interests of business and professional women; to bring about a spirit of cooperation among business and professional women; to extend opportunities to business and professional women along lines of industrial, scientific and vocational activities. National Federation started in 1919.

The Mount Diablo Business and Professional Women's Club of Danville meets on the second and fourth Wednesdays. The meeting is begun with the pledge to the flag and closed with the Collect by Mary Stewart. Members receive a newsletter called "Mount Diablo Beacon."

Past presidents of this organiztion are: Mary Leanora Silva* 1951-52; T. Elizabeth Wolters* 1952-53; Maud Wagner* (deceased) 1953-54; Claire O'Neal* 1954-55; Alice Stevick* (deceased) 1955-56; Dorothy Mullong Rose 1956-57; Scotty Pencovic Loucks 1957-58; Genevieve Bayley (deceased) 1958-59; May Coldren (deceased) 1959-60; Lillian Price 1960-61; Irma Burner (deceased) 1961-62; Charlotte Sherry Hanssen, 1962-63; Esther Ann Vitt and Aldine Allen 1963-64; Lillian Price 1964-65; Irma Burner (deceased) 1965-66; Avenelle Gaines 1966-67; Leona Lobenberg 1967-68; Edna Sherier 1968-69; Leona Lobenberg 1969-70; Jean Treguboff 1970-71; Myrna Marriott 1971-72; Clarice Parker 1972-73; Lorraine Worrall, 1973-74; Ethel Flaten 1974-75; Grayce Garfinkle 1975-76 (this marked their twenty-fifth year); Anna Noll 1976-77. On April 27, 1977 June Brown of Dublin was installed as president for 1977-78, at the Steak and Ale Restaurant in Danville. There are currently twenty active members.

The organization does many worthwhile activities community-wide, including high school scholarships to worthy students. Some of the past presidents also belong to the Nike Club. It was organized in October 1956. Claire O'Neal is a charter member.

In the summer of 1951 Mary Leanora Silva, charter president, hostessed a luau at Mary's Haven. Del Davis was the instructor. Her husband, Cloyce Davis, was master of ceremonies, and some of her students performed the entertainment. These summertime luaus became rather a tradition and for about five years were held at the home of Claire O'Neal, La Gonda Way, Danville, where the performers danced on a large lawn. Other dance groups participating were Dancers of the Pacific and Vivian Schmidt, instructor, and Bill Schmidt, M.C. The Davises and Schmidts are longtime Danville residents. (We Joneses have something in common with the Schmidts. Vivian is a Sagittarian, as am I, and her husband Bill is a Scorpio, as is my husband.)

I wish to thank Claire O'Neal for allowing me the use of her two scrapbooks for my research.

SAN RAMON VALLEY
INTERCHURCH WOMEN'S LUNCHEONS

Even with the club's record (minutes) book at my disposal, I find that because of some omissions it is difficult to determine the actual starting year. However, even before the word ecumenical was in common general use, a group of San Ramon Valley women representing the women's clubs of different churches in the area, were meeting for interfaith luncheons. Two dates stand out prominently as the beginning, 1955 and 1959. From my own personal recollections I will accept the earlier date.

*Denotes charter member.

The first meeting was called by Beth (Mrs. Carl Eugene) Johnson, a Quaker, at her Montair Drive home in Danville. It included women from the two local churches, the Presbyterian (Protestant) and St. Isidore's (Catholic).

The second, third and possibly other luncheons were held at Angel Kerley's Danville home at what was formerly Harrison ranch property. Proceeds traditionally benefited a Valley project. On May 30, 1962, the annual gathering was at the Gordon Ball estate, at the end of Camille Avenue, Alamo, and 400 attended.

A report showed that on April 21, 1966, 220 women, ten clergymen and six of their wives attended the traditional San Ramon Valley Interchurch Women's Luncheon, held at Castlewood Country Club. Women represented all churches in the area at that time: Community Presbyterian, St. Isidore's Catholic, San Ramon Valley Congregational, St. Timothy's Episcopal, San Ramon Valley Methodist, Immanuel Lutheran, All Saints Lutheran, Danville Baptist, and Church of Jesus Christ of Latter Day Saints (Mormon). General chairman was Mrs. Olive Michel of Immanuel Lutheran.

Photo taken at the April 26, 1972 meeting of the San Ramon Valley Interchurch Women's Luncheon Committee at San Damiano Retreat House. Left to right: Nona Senasac, St. Isidore's; Pat Hunt, San Ramon Valley Congregational; Edmee Foley, chairman, St. Isidore's; Vilva Robinett, San Ramon Methodist; Bea Webster, Community Presbyterian; Joan Brandes, St. Isidore's; Pat Ewing, Immanuel Lutheran; Adele Cupit, Danville Baptist; Jean Kurtz, All Saints Lutheran; Helen Tefft, Immanuel Lutheran; Rachel Gaffri, All Saints Lutheran; Cindy Whittenberg, St. Timothy's Episcopal; Elizabeth O'Nion and Betty Mottishaw, both from Church of Jesus Christ of Latter Day Saints. Others on the committee were Loretta McKee, Community Presbyterian; Bettye McIntyre, Danville Baptist; Mary Ann Oesterlee, St. Isidore's; and Nancy Lundin, San Ramon Valley Methodist.

Other annual luncheons were: Thursday April 27, 1967, chairman Cora (Mrs. John) Sparrowk of Danville Baptist Church, with much the same representation as previously. Thursday May 16, 1968, chairman R. F. Jensen of All Saints Lutheran. Thursday May 15, 1969, chairman Mary (Mrs. Donald) Huenink of Community Presbyterian, all held at Castlewood Country Club. It appears that in 1970 and 1971 brunches were held in churches. On Wednesday April 26, 1972, a luncheon was at San Damiano Retreat House, chairman Edmee (Mrs. Robert) Foley of St. Isidore's. The program included music and a short history of Interchurch luncheons given by Olive (Mrs. Earl) Hoffman of Alamo. She told those in attendance that the purpose was to all work together in a spirit of fellowship.

On Thursday April 5, 1973, a luncheon was held at San Ramon Valley Methodist Church in Alamo, with Vilva (Mrs. C. W.) Robinett chairman; on Thursday April 25, 1974, at LDS Church with Gloria (Mrs. C. B.) Kimball chairman; and on Thursday April 17, 1975, at San Damiano Retreat, with Helen (Mrs. Stanley W.) Tefft chairman.

On Thursday, April 22, 1976, at Castlewood Country Club, women of eleven participating San Ramon Valley churches held what was publicized as their twenty-first annual luncheon event, with Adele (Mrs. A. P.) Cupit of Danville Baptist Church general chairman . The program was by Richard King, singer, actor, emcee, musical comedy performer and public speaker. His subject was "The Spirit of Liberty in the Bicentennial Year." He also sang various religious songs.

On Tuesday March 28, 1977, a committee headed by Adele Cupit of the Church of the Valley (Baptist) met for lunch in the Danville Hotel. Discussion was the future of the Interchurch Women's Luncheons, founded over twenty years ago when there were only two churches represented. There were thirteen women present from eight of the ten denominations of the area.

It was the consensus of the group that the purpose and usefulness of the annual luncheon, which was started in a small community, were no longer necessary in so large a community, where other ecumenical organizations offered friendliness and communication. Some of the churches no longer have formal women's groups. The money has always been given to local needs. It was decided to give the small remaining treasury funds to the Senior Citizens group. The record book was given to the San Ramon Valley Historical Society and was placed in their file-safe at the San Ramon Valley Library in Danville. So, after over two decades, the group disbanded and was no more.

ROTARY CLUB OF DANVILLE

Rotary Club of Danville was chartered on January 6, 1955. The club motto is "Service above self—building from within to better serve those without."

The following list of past presidents is alphabetical rather than chronological: Chuck Bloch, Dick Calhoun, Bob Cuenin, Lloyd Daniels, Cliff Forsyth, Norm Holden, Bob Livermore, Ted Merrill, Dick Moulds, Tom Ohlson, Sherm Peters, Don Priewe, Bill Rei, John Roberts, Earle Robinson, Al Rubey, and Mel Whalin.

Officers serving in 1976-77 were Ray Hanks, president; Jim Crossen, vice-president; Jim Graham, secretary; Manuel Giffin, treasurer. Directors were Bob Arrigoni, International service; Charlie Lowell, vocational service; Randy Walker, community service; Bill Littler, club service; Chuck Bloch, past president; Bud Spencer, sergeant-at-arms; Walt Ebbett, bulletin editor; and Kirk Otto, programs.

The following have received the Paul Harris* Fellowship Award from the Rotary Club of Danville: George Vargas (posthumously), Tom Ohlson, and Cliff Forsyth. Danville Rotarians put out a newsletter called "Dantarian." They meet every Monday at the Brass Door Restaurant in San Ramon. Active Danville Rotarians currently number 55.

*The first Rotary Club in the world was organized in Chicago shortly after the turn of the century, by Paul P. Harris, then a young lawyer.

KIWANIS CLUB OF SAN RAMON VALLEY

The Kiwanis Club of San Ramon Valley was chartered September 6, 1956. Past presidents are 1956-57 Walter Wilson, charter president; 1958-59 J. Ward Shannon; 1960 Donald Romer; 1961 Dean O. Smith; 1962 Lawrence Ferrero; 1963 Paul Vergon; 1964 H. Peter Fay; 1965 William Hockins; 1966 Donald Capling; 1967 Samuel E. Statler, Jr.; 1968 Michael Blodgett, Jr.; 1969 Richard Rew (nine-month term); 1969-70 James Benner; 1970-71 Tad M. Heilig; 1971-72 Charles M. Pitts; 1972-73 William McGregor; 1973-74 Donald Defenbaugh; 1974-75 A. William Blendow; 1975-76

William J. Ketsdever; 1976-77 David M. Stegman.

Kiwanians believe in making an investment in their community and being a part of things where they live and where they work. Members hear about and discuss everything from sports to politics, making them better citizens by being informed.

There are nearly a third of a million Kiwanians in clubs across the world. Theirs is a continuing, informal, people-to-people program, where friendships and common purpose transcend international borders, and real world understanding may sometimes be the best result of everything they do.

It is satisfying work resulting in happy people, healthy children, and better towns and villages. There is fun for the whole family at picnics, parties, golf tournaments, and conventions.

The above information was supplied by William J. Wadsworth, current secretary.

MOUNT DIABLO CHAPTER DAUGHTERS OF THE AMERICAN REVOLUTION (DAR)

Mount Diablo Chapter was organized officially on January 10, 1961 to become the 148th chapter in California. Esperanza Chapter of Oakland was the sponsoring chapter. The following officers were installed by the State Regent: Mrs. Benjamin R. Draper, Regent; Mrs. Fred T. Kelleway and Mrs. Lloyd E. Christiansen, vice-Regents; Mrs. W. William Lewis, Chaplain; Mrs. Donald O. Nelson, Recording Secretary; Mrs. Tyko Enbom, Corresponding Secretary; Mrs. Maurice Boevers, Treasurer; Mrs. H. Dean Loomis, Registrar; Mrs. Clyde E. Brown, Historian; and Mrs. Herbert L. Wildenradt, Jr., Librarian, Other organizing members were Mrs. Arthur Brewer and Mrs. John Farmer. Other charter members were Mrs. Guy Green, Mrs. Richard McKillip, Mrs. Robert Read and Mrs. William E. Stock.

The new chapter began its community and conservation program by presenting two six-foot trees to Vista Grande Elementary School in Danville.

Regents have been: 1961-62 Mrs. Benjamin R. Draper, 1962-64 Mrs. Fred T. Kelleway, 1964-66 Mrs. William E. Stock, 1966-68 Mrs. Carl C. Cramer, 1968-70 Mrs. F. J. Clune, 1970-72 Mrs. Henry M. Ferre, 1972-74 Mrs. Edmund R. Young, 1974-76 Mrs. Donald L. Grimes, and 1976-77 Mrs. Milton L. Levy. 1977 Regent-elect is Mrs. Paul Nygreen.

In the following years after the Chapter was chartered, members held many state chairman-ships. When districts were formed, Mrs. Henry M. Ferre was the first chairman of district IV. The first member to hold a California State Office was Mrs. Edmund R. Young, state recording secretary. State appointments have been: Mrs. B. R. Draper, Americanism 1962-66; Mrs. W. E. Stock, vice-chairman of membership 1966-68.

From the original small membership, the chapter now has fifty-seven members who live not only in Danville, Diablo, Alamo, San Ramon (the San Ramon Valley), but also Lafayette, Walnut Creek, Martinez and Hayward. Several who moved out of the area have retained their membership in the Mount Diablo Chapter, although they now live in Placerville, Santa Rosa, and outside the state in Arizona and Arkansas. The largest portion of the membership lives in Walnut Creek, with the majority living in the Rossmoor retirement community.

The nine monthly meetings feature programs following the National Society and State Society objectives: honoring Good Citizens (local high school seniors) selected by the student body and faculty members; holding an American History Essay Contest in February; Conservation Lineage Research; American Indians; American Heritage; DAR Schools (these are supported by all DAR chapters); the flag of the U.S.A., the USO and Veterans service, and reports on the chapter's projects at the state conference and Continental Congress. Chapter representatives are sent to all meetings. At each meeting the President General's message is read, as printed in the DAR Magazine, and a National Defense report is read. Members are encouraged to bring their friends in the community who are eligible for membership and who are willing to work for DAR objectives.

The National theme for 1976-77: "Remove not the ancient landmarks, which our fathers have set." (Proverbs 22:28) State theme: "Proclaim liberty throughout all the land unto all the inhabitants thereof." (Leviticus 25:10)

Meetings are held at 12:30 P.M. on the second Tuesday of each month, October to June, generally in Community Meeting rooms as provided by several Savings and Loan Companies and the Dollar Clubhouse at Rossmoor, Walnut Creek, California.

My thanks to Elizabeth E. Cramer, Press and Public Relations Chairman of the Mount Diablo Chapter, DAR, a resident of Danville, for supplying information to me on this organization.

SOROPTIMIST INTERNATIONAL
OF SAN RAMON VALLEY

Soroptimist epitomizes "The Best For Women." It is a classified service club. "Any woman at least twenty-one years of age, of good moral character and of good business reputation is eligible for active membership, provided that, within the territorial limits of the club, she is engaged in a profession either independently or in an executive or professional capacity; or as a head or deputy or in a professional capacity in a government position; or is an owner, partner, proprietor, corporate officer, manager or executive in a legitimate business or organization."

Code of Ethics: "My business principles exact; full recognition of rights of others; acknowledgment of the responsibilities of citizenship and the duty of discharging the obligations entailed; the use of my position at all times to the end that a higher level of human ideals and achievements may be attained."

Activities: Annual Senior Citizens' Day; presentation of Youth Citizenship Awards; honoring a Woman of Achievement; contributing to the Community Center and the Lung Association; the Training Awards Program (TAP), helping mature women to enter the job market by training in the career of their choice.

Officers: President, Bernice Nemanic, Nemanic's Upholstery; vice-president, Emily Hann, Bert Hann Backhoe; treasurer, Violet Waltz, Wells Fargo Bank; Corresponding Secretary, Arlene Pearson, San Ramon Valley Unified School District; Recording Secretary, Grace Katzer, Carefree Travel Service. Other members are Ann Aldenhuysen, Tamarack Manor; Eunok Benesch, Oak's Oriental Collection; Margaret Bockman, C. M. Bloch, Inc.; Dorothy Ebbett, Mimo Magic; Peg Frolich, A Touch of Yesterday; Marian Holden, Diablo Convalescent Hospital; Mary Jane Jossey, House of Fashion Wigs; Mary Linney, Real Estate Agency; Camille Matthews, Alamo Garden Apartments; Ellen Reisewitz, Frellen's Sunwood; Donna Rodegard, Skil Painting, Inc.; Edythe Sauer, Anderson & Sauer Properties; Beverly Sheperd, Bev's Yarn & Needlecraft; Mary Steiner, Investments and Securities; Janet Stone, The Outhouse; Melva Woods, Wood's Frame Art; Betty Zanzig, Community Center.

Sustaining Members: Phyllis Arbeau, Ruth Farrell, Marjorie Kennedy, Catherine McGregor, and Edna Sherier. Past presidents: Charter president, Mary Ellen Gwynne, 1963-64; Dortha House, 1964-65; Mary Ellen Gwynne, 1965-66; Shirley Phillips, 1966-67; Edna Sherier, 1967-68; Mary Linney, 1968-70; Marion Holden 1970-71; Phyllis Arbeau, 1971-72; Beverly Sheperd, 1972-73; Rena Jarvis, 1973-74; Ann Aldenhuysen, 1974-75; Edythe Sauer, 1975-76; Bernice Nemanic, 1976-77. The Soroptimists meet at noon every Wednesday at the Brass Door Restaurant in San Ramon.

At the Soroptimist Health and Safety luncheon held February 2, 1977, guest speaker Marion Holden, regional chairman of Soroptimist International, spoke on Pollution and Lung Disease. Her emphasis was on legislative impact on long-term care for the chronically ill and elderly. She said, "We are in the midst of a health crisis which is a major social issue in the United States and presents a real challenge. The elderly in our nursing homes today are the people who built the American Dream. They are the pioneers who suffered and worked, sparing no cost, to make our country what you and I enjoy today. Sadly, these people find themselves pinched out and deprived by inflation."

Marion Holden and her husband Norman and two children were our former neighbors when they lived at 14 Gary Way, Alamo, during the 1950s and 1960s. They now make their home on El Pintado Road.

DANVILLE-ALAMO BRANCH
AMERICAN ASSOCIATION
OF UNIVERSITY WOMEN

In 1967 the Walnut Creek Branch, American Association of University Women, established a Danville-Alamo Section, recognizing the growing number of women living in the San Ramon Valley with degrees from colleges and universities. Bethany Hall and Sandy Varco chaired the section for two years. In the spring of 1969, urged by the California State Division of AAUW, the section invited members of the newly formed Half Moon Bay Branch to meet with the local group for advice on formation of a new branch. A meeting was held at the home of Patty Hart. A vote was taken and it was decided to form a Danville-Alamo Branch. Suzanne Fisher was elected temporary chairman. Jeanne Brooding Ryan was selected to chair the first nominating committee.

A charter was granted on June 13, 1969 and the following women were elected as charter officers of the Branch: Sandy Varco, president; Bethany Hall, president-elect; Arlene Baker, first vice-

98

president; Sharon Jensen, second vice-president; Marion Worral, recording secretary; Suzanne Fisher, corresponding secretary; and Kaye Madsen, treasurer.

The following were charter members: Nancy Johnson Adolphson, Norma Humburg Anderson, May Kay Meddaugh Anderson, Dorothy Eggers Baker, Arlene Kay Baker, Janis Morgan Balaban, Jeanne Kinney Brooding Ryan, Dorothy Leiz Brose, Mary Stewart Broussard, Phyllis Fitz Callaghan, Carol Barkstrom Carney, Joann Christenson Caspar, Daphne Lingas Clements, Marillyn Weisbender Cozine, Betty Repasz Cramer, Sue Magnuson De Voe, Judith Peterson Dobbins, Irma McGinnis Dotson, Martha Holbrook Douglas, Judith Larson Edwards, Joan Lawson Enos, Barbara Boysen Evans, Marian Thiel Falk, Doris Smith Feltrup, Suzanne Alexander Fisher, Carole Cardoza Foster, Margaret Stanley Freeman, Barbara Lowrey Gohl, Linda Beck Greene, Winifred Varco Haagensen, Bethany Hoot Hall, Carol Rising Ham, Patty Farrell Hart, Helen Cook Harvey, Julia Pink Henderlong, Lynne Collins Henze, Elaine Stormer Hinkson, Mary Jane Lintz Hughes, Bonnie MacMillan Hutchins, Sharon Smith Jensen, Linda Beers Johnson, Helen Hines Johnston, Laura Beck Lambert, Jean Everett Livermore, Rita Pelz Lucas, Nancy Brown Lundin, Catherine McArthur Madsen, Jeanett McCabe McCluer, Marilyn Brownlee McCurdy, Dona Griffith Morris, Claudia Mauzy Nemir, Marilyn McDonald O'Connell, Norine Palmer Ross, Julia Nan Rodekohr, Claire Schrick Schlaman, Gail Kungel Solt, Sharon Foster Strong, Elizabeth Brown Teed, Colleen Sullivan Tovey, Elaine Holmes Triemer, Carolyn "Casey" Black Underwood, Sandra Carley Varco, Sandra Rose Welke, and Marian Fontaine Worrall.

Since its chartering the Branch has been an effective force in the community, active in the traditional AAUW areas of concern and interest, the community, international relations, cultural interests and education. The branch has implemented an ongoing concern for the status of women and has maintained an active interest in legislation. An early project was the establishment of a balance of nature flannel board ecology show for the primary grades in the San Ramon Valley Unified School District. Annually the Branch sponsors a Conference for Women in the Community. During the Bicentennial celebration, the Branch members designed an historical quilt, stitching squares depicting historical sights in Contra Costa County. They also provided a readers' theater presentation of women in American History for the schools and service clubs in the San Ramon Valley. Each year the Branch has made a Name Grant to the Association Educational Foundation in the amount of $500. The 1973 and 1976 Incorporation attempts were supported by the Branch after extensive study of local government for the Valley. In 1974 the Branch established an award at each of the local high schools, honoring the most outstanding Junior Woman Student of their selection.

Past presidents are: Sandy Varco, 1969-70; Bethany Hall, 1970-71; Elaine Hinkson, 1971-72; Jean Helfrich, 1972-73; Claudia Nemir, 1973-74; Phyllis Callaghan, 1974-75; Sue DeVoe, 1975-76; Linda Best, 1976-77; and Vanette Hicky, 1977-78. 1978-79 will have Florence McAuley at the helm. 1977 membership was 280 members.

My sincere thanks and appreciation to Claudia Mauzy Nemir for the history of the Danville-Alamo Branch of AAUW, and her permission to use it in part or whole.

HOMEOWNERS ASSOCIATION OF TWIN CREEKS, SAN RAMON

Homeowners Association of Twin Creeks, San Ramon, was organized in late 1969, because the residents became concerned about the future development of the empty lands surrounding their homes.

A meeting was held at the home of Arthur and Helen Moore on Playa Court, attended by about thirty homeowners. Almost every occupied home was represented. Acting officers for the first year were appointed as follows: president, Jack Vinding; vice-president, A. C. Olays; secretary-treasurer, Sandy Van Tine; Board members, Helen Moore, Clayton Gonsalves, Harvey Wier, Melvin Mendonca and Glen Wasson.

Past presidents are: Jack Vinding, Robert Nelson, David Swigers and Frank Cassara. Current president is Larry Rothacher.

Original streets were Twin Creeks Drive, Little Creek Court (where the original model homes were), Canyon Creek Drive and Playa Court. The developer was Carl Dame, who named the streets.

Owners of the first homes were Rita Lopez, Canyon Creek Drive, Phil and Kathy Coleman, Playa Court, and Robert and Kaye Nelson, Canyon Creek Drive. All remain as current owners. The home bought by Harold and Mary Page on Canyon Creek Drive is currently owned by V.

Shaw; Clayton and Theresa Gonsalves' home on Playa Court is now owned by Bruce Walton.

The foregoing information was supplied by Sharon Cushing, historian of the organization.

SAN RAMON WOMEN'S CLUB

The San Ramon Women's Club was the brainchild of three women of that area, Coral (Mrs. E. P.) Renick, Anne (Mrs. Jay L.) Ryan and Nan (Mrs. Ted) Williams. An organizational meeting was held in Sunny Glen Center, San Ramon, in 1970, and twenty women became charter members. They applied to Mount Diablo District No. 8 for acceptance into the California Federation of Women's Clubs and were granted their charter in April 1970. By this time their membership had grown to sixty-seven.

Since most of the members are from the Sunny Glen retirement area, and several are widows, the club's chief goal is to provide friendship, companionship, worthwhile programs, activities and outings of general interest. A monthly card section is most popular.

San Ramon Women's Club actively supports the programs of federation of the largest women's organization in the United States. Five of their members have held District Chairmanships and Offices, with three members as District Officers in 1976-77. They are Anne Ryan, president; Gloria Church, corresponding secretary; and Isabelle S. Brubaker, parliamentarian. Their business-luncheon-program meeting is held the fourth Monday of each month at the San Ramon Golf and Country Club.

They have purchased three Pennies for Pines Plantations and supported Pennies for Poppies, Pennies for Art, and the State Foundation Fund; presented three scholarships to deserving students; donated many books to the Los Meganos High School, California High School, Dublin and San Ramon Valley Libraries, and Family Health Center in San Ramon; contributed to Valley Memorial Hospital in Livermore and Laurel Grove Hospital in Castro Valley; sponsored a Girl Scout troop and contributed toward camperships; donated to the Dublin Beep baseball for blind children, Evangelical Free Church in Pleasanton; sent vegetable and flower seeds to the San Quentin Greenhouse program; and endorsed the Diablo Crisis Rape Service.

Members have served as hostesses for the opening of the Family Health Care Center and sponsored a tea for the Snow Queen Contestants.

They have donated funds to the San Ramon Junior Wrestling Team, to the band for uniforms, Children's Emergency Council, Christian Pilots Association, Buena Vista Youth Ranch, Christmas baskets, and Martinez Veterans' Hospital. Through the efforts of this women's club, sixty-five members, neighbors, and friends participated in Operation Identification.

They have supported the following organizations by addressing envelopes, donating prizes, purchasing calendars, speakers, benefits, or money: Crippled Children's Society of Contra Costa County, March of Dimes, Epilepsy Foundation, Arthritis Foundation, American Field Service, Mount Diablo Therapy Center, CARE, Meals on Wheels, and Meals for Millions.

Presidents have been: 1970-71 Coral (Mrs. E. P.) Renick; 1971-72 Anne (Mrs. Jay L.) Ryan; 1972-74 Marie (Mrs. Henry) Vervais; 1974-75 Gloria (Mrs. Robert) Church; 1975-76 Audrey (Mrs. William) Huseman; 1976-77 Dorothy (Mrs. William E.) Walters. Elected to serve as president for 1977-78 was Dorothy (Mrs. Ralph) Foster.

ALAMO-DANVILLE
JUNIOR WOMEN'S CLUB

Alamo-Danville Junior Women's Club was chartered in 1970 by Bonnie Long, with twelve members. The reason for organizing the club was "A need for a young women's Service Club between Walnut Creek and Dublin." It is a part of Mount Diablo District of Junior Clubs and is sponsored by the Alamo Women's Club. Meetings are held the evening of the second Tuesday in their clubhouse in Alamo. Age for membership is between eighteen and thirty-five.

Some of their projects have been: Donated record by Sherrel Milnes, "Songs America Loves," to elementary schools in Alamo and Danville. Put on "Patch the Pony" program for Vista Grande kindergarten class with film strip record, to teach youngsters to stay away from strangers. Delivered March of Dimes packets to the Marching Mothers of the area. Sponsored the fireplug painting contest in the elementary schools for an Americanism Project, receiving approximately 1,500 entries. Ten winners received certificates. Participated in Operation ID (identification of ownership). Designed and built, with JC's help, "Tot Lot" at Community Center. Did "Mr. Smart Spokes," the talking bicycle which teaches bike safety, at Montair School. Helped Lynn School. Sponsored Teenage Art Contest in high schools as well as Art Lecture Series for adults. Gave Halloween Party for Diablo Convalescent Hospital, in costumes.

The club has made money donations from their projects to the Contra Costa Association for the Mentally Retarded, Danville Community Center, and Valley School.

Presidents have been: 1970-71 charter president Donna (Mrs. C. W.) Hostetter, 1971-72 Lois (Mrs. William) Mitchell, 1972-74 Suzy (Mrs. David) Ziegler, 1974-76 Nancy (Mrs. Bill) Polsley, 1976-78 Robin (Mrs. Helmut) Maierhofer. Alma (Mrs. John A.) Brown of the Alamo Women's Club has been Junior Coordinator, 1975-77.

DANVILLE-ALAMO GARDEN CLUB

The Danville-Alamo Garden Club had its organizational meeting on June 1, 1973, and by September had a membership of 125 members. At that time, it was limited to that number and members had to live in the Danville-Alamo zip areas. Now the number is unlimited and members must live in southern Contra Costa County north of Crow Canyon Road.

Objectives of the club are: To stimulate the knowlege and love of gardening; to encourage home and community beautification; to improve the knowlege of horticulture; and to encourage civic planting and conservation programs.

Meetings are on the third Thursday at nine in the morning at St. Timothy's Episcopal Church, Diablo Road, Danville. The calendar year is June to June and annual dues are ten dollars. Club flower is the rose, color is yellow, motto is "Coming together is the beginning. Working together is progress. Staying together is success."

Past presidents: 1973-74 Patricia Cassell and Nina Topping; 1974-75 Donna Hostetter and Dorothy Grossman; 1975-76 Ann Schultzel; and 1976-77 Nancy Goreth of Balceta Court, Danville. The club is a member of Heather Farms Garden Center Association.

ROUND HILL GARDEN CLUB

The Round Hill Garden Club was organized May 6, 1974 under the direction of Alyce Radocay, with 125 charter members. At that time it was limited to residents of Round Hill subdivision, but later was extended to include Round Hill Country Club members as well.

Charter officers who served from May 1974 to May 1975 were: Jackie (Mrs. Gregory) Haddad, president; Barbara (Mrs. Charles) Sumner, vice-president and program chairman; Marcia (Mrs. Jack) DeMent, treasurer; Kay (Mrs. Richard) Bartlett, financial secretary; Ginny (Mrs. Robert) Anderson, social coordinator; Linda (Mrs. Ronald) Beale, parliamentarian; Bess (Mrs. Larry) Parrish, membership officer; Thelma (Mrs. L. Gram "Bud") Weigand, recording secretary; Shirley (Mrs. Robert) White, corresponding secretary; Joan (Mrs. George) Dirth, publicity; Anne (Mrs. Charles) Haist, horticulture advisor; Joyce (Mrs. Craig) McConnaughey, bulletin editor; Elsie (Mrs. Wally) Davis, garden club representative; Dee (Mrs. Anthony) Silva, communications officer; Alyce Radocay, club advisor.

Club flower is the rose; club colors green and white; club motto: "Who loves a garden still his Eden keeps." (Alcott). Object of the club is to stimulate the knowledge and love of gardening and to encourage home and community beautification, to improve the knowledge of horticulture and to encourage civic planting and conservation programs. The club is a member of Heather Farms Garden Center Association.

Mrs. Jack (Marcia) DeMent was the second president, serving 1975-76; Mrs. William (Deedy) Linforth was president during 1976-77. Installation of new officers to serve from May 1977 was held at a luncheon at Round Hill Country Club on Monday, April 4, 1977. Marcia DeMent, past president, was installing officer. Officers are: Elsie Davis, president; Valerie Wollman, vice-president; Sadie Pizanis, social coordinator; Betty Church, membership; Erna Segal, financial secretary; Joyce McConnaughey, treasurer; Thelma Weigand, recording secretary; Diane Barley, corresponding secretary; Rosellen Breuner, parliamentarian; Liz Hanson, publicity; Dee Silva, bulletin; Mary Naughton, garden center representative; Barbara Hahn, horticulture advisor; and Jackie Haddad, communication officer. Their annual fund raiser was May 2, 1977, a fashion show luncheon with the theme: "Fashions and Flowers."

WHITE GATE
HOMEOWNERS ASSOCIATION

White Gate Homeowners Association was organized by Century Homes (Harold Smith Company) in January 1976, and an interim board of directors was appointed. They were William Kinney, Douglas Putnam, Harold Smith, Randy Smith, and Del Tacconi, who served as president. Four months later, April 1976, the first election of a board of directors was held by the property owners. At that election the board was expanded to seven members. Those elected to the first board were Carol Edic, Harold Smith, Robert Galbreath, William Kinney, Stephen Lea Vell, Douglas Putnam, and Randy Smith. Stephen Lea Vell served as president from May 1976 to April 1977.

The first house was completed February 3, 1973 and was occupied by Mr. and Mrs. Tracy Slaughter, the subdivision's first residents. Their address is 1004 White Gate Road.

Other streets are Ray, Todd, Seville, Nina, Toni, Shandelin Courts and Vagabond Court, Vagabond Way, Piedras Circle and Court, Park Meadow Drive and Court, Partridge Court, Lackland Drive and Court, Parkmont Drive and Shantilly Court. There are some streets planned but not yet named. There are also open space and green belt areas.

TOASTMASTERS

Toastmasters has held several organizational meetings during March and April of 1977, for the formation of a group in Alamo, Danville and San Ramon areas which will be a part of Toastmasters International, a non-profit, non-partisan, educational organization of Toastmaster clubs throughout the world, open to men and women.

The Club will provide a professionally designed program to improve abilities in communication, and to develop leadership and executive potential. Members will have the opportunity to deliver prepared speeches and impromptu talks, learn conference and committee leadership and participation techniques, understanding of parliamentary procedures, and to learn to evaluate themselves and others.

Meetings are held Thursday evenings from 7:30 to 9:00 at the San Ramon Valley Library, 555 South Hartz Avenue, Danville.

Pro-tem officers elected were Jerry Wijnen, acting president; Perry McCown, education vice-president; Sylvia McCown, secretary; and Gail Wijnen, treasurer. Member Ronald I. Wallace was helpful to me with this information.

My husband, Al Jones, has been an active member of the Las Juntas Chapter of Toastmasters for several years and was their president in 1973. They meet on Friday at noon at the Contra Costa Board of Realtors Conference Room.

SAN RAMON VALLEY ELKS LODGE

The newest service organization in the San Ramon Valley is the Elks Lodge which was proposed in the spring of 1977. Charter officers are Ed Gregory, chairman; Ted Wilson, first vice chairman; Denis Behen, second vice chairman; Frank Geasa, recording secretary; John Molina, corresponding secretary; and Larry Riera, treasurer. Committee chairmen are Sam Blair, sites; Don Bechtel, membership; and Don Bell, public information. Their organizational meeting was held at the Brass Door Restaurant in San Ramon.

WHITE GATE FARM
40 Shandelin Court, Danville
Built 1856 by Howard Bros.

Chapter Six
Modern Day Pioneers
in Their Fields

XAVIER FAMILIES

John Xavier (1882-1955) was born May 11, 1882 in the Azore Island of Faial. He came to Danville in 1911 and worked as a cook for the Hay Press. The cookhouse was horsedrawn and went from place to place in the surrounding area. He later worked about three years for Manuel J. Medina as a shoe repairman, his trade from the old country. The shop was located on Hartz Avenue (now Bev's Yarn Shop). Mr. Medina passed away and John Xavier later married Mrs. Olivia Medina. They moved to West Oakland, where he had a shoe repair shop on Seventh Street. They later moved to San Leandro for about seven years.

They returned to Danville about 1929 and located a shoe shop on Hartz Avenue, just about across from the present Thrift Station (former Xavier's Sporting Goods). The depression hit and the business was lost. He then started a small shoe repair shop on Hartz Avenue where the ARCO gas station is now at Linda Mesa. After about two years he moved into a building, also on Hartz Avenue, next to the present Thrift Station (building no longer exists). In 1940 he moved into the building which is now the Thrift Station and his son Walter went into the business with him.

John Xavier and his wife Olivia divorced in 1932. She opened Olivia's Variety Store across the street on Hartz, which operated for years. (I remember it well.) It was then next to the Williamson's Market, which later became the Square Deal Market (and later the second P-X Market (RA)). It was owned by Daryl Green and Dean Springer. Next door to the south was the old Bank of America building, on the corner, now Jean Harris' Art & Apparel.

Walter attended grade school, first in Green Valley School (RA), near what is now Los Cerros School. (Green Valley School was the former home of Eric and Lydia Turner, who owned Turner's Hardware in Danville for years.) Walter later attended the old Danville Grammar School (now Community Center). He graduated from San Ramon Valley Union High School, where he played football. Manuel J. "Bing" Medina, Jr. (RA), Walt's half-brother, also attended all local schools and graduated from the local high school. He is now retired from his position as purchasing agent for the Fremont schools and makes his home in Fremont.

Walter and Louise Dondero, daughter of Louis and Esther Dondero, were married April 28, 1940, in St. Paul's Catholic Church, San Pablo. They came to Danville as newlyweds and resided on Green Valley Road for eighteen years. In 1958 they purchased the James L. Rich property of three and three-quarter acres with several buildings and their home at 977 Danville Boulevard, Alamo. It was the former Harrison property and is known as Xavier Apartments.

The Xaviers had five children. Gary Walter Xavier was born August 13, 1941 and married Lois Lynn Pfaff of Fort Worth, Texas. They have a son, Anthony Joseph, born October 11, 1965. Gary graduated from San Ramon Valley High School in 1960, where he had a band called "The Starlighters." He and his family reside in Los Angeles. He plays piano with a band called "The Fun Factory," and travels all over the country. They play in Las Vegas and Tahoe and are currently preparing to tour Europe.

The second son, Richard David, died at six months.

Sharon Louise Xavier was born September 19, 1948, married John de Souza, son of the de Souzas of Portugal. Sharon is a 1966 graduate of San Ramon Valley High School and the College of Holy Names. She earned her teacher's credential at California State University at Hayward, and has one child, John Marcus de Souza, born

April 25, 1974. Her husband is with Equitable Life Insurance Company in the Fremont area.

John Michael Xavier, born February 11, 1956, was named for his paternal grandfather. He graduated from San Ramon Valley High School in 1974 and attended California State University at Hayward. He presently works for Walt's Shoe Repair. He went to Europe with the San Ramon Valley Jazz band and is active with Adult Jazz Workshop. He plays trombone and is also in a band called "Mosaic," in which he plays trombone and organ. He also plays piano and trumpet.

Jane Anne Xavier, born December 4, 1962, attended Rancho-Romero, Stone Valley and Los Cerros schools and is a freshman at San Ramon Valley High School. She is a competitive ice skater.

Xavier's Sporting Goods Store, handling sports and athletic equipment, men's clothing and shoes, was sold to Tom Kalmanir, Faunce and Robbins in 1968. Walt then moved to the 7-11 Shopping Center in Alamo and is still there as Walt's Shoe and Saddlery Repair Shop. In 1974 he leased his building to the Thrift Station.

SANDKUHLE FAMILY
Sunset Nursery

Herman J. Sandkuhle (died 1944) and his wife Juliet (Settenbez) Sandkuhle (died June 13, 1963) came to Danville in the summer of 1925 from Oakland, with the three children, Dorothy, Herman, Jr., and Raymond. They bought seven acres on the southeast corner of Danville Boulevard and El Portal, on the cusp of Alamo-Danville. It was the Kendall property and had two cottages of about 1913 vintage. They intended the home for summer and weekend use, as their business was the Sunset Nursery Company in Oakland. The business was started in 1906 and ended in 1967.

They began to plant to improve the property and in the fall enrolled the children in the Danville school, as they continued to tend to the plants' needs. They said, "We will move back to Oakland for Christmas," but, according to Herman Jr. "Sandy," Christmas never came and Danville became their permanent home.

Dorothy Sandkuhle married Frank Vasallo, who was a teacher and counselor in the local school district. They live on La Questa in Danville. Raymond married Audrey Zimmerman of Danville, and they live in San Jose.

Herman J. "Sandy" Sandkuhle, Jr. lived on the nursery property until 1939, when he married Henrietta Jones of Danville. They built a home on the hillside of Del Amigo Road, Danville. She passed away in 1941. From 1943 to 1947 he was in the military service, and was stationed in the Pacific. He met Muriel "Brandy" Parker on Iwo Jima. They were married and had three children, Barry, Becky, and Judy B., and made their home in Danville. The children attended local schools. "Brandy" passed away of cancer on June 1, 1963, and the children went away to school. Barry went to New Mexico Military Institute at Roswell, and Becky and Judy B. to San Dominican in San Rafael. Barry graduated from UC, Davis, and manages the Danville Sunset Nursery. Becky graduated from Chico State and teaches in San Leandro, and Judy B. graduated from Cal Poly at San Luis Obispo, and runs the greenhouses at the Nursery. Sunset Nursery are master nurserymen and have been in business continuously since 1925, one of the oldest businesses in the area.

Herman "Sandy" J. Sandkuhle, Jr. was married on April 6, 1966 to Bernie Dykes of Alamo. She has three sons, Jim, Gary and Robert, who attended Alamo schools and graduated from San Ramon Valley High School. Jim Dykes was in the class of '63, with our son Gary Jones. Jim is a graduate of the Military Academy at Vallejo and is now ship's captain of the SS *Monterey* (at age 31). He lives in Ygnacio Valley with his wife Rita (Gianichini). A first baby is due May 1977. Gary Dykes graduated from St. Mary's College, Moraga, and is a dental laboratory technician at Tahoe. He lives in Nevada and is unmarried. Robert graduated from UC, Berkeley, and is in the contracting business in Gardenville, Nevada.

The Sandkuhles, "Sandy" and "Bernie," make their home in Danville on Del Amigo Road.

BYINGTON AND FAGAN REALTY
OF ALAMO - 3195 DANVILLE BLVD.

Frank J. Byington of Alamo and Edward G. Fagan of Oakland, and later Danville, started in the realty business in 1932 in Alamo. Their slogan was, "San Ramon Valley is the coming place to live." (How right they were!) Offices of the "pioneer firm" were in what was claimed to be the oldest building in Alamo. (Doubtful, as the Henry Hotel (RA) and Silas Stone home (RA) were older.) The structure was erected in about 1870. It was built to accommodate the lot—rather long and slender with a hallway right down its center and rooms to either side. Later an addition was added to the rear, a kitchen, eating area, screened porch and bathroom.

At one time the George Smiths resided there. His wife was called "Grandma Smith" and smoked a corn cob pipe. She especially enjoyed doing so on the front porch. "Grandpa Smith" carried the Alamo mail from the post office to the Alamo Southern Pacific station at Hemme by horsedrawn cart. They had a son George, and another son became Constable Truby Smith. He, his wife Lulu, and their children, a son Ellsworth and daughter Evelyn, lived in the home later.

The first Mrs. Walter Cross (RA), Mary Ellen (Feely), purchased the building from George Smith the son. For a time Anthony "Tony" Linhares (RA) and his wife Bertha (Bell) rented it from Mrs. Cross. It was she and Walter Cross who also rented the building to Byington and Fagan for their real estate business.

Over the years the building at 3195 Danville Boulevard, Alamo, had been used for many things besides a residence. For a time it was the site of the Alamo Library, and the Alamo Women's Club used it on occasion. One historical reference even mentioned that for a very brief time it was used as a meeting hall by the Alamo Lodge of Masons (RA), when their brick structure fell in the October 21, 1868 earthquake. (Doubtful, as they went to Danville briefly, then to Walnut Creek.)

By 1957 Byington and Fagan Realty claimed to be the second oldest in the area* and had accomplished much, with some of the finest developments in the entire Valley. In 1957 the business was run by Charles T. Byington, nephew of the founder. In 1934, their first subdivision, and probably the first in the Alamo-Danville area, was created when they cut up the 160 acres of the Smith Ranch into farms of two to ten acres. They named this subdivision Alamo Oaks, because of the bountiful oak trees that grew there. Other developments to their credit were Finley Lane (RA), Jackson Way (RA), Alamo Way, Livorna Heights Road (RA), Acacia Lane, Gaywood Road, and La Colina, all in the Alamo area. They also developed the Fred Houston Ranch in Danville and named it Danville Estates. Tony Linhares removed the sheep sheds and barns in 1946 to make room for the subdivision. In 1957 they helped subdivide Escondido Estates (RA) off Camille Avenue (RA) in Alamo.

In the late 1950s and early 1960s the staff was Charles T. Byington, Frank J. Byington, Robert E. Cook, Harold Frybarger, Col. Allison Hartman, and James R. Lawson.

In 1970 Betty Stonebreaker took over Emerson Associates, a real estate business, from Jim Emerson. He moved out of the area. In 1971 Harold Frybarger and J. Allen (Al) Madison became partners with her. Al Madison first went into the real estate buisness in 1948 for William F. Anderson (RA) in Walnut Creek. On September

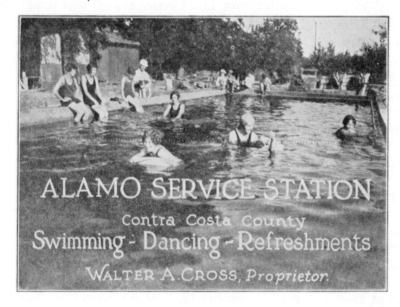

ALAMO SERVICE STATION
Contra Costa County
Swimming - Dancing - Refreshments
WALTER A. CROSS, Proprietor.

This was an advertising postcard of Alamo's first Service Station (RA). It included the first public swimming pool in Alamo, an open-air dance pavilion and refreshments, and was in the vicinity of and behind the building at 3195 Danville Blvd. In the photo, which was taken in the 1920s, is Walter A. Cross (in white hat), the proprietor, and his pet dog. Enjoying a swim are his three daughters, left to right: Gloria (Mrs. Harold J. Doebler of Florida (RA), Imogene (Mrs. Oscar W. "Pete" Peterson of Alamo (RA), and Alma (Mrs. Everett S. Crosby of New York.)

*John Wayne (RA) (deceased) of Alamo had seniority for early real estate in Alamo. He was in the business and worked out of his Alamo home for years.

13, 1974, Madison took over the Alamo-Danville Realtors when he purchased the building from Alma (Cross) Crosby (RA) of New York, along with the adjoining former Cross residence. Since that time that residence has been the home of Scott Allen Madison, son of Al and Mary Madison.

During the war years Gloria (Cross) Doebler (RA) and her children, Joe and "Murphy," lived in the building while their husband and father, Harold J. Doebler, was away serving in the war.

BLEMERS

Lisa Lippincott, born in 1961, and Abby Lippincott, born in 1964, are fifth generation native Californians. On their grandfather's side, the genealogy is: George Whitney married Sophia Greenwood; James G. Whitney married Octavia Fernandez; Mabel A. Whitney married Charles H. Blemer; John Whitney Blemer married Ethel Nichols, and Lois Ann Blemer married Alan Lippincott.

On their grandmother's side, the genealogy is: Hiram Tubbs married Susan A Staniels; Abby Ann Tubbs (1854) married Sheldon Kellogg; Ethel Lois Kellogg (1877) married Henry D. Nichols; Ethel Nichols (1907) married John W. Blemer; Lois Ann Blemer (1933) married Alan Lippincott. On this side, most were born in the Oakland area.

John Whitney Blemer was born in Sacramento on February 1, 1901. Ethel Nichols was born in Piedmont on March 15, 1907.

Dr. John Blemer "was there!" April 18, 1906, the day of the San Francisco earthquake. After the quake, fire forced the family to leave their Union Street home. They used his red coaster to haul heavy baggage to the beach, and later to Oakland. Then they went on to Spring Valley Ranch (the large Whitney ranch) in Rocklin (Placer County), where Dr. Blemer's mother had been born in 1875. (The handsome Whitney home was torn down soon after the Blemers were married.)

The childhood and adolescent years of Dr. Blemer were spent in Placer County, where he attended Loomis Grammar School. In 1918 he moved to Sacramento for high school. Following graduation he entered the University of California at Berkeley and received his medical degree from the University of McGill in Montreal, 1930, serving his internship there and at the University of California at San Francisco, before starting practice.

Dr. Blemer was a medico with Dr. Hartly Dewey at Lewis Memorial Hospital, Yosemite Valley, for over one year. While still on the job, worrying about patients, he married Ethel Nichols in the Old Court House in Mariposa, on March 15, 1933. The ceremony was performed by Judge Trabuco. For a quick get-away honeymoon, a party of one cook, one ski instructor, one ranger, five assorted female skiers, and the newlywedded Blemers climbed Tenaya Trail to the Ranger Lodge on Basket Dome, across from Half Dome, for a week's excellent skiing.

Later they had another honeymoon, a trip to Mexico City, the arduous way. They drove to El Paso, Texas, and then flew in an early-type biplane, with three stops en route, over the Easter holidays. All the photos they took were blank— shutter closed! When city residents went to the seacoast or mountains, and all the Mexican Indian natives trooped into the city parks, the Blemers returned home to live in the Nichols summer home at Diablo. Dr. Blemer was assistant to Dr. Mel Bolender in his Hartz Avenue, Danville, office. In 1934 Dr. Bolender left for a Walnut Creek office and Dr. Blemer took over the Danville office.

The Blemer's home was built in 1936 by Tantan and Stockholm, on the over-thirty acres purchased from Mrs. Nolan. All utilities had to be brought in. Their closest neighbors were over one mile away—and so remain. In 1965 they sold twenty acres to the San Ramon Valley school district, and Los Cerros School was built. The road was widened, high wire mesh fencing put up, and a sewer installed, but security and peace remained. In 1976 the school put up a sign at the Green Valley Road junction, "Los Cerros School— Blemer Road." This was a very pleasant surprise, and the Blemers later put "950 Blemer Road" on the entrance gate. Nurses serving Dr. Blemer over the years have been Miss Roberta Smith, known affectionately as "Smitty," for twelve years, and Mrs. Polly Sorensen, for over seventeen years. She is his current nurse.

The Blemer's only child, Lois Ann, was born December 8, 1933, in Oakland and attended Danville Grammar School, Anna Heads in Berkeley, and Stanford University, from which she graduated in 1955. She married Dr. Alan Lippincott, December 12, 1959 at Carson City, Nevada. They have two daughters, Lisa, born September 18, 1961, and Abby, who arrived May 29, 1964. The Lippincott family make their home in Pleasant Hill. Lois is a docent for Steinhart Aquarium in San Francisco. They both enjoy diving for fish specimens, bringing them from trips to Hawaii, Cayman Island, Belize, Honduras, Baja and other holidays they've shared for the past eight years. They also maintain a small vineyard and sell their grapes and make a bit of wine for their own use in a very small one-room winery.

It would be remiss of me not to mention that Dr. Blemer's lifelong hobby has been playing golf.

Alfred L. Tubbs (1827-1896) came from Boston to San Francisco in 1850, to sell two shipments of goods from the east coast. After that success he decided to remain.

In the fall of 1850 he formed a partnership, the Folger & Tubbs Ship Chandlery, with elderly Captain William Folger, of the family that later became Folger's Coffee.

In 1853 Alfred sent for his brother Hiram Tubbs (1824-1897) to join him. Hiram and his wife, Susan Ann, left Boston by boat in 1853. They crossed the Isthmus of Panama by mule and train while watching the Canal being built (1850-1855). On the Pacific side they boarded the Pacific Mail steamship *Tennessee* for California. In a fog the *Tennessee* missed the Golden Gate and ran aground on the Marin Coast. All were safe and departed with their belongings. Hiram and Susan made it to Sausalito, and a barge took them from there to San Francisco.

After Captain Folger retired, the Tubbs Brothers decided what San Francisco needed was a cordage mill. Tubbs Cordage Company was established in 1856. Hiram returned to his native New England and brought back rope manufacturing machinery and men to run it. Tubbs Cordage Company is still very much in business and still run by descendants of its founders.

Alfred Tubbs remained in San Francisco. His side interest was in the Napa area where in 1882 he built Chateau Montebella Winery. Both A. L. Tubbs and Captain Folger served on the Vigilance Committee in 1852 and were also members of the Volunteer Fire Companies. Alfred L. Tubbs was State Senator from San Francisco, 1865-69. He fathered the bill to create Golden Gate Park. A. L. Tubbs was invited by his friend Leland Stanford to be a trustee of the University which Stanford was founding.

Hiram Tubbs moved across the bay to East Oakland, where he built a home and hotel. Tubbs Hotel was built in 1871 and destroyed by fire in 1893. Hiram was also one of the founders of Mountain View Cemetery. He too, was on the Vigilance Committee and served on its executive board in 1856. The old Tubbs home was torn down soon after Mrs. Blemer's great-grandmother, Susan Ann Tubbs, died in 1905. Her brother, Herman D. Nichols, was the last child born in that old home, in 1901.

MAY FAMILY
Shoe Stables

John W. and Margaret May arrived in Danville the day after Thanksgiving 1951. They had been married in 1941. They were from Los Angeles, where they had attended the University of Southern California together. They purchased the Eggert home, which was built in 1939 on Danville Boulevard, in the north end of Danville on the cusp of Alamo (Creek is the dividing line). Their daughters, Diana Wynne, known as "Deedy," and Susan Ellen, known as "Toody," were in third and second grades at Charlotte Wood School. Marilyn Margaret was ten months old. Two more daughters arrived, Barbara Ann, born in 1952, and Melinda Virginia, born in 1961.

John May was sales representative for a mid-Western women's dress shoe line, and he continued until 1958, traveling Oregon, Washington, California, Arizona, Nevada, Alaska and Hawaii.

In 1958 they purchased the home of the More sisters, Mary and Mira, on the corner of Diablo and Rose Streets, across the street from the family home of James and Lillian Close. The older home was converted into the Shoe Stable, the rooms, in their original design, used as selling rooms for the family shoe store.

Two years later, their close friends Marjorie and Charles Carson (who went on their honeymoon with them in 1941) became partners in the concern. A second store was opened in Lafayette. A third store was in Pleasanton for six years and was sold in December 1976. In February of 1977 the newest Shoe Stable was opened in the Village Town & Country Shopping Center, Danville, featuring shoes and women's sportswear.

Four May daughters have graduated from San Ramon Valley High School. Diana "Deedy" was the first girl to become vice-president of the student body. (Teresa Cady was the next girl veep, seven years later.) "Deedy" graduated from USC, and went to Washington, D.C. as liaison area person for Governor Ronald Reagan.

There she met Christopher Ogden, graduate of Yale. They were married August 12, 1967 at St. Mary's chapel, Moraga, California, with a reception in the family's Danville home. They have a son, Michael May Ogden, born March 26, 1971, and another baby is due in July 1977. Chris is *Time* correspondent covering the Secretary of State. They are world-traveled due to his assignments. In 1977 they have resided in the U.S.A. for the first time.

Susan "Toody" was head pompon girl in high school and a graduate of San Jose State. She went to Washington, D.C. and worked for Congressman Jerome Waldie and then Senator George Murphy. On July 25, 1971 she married John Wiseman "Jeff" Foord of Pennsylvania, in the San Ramon Valley Methodist Church. A baby is due in May 1977. She does all of the advertising for all the Shoe Stables and is an active travel agent. Jess is manager of the new Shoe Stable Village store.

Marilyn was graduated from UCLA and will be married August 20, 1977 to Paul Gardner of Colorado Springs, in a garden wedding at the family's Danville home. She is a CPA and works for Price Waterhouse in San Francisco.

Barbie graduated from San Jose State and met her husband on campus. He was a member of the All-American water polo team. She was married on May 23, 1976, to Ronald Rory Young of Palo Alto, at a home garden wedding. He was a physical education coach at Campbell High School in San Jose, but they gave it all up, bought a boat and are commercial fishermen. They have been selling fresh fish on the highway on her parent's property.

Melinda is a sophomore at San Ramon Valley High School. She is a serious gymnast, takes lessons, and is on the high school team. She, like her sisters, is horse-minded and owns a horse.

Gary Leith Memorial Walk was named for Gary Leith (deceased), who was John May's first salesman while he was still in high school.

At the west end of the rear of the May property for years was a gravestone. The story goes something like this: In the mid-1930s a worker on the trestle of the Southern Pacific railroad track died. His fellow workmen put him in a box and buried him there. Years later, his family removed his body and took it to Mexico, where they gave him a proper burial. But in his memory they put up a gravestone. In about 1975 the headstone dis-

appeared. Another story goes along with it: As one utility company was putting in new pipes with large machinery a workman on the rig saw the tomstone and left in a hurry. He wanted no part of digging up any body! His supervisor assured him there was no longer a body there, and with coaxing the workman returned, crossed himself, and went back to work on the rig.

MAGEE

Harry H. "Hap" Magee, son of Harry H. and Juanita (Ghirardelli) Magee of Oakland, is a graduate of Piedmont High School, class of 1941, Willis Business College and UC, Davis. On March 28, 1953, he married Ruth Julian, daughter of Joe and Clara Julian of Yerington, Nevada. They have one daughter, Julie*, sixteen, who attends Carondelet High School in Concord and is a good help on the ranch.

Geographically the Magee Ranch is in Alamo, as are all the homes on the north side of El Portal. Before home delivery was extended to Alamo, they chose to take Danville as their address on La Gonda Way. They came to La Gonda Way from Yerington, Nevada as 1952 was a bad year in cattle, so they moved to better grass. Hap owns HH Magee Ranches, which has been in cattle production and specialized in sales, rentals and "truckportation" of cattle, horses and feed since 1946. There are 993 acres of Alamo and Danville property, purchased in 1941, and Diablo land, purchased in 1950. Hap also leases 20,000 acres in four counties, and also operates cattle ranches in Nevada. The seventeen acres where the Magees live was purchased from the San Francisco Protestant Orphanage by the senior Magee in 1946.

Hap is a brand collector and owns the brand made by Daniel Inman (see Chapter Two, *Early Pioneers*), who was owner of Danville's first business. Hap has over 1,500 irons in his current collection and all were at one time registered. He started his hobby of collecting brands in the summer of 1935 when he found an old iron at "Hog Camp," the previous headquarters of their Mason Ranch in Yerington, Nevada. He was sixteen years old when he started collecting. For a time, he lost interest and gave away most of his collection. Soon thereafter he realized his error and began his hobby again.

Hap now boasts the only international collection in the world. There are about seven branding iron collectors in the world and they are in constant correspondence with each other. Hap's collection includes some from Australia, England, Argentina, Canada, and Hawaii; however, most are from California and Nevada. Some are from "VIPs" (Very Important People) like Bing Crosby, Beatrice Kay, Miller-Lux, the King Ranch, C. H. Howard and Safeway Stores. Some go back to early California and belonged to Indians and Spaniards. Hap's joy in collecting is that there is a story which belongs to each brand exclusively, and he truly enjoys spinning these tales for listeners. He says, "I don't want an iron just to have it. It isn't worth anything to me unless there is a story to go with it!" Collecting branding irons can be somewhat expensive. He tells this story on himself: "I used to be a heavy smoker, but no longer have the habit. At one time, I spent $15 a month on tobacco (Wings cigarettes at fifteen cents per package). I now allow myself that money for my hobby. It's a lot more practical and so far I haven't exceeded my budget!"

All brands must be registered. There are approximately 35,000 brands in California, no two alike. Branding laws went into effect in Nevada in 1872. Hap's oldest iron belonged to John Childs of Genoa, Nevada, and was recorded in 1850.

THOMAS W. OHLSON

Dr. Thomas W. Ohlson arrived in Danville in September 1954 with his family of three daughters, Dace, Nancy and Janice, and his wife, Gloria, who was pregnant with their first son, Bart. They came from two years of veterinary practice in Modesto, with two years in Stockton prior to that. Their first home was in downtown Danville on Rose Street. There they converted the detached garage into Danville's first veterinary

* Julie is a junior and for two years has been the only member from the high school on the rodeo team. She participates in District 4 (there are seven districts) and competes in California rodeos and the Grand National. She will graduate in June 1978.

Hap Magee told me, during our visit in April 1977, that they will be moving to Nevada following Julie's graduation. Their seventeen and one-half-acre La Gonda Way ranch will be sold. When he gets settled in Nevada he hopes to finish his book, which he has been working on for almost ten years. He has copyrighted the title, "Windshield Cowboy." It will be about his experiences and the business of "Truckportation," as well as interesting sidelights.

hospital. Dr. Ohlson was then the only veterinarian between Pleasanton and Walnut Creek. He took care of both small and large animals. It was not uncommon to see Dr. Tom treating a horse tied to the front fence of his home.

Tom and Gloria are second generation Californians. Both graduated from Fremont High School. Tom saw military service and then went to Washington State College for his veterinarian degree since, at that time, there was none available in California. He also attended San Francisco City College. Gloria received her nurse's training at Merritt Hospital in Oakland. In the early forties nurses in training (as in many other occupations at that time) were not allowed to marry. So in order to follow the destinies of their hearts, they went to Santa Cruz to be married on December 28, 1943. And Tom went off to serve in the Navy.

The Ohlsons have six children. All started kindergarten and went through the expanding San Ramon Valley schools. They are Dace, who is married to Bob Hawkinson (brother of Darlene Calhoun* of Danville). They live in Montana with their two sons, Cole Thomas (named for his maternal grandfather), born December 12, 1972, and Joshua Leroy (named for his paternal grandfather), born March 4, 1975. A third child is due June 1977. Nancy is married to William Barnwell from a Pleasant Hill family. They live in San Jose. Bill is manager of the Hungry Hunter in Pleasanton and Nancy is a dental hygienist. Janice is divorced after two years of marriage. She lives in Reno, Nevada. Bart, 22, Kurt, 20, and Darla, 18, all live at the family home. They all graduated from Monte Vista High School except Dace, who was a graduate of San Ramon Valley High School.

Both Tom and Gloria have been very active in community affairs. He served eight years on the local school board. He was president of the Chamber of Commerce (RA), Danville Rotary, Vista Grande P-TA (jointly with Gloria), and Veterinary Association of Contra Costa County, in which he is still active. They are both directors of Diablo Cotillion. Gloria has been president of P-TAs and served as regional representative of the San Ramon Valley area also.

For need of more room and better parking facilities Dr. Ohlson moved his veterinary hospital to its present location south of Danville on Camino Ramon in 1966. The Ohlsons have made their home on El Pintado Road in Danville since

1960. There are now ten veterinarians serving the San Ramon Valley area.

Our dogs, Blondie and Sparky, and cat, Mitzie, were well cared for by Dr. Ohlson over the years before their deaths.

HOWELL SWIM SCHOOL

How often have we heard of unsung heroes? Here is its counterpart—a very deserving heroine, Jae Howell of the Howell Swim School on Stone Valley Road, Danville, on the cusp of Alamo. For all her accomplishments and years of generous contribution to the community it is hard to imagine that she has not been named "Citizen of the Year," when others less known and less deserving have been so named.

It's sad to learn that the school's beginning was a matter of necessity when Jae's husband, John, became ill in 1951. Jae started the school in Walnut Creek that year, teaching babies, pre-schoolers, school-age children and adults how to swim. Due to its success, it was moved to Danville in 1957 for a larger pool and better parking facilities. The Howells bought Robert "Johnnie" Johnsen's former home at 170-C Stone Valley Road—it was later renumbered 2701.

In 1958, when John Howell passed away, the school became more than a part time fun activity, as there were three children to support. They are son Jack and daughters Dianne and Debbe. As a youngster, Jae had been in A.A.U. competition the national level, so she formed her own team. That year they saw the National A.A.U. Championships in synchronized swimming. Though the speed swimmers and diving team had won many medals and trophies, Jae decided to start a synchronized swimming team.

It began with about ten girls, including her own two daughters, Dianne and Debbe. By 1960 Dianne Howell had won the national twelve-year-old-and-under championship and a trip to Europe with an exhibition at the Rome Olympics. Jae was one of the coaches for the American team, which toured nine European countries. They exhibited and participated in the International Championship in Barcelona, Spain prior to going to Rome. Dianne and Marion Whitney,

her partner, won the International Duet Championships.

Jae continued teaching the basics of swimming and diving, and many of her students graduated to the team. Children associated with other speed teams around San Ramon Valley came for stroke analysis and to "bring down their times."

The synchronized team participated in A.A.U. competition all over the world—Europe, Japan, Mexico, Canada, and in all parts of the United States, including Hawaii.

The girls were thrilled when they finally received the status of V.I.P.; when they were boarding a flight the pilot would announce, "The Famous Howell Swim Team from Danville, California, is now boarding. They are competing in the National Championships in . . ." (and would name the destination). When there was a stopover, they would be escorted to the V.I.P. room and they met many distinguished persons. The movie stars appealed to the girls most, since they were in their early teens.

The team appeared on ABC's "Wide World of Sports" nine times, and was interviewed on other television programs. They appeared in headlines in the sports pages all over the world. They had a three-page spread in the *Parade* section of the *Oakland Tribune*. Their achievements were greater than the space the local newspaper found to cover them*.

Some of the Far Western team champions with their trophies. Left to right: Nancy Lee, Kathy Ahlf, Kathy Knibbe, Gail Gardner, Jae Howell, instructor, Kathy Craig, Debbe Howell, Gail Johnson, and Melinda Sellers.

*Darlene Calhoun is the wife of Superior Court Judge Richard Calhoun. They make their home on Love Lane, Danville.

In 1965 the team was ranked second in the nation and second in the world! All of these honors and the notoriety meant that they could achieve success by working hard. They were asked to give clinics for coaches and competitors throughout the nation and in Canada. The Japanese National champions, accompanied by Dr. Takahashi and Dr. Kitamure of the Japanese Swimming Federation, came to Danville to study under the local team for two weeks. Various team members housed the team and Round Hill Country Club supplied pool use. Many of the Japanese girls could not speak English and so gestures and body language made a real workout for all.

In 1967, after ten years, twelve hours a day, seven days a week, Jae decided she would have to dissolve the team and use all her energies towards the swim school. They had acquired 197 A.A.U. Pacific Association, Far Western (thirteen western states), Junior Olympics, and Junior and Senior National Championships. The team had approximately forty-five members, although several hundred had been members over the ten-year period.

Original team members were: Dianne Howell, Pacific A.A.U. Junior and Senior, Far Western,

Junior Olympics, Junior National A.A.U. solo, duet and team champion, Senior National A.A.U. team champion and International solo and duet champion; Debbe Howell, Pacific A.A.U. Junior and Senior, Far Western, Junior Olympics and Junior National A.A.U. solo, duet and team champion; Kathy Craig, daughter of Eleanor (deceased) and Richard Craig, Danville, Pacific A.A.U. Junior and Senior, Far Western Junior Olympics, Junior and Senior National A.A.U.; Carolyn Deardorff, daughter of Gerry and Mel Deardorff, Danville, Pacific A.A.U., Junior duet and team champion; Kim Welshons, daughter of Bob and Katherine Welshons, formerly of Danville, now Santa Clara, Pacific A.A.U. Junior and Senior, Junior and Senior National A.A.U., Far Western, Junior and Senior National A.A.U. solo, duet and team champion, and International solo champion; Kris Welshons, Pacific A.A.U. Junior and Senior, Junior and Senior National A.A.U. solo, duet and team champion; Gail Johnson, Walnut Creek, now San Jose, Pacific A.A.U., Junior Olympics, Junior and Senior National A.A.U. solo, duet and team champion.

On special teams were: Janie Johnson, daughter

Howell Synchronized Swimming Team. In the center are Dianne Howell and Kathy Craig. Left to right: Melinda Sellers, Gail Gardner, Nancy Lee, Kathy Knibbe, and Debbe Howell.

111

of Jack and Fran (deceased) Johnson of Danville; Nancy Looney, daughter of Jack (deceased) and Barbara Looney, Danville; Debbie Ibsen, daughter of Keith and Barbara Ibsen of Danville; Sarah Drennan, daughter of Russ and Virginia Drennan of Alamo. For four years this team captured every event in the Junior Olympics and Far Western Championships in ten-years-and-under and eleven and twelve-year-old events.

"B" team, Nancy Ohlson, daughter of Tom and Gloria Ohlson, Danville; Patty Torrenga, daughter of Don and Fran Torrenga, Pleasant Hill; Nancy Lee, daughter of Dr. and Mrs. Ted Lee of Oakland; and Gail Johnson, Danville won the Junior National team championships in 1966.

Melinda Sellers, daughter of George and Flo Sellers of Walnut Creek; Kathy Knibbe, daughter of Paul and Marion Knibbe, Pleasant Hill; Gail Gardner, daughter of Gene and Sue Ahlf of Pleasant Hill; Kathy Craig; and Dianne and Debbe Howell made up a team which was ranked second in the nation and in the world when they disbanded in 1967.

Currently the swim school has between 600 and 1,000 students a year. Students are all ages, from six-week-old babies to oldsters in their eighties. Some of the small ones are the third generation of their families to attend.

To sum it up, Jae Howell is very modest and humble, and says she is fortunate that her work has been a very gratifying type of activity.

All the Howell children attended local schools. The two oldest graduated from San Ramon Valley High School, while Debbe graduated from Monte Vista High School. Jack is married to Janet Despinoy of San Ramon. They have two daughters, Tiffany, born June 3, 1970, and Monica, born May 6, 1974. The family lives on Montair Drive in Danville. Jack is in real estate. Dianne is married to John Skaife, formerly of Alamo. They live in Walnut Creek and have a son Justin, born June 26, 1974. Debbe lives in North Carolina.

*The local publisher said the team was getting too much coverage elsewhere, but Jae felt too many articles in the local newspaper covered teenagers in trouble while her teams were making good accomplishments. These accomplishments brought headlines in other areas and deserved more local mention. Most large cities throughout the nation subsidized their teams, in supplying pool facilities, suits, trips to meets, etc. The parents club held functions, including teas, rummage sales, cake sales and carnivals, and Jae donated her pool.

Our son Gary took diving lessons from Jae Howell at one time while in school.

Chapter Seven

Places

MOUNT DIABLO

Diablo Mountain (RA) was referred to as Sierra de los Bolbones by early Calfornians, for many years after the Americans came. Diablo, they claimed, was the name applied to the smaller peak, now known as North Peak. Legends of the mountain are many. The early inhabitants, the Indians, called it "Pupunia" or "evil spirit."

In 1876 the U.S. Coast Geodetic Survey detailed Professor George Davidson and his party to erect a signal station on the summit of the mountain for the triangulation survey which now extends across the continent. Davidson's party calculated some of the heights and distances indicated by pointers seen on the view platform on the summit today. From the U.S. Department of the Interior, General Land Office, is this information: "...the initial point of the Mount Diablo Meridian was established on Friday, July 18, 1851, by Leander Ransome (RA), deputy surveyor, under instructions issued on July 8, 1851, by Samuel D. King, Esq., surveyor general of California at San Francisco." Colonel Ransome and a party of six completed weeks of work on that date and placed a marker on the summit establishing the east-west base line and the north and south meridian, still the central survey point for northern and central California and Nevada. His survey marker gives the elevation of the peak as 3,849 feet. In July 1891 an observatory platform and telescope used by guests of the Old Mountain House were destroyed by fire, and the hotel itself burned on the south side on July 29, 1922.

Mount Diablo, July 1976. (Courtesy Bill Hockins, photographer)

113

Egon A. Pedersen, five-year resident of Diablo and a director of the San Ramon Valley Historical Society and its chairman of the Mount Diablo landmark project, represented the Society at the State Historical Resources Commission at their recent meeting in the Old State Capitol Building in Benicia. Mount Diablo was unanimously approved to be registered as an historical site. The commission, which recommends landmark status for buildings and sites to the State Department of Parks and Recreation, approved the registration on Thursday, November 4, 1976. Pedersen said Mount Diablo was a "unique integration of history and beauty," and cited its vast archeological heritage. Fossils 150 million years old, of prehistoric elephants, camels, three-toed sloths and saber-toothed tigers have been found. Indians lived there 5,000 years ago and some of their sacred grounds are still intact. The mountain also guided early explorers, first the Fages-Crespi expedition in 1772 and later the De Anza group with the first encirclement in 1776. Pedersen also noted the mountain's extensive wildlife and 400 plant varieties, seven of which are endemic and found nowhere else on earth!

A plaque will be dedicated at the summit in the fall of 1977 sponsored by the local Society.

Mount Diablo

Old toll gate at Mount Diablo Park. (Courtesy Vivian Coats Edmonston)

Mount Diablo from another angle, 1974. (Courtesy Bill Hockins, photographer)

OLD MOUNTAIN HOUSE

Old Mountain House was the brainchild of a Yankee from New Hampshire, Joseph H. Hall. He planned the building of a resort near the summit to attract people from all parts of the state and from across the nation.

He was also instrumental in the construction of the two roads up the mountain, the first from Ygnacio Valley to the summit of Diablo through Pine Canyon and the second from Danville through Green Valley, meeting the first road a mile from the top. These roads were opened May 2, 1874 and stage lines were started. Two stages ran twice daily over the roads, which met about 300 feet southwest of a spring from which a good-sized stream ran down the mountain to join the water of a creek above the head of Pine Canyon.

It was 100 feet west of the spring that Hall built his Mountain House, aptly named. The two

Mountain House Hotel, 1880.

stages arrived daily from Pacheco, Martinez, and the west, and from Oakland and that area through Danville, and stopped at the hotel, a mile from the summit. From there the ascent to the top was by hiking or horseback.

Old Mountain House had sixteen rooms, filled with all known conveniences. There was a huge dining room where epicurian meals were served. In its heyday the register of the Mountain House showed names of people from all over the world. Often couples were married there.

Ranchers and property owners objected to the hotel because they claimed sightseers overran the once peaceful slopes of the mountain and many

times were the cause of fires, which ruined pasture lands. Ranchers petitioned the Board of Supervisors to close the mountain roads. The petition was granted, an ordinance was passed, and gates and fences were installed and armed guards posted to keep out the public. Finally the old hotel was burned. The ranchers and property owners could not fight progress forever and with financial assistance from the county, Mount Diablo State Park was established by the state park commission in 1931, though it was never designated as a state landmark. It includes 2,300 acres of land at the summit of the mountain, with 255 picnic and 55 camp sites. Original roads are still used. Although widened and paved, they essentially follow the fifteen-foot dirt roads of 1874.

The natural stone observation tower and platform, built with stones quarried on the mountain, was begun in 1932 and completed in 1933.

Another plan was to build a tower of medieval architecture to be called Torre del Sol, Tower of the Sun, a three-story structure to be topped with a tower. It was to have sleeping apartments, dining rooms and house guest conveniences. The plan disappeared when the U.S. entered the war.

From Mount Diablo can be seen scenic wonders surpassed only by those seen from one other mountain in the world, in Africa. From the top can be seen 734 square miles of Contra Costa County and a total of over 60,000 square miles of the earth's surface.

Stagecoach from Martinez in front of Mount Diablo Hotel servants' quarters, c. 1880.

SAN RAMON
CIVILIAN CONSERVATION CORPS

The following is from a 1957 newspaper article.

Central and south Contra Costa would not be so lovely an outdoor area as it is today [1957] if it had not been for the work of a group of men and boys whose contributions now are virtually forgotten. These were the workers in civilian conservation corps camps, a nation-wide agency which provided employment and useful work for thousands of young men during the Great Depression.

The San Ramon CCC Camp operated as a soil conservation force working on privately owned agricultural land in cooperation with the owners who cooperated and assisted them in planning and installing soil and water conservation practices which saved many an acre of eroded soil.

Camp field operations were carried on in consultation with the agricultural extension service and other federal, state and local agencies and with the county soil conservation committee. The committee chairman was Thomas S. Vanasek of Ygnacio valley, who is still very much involved in county conservation practices although the CCC vanished at the beginning of World War II. The nation's manpower had to be mobilized for an all-out war effort.

CCC work crews were restricted to work which required special equipment or skill which the farmer did not have available. This included earth-fill stock ponds, masonry check dams, and diversion ditches. Hillside erosion was stopped by the planting of trees and shrubs.

The veterans branch of the CCC constructed the museum on top of Mount Diablo. This 200 man company, No. 2932 of Mount Diablo SP-9, was called the crack company of the Sacramento district. These men, all veterans of World War One, built the fossilized stone museum quarried six miles down the slope.

Many miles of roadway were built and some of the dangerous curves widened on the mountain. Grades were leveled in many places. The parking area at the top was leveled and rock-walled. This veterans company also built 28 picturesque picnic sites with parking spaces, piped water, stone fireplaces, and made tables and benches.

They also constructed fire trails, built water storage facilities and installed telephone lines. Many of them also took courses at night at San Ramon Valley High School in mineralogy and general and military photography. They did this as a national defense effort to help the government's quest for strategic minerals.

The classes were taught at San Ramon Valley Union High School by principal George V. Cooley and state division of mines technologist George L. Gary and aerial photographer Roscoe P. Ricard.

My husband Alfred Jones, whom I always call Fritz or Jonesie, worked under the CCC program for Steve Johnson, Sr., who had a contract with the CCC authorities to hire local men to haul lumber up the mountain. Since there were more young men applying than there were jobs, in fairness Johnson formed crews and each crew had an opportunity to work for a period of time, thus giving more men an opportunity to fill the available jobs. My hubby remembers it was very windy on the mountain. Once some one-by-twelve boards got blown about as if they were kindling!

April 1939 news item: William Timm of Walnut Creek and Associates reopened the old coal mines on Diablo.

WHITE GATE FARM

The Spanish and Mexican governors had the power to grant unoccupied lands to petitioners who would stock the land and make it productive. Jose Garcia (RA) (of the Alamo adobe) received a grant and was the first official owner of White Gate Farm. When his daughter Maria married a Captain Merrithew, Garcia gave the couple a stretch of land that Maria could cover on horseback in one day from sun-up to sundown. It is said that Maria lost one spur, which was found later when settlers explored the area. Later a spur with Maria Garica's initials was found in a spring on the then Al Davies property (in the vicinity of the present Round Hill Country Club). It was a perfect match to its mate on display at Bancroft Library in Berkeley.

A home was built in about 1847 near some large trees, to the left of the present White Gate Farm home. It later burned down. In 1856 brothers Nathaniel and Charles Howard built the present home. It was a duplex of Colonial New England design. The well-built home was of logs from Redwood Canyon, which were taken around the Horn by ship to Maine, where they were milled into lumber and then returned. The house included redwood mud sills, hand-cut and hand-finished doors, and double hung windows, and Georgia pine cupboards.

White Gate Farm was on the road from Alamo's Henry Hotel to the coal mine area at Nortonville and Somerville. Stables and bunkhouses provided a stopover for drivers and animals. The original trail for the route is still visible in the hills behind the farmhouse.

Some of the upstairs rooms were used as a

school until 1865, when the first Green Valley schoolhouse was built. At one time there were nine students. To this day, some of their names and birthdates (one 1804) are still on one bedroom door. One name was Knox, for whom Knox Road was named. Later it was to have been called Kentwood Drive, and presently it is known as Green Valley Blind. At one time there were four forty-acre parcels that belonged to the families of Hall, Love, William Z. "Pap" Stone, and Cope.

In 1886-87 the property came into the possession of Judge Warren Olney. In 1898 Judge William H. Donahue (great uncle of the present owner, Ray Donahue) and his wife Annie bought White Gate Farm, but continued to live in Oakland by Lake Merritt, in a home that is still standing. The judge later had a suite at the Claremont Hotel, Berkeley. He died in 1949. His law firm offices still function at 29th and Broadway, Oakland.

During this four-year period different people and caretakers lived at White Gate Farm. The land was good for growing grain and grazing cattle. The sandy soil was good for the animals' hoofs. The original "Man O' War," predecessor of the racing champion, was foaled at White Gate Farm. Horses were trained at the track at Diablo, the present site of St. Timothy's Episcopal Church, Cameo Acres, and Diablo Hacienda subdivision. Originally there were plentiful orchards, fruits of all kinds, nuts, olives, and grapes. The first almond orchard was removed in 1927.

In 1902 John Joseph Donahue and his wife Ellen Collier (Collier Canyon, Livermore, was named for her family), lived at White Gate Farm. Their children were Mary, who died when nineteen years old; Frederick L., born in Altamonte; Mervin; Bernice (now of Rossmoor); Maude; Grace (lives in Quincy); William (lives in Cottonwood); Francis, born in Pleasanton; and John.

Frederick L. Donahue married Ruth Marie (Mortensen) at St. Isidore's Catholic Church. They had two sons, Raymond L. and Edward P., both born at White Gate Farm. Both attended local schools and graduated from San Ramon Valley Union High School. Ray was baptized and confirmed by Archbishop Hanna. He is a bachelor and has continued to make White Gate Farm his home. Ed married Elaine and they had a daughter, Linda. Their mother died in September 1973 and their father in January 1974.

The home at White Gate Farm has three acres around it. Ray Donahue has been restoring and remodeling the house for thirty years. An addition designed by his mother was added in 1970 and is now the beautiful living room. Ray did all the interior decorating and selection of materials, assisted by Eleanor Shipley of Danville. When a fireplace was removed from the original parlor, under the brick hearth was found the original carpet, an 1854 Alexander Smith, the label showing an Alabama address. They are still in business.

White Gate, 1862.

White Gate Farm in 1977, after much remodeling and restoring. Addition at left was designed by Ruth Donahue and added in 1970. It is the living room and holds many lovely antique treasures.

117

Ray wrote, describing the carpeting, and the company sent representatives from their San Francisco offices out to see it. It is the Rose Garden pattern. Ray had new carpet of that pattern loomed for the home. Original furnishings include two Lincoln sofas, now rebuilt; a pair of rockers, now also swiveled; marble-top tables; Gone-with-the-Wind lamps; hanging lamps; and piano lamps, all wired and in use. An interesting fireplace poker was once on Ray's great-great-grandfather's ship (John Joseph's father). James and Peter Donahue owned the Donahue Iron Works in San Francisco, where they made boilers. There is a monument to James Donahue in San Francisco.

WHITE GATE SUBDIVISION

In 1969 Fred and Ruth Donahue sold 184 acres to the Harold W. Smith Company, developers. The realtor handling the deal was Henry "Gary" Garabaldi (deceased). White Gate Subdivision was started in 1969 and at completion there will be 240 family homes. Some area of green belt will be preserved. Riding and hiking easement will be dedicated to the county when needed.

Some street names are White Gate Road (the registered name of the place), Donahue Lane (named for the family), Ray Court (named for one son), Shandelin Court (named in honor of John Joseph Donahue, the grandfather, who always referred to the home as "Shandelin Hall"), and Tony and Todd Courts (named for the grandsons of Mr. and Mrs. Henry "Gary" Garabaldi the realtor).

PRESBYTERIAN CHURCHES

The research on the Presbyterian Churches comes from many sources and several years' accumulation of materials. The difficulty has been to sift out and work with several references, all presuming to be accurate, but with some conflicting dates. Most recently my thanks go to Sonnie Edgecomb of Danville for her assistance and the use of church records, among them the church history, written by its former pastor, the Rev. Wesley H. "Van" Van Delinder. Bear in mind, at times, there was more than one church.

Records seem to show that the California Presbytery of the Cumberland Presbyterian Church (RA) received into membership the first Protestant Church in Contra Costa County on April 4, 1851, officially recognizing a small group of ten members. It is said to have been the result of a ten-day Camp Meeting (RA) organized by Alamo pioneers John M. and Mary Ann (Smith) Jones (RA). (They returned to settle in Alamo November 10, 1851.) By 1870 it was the largest church in the California Presbytery, with forty-five members and 225 Sunday School pupils. It declined in strength and by 1884 had but one member. From 1884 to 1906, Mary Jones, also known as "Grandma Jones," (RA) continued to operate the Sunday School and to arrange for preachers for the Sunday services. Meanwhile many of the former members began to attend a Presbyterian Church that had organized in Danville in 1863. In February 1863, the Rev. H. R. Avery was sent by the board of home

White Gate in 1914. The Donahue Ranch is now White Gate Subdivision.

118

Danville Presbyterian Church, built in 1875, burned on May 27, 1932. Pastor shown is believed to be Reverend R. S. Symington.

In 1875 the church building was moved to the center of Alamo, on the west side of Highway 21 (present site of the street Lunada Lane, near the Alamo Post Office). "Grandma Jones" remained loyal to that church, which was on Jones property (a portion of "Rancho Romero" (RA)) until 1906, when the Cumberland Presbyterian Church and the Presbyterian Church of the U.S.A. merged, uniting with the First Presbyterian Church of Danville.

The picket fence was first. The wire fence came later.

missions of the Presbyterian Church, U.S.A., and he began the establishment of the oldest church in the San Ramon Valley. Preaching points were established at Alamo, Green Valley, San Ramon and Pacheco. This work continued under the name of the Central Contra Costa Presbyterian Church until May 1875, when it was consolidated as First Presbyterian Church of Danville.

Another reference shows that Protestant church services were first held in 1857 in a private home by the Rev. David McClure of Union Academy (RA), in Alamo. The Cumberland Presbyterian Church (RA), first Protestant church in the then large Contra Costa County, including Alameda County, was built in 1856 on the south end of Alamo, north of the present Sunset Nursery, opposite the Union Academy. First preachers came from San Jose, recruited by "Grandma Jones," a former resident of that area. Early preachers were the Rev. Cornelius Yager, spring 1852, Mr. Trusdale, and the Rev. T. M. Johnston.

In 1875, several denominations were thinking of organizing into one Protestant church. A vote was taken and it was decided whichever church won would be supported by all the Protestants in the community with their attendance and financial aid as needed. The Presbyterian Church founded by the Rev. H. R. Avery in 1865 won the election. The Rev. R. L. Symington was selected to be the pastor. The church was incorporated and named the First Presbyterian Church of Danville. A beautiful colonial New England style church with a tall slender steeple was built. The cornerstone was laid on October 1, 1875 and dedication was on June 18, 1876. (I also found the month of January 1876 used in some references). It was on Front Street, the main street of that day. A beautiful California redwood tree was planted in front. It is still standing.

The Rev. R. S. Symington was pastor for many years. This handsome church, known by all for miles around, burned May 27, 1932 in a three-

119

hour long fire which started at midnight. After the fire the congregation met in the Grange Hall (present site of Village Theatre) next door. In 1933 a new church building was built on the present site of Lynn School. This building remained as the church (where I attended many Sundays) until 1951, when it outgrew its Front Street location. The plaque at the over-100-year-old redwood reads: "This Tree Planted in 1876 is Dedicated to the Memory of Rev. R. S. Symington, First Pastor, Danville Presbyterian Church. Tree and land donated by Mr. and Mrs. E. C. Wiester, May 14, 1950."

On January 1, 1876, trustees were Robert O. Baldwin, David Glass and J. J. Kerr. Elders were Joseph Wiley and A. J. Young, who had both served as elders of the central county church. They were ordained May 14, 1871. On that day Rev. H. R. Avery left to assume duties at the Tomales Church.

Some church records were lost in 1898, but existing records show there were fifty-nine members in 1876 with no additions until 1882. The next records show a membership in 1913 of fifty-four, with eighty-six in the Sunday School. When the Rev. H. W. Van Delinder came in 1949 there were 199 members. By 1957 there were 723.

From 1875 to 1955, there were but two clerks of the session. A J. Young served for fifty years and Will E. Stewart (RA) for thirty years. Dr. Wilson E. Close, who served as elder in the mid-fifties, is a descendant of one of the charter members, Mrs. L. M. Close. Miss Sarah Young, the daughter of A. J. Young, was organist for forty years. The late Congressman John Finley Baldwin was a grandson of Robert O. Baldwin, one of the original trustees. Mary McPherson Podva and Joel H. Boone were also charter members. Ina Boone Root (deceased) joined the church June 10, 1886. Mrs. Josie Close united with the church September 1902 and Carl Dauth September 1909 (both deceased).

Some pastors over the years have been: T. R. Bradshaw, 1870; T. M. Johnston, September 1859 to September 1869, when he moved to Stockton, then Monticello; W. H. Tubb, January 5, 1872-1883. (He was a mural painter. His work depicting scenes from Kentucky was seen in the Tom Flournoy home.) Other pastors were: John M. Cameron; Samuel Briggs; Wm. R. Bishop; R. F. Trousdale; R. S. Symington, D.D., January 1, 1876-86; J. C. Burgess May 1, 1886-1899; R. S. Eastman, D.D., May 6, 1900-03; James G. Ander-

sen, May 3, 1904-07; F. S. Fraser, November 17, 1907-08; Charles F. Woodward, November 6, 1908-13; John A. Ainslie, July 1, 1913-18; Duncan A. McRae, February 2, 1919-20; Alexander Eakin, August 29, 1920-24; M. E. Coen, September 5, 1924-26; John E. Stuchell, 1926-32; William E. Clawson, 1933-36; William Earl Terry, 1936-38; William W. Rasco, 1938-43; Alan L. Searles*, 1943-48; H. W. Van Delinder, August 1949-?; and Orville L. Shick, from 1961 to the present.

Among the early elders of the church were: Joseph Wiley, January 14, 1871, A. J. Young, January 14, 1871; V. Craig, March 12, 1882; R. O. Baldwin, January 18, 1887; August Hemme, February 7, 1886; Hugh Wiley, January 11, 1891; Albert B. Hoag, November 15, 1903; William G. Love, September 20, 1908; William E. Stewart, September 20, 1908; and William J. Williams, September 20, 1908. Other elders on the church register are: Charles O. Love, April 11, 1920; George Cheshire, 1927; John F. Baldwin, Jr., 1933; Delbert Main, Joseph Rogers, Chester Love, Dr. Wilson E. Close, 1947; Dr. Paul Wendt, 1947; Dick Starkweather, 1946;.W. D. Barton, 1948; C. L. Anderson, 1948; C. C. Morse, 1950; LeRoy Riddle, 1950; Fred Groesbeck, 1950; John Graham, 1950; Thelma Tromp, 1950; E. H. Baldwin, Horace Van Gorden, 1951; John G. Sullivan, 1951; Joe Brugger, 1951; Loren Meigs, 1951; E. O. Oliver, Roscoe Jones, Jr., George Conner, Marion Frank, John Rock, Don Brownlee, W. C. Carr, Fred Dull, Sidney Gleb, 1952; Lyle Pember, 1952; Robert Shipley, Richard Thornton, Claude Andreason, Joseph F. Smith, Jr., O. D. Paulson, Herbert Polk, Melvin Katzer, Glen Worthley, Duane "Bud" Spencer, Tom Williamson, Keith Noble and Robert Ausfahl.

From the *Pacific Cumberland Presbyter* newspaper dated August 1861: "The ecumenicity of the Alamo Cumberland Church is shown by the fact it allowed its building to be used by Methodists and Baptists." Apparently others used their facilities as well, but all the issues of the *Pacific*

---

*Alan L. Searles christened our son, Alfred Garrett Jones, on Sunday November 4, 1945, at "Rancho-Romero" at a private home christening. His godmother was Mary Frances (Lax) Brear and his godfather was Frederick Gillette Brear. Our son, known as Gary, shared his christening with his paternal cousins, Marilyn and Gregory Alden Jones. There were twenty-five close friends and relatives in attendance, almost all from the San Ramon Valley area.

Cumberland Presbyter carried the notice that Methodist services were held the first Sunday of the month, Baptist services on the third Sunday, and Presbyterian services on the second and fourth Sundays.

Homecoming Sunday was observed May 28, 1950, to celebrate the 75th Anniversary of the Community Presbyterian Church in Danville. At the 11:00 A.M. worship service the pastoral prayer was by the Rev. R. S. Eastman. The sermon, "The Communion of Saints," was given by the Rev. H. W. Van Delinder, and ground-breaking was by C. L. Anderson. There was a 12:15 picnic lunch, with a "Recognition of Long-time Members" at 12:45. At 2:00 P.M. the dedication of the redwood tree was held. Other events of the day were the presentation of the deed by Mr. Ed Wiester to John Graham; the unveiling of the plaque by Mr. W. E. Stewart, a tenor solo, "Trees," by Joseph Funk of Camille Avenue, Alamo (my neighbor), and a prayer and benediction by Rev. W. E. Clawson.

The Community Presbyterian Church of Danville, at 222 West El Pintado, was dedicated on December 23, 1951. Additional facilities were dedicated in April 1952 and the third unit in April 1956. The present buildings are situated on a five-and-one-half-acre site. Mr. Shick, a native of Pennsylvania, earned his master of theology degree in Dallas, Texas and served in the Army as a chaplain. He previously served churches in Maryland and Virginia and came to the San Ramon Valley in 1961. His wife, Esther, is a native Californian. They currently make their home on Roan Drive, Danville, in Diablo Hacienda. The church now offers three services for its 1,000 members. Associate pastor is Jim Rueb, and a second assistant is expected during 1977.

1977 expansion plans call for a 700-seat sanctuary and an all-purpose room for services, programs, community activities, concerts, forums and other public presentations. There is an active group involved in youth fellowship, with some 200 to 300 of high school age meeting each week. The church has an open door policy for other groups, among them the San Ramon Valley Clergy Association, Alcoholics Anonymous (AA), Alanon, Scout groups, Christian Men's Breakfast, and Interdenominational Bible Study Group. The local church is ruled by the church session, made up of eighteen ruling elders, who make most of the decisions.

At the end of April 1977 I was given the program for the 1875-1925 Fiftieth Anniversary of Laying of the Corner Stone of Danville Presbyterian Church. There was a morning service at 11:00 A.M. with an Anniversary Service at 2:30 P.M. Ushers were Waldo Wood, Gordon Turner, Ben Johnson, Charles Wells, and Virgil Kelley. Committees were: Invitation - the sessions; Program - Miss Sarah Young, S. H. Johnson, M. E. Coen, A. J. Young; Entertainment and refreshments - Ladies Aid, Miss Laura Flournoy, president; Reception - Mrs. Anne Van Gordon and S. H. Johnson. The Board of Trustees was: A. M. Burdick, chairman; Miss Laura Flournoy, secretary; Mrs. Nellie Baldwin, treasurer; and C. W. Close, C. O. Love, E. H. Baldwin, Frank Mariana, Josiah Boucher, S. H. Johnson and John Baldwin.

ST. ISIDORE'S

Mass was first celebrated in the Danville area* in 1875 at the home of Edward McCauley in Green Valley by the Reverend James H. Aerden, O.P., on the occasion of a sick call. During this visitation Father Aerden arranged for the celebration of Mass at the Alamo Hotel Hall on the fifth Sunday of the month. This arrangement continued until 1883, when the Rev. Lawrence Serda, pastor of Sacred Heart Church, Oakland, took charge of Walnut Creek, Lafayette, and Moraga Valley and celebrated Mass for the congregation of ten families in the Grange Hall in Walnut Creek on the second and fourth Sundays of the month. Making the journey of over twenty miles by winding dirt roads to Walnut Creek on Saturdays, Father Serda spent the night at the home of Mr. and Mrs. Erastus Ford or that of Mr. and Mrs. Antone Silva Botelho.

In August 1884, Mr. Botelho donated land for a church at the southwest end of Main Street, Walnut Creek. A subscription for the new church started and when Father Serda had secured $2,500, the total cost of the building, construction started. The Most Rev. Archbishop Joseph Sadoc Alemany officiated at the dedication on October 12, 1884. The congregation remained under the care of Father Serda until 1892, when the Dominican Fathers from Martinez took over the care of the church as part of the Martinez Parish. Rev. Joseph F. Barrigan, O.P., chaplain of the Novitiate of the Christian Brothers at Martinez, took care of the parishioners during that period.

On April 20, 1910, Archbishop Patrick W. Riordan established Danville as a parish center.

The Rev. John I. Collins was the first priest. St. Mary's Mission of Walnut Creek was then detached from Martinez and transferred to the Danville parish. Father Collins gathered his small flock for Sunday Mass at the Danville Grange Hall. He lived at the Danville Hotel until the church and rectory were completed.

The building of St. Isidore's was one of the biggest building projects of that time. It took one year, three and one-half months to complete the two buildings, at a cost of $11,000. Dedication was on July 28, 1912 by Archbishop Riordan. The dedication sermon was preached by Father Peter C. Yorke. The new parish of St. Isidore's embraced boundaries from Livermore and Pleasanton, touching Hayward and Oakland Parishes on the west. It included Moraga Valley and Orinda, with the boundaries of the Martinez and Concord parishes to the north, and the eastern slopes of Mount Diablo, St. Mary's Parish in Walnut Creek, Santa Maria in Orinda and St. Perpetua's in Lafayette. The mother church is now limited with a northern boundary at Livorna Road in Alamo, and the Norris Canyon area to the south. It takes in the Morgan territory road on the east.

During the first twenty-five years the parish enjoyed the quiet of a typical country parish. By 1937, with the completion of the Broadway Tunnel, many people began to come and enjoy the Valley. In 1956, the late Father Plunkett, realizing the growth would continue, purchased property on La Gonda Way for a new parish plant, at the cost of $22,500. The first building constructed was a hall to serve as a meeting place. Its cost was $165,000. The parish plant now includes the church, rectory, convent, school, parish hall and religious education center. A new church with a capacity of 900, at a cost of $226,000, was dedicated December 22, 1961. In 1962 the parish opened a parochial school staffed by the Franciscan Sisters in Philadelphia. In the past seventeen years the parish has increased in size, from 600 families at the time of the Golden Jubilee in 1960, to 2100 families in 1977.

The old church building was demolished on Wednesday, December 11, 1963. A familiar Danville landmark, it had occupied the corner of Hartz and Linda Mesa Avenues for over fifty years. (Now a new shopping center is there.)

Anthony Cabral watched the wrecking of his church that he had attended regularly since February 15, 1887. It was the church he had helped build. In 1910, when Tony was twenty-two years old, he was hired by the Oakland construction firm of Stanley and Archer. Mr. Stanley, Mr. Archer, Stanley's son, Bob Podva, and Cabral were the crew and they all worked. Cabral said only the finest materials were used in the church and rectory buildings. It was fine pine and better built than buildings of today [1963], according to Cabral. He took the wrought iron railings and a giant eight-by-eight post which he planned to use at his Prospect Avenue home. (Stanley and Archer also built the Hannah Harrison house on Hartz Avenue, the Juul residence on School Street, and the Fred Booth home.)

There were many memories by eyewitnesses to the demolition. Mrs. Alice Selzer watched and felt a part of her life leaving. As a little girl she had put flowers on the altar. Rose Brazil had memories too, as did Miss Lena Fereira, whose mother Mary cared for the altar and did much of

St. Isidore's Catholic Church, Danville, was dedicated on July 28, 1912. It was later covered with white Pabco shingles, eventually was wrecked and removed, in 1963.

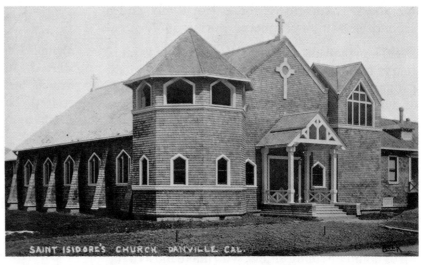

SAINT ISIDORE'S CHURCH DANVILLE CAL.

122

the maintenance work in the church for thirty-five consecutive years.

The following is taken from *Valley Pioneer* newspaper clippings dated December 18, 1963 and November 19, 1970, with some editing:

"Thanksgiving Day Mass; Parish Observes 60th Year"—To commemorate the 60 years of existence as a Catholic Parish, St. Isidore's Church, a Concelebrated High Mass was held on Thanksgiving Day 1970. The Rev. Roy Brown, O.F.M. of San Damiano Retreat House delivered the sermon with the Rev. Julius Bensen, pastor; the Rev. Thomas O'Shaughnessy, assistant pastor, and the Rev. Mr. Paul Vassar, deacon. During the celebration of the Mass, special liturgical music was presented by the St. Isidore's choir under the direction of Donald Fantz and the St. Isidore's teenage instrumental group with Miss Patricia Crossen directing.

The present pastor of St. Isidore's is the Rev. Julius Bensen, who has served the Parish since 1957. Father Bensen said: "As we look back on the last sixty years of the Parish we marvel at its fortitude in trying times and glory in its achievements, both physical and spiritual. It has been fortunate in the good men who served as pastors and it has been blest by the generations of men and women and also children who have been true to their faith and their parish. May God bless this parish for many years to come."

Following the 1970 Thanksgiving Day Mass in observance of the Parish's 60th year, there was a dedication ceremony of the original cross that stood on the roof top of the old St. Isidore's Church. The cross, located adjacent to the rectory, bears the names of all former pastors and administrators of St. Isidore's*. The bell, rescued from the rubble of old St. Isidore's, was mounted as a memorial to the late President John F. Kennedy. It was a joint effort of the Father's Club and the Holy Name Society of the Parish. They felt it a fitting tribute to the late President Kennedy. It was erected near the creek. (The bell was donated to the church in 1911 by Concelho No. 3 of U.P.E.C., a Portuguese Lodge active in the area.)

Former Pastors at St. Isidore's are: Rev. John Collins, 1910 (start of parish); Rev. Martin J. Concannon, 1912; Rev. J. J. Hennessy, 1912; Rev. J. W. Galvin, 1917; Rev. Patrick McGratton, 1919; Rev. Patrick Bresnan, 1922; Rev. Hugh Bohan, 1924; Rev. W. Emmett O'Connor, 1928; Rev. Timothy J. Shanahan, 1929; Rev. Louis Miller,

1935; Rev. Henry J. Lande, 1941; Rev. Martin J. Egan, 1948; Rev. Thomas Collins, 1950; Rev. Henry Plunkett, 1952; Rev. Bartholomew McCarthy, 1957; Rev. Julius M. Bensen, 1957 to present.

At St. Isidore's Church School, grades one through eight are taught by Franciscan Sisters and lay faculty. Full enrollment is 320 students. Present plans (1977) are for a new multipurpose building to be started soon to serve the growing needs of the expanding parish. There are religious education classes for students attending public schools, with 150 pre-school students, 1,155 elementary and junior high students, 145 high school students, and a faculty of sixty-one teachers, with two Sisters of St. Dominic.

There are three priests at St. Isidore's currently: Msgr. Julius Bensen, Father John Egan, father in residence, and Father John Manning, the associate pastor. Msgr. Bensen is a native of San Francisco. He is a graduate of Star of the Sea parochial school, San Francisco, and attended St. Joseph's College in Mountain View and St. Patrick's Seminary in Menlo Park, and was ordained in 1940. He has served three churches in San Francisco, St. Anne's in Lodi, and a church in Half Moon Bay.

The local diocese includes two counties and eighty-four parishes. Bishops attend regional and national meetings. The Priest Senate is made up of fifteen priests, more or less. St. Isidore's has a parish council with fifteen members, twelve lay members elected by the people, and three appointees.

My thanks to the Rev. Julius Bensen for information.

The 1977 directory of San Ramon Valley now lists some fourteen churches of other denominations and faiths in the area.

LACEY'S ARABIAN CENTER
Home of Champions (formerly Rogers Arabians)
"PORTUGEE GULCH"

In the late 1800s a colony of Portuguese people settled in the area out Miranda Avenue, Alamo, which years before had been Stone property. The settlement became known as "Portugee

*Though St. Isidore's Catholic Church came into being with the establishment of Danville as a parish center in 1910, its history dates back to 1772. In that year, the Fages-Crespi Exploration Party (RA) spent a night camping on the future site of Danville/Alamo.

Gulch" (said to have been named by one of the Ventura boys), and to this day some people refer to it as such. There were four major families: Bispo, Marengo, Nunes and Ventura. Two of the homes still remain, those of Nunes and Ventura.

The Marengo Place was known for its vineyards and winery that went into the hillside with large storage tanks. James and Angiolina Marengo had three daughters, Annie, Mary and Stella. In adulthood they became the mesdames Artero, Borlandelli and Borghini, now all deceased.

Eighty-eight acres were acquired by Manuel and Maria Ventura of Pico, the Azores. Manuel came to America in 1874 and farmed in the Sacramento Valley for nine years. He worked for fifty cents per week and had to pay room and board. He came to Contra Costa County in 1883. He and his wife had seven children. Mary, Joseph, and Manuel, now all deceased, were born on the ranch in a home which burned down. Amelia, Elvira "Vi," Rose and Gertrude (deceased) were all born in a home which is still standing.

Mr. Ventura sold his property to his son-in-law Manuel Caspar (deceased), who was married to Mary, and the Venturas moved to Walnut Creek. Mr. Ventura passed away in 1935 in Pinole, at the age of eighty-two; his wife died in Martinez. When in his early forties, Mr. Ventura experienced a stroke, and his right leg and arm were enough affected to leave him handicapped, but his mind was alert and he continued to work.

Mary (deceased) married Charles Voll (deceased) and had two children, Agnes and Charles (both deceased). They divorced and she married Manuel Caspar. They had twins, Eleanor and Edwin, and Rosalind and Joe.

Joseph (deceased) married Delphina Cordera and had two sons, George, who lives in Vista, California and Robert, who lives in Oregon. Joseph was a volunteer fireman for Walnut Creek and worked for the Farm Bureau for many years.

Manuel (deceased) married Evelyn Todoroff (deceased). They had no children. She died before him.

Amelia married Manuel Rose (deceased 1956) and they had five children: twins, Edwin, who lives in Washington state, and Edward, who lives in Walnut Creek; Ernie of Grass Valley; and daughters Gloria Harvey of San Ramon and Geraldine Correy of Santa Rosa. Amelia has thirteen grandchildren and ten great-grandchildren, and makes her home in an Alamo apartment.

Elvira "Vi" married Constantino Vallado and they had three children: William Robert lives in Chicago; Leonard Eugene lives in Walnut Creek; and Helen Davis lives in Concord. They divorced and "Vi" married Joe Nunes of Pinole. They had Teddy Chismer, who lives in Martinez. "Vi" has twelve grandchildren and three great-grandchildren and lives in Martinez.

Rose married Earl Ward of Oklahoma, and they had six children: Marlene Vasta lives in Mendocino; Loretta Ludvigson lives in Concord; Betty Flanders lives in Concord; Melani Cordova lives in Benicia; Jennie Ortiz lives in Mendocino; and Earl Ward, Jr. lives in Concord. Rose has thirteen grandchildren and five great-grandchildren. She lives in Mendocino and is widowed.

Gertrude (deceased) married Herb Thompson and their children were: John, Bill, and Don, all deceased, Pat Robison, who lives in Martinez, Bobbie Epperson, who lives in Vacaville, and Ronald Thompson, who lives in Lake County. There are nine grandchildren.

John Texeira Nunes (pronounced Noons) was born in St. Jorge, Azores. He was the only member of his family to leave Portugal. His bride, Mary Martin, was born in Providence, Rhode Island. She came to California with her family and settled in San Leandro, where she met and married John Nunes and their first daughter Annie was born. The Nunes family moved to Alamo and had seventy-four acres, which they farmed. Three more daughters were born there, Belle (deceased), Mary and Bernice. Annie lives in the San Joaquin Valley with family members. Mary is in Bakersfield and had two sons. Bernice married a widower, Louis Vezzani, with two sons. They had no children. She graduated from San Ramon Valley High School with its second class, in 1915. She graduated from the University and taught in Oakland for many years. She is now retired and widowed and makes her home at Rossmoor.

In March 1977, when "Vi" Nunes was interviewed, she recollected some thoughts of early days in Alamo. She said they raised cattle and pigs and had eggs, etc., which they took to Washington Street in Oakland. They took the horse and buggy to town. Ashby Avenue was all in dairy farms. Her father would buy the "drop calves," and take them home to Alamo to fatten them up for eating or selling. Twice a year they went to Hayward to buy supplies, and paid for them when the crops came in. They skimmed cream and made their own butter. She remembers the big auctions of livestock or equipment held at large ranches.

In more recent times, approximately twenty-five years ago, the property was purchased by John Rogers from a Mr. Botelho and used for training and breaking Arabian Horses. Murrel Lacey was his ranch manager and trainer for seven years. Mr. Lacey then leased the ranch and continued its operation for three years. He is well known in his field and for a time was the manager of Wayne Newton's horse ranches in the Las Vegas area. Murrel and his wife, Randi, have a home on the premises.

In August 1975, Herb Biddulph and his wife, Margaret, of Las Vegas, purchased just under 170 acres in three different parcels from Rogers, who moved to Washington. Included in the purchase were the three homes, several barns and the enclosed arena.

The Lacey's Arabian Center is a corporation formed by Biddulph and Lacey and will continue to breed and train Arabian horses. They have an active apprentice program with four participants. They sponsor an annual horse auction at the Center as well as a Junior 4-H Auction. Requirement to participate is that the young horse bidders be members of 4-H, Future Farmers, or some other youth organization interested in horses.

In the spring of 1977 the Biddulphs were building their eight-room ranch style home against a hillside overlooking the working part of the Center. Tom Mayes is the builder, Paul Zimmerman the architect.

The former Ventura house is now used by those in the apprentice program. The former Nunes home is occupied by the Biddulph's daughter and husband, Markey and Coury Pontrelli, who expect a child in July 1977.

In March 1977, I was invited to visit the Center by Lorraine Soltau of Danville. Jennifer Jones and I looked over the operation, met Murrel Lacey, and talked with some of the apprentices. The following is excerpted from a copy of the original deed given to me by Mr. Biddulph with his permission to use. Terminologies of measurements are interesting; I share it with you: Property Deed in book 37/38, signed by C. Ed. Miller, County Recorder and J. M. Stow, Notary Public, recorded at the request of James Foster, July 24, 1879 at 11 minutes past 11 a.m. Deed between

Antone V. Pacheco of Contra Costa County and the state of California and Antone Guera, for $800 in gold coins, parcel of land, bounded and particularly described as follows: to wit Commencing at corner to Sections 5, 6, 7 & 8 Township One, Smith Range on West, thence 88⁰ 2' east on line between sections 5-18, 28, 50, to Station marker G.P. north, 18' east 26, 82 thence to Station marked G.P. No. 2, thence North 78'9' west, var. 16'42' east 28.75 to Station. Thence south 31.56 to point of beginning containing 69¾ acres. Receiving the right of a private roadway across the above tract from the east line of said tract to east line of lands belonging to Jo. Alameda.

In regard to the Marengo place, portions from an original legal document were in the library show. Angiolina Marengo died in March 1910. At that time her daughter Annie was fourteen years old, Mary was about nine, and Stella was seven, all residing in Alamo. Following Angiolina's death, the Appraisers of the estate named by Superior Court of the County of Contra Costa were Frank Trevitts, A. L. Stone and August Humburg.

It has come to my attention that a C. P. Borlandelli, grandson of James and Angiolina Marengo, has a copy of the original deed dated 1883. He said James Claude Marengo first worked in the coal mines at Sommerville and Nortonville as a powder man. He continued his work of drilling and operating in the mines up to prohibition.

DANVILLE RAILROAD STATION
SOUTHERN PACIFIC DEPOT
DANVILLE, CALIFORNIA
355 Railroad Avenue

By spring of 1891 the railroad tracks were all laid and the railroad had come to Danville. The two-story Southern Pacific Depot was finished and business was booming! All Southern Pacific stations are built according to company plan and follow much the same design, structure and color. Danville's was no exception, but it was an attractive addition and it brought business to the town. It was a very busy place, and of great interest to the townsfolk who enjoyed its usefulness and recognized its necessity.

The first station agent was a Frenchman named Montague. He was followed by Seward Higley, who, with his wife Jessie, was well experienced as they had served somewhere in the east. They

Southern Pacific Depot in Danville.

came to take up duties in Danville in 1917 or 1918. Jessie had learned telegraphy and helped her husband at the station. When they arrived, the station was in need of housecleaning and the apartment on the second story was in deplorable shape. Jessie, who was naturally artistic, took the task well in hand. However, one obstacle was that colors designated by the company were to be used and no others. Jessie, an outgoing likeable person, discussed the issue with the painter who had arrived with the standard paint—brushes ready to go. He must have been a very understanding man, realizing her talents to make the apartment an attractive and better place to live. His comment to Jessie may have been something like this, "I'm going to town for lunch. Whatever you do to the paint while I'm gone will be your business. When I return I'm hired to paint!" Those who visited the Higleys in their apartment have said how attractive it always was. They were there about ten years when Seward Higley became ill and was taken to the Southern Pacific Hospital in San Francisco, where he died. She left Danville and later remarried and lived in Hayward, where she passed away some years ago. Hazel Wiester of Danville was a close friend of Jessie.

In those days and for many years, shipping by train was a big business and all kinds of grains and fruits, as well as other items, were shipped in that manner. Hazel Wiester remembers the wonderful cherries from orchards at Alamo that were shipped.

The last station agent was Mr. Jacobson, known as "Jiggs." He came in the late 1920s and is remembered by many.

In between times the apartment was rented by other people not affiliated with the railroad.

Joseph J. Ramos (deceased), a native of Danville, born in Tassajara in 1886, bought the railroad station in 1950 and it became Danville Feed and Supply. It remains today as Danville Feed and Garden Supply and is owned and managed by his son, Joseph B. Ramos. Joseph J. and his wife raised two daughters, twins Louise and Lucille (both deceased), and four sons, Wilfred (deceased), Eldred, Joseph B., and Donnie (deceased), all born in Gustine, California except Donnie, who was born in San Ramon. The Ramos children attended San Ramon school while they lived on Thorup Lane. Later, when they lived on Prospect Street, they transferred to Danville schools and graduated from San Ramon Valley Union High School.

Eldred Ramos lives in Palm Springs and is married to Margery Graham. They have four sons. Joe Ramos lives with his wife, Dorothy, in Danville. He has a son, Michael, who works in the local business.

Note: I have researched the following extensively and hope that proper dates will be applied and used in the future.

HISTORY OF DANVILLE HOTEL

Sometime in 1858, the *original* Danville Hotel (Hostelry) was built at the junction of the then County Road (now Front Street) and Tassajara Road (now Diablo Road), near a street some say was then called Post Street. (This site is possibly where the Mobil Service Station now stands.) The hotel was operated by Henry W. Harris, who was also Danville's first postmaster. Fifteen years later, on July 9, 1873, the building was *completely devoured* by fire and was gone and no more. (finis)

126

RAILROAD HOTEL

Eighteen years later, in 1891, the Railroad Hotel was built on Railroad Avenue and Short Street, facing west. It faced the Southern Pacific tracks to the west, when the Southern Pacific extended its line to Danville and San Ramon. It was used mainly for the convenience of the railroad men and some transients. The site is now part of the parking area for the new Danville Hotel Restaurant and Saloon.

The two-story building was designed with the simple architectural lines of that day and always painted a clear white. It had four double hung windows across the front on the upper floor and two windows and two doorways below (see photo). For many years it was operated by Mr. and Mrs. Edward McCauley and their two daughters, Mollie and Nellie, known as "the McCauley sisters." The mother did the cooking and was a very good cook and an exceptional baker. Mollie (who never married) and Nellie served the meals in the downstairs large dining room which had the stove that heated the entire building. There was, of course, a wood cook stove in the kitchen.

The Railroad Hotel was later renamed the Danville Hotel. An attractive railed veranda was added across the front and down its south side on the upper story, and two more posts were added to its original five supports downstairs. The saloon on its southeast corner had its own entry door and at one time was run by Manuel Rose.

As newlyweds Ed and Hazel Wiester[1] lived in the upstairs front room (left side) of the Danville Hotel, from November 1912 to March 1913. Hazel remembers that Mrs. McCauley's cranberry pie was delicious. She further remembers there was no heat upstairs and a very long hall to the one and only bathroom, which was shared by all! At one time there was a blind woman entertainer who also lived at the hotel. She would entertain in the Grange Hall. Her talents were not remembered by Mrs. Wiester.

Sometime thereafter, about 1927-28, when Hartz Avenue became the main thoroughfare, the Danville Hotel was moved and completely turned around to face Hartz Avenue. (This is the present site of part of the Danville Hotel Complex shops.) It was still operated by the McCauley family. (I'm told their former home is still on the corner of Hartz and Short.)

From my own personal recollections, from May 1937 onward, I can remember that the Danville Hotel was successfully operated by a German chef named Paul Zeibig of San Francisco. He took great delight in always wearing his chef's hat as he strolled up and down Danville's "main drag." He earned national acclaim via Duncan Hines, which recommended good places to eat across the nation. A sign given to him which stated this acclamation was attached to the side of the building. Most of his waiters also came from San Francisco, and his trade came from all over the Bay Area. It is said he often gave dinners by invitation. I can remember that his was the first establishment where I experienced finding an assortment of salads from which to choose. When the war came, with gasoline rationing, his trade began to dwindle and the local population was not large enough for him to continue to serve his epicurian meals. My husband remembers an incident when a cherry jubilee dessert caused a fire. Ruth Martin of Alamo Oaks told me he was a chef on the *Matsonia* in 1960—when they took the steamer to the Hawaiian Islands.

Russel Glenn learned his restaurant business experience when he was a sales manager for Duchess Inc. of Oakland. They also did catering. In 1952 Glenn became the owner of the then rundown Danville Hotel[2]. The building known as the Danville Hotel was then sixty-one years old. (Some sources and newspaper clippings, also an Historical Society publication, erroneously said it was 108 years old! No way!) Glenn redecorated the building, painted it bright red with white trim, and added his collection of antiques and gold rush memorabilia. He built a "Ghost Town Patio" with an outdoor atmosphere reminiscent of Virginia City. The newly constructed Ghost Town, all facades (store fronts), included a Wells Fargo Bank, Chinese laundry, jailhouse, barbershop and others. On balmy evenings it was enjoyable to be served dinner out-of-doors and then look at "the sights!" It was a tourist attraction and a place to take out-of-town guests.

Diablo Decorama (RA), sponsored by the Mary Doyle Unit of Mount Diablo Rehabilitation Center (RA), was held October 1 through 11th, 1959, at the hotel. Ten professional decorators (two were local) showed their talents by decorating upstairs rooms. It was then that the upper level was renovated and an attractive apartment included for Glenn's private use, built by Danville builder Vern S. Ryan.

Glenn sold the business in 1962 and planned an indefinite cruise of the Caribbean with his family.

The four businessmen who purchased it removed the Ghost Town patio to make way for a motel which never materialized and after about four months they went through bankruptcy and Glenn again assumed ownership.

Over the years he bought up the block on which the hotel sat, bounded by South Hartz Avenue, Short Street, Railroad Avenue and Prospect Avenue. This included a number of frontier-style small shops, which he added to his tourist attractions. He added a red and white striped covered wagon entrance to the Danville Hotel Restaurant and Bar. Over the years several piano players and different types of pianos were featured and toward the end a piano bar was popular with patrons.

In 1965 Glenn added the Danville Hotel's Silver Dollar banquet room to accommodate 295 people. It was built at the back on Railroad Avenue and faced the railroad tracks. Once again he commissioned builder Ryan for the job, assisted by several local sub-contractors. The Silver Dollar Room was controversial—there were those who liked it very much and those who disliked it very much, because of its "carnival appearance!" But it did attract attention and the building has often been used as a background in publicity. The Silver Dollar Room was designed by Leon Ericksen, owner Glenn, and a crew of two set designers from independent studios in Hollywood, Al Locatelli and Ernest VandeBovenkamp (originally from Holland). VandeBovenkamp came to Canada at seventeen years of age and worked for a Dutch construction company. He entered the U.S.A. in 1962 when he had learned to speak English. Open House for the Silver Dollar Room was June 23, 1965 and of course the Joneses were there!

The old spiral staircase, visible on the north side of the Danville Hotel, was once in service at the old Union Bank in Oakland. After fifty years the bank was demolished and Glenn brought the staircase to Danville.

In mid-1976 the eighty-five-year old Danville Hotel building and complex were purchased by Jerry E. Carter[3], a Danville resident. He remodeled the entire complex, with its many specialty shops to represent the late 1800s, which was the buildings' true era. Carter, with two experienced restaurant men, Jack Barnette and Larry Moblad[4], and Marvin A. Bamburg of San Jose as the architect, designed the Danville Hotel Restaurant and Saloon. It represents an early California hotel

The Danville Hotel, built in 1891 at the corner of Railroad Avenue and Short Street, was turned to face Hartz Avenue in about 1927. It is now part of the Danville Hotel Territory.

with elegance and a touch of class! The restaurant has three dining rooms, each decorated with attractive antiques, light fixtures, and lace curtains as well as draperies. Cheerful fireplaces have been added. Thompson Floor Company on Hartz Avenue imported from Belgium the floral patterned Axminister carpeting representing the period of the late 1800s. Many furniture pieces are authentic antiques, including some light fixtures, the organ, sideboards, and the china cupboard. Nemanic Upholstery & Draperies, Alamo, upholstered the antique furniture and booths and did the drapes. Aileen Carter, the owner's wife, did all the interior decorating. She has a natural flair.

The head chef is John Parsons. The menu, with its varied specialties and unique titles, is representative of early California foods. Some menu specialties are the Big "S.O.B." (slab of beef), "Swinging Door Specials," which include meats, seafood and Mexican fare, and a special children's menu called "Little Miners."

The Danville Hotel Restaurant and Saloon uses 155 South Hartz Avenue as its address. It was open to the public for business December 3, 1976, but closed for Sunday December 5, 1976, when a benefit opening was sponsored by the Contra Costa Lawyers' Wives. Its trademark is a pair of swinging doors. It is on the general site of the 1891 hotel, perhaps less than 100 feet from that building.

The San Ramon Valley Historical Society, at their February 3, 1977 Annual Meeting, voted the

Danville Hotel, now known as the Danville Hotel Territory, to be designated as one of San Ramon Valley's landmarks. A plaque dedication spon-sponsored by that group will be held on November 19, 1977.

Reconstruction and remodeling of the second story of the 1891 Danville Hotel building, to add more office space and to accommodate a private office for Carter, are being done now.

MOUNTAIN VIEW HOTEL

It is said that J. H. Gernant and his wife opened a twelve-room hotel on August 1, 1891, and named it Mountain View Hotel. It was located at the southwest corner of Hartz Avenue and School Street, Danville (present site of the three-story Balford Building).

In the very early 1900s Ella Elliott (Mrs. Charles) Gust operated the Mountain View Hotel. During the historic 1906 earthquake and fire she housed some "refugees" from San Francisco. Research tells us that for a time it was used as a private residence and one family who lived there were the Andreasens. After the war a Freitas ran a boarding house there.

Stephen Johnson operated a tea room with lovely antiques and I believe it was he who named it the Carriage House. I recall it was very attractive and well done. Adkins opened it as a furniture store featuring maple furnishings and continued the Carriage House name. He operated it until 1960 when it was razed.

Like so many of the old, oldtime buildings, it once served as a stagecoach stop.

In more modern times, a group of local men erected Danville's "skyscraper", a three-story building named Danreco Building, and opened it for office space and business rentals. Its claim to fame was that it contained Danville's first office elevator! The building is a box-shape and many thought it ugly. In more recent years it has had new ownership, and in 1975-76 was renamed Balford Building. It continues to house several local businesses.

169 FRONT STREET, DANVILLE

I have been researching this building for some time and finally feel that my information is correct, following an April 1977 interview with Isabel (Vecki) Myers of San Francisco, one time resident.

The two-story building at 169 Front Street, Danville, was built by the Howard Brothers, perhaps as early as 1866. They used lumber which went around the Horn. In its history the building has been used for many things. It was built for the Michael Cohen family (pronounced Con), who had a general store on the same street. It was a large family and they lived there several years while the children were growing up. One of the daughters, Linnie, married George Wiley, who was the ranch manager of Dan and Seth Cook's ranch at Diablo. Later he became county treasurer. M. Cohen may have sold in about 1888.

At one time the building was the private home of John P. Chrisman, who later sold it to Dr. Victor John Vecki and his wife Claire, who moved there in the early 1900s. They had a daughter, Isabel, and son, Victor Jan, who attended local schools and graduated from San Ramon Valley Union High School. Dr. Vecki was a dentist, a graduate of Physicians and Surgeons of San Francisco. He practiced for a short while in Oakland.

One day while the Veckis were visiting at the Danville Hotel, someone complained of a bad toothache and Dr. Vecki gave assistance, where-upon their good friend John Van Gorden said why not practice here in Danville. So he purchased a barber's chair and set up offices in his home at 169 Front Street, where he practiced for many years. I've been told by some of his former patients still living in the area that they still have his fillings in their teeth.

The Vecki property on Front Street extended to the corner, which was Tiger Alley (later

This photo of the Vecki home at 169 Front Street, Danville, was taken in about 1910. The house was built in about 1866 by Howard Brothers. Lumber used was "bridge" lumber which came around the Horn. (They say "no termites" ever!) In the photo, left to right, are Mary N. Allen (Mrs. Vecki's mother), Claire Vecki, Dr. Victor John Vecki, and his mother, Isabel Vecki. The children are Victor Jan and Isabel.

Prospect Avenue) and down to Hartz and included a large almond orchard, fruit orchard and garden areas.

The longtime rumor that motion pictures were filmed in Danville, particularly "Rebecca of Sunnybrook Farm," starring Mary Pickford, is untrue. It, like several others, was filmed in Pleasanton, California. Many movies, mostly westerns, were filmed in Niles, California, including Charlie Chaplin's famous "The Tramp." The early movie, "Once to Every Woman," starring Dorothy Phillips and directed by her husband, Alan Holubar, *was* filmed in Danville. The movie company asked the Veckis' permission to take pictures of the exterior of their attractive home and soon the Vecki family found the cameramen filming inside as well. The Vecki children and other neighborhood children were also used in the film.

The Veckis sold the property in the late 1930s and moved to Walnut Creek, where they built a new home on Almond Avenue and Dr. Vecki continued his dental practice in the Acree Building.

I have been told that a Manual Brown owned the building at 169 Front Street for a time, and that it was he who covered the wooden structure (which was board and batts) with stucco and removed some of the ornate Victorian "gingerbread" trim (see photo). While William E. and Lucile Nickerson owned the building, they rented it to the Pentecostal Church, and singing and sounds could often be heard by neighbors and passersby. Henry and Charlotte Neidenbach and their children lived there for a time, I was told.

In more recent years the building was leased by Jimmy Styles (deceased), Gertrud Stockton, and Maureen Oestreich, who bought the building with the hopes of having an Art and Design Center where all three could have their talents under one roof. The plan never quite materialized. In 1961 Bill Hockins and Maureen Oestreich bought the building. Current owners are Bob and Sunny Read, who purchased the building in March of 1971. The main building has nine rooms and two bathrooms. On the south side of the building toward the back is a separate building, "Mark Coiffures," operated by Corrina Willet. Tenants in the main building are Rick Barry and Associates, "Top of the Line" Club, Insurance by Hockins, Petersen Associates, construction development consultants, and Sunny Read Realtor, managed by Louise Bisset.

On April 13, 1977 Dr. Wilson E. Close and I, representing the San Ramon Valley Historical Society, and to gather material for this book, were invited to visit Isabel (Vecki) Myers and her husband Clarence in their St. Francis Wood home in San Francisco. We had a very pleasant conversation, reminiscing for several hours, followed by a delightful luncheon and a tour of their lovely home of ten years. Isabel mentioned that she had her dancing and piano studio at the 169 Front Street house at one time, and Wilson remembered that he had been one of her piano pupils.

Isabel was interested in the theatre and in 1932 played in Los Angeles in the Greek classic, "Lysistrata[5]," starring Nance O'Neill. In June 1936 she was the leading lady with a Honolulu Stock Company and many times was the leading lady at the Alcazar Theatre. She played the ingenue, Christianne, to actress Nance O'Neill in David Belascy's play "The Lily." Mr. Hickman, Nance O'Neill's husband, played the father. She also had a part in John Colton's "Lusitania Night." "The Lily" also ran on radio. She showed us some of her publicity photos and articles in leading magazines, including *Radio Stars*, March 1936, when she was a member of the NBC radio acting staff. She met her husband, Clarence Myers, in radio. He was in newscasting and went to England with the OWI. He was also with *Call Bulletin* for Hearst. In the meantime Isabel took up ballroom dancing and, with dance partners, toured the northwest and other areas. Clarence Myers' uncle, Edmond Wunsch, lived in the area of Round Hill Country Club for eighteen years. He owned an acreage with a large home, barn and a second house which he recently sold. He is ninety-three years old.

Isabel has remained active in theatrical interests. She has been president of San Francisco Musical Club and St. Francis Wood Club. Just a few years ago an entertainment was given at the old 365 Club and she performed the Viennese waltz with a dance partner. She remains active on many cultural committees. Her mother, Claire Vecki, passed away in about 1968 in San Francisco. Her brother Victor, who was a City Clerk of Walnut Creek for many years, is married to Charlotte Doud of the Carmel-Monterey area and lives in Pebble Beach, California. He was in real estate until his open heart surgery.

I was told years back by another source that

"the drummers" came to 169 Front Street, usually from San Francisco or Sacramento, to sell their varied wares to the local townsfolk. They arrived with their suitcases and stayed for the weekend of their sales in the house. One could often see them rocking on the chairs which were lined up on the front porch.

Another movie star who has owned property in San Ramon Valley is Marjorie Rambeau, who had a ranch where Pariaso is now (Herman Tiessling development). The actress and her mother had a house south of town, later owned by Mrs. Ferdinand Hansen. Mrs. Rambeau "did" some of the building, I read. Bing Crosby has also owned property in San Ramon and may still.

SAN RAMON VALLEY BANK

The following is from the *Walnut Kernel*, Walnut Creek, California, August 1957.

Joseph L. Silveira started the first Walnut Creek bank in his general merchandise store in 1906 (corner of Main Street and Mt. Diablo Boulevard, Walnut Creek). On June 28, 1907, the San Ramon Valley Bank was organized and on that date the private Silveira bank was incorporated into the new bank. Some of its officers during the first few years were Captain John Hackett, president; A. H. Cope, vice-president; Arthur Burton, second vice-president; Joseph L. Silveira, cashier and manager; R. O. Baldwin, president; N. S. Boone, first vice-president. Among early directors were Ralph Harrison, S. P. Borger, W. K. Cole, Charles G. Goold, and F. V. Wood. Branch offices were begun in Danville in 1907 and in Concord in 1912.

From the Bank of America, Archives #3218, San Francisco Headquarters, I received the following:

Book of by-laws of the San Ramon Valley Bank, adopted June 29, 1907, amended July 6, 1914, indicates this bank was incorporated in Walnut Creek on June 28, 1907. Article IV, Section 4 of the by-laws gives the bank's directors power to establish a branch at Danville "when they deem it advisable." The Minute Book and Journal of Meetings of Directors and Stockholders of the San Ramon Valley Bank indicates that an application to establish a branch at Danville was procured August 3, 1907. The Annual Report of the Superintendent of Banks of the State of California, dated October 31, 1910, indicates that the San Ramon Valley Bank, Danville Branch was incorporated December 20, 1905.

The first president of the San Ramon Valley Bank was J. L. Silveira. He was succeeded as follows: Captain John Hackett, 1907; A. H. Cope, 1908-1913; N. S. Boone, 1913-1922; B. G. Ensign, 1922-1924; and C. R. Leech, 1924-27. The minute book indicates a Mr. James C. Jones of Alamo was elected a director on August 8, 1923 and served as such until the bank was purchased by Liberty Bank of America on February 8, 1927. On February 19, 1927, the Libery Bank of America was purchased by the Bank of Italy.

The 1977 San Ramon Valley Directory lists six banks, and there are at least three more, and it lists five Savings and Loan Associations.

The San Ramon Valley Bank, Danville branch, at the corner of Hartz Avenue and Tiger Alley (now Prospect Avenue, before any additions.

This photo shows the Freitas and Peters Store. Building was wrecked in 1959.

The Peterson Ranch (Blackhawk Ranch) in May 1977. (Photo by Bill Ketsdever, editor of *Valley Pioneer*)

BLACKHAWK RANCH

Blackhawk Ranch was started by Easton & Ward in 1916. Ansel M. Easton, prominent Bay Area resident, purchased 1,250 acres of land near Mount Diablo and named it Blackhawk Ranch. A part of the ranch was situated on the southern slopes of historic Mount Diablo. At various times geological discoveries have been made there including bones of prehistoric animals.

Easton and his son-in-law, William A. Ward, and their wives, both named Louise[6], settled there. (See Chapter Five, Clubs and Organizations, China Club). A fifteen-room house, nestled in the hillside, was built in 1916. It was stucco of Spanish style and U-shaped, and had a tower room above one of the entries. The shingled roof was replaced in about 1927 with flat tiles. The

architect was the well-known Bernard Maybeck of Berkeley. Midway through construction it burned down, but was immediately rebuilt and completed by 1918. It had many fireplaces (see photos) and eight bathrooms. It included a large servants' wing for the cook, the butler (Walter Wallis), maids, the chauffeur (first Wilmar Strout and later Charles Roberts), and several gardeners. Ranch manager was Edward Lovell.[7] There was a partial basement for Mr. Easton's woodshop. The house was surrounded with magnificent gardens, courtyards and fountains.

The Eastons made many trips to the Orient and had a wonderful collection of porcelain, brass, ivory, wall hangings, and carved and silk screens, making it an interesting home, according to their granddaughter Betty Ward, now Mrs. A. K.

132

Goodmundson of Oakland. She remembers that her grandmother did not like the stucco exterior so had trellises with vines to cover it.

Easton & Ward spared no expense or effort in building their stock of the world's greatest Shorthorn breeders. They imported the finest of purebred cattle and prize-winning Shire horses. A huge and costly horse barn was built. It was also used for display showing of their stock. Other ranch buildings were elected (see photo) and some 160 acres were planted in walnut orchards. Nature's wild life roamed about.

From 1920 to 1930, Blackhawk Ranch became world famous as breeders of purebred Shorthorn cattle and prize Shire horses. It was said to be the finest world-wide. Top honor winners at the American, International, and shows everywhere, Easton & Ward took more prizes than any other breeder had ever won in a single year! Cattlemen from all over the world came to the Blackhawk to witness the prize showings. Among prize winners were the imported "Collynie Price Lavender," Shorthorn champion, and "Blackhawk Chessie," champion Shire mare, both winners of many awards.

In 1934 Easton sold the Blackhawk holdings to Raymond C. Force, retired president of Caterpillar Tractor Company of San Leandro. He operated a prize Arabian horse ranch called Rising Sun Ranch at Livingston. Force moved his Arabian horse activities to the Blackhawk. When he later started his huge Hereford cattle operation, he sold his Arabian horses. He also purchased several adjoining ranch properties from the Freitas, Souza, Frick and Goold families, and his acreage was increased from the original 1,250 to 6,500 acres.[8]

The Force family resided in Piedmont, California from 1934 to 1941, using the Diablo estate (Blackhawk) as a summer house. In 1941 they moved to Blackhawk. Upon the death of Al Hauschildt, ranch manager, in 1940, Force hired the well-experienced Lorens Foard as manager of the ranch. Additional improvements, including miles of roadway, a walnut dehydrator, stock ponds, pens and more buildings, plus a swimming pool and cabana area, were added. Anchor wire fences were installed to keep out the deer. While there, they remodeled and the style of the home became French, with the interior in French Provincial furnishing. (Two sources told me that Force shingled the exterior and remembered it

that way, although most people I interviewed claimed that it remained stucco, as it is today.) Leslie H. "Les" Kerns was in charge of tending the seven acres of landscaped gardens which surrounded the home, watered by springs from the canyon.

In 1951 Raymond C. Force passed away and his widow Florence was in charge. In 1956 she sold to Castle & Cooke Ltd.[9] and Helemano Company Ltd. of Honolulu. She returned to Piedmont.

In 1957, under Lorens[10], there were about 1,000 head of Hereford cattle and 500 acres planted in hay and grain for the livestock. The large walnut orchard of 160 acres was considered among the best producers in Contra Costa County. Over the years, Blackhawk Ranch has brought much fame to the county.

(Author: This next seven year period I have been unable to research for you.)

In 1964 G. Howard Peterson[11], of Peterson Tractor of San Leandro, bought the ranch from Castle & Cooke. He had been interested in it before they purchased it from the heirs of Raymond Force. Nelson Wright of Geldermann Realtors had the listing and Bill Flett closed the sale. The large home and the grounds were run down. Peterson brought in Easy Bay water to supplement the supply available. He did extensive remodeling. He added overhangs and a heavy shake roof, replaced all the windows (which were small casement—see photos) and added many more, replaced all doors to eight-foot size throughout, including a beautiful carved pair. He lowered some ceilings and changed the entry, extending it and using rock on the exterior. He enlarged the master bedroom wing and altered and improved many areas, creating a 9,000-square foot house. The maids' quarters were made into a three-car garage with automatic door. The main fireplace, which was specially hand carved forty years ago in marble, has been used in three homes of the Petersons. It is presently in their Round Hill, Alamo, home on Joseph Lane.

Peterson and his wife Marion made extensive improvements in the huge garden areas. Hedges and fences were removed in some areas to open up and make the rear garden one large sweeping lawn with an enormous flagstone patio. Four large European plane trees had been planted on the square by Easton. Peterson removed one pair so the beautiful rock waterfall could be enjoyed.

Fifteen-room Easton-Ward residence under construction in 1916. Men at left may be Mr. Easton and Mr. Ward. (Courtesy Betty Ward Goodmundson, granddaughter of Easton and daughter of Ward)

Easton-Ward residence in 1919, showing other entrance under flag pole below Tower Room at right. Possibly Ansel Easton in foreground. Note old-fashioned touring car at extreme right of photo, in front of servants' wing. (Courtesy Betty Ward Goodmundson)

Blackhawk Ranch, Easton-Ward home, in 1925. Note roads, driveways, garden areas and landscaping. (Courtesy Betty Ward Goodmundson of Oakland)

Early photo of Blackhawk. Shows the courtyard which led to the main entrance and the tower room at right rear. Note all the chimneys. (Courtesy G. Howard Peterson, Alamo)

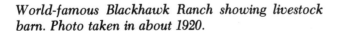

World-famous Blackhawk Ranch showing livestock barn. Photo taken in about 1920.

To the huge sycamore trees, several along the creek, and some older pines and eucalyptus, the Petersons added many more trees and shrubs in the eight-acre garden areas. Huge beds of rhododendrons, azaleas, camellias, and ferns, outlined in some places by redwood trees, were planted. The original pergola with its four posts was reconstructed, with trellis and benches added. A bridge was built with huge garden plantings on each side. The rose garden is uniquely terraced and watered by a sprinkler system with its heads set for each to cover four roses at the proper height, not to water overhead.

Howard and Marion Peterson graciously took my husband and me on a complete tour of the heavenly gardens and the home, with a garden view from every window, on an evening in May 1977—truly a "Garden Show." My husband questioned the zig-zag paths visible on the hillside. Mr. Peterson explained they were put in by Chinese labor as paths for riding or climbing, with distance markers. My husband tells that when he was a small boy visiting Blackhawk with his father, he became interested in a small drop calf, whereupon Mr. Ward made him a present of it and he manually lifted it up and placed it in the Chrysler phaeton touring car of the Joneses. When it was grown my husband sold it for about $17. He then thought he would go into the cattle business when he grew up, as he was given the calf, was supplied the feed at Rancho-Romero, and was able to keep the money upon the sale. Not bad!

In the mid-1970s Peterson sold to Blackhawk Development Company, retaining 300 acres at Blackhawk, including the house and surrounding gardens, where they resided until 1976. Blackhawk Development Co., with Robert Carrau as president, and Wayne Hawkins and Bill Morse, had hoped to do a 4,000-lot planned unit development. In early spring, 1975, there was a turnover of management and Owen C. Schwaderer was made president with Stephen P. Beinke, vice-president, and Neil Stone project engineer. There will be 206 homesites in Phase One. Blackhawk properties has undergone several delays in its development, but construction is now going on and what was at one time the property of very few will in the future be homes for many. Progress always happens with growth and more people!

In May 1977 Peterson sold the remaining 300 acres with home and gardens to Dr. Daphne

Chisholm. Jim and Wendy Geldermann handled the real estate transaction. Dr. Chisholm will develop Renaissance West in Danville, a health and beauty spa. Nira Carol Pratt will be resident director.

TAO HOUSE

Tao House (RA), Corduroy Hills Ranch, sits high in the hills of the Las Trampas Range in Danville, thirty miles east of San Francisco (O'Neill's favorite city). Eugene O'Neill[12] and his wife, Carlotta Monterey (Hazel Neilson Tharsing), arrived in the Bay Area in December 1936. They were seeking their dream home and found the site for it facing majestic Mount Diablo. His Nobel Prize for Literature money, awarded him in 1936, enabled them to build Tao House. (He was the first American playwright to win the Nobel Prize.) They lived at Tao House longer than any other place, from 1937 to 1944. O'Neill has been quoted as saying "he liked Tao House best"—"really have an ideal home"—"pure country without the taint of suburbia"—"my final harbor." "Tao" means "the Way," and is pronounced "dow."

While at Tao House he wrote "Long Day's Journey into Night," "Hughie," "The Iceman Cometh," and his final play, "Moon for the Misbegotten," which won four Tony awards in 1974. His daughter, Oona Chaplin wrote, "My only conscious memories of my father are in that house, against the slopes of Mount Diablo, which I found very beautiful."

O'Neill's failing health and the lack of servants during the war forced them to move to a San Francisco hotel in 1944, where medical treatments were more readily available. The house and surrounding 160 acres were sold to Lieutenant Commander and Mrs. Arthur W. Carlson. They and their son Richard moved in August of 1944. Mr. Carlson was in the Coast Guard, with an office in San Francisco. He was very active in Republican politics. From 1939-43 he represented Piedmont in the State Assembly. When they moved to Danville, he was head of the Republican State Central Committee for two years. A native of Minnesota, he died March 29, 1953. Charlotte was married in August of 1954 to Hugh Guy Miller and they enjoyed Tao House at Corduroy Hills Ranch. They sold it in the spring of 1965 to Empire Realty Company (Japanese cartel). They defaulted and the Millers repossessed the property in March 1974. Miller, a

BARN

BARN

TAO HOUSE

SWIMMING POOL
& BATH HOUSE

CARETAKER'S
HOUSE

Tao House.

136

native of Wisconsin, passed away March 5, 1969.

During 1959-60 Charlotte was on the Republican State and County Central Committees and served as Precinct Chairman of Contra Costa County for two years. She married Stanley B. Gerdes, March 25, 1971 and they make their home on Crocker Avenue in Piedmont. Her paternal grandfather was I. H. Ham, a California pioneer who arrived in San Francisco in 1849. He was in the Commission business there several years, and later moved to Tulare (San Joaquin Valley), where he operated a flour mill and lumber mill. He built many of the town's buildings, several still standing. Charlotte's maternal grandfather was George H. Collins, who came to California and the San Francisco area at the close of the Civil War. He was in the lumber business in San Francisco all of his life. Charlotte and her mother were born in Oakland, her father in San Francisco.

Charlotte's son, Dick Carlson, attended Danville Grammar school and graduated from San Ramon Valley High School in 1953. He graduated from UC, Berkeley in 1957, spent five years in the Navy and earned his masters at California Business School. He has a real estate license and has been in that field. In 1969 he married Frances Mullane, daughter of Lieutenant Colonel and Mrs. Walter R. Mullane of Saratoga, California. They make their home in El Cerrito with their two young children, William Raleigh, called Bill, born June 13, 1975 and Catherine Elizabeth, born January 3, 1977. Dick presently is in his second year at Boalt Hall; apparently he wants to be an attorney. (He attended high school with my niece, Marilyn Jones. I can remember how well he played the piano.)

THE EUGENE O'NEILL FOUNDATION

To preserve Tao House, a small and dedicated group of San Ramon Valley and East Bay residents joined together in late 1974 to form the Eugene O'Neill Foundation. It was the successor to the original Eugene O'Neill National Historic Site Association, founded in 1968, spark-plugged by Thalia Brewer of Danville.

Other agencies which have been involved are the National Park Service, California Arts Council, State Parks Department, Contra Costa County and East Bay Regional Park District. In May of 1971, Tao House was placed in the National Register of Historic Places. In August of 1971 it was included on the list of United States land-

Carlotta and Eugene O'Neill at Tao House with slopes of Mt. Diablo in the background.

marks. Only two previous homes of persons in the field of literature have received that distinction from the U.S. Congress in its 200 years of history!

Following a membership drive, Foundation members held a major benefit in 1975 in Berkeley. Jason Robards and Jack Dodson donated their talents and time to produce "Hughie" in Berkeley and Los Angeles. A second benefit, in July 1976, was the outdoor production of "The Hairy Ape" by Hanover College Theatre players of Indiana, held at Tao House. This was a first!—an O'Neill performance at O'Neill's home.

Two years of concerted effort by the Foundation resulted in two major milestones in turning Tao House into a western center for the theatre arts. Assembly Bill AB4539 by Assemblyman Dan Boatwright and Senator John Nejedly was signed into law September 22, 1976, in Sacramento. On October 19, 1976 President Ford signed a bill in Washington, D.C. co-authored by Congressman George Miller and Senator Alan Cranston, designating Tao House a National Historic site. The state bill provides funds from the Collier Fund for acquisition. Federal funds will perpetuate it as a memorial to Eugene O'Neill in honor of American literature and drama.

With the cooperation of the State of California and the U.S. Department of Interior, Tao House will be the only place on the west coast that is a major center for theatre arts. The Eugene O'Neill Foundation boasts a "VIP" roster. It is probably the only world-wide organization with three knights as members—Sir Charles Chaplin, Sir Laurence Olivier and Sir Ralph Richardson. Other honorary members include: Colleen Dewhurst, Ingrid Bergman, Oona O'Neill Chaplin, Lynn Fontanne, Helen Hayes, Jack Lemmon, Alfred Lunt, Charlotte Morrison, William Penn Mott, Jr., Jason Robards, Louis Sheaffer, Elbert M. Vail, Richard C. Trudeau. In January 1977 actress Katharine Hepburn spent two hours at Tao House and was very enthusiastic. She was in San Francisco for her run of "A Matter of Gravity."

Officers of the Foundation are Darlene Blair, president; Thalia Brewer, first vice-president; Dyke Brown, second vice-president; Lois Sizoo, secretary; and H. L. Davisson, treasurer. The thirty directors are: the officers, Travis Bogard, Harry Campbell, Ann Cavanagh, John Esau, Sally Ewing (resigned spring 1977), Armand Gentile, Barney Gould, Jean Harris, John Hartwell, Marjorie Humphrey, Helen Kelly, Manfred Lindner, I. L. Leiber, Graham Moody, William Penn Mott, Jr., Hilda Perlowin, Charlotte Riddle, Cynthia Savell, Sandra Silberman, Randall Smith, Ray Stansbury, Elinor Stark, Dwight Steele, Norma Taylor, and Mildred Winslow.

On January 18, 1977, a letter addressed to the Board of Supervisors of Contra Costa County asked that they serve in a temporary supporting position in order to permit the appropriation of $255,000 from the Collier Park Preservation Fund for acquisition of Tao House and 13.9 acres. The Supervisors agreed that the county should act as a participating public agency for acquisition of the property.

People ask the Foundation, "Why do you care so much about saving that house?" Victor Hugo said in 1832, "Let us, while waiting for new monuments, preserve the ancient monuments." In O'Neill's own words: "I think that any life that merits living lies in the effort to realize some dream, and the higher that dream is the harder it is to realize."

Membership and contribution information at several support levels can be had by writing the Foundation at P.O. Box 402, Danville, California 94526.

Eastern facade, Tao House, 1974.

THE
Eugene O'Neill
FOUNDATION,
TAO HOUSE

POST OFFICE BOX 402
DANVILLE, CALIFORNIA 94526

Tao House.

138

OIL DRILLING IN DANVILLE JUNE 1963!

Here's another bit of San Ramon Valley history unknown to new residents and perhaps even somewhat difficult to accept:

The McColloch Oil Corporation of California leased oil rights on the property called Corduroy Hills on Las Trampas Ridge, owned by Charlotte and Hugh Miller. (She is now Mrs. Stanley B. Gerdes.) Richfield Oil Corporation purchased half of the lease. Equipment was taken up the dusty road beginning Friday, June 21, 1963. Drilling was started the early morning of Sunday, June 23. R. B. Montgomery Drilling Co. and Borst & Giddens of Ventura assisted McColloch. Over twenty sixty-foot rigs, each weighing 96,000 pounds, were used. At the 1500-foot level a huge oil derrick was erected almost overnight—all this on the property once owned by playwright Eugene O'Neill. Four five-man crews worked around the clock. Each day samples at various levels were sent to Richfield in Los Angeles for chemical and physical testing.

The first rig, the largest then owned by Mc-Colloch, stood 145 feet tall. L. D. Banderob was project foreman and a resident of Danville during the job. By Tuesday, after the installation on Sunday, the bore was down to 735 feet in an old sea bed, said to be twenty to thirty million years old. They expected to go 8000 feet.

One year later, in July 1964, a second attempt at oil discovery in the Danville hills of the Las Trampas Ridge was made by Phillips Petroleum Company. Their derrick was installed in Miller's meadow, up from Camille Avenue, near the Gordon Ball property. To residents below, for miles around, the towering framework, when lighted at night, looked like giant Christmas trees! It was truly an illuminated spectacle! I remember it well.

Some oil and natural gas were found, but not in commercial quantities. The work ceased and the wells were capped. The caps are still visible and have been spotted by hunters and hikers in the Las Trampas area, but the exciting adventure of oil discovery became history.

LONE PINE RANCH

Lone Pine Ranch at 2590 Stone Valley Road, up Lone Pine Lane, Danville, consisted of 175 acres with a house, large barn, windmill and beautiful large oak trees, when Leroy F. and Harriet (Hume) Krusi purchased it from realtor Frank Marshall of Walnut Creek in 1940. The Krusis were from Alameda. They used the home for weekends and their summer home. During the war years it became difficult to travel because of gas rationing and the blackout (RA), so they didn't come out as often. When building materials became available following the war, they built their present home—in about 1950. They have four children: his sons Leroy H. Krusi and George S. Krusi; their son, the Reverend Carlisle H. Krusi; and daughter Susie (Mrs. L. H.) Dyke, who lives in Arroyo Grande near San Luis Obispo.

It is said that years ago "Indian Joe" lived up in the canyon in a small house. He would go down into Alamo and "set up shop" and sell his eggs and chickens under an available tree on the roadside. One day years ago, he just didn't return home.

Lone Pine Ranch has long been so named for a large digger pine which fell down about five years ago. Part of its stump is used for a horse jump. The lower section was full of lead, apparently from target practice over the years. Lone Pine brand is still a registered brand.

An original house was built up in the canyon, possibly in the 1880s. Many parties were said to have been enjoyed there over the years. At one time there was a dairy farm and the cream separator house still remains. There is a large training arena and tack room. Horses roam the hillside. Over the hill was the Emmons Ranch of 640 acres (full section) and the original Twin Creeks Ranch of Robert Mulvany (deceased). The canyon goes into Green Valley Blind, which used to be called Stone Valley Road dead end. Mr. Krusi rides trail every Tuesday. Mrs. Krusi's hobby is playing golf.

The ranch foreman and his wife are Don and Lupe Saldana, who live in the former home. Fifteen-year-old Julie Munger, daughter of Maynard and Mary Munger of Orchard Court, Alamo, is one of the riders sponsored by Mr. Krusi. This season, 1977, is her sixth year of riding competively in races and trail riding. She has a large collection of trophies and awards. One hundred sixty acres east of Round Hill Country Club and north of the home have been green belted.

HUMPHREY'S ARENA

The Humphrey's Arena on Stone Valley Road, Danville, came into existence in August 1954, because of an International horseshoe champion! Whey Guy Zimmerman won the horseshoe pitching contest, community leaders, merchants and townsfolk in general wanted to honor him with a parade. All parades need horses! A group of horse-minded young people from the San Ramon Valley area wanted to participate. Ray McCoy (RA) (deceased) was selected to assist and prepare them, and became their drill master.

Twenty youngsters formed the Danville Junior Horsemen's Association. The name "Double D Riders" was taken from their home towns, Danville and Diablo. Under the banner of "DD Riders" they performed in many parades and county fairs and became an expert drill team.

Dave and Marjorie Humphrey, whose sons, Dave and Bill, were charter members, decided that the group needed a place for practice, riding lessons and horse shows. A portion of their ranch became headquarters for the Danville Junior Horsemen and the San Ramon Valley Horsemen's Association. The dedication took place on October 23, 1955, with volunteer labor. In the summer of 1976 the arena was rebuilt and spruced up for continued use.

The original twenty participants were Nancy Bigelow, Barbara Dean, Lee Ditzler, Diane Endsley, Loretta and Pat Foard, Bren Griffin, Diane Glines, Bill and Dave Humphrey, Barbara and Virginia Mitchell, Kathy Morrison, Mickey Nikolai, Martha Pasquale, Nancy Pond, Ann Richardson, Roth Rose, Tam Tison, and Dick Von Wald.

The land remains Humphrey property, but the arena is the responsibility of the riding club members. Danville Juniors has over 150 members, both boys and girls, between the ages of eight and eighteen.

Norman and Lois Sims of El Pintado Road have worked with the group since 1964 and remain the advisers. The following have served as president: 1964 Don Saulsberry, 1965 Maggi Freeman, 1966 Sharon MacDonald, 1967 Sue Gibbs, 1968 Kris Van Nuys, 1969 Jim Makepeace, 1970 Chris Ives, 1971 Teresa Cross, 1972 Teresa Cross, 1973 Scott Sims, 1974 Bob McCoy, 1975 Laura Kellejian, 1976 Pam Stark, 1977 Angie Sussman.

Trees have been planted to help screen the arena. Several were donated by members and friends. Plaques can be placed where desired by the donors.

SAN DAMIANO RETREAT

The Franciscan Fathers and Brothers have dedicated San Damiano Retreat House to the memory of San Damiano, a little old church near Assisi in Italy. St. Francis, beloved of God and

San Damiano Retreat House.

man, prayed there in silence when he was a young man.

The sixty acres of land was purchased on January 10, 1960, from Andrew Abrott. The real estate transaction was handled by Lou Frank of Castro Valley. Construction began in July 1960 by the Reardon Construction Company of San Francisco.

San Damiano Retreat rests 1,000 feet above San Ramon Valley, in Danville, on a wooded plateau, looking down upon the beauty of the Valley and across to Mount Diablo. The main structure is patterned after California mission styling, with tile roof, arched passageways, and verandas typical of Spanish architecture in beauty. All is surrounded by well-kept Spanish patio gardens offering quiet reflection and fruitful meditation. There are several fountains. The main one on the central patio takes its design from a Spanish colonial chalice. It reminds one of the days of the Dons. Benches are provided for restful thought, with views from any angle of pure joy and beauty, peace and quiet.

The first religious Superior of San Damiano was Fr. David Temple O.F.M. He continued until September 1976. The Friars first took residence on September 20, 1961. In 1977 the Superior is Fr. Michael Weishaar O.F.M. The staff consists of seven Friars, two priests, and five Brothers.

The purpose of the Retreat House is that anyone can go there to reflect and "retreat," away from home and the cares of everyday life. "Making a retreat" is becoming an everyday expression. San Damiano offers weekend retreats which begin Friday evening and continue to Sunday afternoon. They are planned for men, women or married couples.

San Damiano is a place where in meaningful silence you can encounter your God, and then go out to meet the challenges of today—with the changes you find are needed in your own heart.

Upper patio gardens of San Damiano Retreat, centered around a fountain and planted with citrus, palms, and other trees, and many flowers.

Silas Stone in 1853
(1792-1864)
Alamo Pioneer

SILAS STONE'S RESTAURANT

The Silas Stone's Restaurant opened on July 4, 1977, at 3168 Danville Boulevard in Alamo, not more than one mile from where the real Squire Silas Stone (RA) lived. He was an early day Alamo pioneer, who crossed the plains in 1853 and settled in Alamo. The restaurant, with 3,100 square feet, was designed and built by general contractor Tom Beck of Danville, who is the owner-manager.

It does not offer a full service of food, but specializes in soups and salads with homemade bread and desserts. Hours are 11:00 A.M. to 10:00 P.M. The decor is Early California, with photographs of the historical background of the area. The seating capacity for service is one hundred. The logo is the Silas Stone home which was on Stone Valley Road until October 1954, when it was torn down.

Tom Beck and his wife, Mardi, live on Danville Boulevard in Danville, near Nadine Place. She is the daughter of Dr. and Mrs. Dudley A. (Rosemary) Robnett, who make their home on Las Trampas Road, Alamo. Mardi attended local schools and graduated from San Ramon Valley High School.

You've heard of intuitiveness, E.S.P., mental telepathy—right? Well, call it what you will, but Tom Beck has had "that" feeling toward Squire Silas Stone. Sometimes we are drawn to someone and so it was natural for him to name his new restaurant Silas Stone's. Tom contacted several descendants of Silas Stone for the initial reaction and received the full "go-ahead." My personal opinion as an in-law is that Silas Stone would be proud to have a business establishment named for him and in keeping with historic Alamo.

1. Ed and Hazel Wiester purchased two acres on the southwest corner of Danville Boulevard where now are condominiums, near the Congregational Church and later bought an additional strip of land to straighten out the shape. They lived there from 1913 to 1961. Mr. Wiester passed away in 1963. Hazel moved to Esther Lane in 1961. She still lives there and is in her eighties.

2. I hostessed a surprise dual birthday dinner at the Danville Hotel in October 1955 for a party of four. Honorees were my Moms, Bertha Morris Boggini, a Libra, and my hubby, Alfred Bensen Jones, a Scorpio. Our total bill for four Porterhouse steak dinners, complete, including ten percent tip and tax, was $16.95! Following dinner we experienced quite a severe earthquake. The Danville Hotel suffered damage to the plate glass windows, and worst of all, the stock of liquor, behind metal grillwork, all broke and came waterfalling down all over the floors and in the walking area.

3. Jerry E. Carter, with his wife Aileen and three daughters, Le Ann, Cathleen and Donna, who all attended local schools and graduated from San Ramon Valley High School, were early residents of Greenbrook, moving to their Harlan Drive home in 1965. They also own the Clothes Barn, women's and girls' clothing chain.

4. Jack Barnette was raised and schooled in Martinez, now makes his home in Danville. Larry Moblad was raised in the Los Altos area and currently lives in neighboring Walnut Creek.

5. On the Opinion Page (letters to the editor) of the *Contra Costa Times*, Friday, March 25, 1977 was an interesting letter from Kendric R. French of Walnut Creek — "Aristophanes, whose 'Lysistrata' recently played in Walnut Creek, was once a culprit in the eyes of the Los Angeles Police Department. In the early Thirties, 'Lysistrata' was produced by a troupe of West Hollywood amateurs. There was a police raid. After arresting the players, the police lieutenant asked, 'Who was the playwright?' The answer, 'A Greek, by the name of Aristophanes.' 'A Greek guy? We'll go out and pinch him too!'" When I mentioned this to Isabel (Vecki) Myers, she remembered it well.

6. The following is a newspaper obituary: (no date) "Rites Tomorrow for Mrs. Easton—Services to Be Held At San Mateo. Services will be held at 3 p.m. in St. Matthew's Episcopal Church, San Mateo, for Mrs. Louise Adams Easton, widow of Ansel Mills Easton. Mrs. Easton died Saturday at the Ross home of her son, Laurence. She was 88.

Cremation will be at Cypress Lawn. Her husband owned much valuable Market Street property and also considerable land in northern San Mateo county. He founded the town of Easton, now a part of Burlingame's Broadway sector.

For many years they lived on a 1200-acre stock ranch on the slopes of Mount Diablo. Mr. Easton died in 1941.

Mrs. Easton's father, too, was a big Penninsula landowner and at one time held much of the Menlo Park area.

In addition to her son, Mrs. Easton leaves a daughter, Mrs. William A. Ward, of Angel's Camp, four grandchildren and three great-grandchildren."

7. Edward Lovell's daughter Laverne married Walter Wallis' brother, known as "Em" Wallis, who worked at Blackhawk Ranch. They are residents of Pleasanton. Walter Wallis and his wife, Margaret, who had a daughter Mary, at one time, in about 1939, operated a restaurant which later became Root's Bar in Danville. They then went to San Simeon.

8. As a point of interest, during the early 1860s land in Sycamore Valley sold for about $1.25 per acre. Within a ten-year period the price rose to about $10.00 per acre. Inflation!

9. A newspaper article from the *Oakland Tribune*, Contra Costa section, April 6, 1956, says "Danville Ranch Bought—Black Hawk Site Purchased by Honolulu Firm. The 6,556-acre Black Hawk Ranch, a well known stock farm, was sold today for $1,250,000 to Castle & Cooke Ltd., of Honolulu.

"The transaction was announced by John E. Morris, Oakland real estate man, and A. G. Budge, president of Castle & Cooke. The ranch was purchased from the family of the late Raymond C. Force, former president of the Caterpillar Tractor Co., who had owned the ranch since 1934.

"Budge said the property probably will be operated by a subsidiary Hawaiian company, but for a time operations will continue under the present management. Two-thirds of the area is in use as ranch and crop land, and about 1,000 head of Hereford cattle are ranged there. Walnut orchards occupy 134 acres and a 25-acre game preserve including two lakes is maintained adjacent to Mount Diablo State Park.

Eventually part of the ranch land—perhaps, 2,000—acres—will be subdivided, Morris said. 'But that's five or six years in the future.'"

10. I was told Lorens Foard and his wife Daisy are now in Paso Robles, at a Castle & Cooke holding.

11. G. Howard Peterson and his wife Marion, of Joseph Lane, Alamo, have 7,000 acres in Lake County at Middletown, which they enjoy and visit often.

12. Eugene Gladstone O'Neill (1888-1953) was one of the greatest of modern American dramatists. His plays are of varied types, including realistic, romantic, and satirical works. O'Neill adapted ancient Greek dramatic techniques to playwriting. He was born in New York City, the son of the famous American actor, James O'Neill. He studied at Princeton University. At Harvard University he took the George Pierce Baker playwriting course. He worked as an actor, sailor, and reporter before his start in writing plays in 1914. Three of his plays won the Pulitizer prize for drama.

Chapter Eight

Schools and Education

In this business of research and history writing, the more one digs the more one finds. Just before Easter 1977 I was given the loan of two early issues of *The Valley Kernel*, San Ramon Valley Union High School yearbooks, 1914 and 1918. George C. Wood presented them to me. The 1918 issue, brand new, will be donated to the San Ramon Valley Historical Society files at the SRV Library in Danville.

The 1914 issue was dedicated to Miss A. Maude Cornwall. "To Miss A. Maude Cornwall, who has so faithfully served as a member of the faculty since the organization of our school, we, the Student Body of San Ramon Valley Union High School, respectfully dedicate our first annual." Also in that issue: "In Memoriam: Whereas it has pleased divine providence in Its inscrutable wisdom to call from his earthly home Gardner Gay Goold, who departed this life April 14, 1914, we, the students of the San Ramon Valley Union High School, do offer this page of our first annual to the memory of a fellow student who attended our high school the first year of its organization."

The faculty was: Mrs. Elma Galvin, Principal (English, Latin and American history); Miss A. Maude Cornwall (mathematics, M. & M. history, and bookkeeping); Miss M. Virginia Stuart (Spanish, chemistry and physics); Mrs. A. G. Leeson (drawing).

Classes: Seniors: Ora Bell, Viola Lynch, Astrid Olsson, Alice Bell and Ruth Weinhauer. ("Jane Kendricks was one of the Seniors until about a month ago, when, on account of poor health, she was forced to leave school. Her Senior classmates regret very much her inability to be one of their number on Commencement night.")

Juniors: Frederick Humburg, Bernice Nunes, Henry Anderson, Edward Anderson.

Sophomores: Lloyd Williams, Lloyd Abrott, David Boucher, Lorenz Humburg, Florence Bur-

ris, Bernice Donahue, Loretta Coakley, Ruth Crozer, Valdo Otto.

Freshmen: Ila Boucher, Raymond Andreasen, Christine Andreasen, Marie Coakley, Undine Horton, Morall Smith, Hazel Clausen, Howard Wood, Roy Bell. There was a total of twenty-seven students. The cover was done by Loretta Coakley.

The Seniors' Farewell was written by Bernice Nunes, Class '15: "How dear to our hearts are the days in our High School. When in May we will leave it no more to return; Our English, our civics, and hard mathematics, And all the old studies, no longer must learn. In our old-fashioned school-house, The almond trees by it, That stands in the heart of our San Ramon vale. 'Round the world,' says Miss Alice, 'I'll travel some day.' How skillful Miss Olsson as musician will play! Miss Weinhuaer will patiently nurse the sick well, Teaching kiddies their letters, tempt Miss Lynch and Miss Bell, In some old-fashioned school-house, With almond trees by it, That stands in the heart of some far distant vale."

"An Historical Sketch of San Ramon Valley" by Friederiche Humburg, March 9, 1914

"And what is so rare as a day in June? Then, if ever, come perfect days; Then Heaven tries the earth if it be in tune, And over it softly her warm ear lays."

It was on such a perfect day in June 1847, that a canvas covered wagon drawn by oxen, slowly wound its way through a beautiful valley. This "prairie schooner" carried a little family of home seekers [John M. Jones (RA), his wife Mary A., and two daughters], and as the oxen moved laboriously along, the scene which greeted the eye at every turn of the winding path, called forth exclamations of admiration from the occupants of the wagon. At length the travelers halted the oxen, that they might better gaze and admire the picture of beauty and serenity, that was spread before them. On every side, the valley and surrounding hills were covered with thick, velvety clover, and wild oats standing waist high, and waving and rippling in the summer breeze, like the bosom of a lake. The western hills were clumped with oaks, maples and shrubs; willows and mottled trunked sycamores fringed the little stream at their left; while the mountain, which formed the eastern wall of the valley, seemed ever at their side as they journeyed southward. Cattle grazing on the luxuriant grasses, the chirp and twitter of birds, and the drowsy hum of insects, completed a picture of beauty, peace and contentment. Save for the bridle path which was the only guide of our travelers, and for a tule thatched hut near the stream (used as a rude shelter by Spanish vaqueros when night overtook them in this region), there was nothing to show the hand of man.

This was San Ramon Valley as it looked when first viewed by Americans, when they stopped their ox team on that June day so long ago, just north of the spot where the village of Alamo now stands. No wonder that the head of that little family bared his brow as he stook amid the wild oats, and exclaimed half in prophecy, half in determination, "Some time we will have a home in this valley." This was before the discovery of gold in California, and this little family were home seekers, not gold hunters. But because of the Mexican war which was raging at that time, they sought a settlement for protection, and Pueblo (now San Jose) was their destination.

Four years later, the year 1851, our home makers were back in the San Ramon Valley, accompanied by another family. These two families with two others who joined them later, purchased four leagues of land in the Romero Grant, paying for it four thousand dollars.

Is not our pride in our valley justifiable, when one considers that these people who had journeyed by wagon and ox team over half a continent, and who had the whole state of California to choose from chose for their home the heart of the San Ramon?

Some changes marked the valley during the four years that had passed, notably the building of adobe houses, which were the homes of Spanish families. Viewed through the lapse of years, we associate the adobe with the romantic and the picturesque. Built of adobe bricks, dried in the sun, their thick walls and deeply framed doorways and windows afforded warmth in winter and coolness in summer. Every adobe house was surrounded by a 'portico' about whose rude pillars clambered vines of the mission grape, and in every door yard bloomed the fragrant Castilian rose of old Spain. The adobes call to mind tales of the gay, carefree life of the Spanish days in California. We think of the fandango, the soft music of the guitar, and the horsemen with their wide sombreros, their bright colored serapes, their jingling spurs, and their horses no less gaily bedecked in silver mounted bridles, and saddles with monstrous tapaderas.

But one may ask why, in our valley today, we find no descendants of these gay, pleasure loving people. That question may be answered in two words, the "manana" of the ease loving Spaniard, and the "today" of the hustling, progressive American.

Soon after the coming of the first American home makers in 1851, others followed, and the fifties saw the arrival of many settlers in the valley. There followed a season of prosperity. Farms were improved with houses, barns and granaries, a few fruit trees were set out, and gardens planted. The fertile land, little of which had ever know a plowshare, under American thrift was cultivated and made to produce abundantly.

In the midst of this prosperity, a heavy blow fell upon the residents. The Spanish grants under which title the people had bought their land, became the cause of years of litigation, and many residents were forced to pay for their land a second time.

In those days all were neighbors in the fullest sense of the word; helping one another by an exchange of work; all joining together in their few social affairs; and ready to aid when sickness or death entered a home. Doctors were far away, and trained nurses were unknown, but it was nothing unusual for a pioneer mother to ride miles on horseback, often with a baby in her arms, to care for a sick neighbor.

The first post office in San Ramon Valley was established in 1853, [author: not so; it was May 18, 1852 and is so recorded in the Post Office Archives in Washington, D.C.] and named "Alamo"—a Spanish word meaning poplar tree. The post office was given quarters at the home of John M. Jones, who lived in a adobe house that crowned the knoll of the J. O. Reis home site just north of Alamo. [author: site of the present Alamo Safeway Store] Mr. Jones was the first postmaster, and his wife, Mrs. Mary A. Jones, was his deputy. For many years Alamo was the only post office between Martinez and Mission San Jose. The mail was carried between those two points by a man with a horse and cart, who made a round trip twice each week.

Alamo is the second oldest town in the county, Martinez being the oldest. The first house in the town of Alamo was built by a man named George Engelmeyer. He at first had a shoe shop, but soon enlarged his shop to a general merchandise store, and did such a thriving business that in a short time he had to employ a clerk. Other shops soon followed—blacksmith, harness and butcher shops, and a hotel. In 1858 the frame building still standing under the maples and walnuts on the west side of the street, was built. [author: torn down July 1954] The lower floor of this building was used as the general merchandise store of Lomax and Smart, while the upper floor was the Masonic Lodge room, Alamo Lodge No. 122 F. & A.M. which now holds its meetings at Walnut Creek, was organized in Alamo in 1858, and this old building was its first home. In 1860 a two story brick structure was erected on the west side of the street, on the property now owned by Mrs. George Smith. Wolfe and Cohen were the owners of the general merchandise store which occupied the lower story, while the Masonic Lodge moved from its first location into the more commodious quarters of the upper story of the new brick building.

The bricks of which this building was constructed were made by G. W. Webster, who lived on what is now the Van Gorden place. The brick kiln was situated on the Rancho El Rio, just across the creek from the Van Gorden pear orchard. In the great earthquake of 1868, the building mentioned was badly damaged, and was soon afterward torn down.

The ruin known as the Foster house is of historic interest. It was erected in 1857 by James Foster of Maine, and the staunch timbers of which it is constructed were made from trees which grew in the Maine woods. The lumber for the house was sawed, shaped and fitted, all ready to put together, then shipped around the Horn to its destined home.

Mr. Foster was a wheelwright, and wagons, carriages, furniture and even coffins, when occasion required, were turned out from his shop with a neatness and finish that would do credit to the present day.

In 1854 the first school in San Ramon Valley opened its doors in a little house which stood in the northern part of what is now the Kendall property, near the cemetery. Richard Webster was the first teacher. Soon after, a church (Cumberland Presbyterian) was built near the schoolhouse, on the lot which is now a driveway leading to the cemetery.

For awhile, a school was conducted in a little house that stood on a bedrock knoll, a short distance north of the point where the Southern Pacific Railroad crosses the county road between Alamo and Walnut Creek. This was known as the "Wall" schoolhouse, being near the home of Captain Wall, at that time the owner of the Foulds ranch.

In 1859 leading residents organized the Contra Costa Educational Association, and erected the Union Academy, a boarding and day school. The Academy opened for instruction in June 1860, with Rev. David McClure as its first principal, while Silas Stone, John M. Jones and Robert Love comprised its first Board of Trustees. The Union Academy was a large three-storied structure, centrally located between Alamo and Danville, on the west side of the county road, on land that is now a prune orchard belonging to E. B. Anderson. The fine locusts which grace the roadway at that spot were planted in the days of the Academy, to adorn the entrance to its grounds.

John H. Braly, in later years principal of the San Jose Normal School, succeeded Dr. McClure as principal. Mr. Braly's successor was Rev. Robert King, and in 1868, during his principalship the Academy was destroyed by fire, and was never rebuilt. The church building almost directly opposite the academy site afforded temporary school accommodations. In the meantime other towns had sprung up—Danville (so named for Daniel Inman, its first resident), Limerick (now San Ramon) and Walnut Creek, situated at the junction of Walnut and San Ramon creeks. District schools were established at Alamo and at these younger towns.

In 1910, by popular vote of Danville, San Ramon, Alamo, Green Valley, and Sycamore districts, a high school was established at Danville, and named the San Ramon Valley Union High School. Although still in its infancy it gives promise of becoming a power in the land.

In nothing does history show progress in greater degree than in modes of transportation. Beginning with that ox team which "gee hawed" its way through our valley in 1847, we may trace the means of travel next by the saddle horse, then by carriages, drawn by horses. Next came the steam railroad with the advent of the Southern Pacific in 1891; in more recent years, by scores of automobiles; and now in 1914, the Oakland, Antioch and Eastern electric railroad lands us in the metropolis in less than two hours.

Since the coming of our first American settlers in 1851, the years have brought many changes besides those of transportation. Many of the big ranches have been divided into smaller holdings. With the increase of population and more intensive farming, land has steadily increased in value, and instead of being sold by the "league" it is measured to the hundreth of an acre. Instead of the scattering farm houses of the fifties, the valley and foothills are dotted with comfortable and attractive homes.

Better facilities for handling perishable products have changed many grain fields into orchards, and fruit from the San Ramon Valley now commands the highest prices in the markets of eastern cities.

We of the San Ramon Valley have much for which to be thankful—thankful for Nature's gifts of ideal climate and fertile soil; for a varied and beautiful landscape; for educational and commercial facilities of modern times; for the touch of romance that has come to us from olden days; for musical names—relics of the sons of Spain; but above all are we glad and thankful that we are descendants of men and women who, thrilled by the tales of the "Pathfinder," braved the dangers and hardships of the long journey across the plains, bringing with them little of material riches, but a wealth of courage, fortitude, energy, industry, and integrity. As inheritors of this wealth, may we of the present day live up to the high standard set by our forefathers—the pioneers of San Ramon Valley. (Friederiche Humburg 3-9-14.)

Also in the May 1914 yearbook I found the following:

Athletics

Track: Henry Anderson, manager; Valdo Otto, David Boucher, Lloyd Williams, Lorenz Humburg, Edward Anderson, Raymond Andreasen and Lloyd Abrott. This is the first year we have started a track team. All of the boys that are to take part in the track meet are training every day. There are only a limited number of boys to pick from, but they all go in for the track enthusiastically. The boys train about three hours a day. We have a Track Meet with Concord high school March 21, 1914 and will take part in the County Track Meet at Concord April 4, 1914.

Football: We played American football in 1912. The team was composed mostly of high school boys, but a few others not in high school were on the team. We did not have enough boys in the school. William Meese coached us. This was the first year we played football.

The first game was at Antioch. We played the game in two thirty minute halves. The first half was interesting. In the last half they scored most of the points. Score 31 to 0 favor Antioch. We played two games with Vallejo High School. The games were both played at our home grounds. The scores were 38 to 0 and 28 to 0, favor of Vallejo. We played a game with Pleasanton—there. Very interesting. Score was 0 to 0.

Last year we played Rugby. We did not have any coach and trained ourselves. We did not have enough players in the school, so had to use others outside of school. We played one game with Concord there, score 31 to zero, favor of Concord.

The 1918 issue of the yearbook of the San Ramon Valley Union High School, *The Valley Kernel*, was professionaly printed by Standard Print of Martinez. The dedication was: "To our boys who are with the colors we, the students of the San Ramon Valley High School, proudly and lovingly dedicate this issue of *The Valley Kernel*. In Memoriam: Edwin Dobson attended 1910-11, Hugh Riley 1913-14; Corodon Sharp 1913-14."

The book contained a photograph of the brand new high school at the site where it remains today. Trustees were: Mr. Josiah Boucher, Chairman: Mr. William Stewart, Clerk; Mr. William Meese, Mr. August Humburg and Mr. Elmer H. Baldwin.

Class Roll: Mayme Belle Kelly, Braddick T. Peterson, Durward Van Gorden, Claude G. And-

reasen, Catharine Louise Stelling, Leo G. Lynch, Edythe Bernice Love, Reuben Theodore Olsson, Charles Edward Stelling, Alberta Wiedemann, George Clifford Wood, Philip John Harris, Clara Vivian Coats. Class Motto: "Give to the world the best you have, and the best will come back to you." Class Colors: Red, White and Blue. Class Emblem: The American flag.

Under the Service Flag were listed: Lieut. Edward C. Andersen, hdqtrs. Military Police, Field Artillery Replacement Depot, Camp Jackson, South Carolina. Henry M. Anderson, 85th Aero Squadron, A.E.F., England. David Boucher, Naval Reserve Training Camp, San Pedro, Calif. Angus Cameron, Co. B, 319th Engineers, Camp Fremont, Calif. Raymond L. Clarke, 86th Co. 7th Regiment, U.S.M.C., Santiago, Cuba, c/o Postmaster at New York. Merton E. Groom, F Troop, 13th U.S. Cavalry, Sam Fordyce, Texas. Lorenz Humburg, Battery C. Co. 347, Camp Lewis, Wash. Lester Lawrence, Co. 17, 1st Motor Mechanics, Regt. S.C. American E.F. via New York. J. Lyman Labaree, 6th band, C.A.C., Fort Warden, Wash. Valdo P. Otto, 132nd Ordnance Depot, Camp Fremont, Calif. Braddick T. Peterson, Alamo, Calif. Hugh Riley (Deceased); George Samuels, Co. E, 159th Infantry, Camp Kearney, Calif. Chadbourne Stow, Co. G, 160th Infantry, Camp Kearney, Calif. Russell Stow, School of Artiface, Mare Is., Calif. Irving Weik, Co. I., 363rd Infantry, Camp Lewis, Wash. Perry Wing, Co. F, 159th Infantry, Camp Kearney, Calif. Lloyd Wood, Co. A., 159th Infantry, Camp Kearney, Calif.

The faculty was: Mrs. Elma V. Galvin, Principal (English and History); Miss Anna Morgan (mathematics and drawing); Miss Dorah Lucas (Latin, Spanish and commerical courses); Miss Hilda F. Webb (physics, chemistry and sewing). There were thirteen seniors, eight juniors, twelve sophomores and fifteen freshmen, a total of forty-eight students in the entire high school.

The following is an article taken from the 1918 yearbook:

"War Work"

The school has been very active in war work this year, and we have contributed a very large sum to the Red Cross considering how small our school is compared with others in the county.

At the time when all the students were requested to become members of the Jr. Red Cross, our school joined immediately. From March 19 until April 18, 1918, we have turned in $93.25 for the Jr. fund, $33.55

of which was disbursed leaving a balance on hand of $59.70. The boys and girls have not had very much time outside of their school duties to do a great amount of work for this chapter but our sewing girls, with Miss Webb's assistance, have indeed done their part. They have turned out 7 girls' dresses, 6 boys' shirts, 4 knitted army sweaters, and 4 pair of socks. The articles belonging to the infants' layette were one knitted cap, one knitted sweater, two dresses, two cloaks, one shirt, four pairs of bootees and two jackets.

Miss Sally Hampton gave a very true and inspiring talk to us one afternoon in February about the Belgian Relief Work. We became very much interested in the cause and have given a small program every Friday afternoon for their benefit. We charged each student a cent for admittance but naturally did not object to receiving more. The programs consisted entirely of SRVUHS talent and we became very proficient in delivering addresses. Since Feb. 28th we have turned in $23.50 for our little hungry friends. We were required to turn in $8 at the end of the school term so we have exceeded our quota.

When the Y.M.C.A. drive was being carried through, each class in school pledged the amount it wished to donate. The Seniors gave very generously and the total sum from the sudent body was $45.

We have only one boy scout in school at the present time. He has done marvelously well selling war stamps and Liberty Bonds. Next year, when the young boys enter school as Freshmen, we hope they will endeavor to become Boy Scouts and help the cause. The big Red Cross drive was well supported by the Junior Red Cross members. Our faculty and student body went "over the top" and gave $101.85, as our donation from personal pledges.

We realize how easy is our lot compared with that of the ones who are suffering and dying in the war zone, in order that freedom may exist over the world. Our deprivations, our sorrows, our needs are as nothing placed side by side with what they have to endure.

The money and assistance that we have given for our soldier boys came from the depths of our hearts and we hope it has somewhat relieved the horror and sadness of the war.

UNION ACADEMY

The following was taken from the Pacific Cumberland Presbyter newspaper with reference to the Union Academy:

"The Union Academy"

The traditional interest of Presbyterians in education was shared by the Alamo Cumberland Presbyterian Church. Not only were its members active in organizing public schools, but by 1859 they had been instrumental in organizing an Academy giving instruction on a high school and college level. Rev. David McClure was its first headmaster, he was followed by John Braley, later to become a Cumberland Presbyterian minister in San Jose, and by a Mr. King. The Academy was destroyed by fire in the summer of 1868. The following are quotations concerning its work:

Dec. 1860 — "The inhabitants of our own beautiful Valley have not been indifferent to the great subject of education. The traveller cannot but admire the great number of neat comfortable school houses that dot the valley over from one end to the other. But the most conspicuous are the Union Academy buildings. These buildings have been erected by a Joint Stock Company at a cost of about $5,000. The building is a neat substantial frame, with a good, convenient, well arranged boarding department attached to it. The school rooms are fitted up with taste and convenience and will accommodate about 100 students. It is an ornament to our beautiful valley, and speaks well for our citizens."

Nov. 1861 — "This institution has recently been purchased by some five or six of our most responsible citizens, and placed in charge of Mr. John Braley, A.B., and his sister Miss Lizzie Braley, who will open it on the first Monday of prox, for the reception of students. They will also open a first-class boarding department in the Academy building, under their own supervision; and that the public may understand precisely the expenses of educating their children or wards at this Institution. Mr. Braley has furnished us with the following specific list of charges:

"The school will be divided into 4 sections, based upon the branches studied. Sec. 1st. Embracing Reading, Orthography, Primary Geography, Primary Arithmetic. Terms, $3.00 per month. Sec. 2d. Embracing Arithmetic as far as through Fractions in 'Ray's Part Third,' Intermediate Geography, English grammar commenced , with Reading, Writing, and Orthography. Terms, $4.00 per month. Sec. 3d Embracing Mathematics through Elementary Algebra, English grammar, Geography completed, Physiology, History of United States, Reading and Orthography continued. Terms, $5.00 per month. Sec. 4th. Embracing higher branches of Mathematics and all other branches embraced in a Scientific Course. Terms $6.00 per month. With Greek and Latin $7.00.

"Instruction in Piano Music, with use of instrument, $8.00 per month. Embroidery, Drawing, and Painting, each $2.00 per month. Boarding and rooms in the Academy per week $5.00. Washing and ironing per week $1.00. Rooms furnished with bedsteads, mattresses, washstands, bowls and pitchers, tables and chairs. Other articles necessary to complete outfit, such as bed clothing, towels, etc. and carpets if desired, students will themselves furnish. Board bills payable per half session in advance; otherwise two per cent a month interest will be added.

"There is room in the Academy building for twelve students—six males and six females—and no more. For that number there is good rooms, and good accommodations will be afforded. None are wanted but those who will willingly, promptly, and pleasantly observe all the regulations of the Academy.

"No student admitted for a less time than one month, and tuition will be charged per month. Money refunded and deductions made in cases of absence owing to sickness and other uncontrollable circumstances."

Jan. 1, 1863 — "Grand festival at Union Academy gotten up by Ladies for benefit of Academy, Large crowd, huge Christmas tree, presents for everyone. Supper wonderful." "Complete success, but some opposition to it in neighborhood, called a 'swindling arrangement and lottery.' 'What a pity that there can't be unanimity in a neighborhood, when the general good is the thing to be consummated.'"

May 1862 — "Students issued first number of their Academy paper, 'The Waifs' on May 18th. Parents night. Young ladies and gentlemen read extracts and declamations."

July 1862 — "Article on closing exercises on June 27, commends eloquence of student speakers. 'House was filled to overflowing!' Commends the student newspaper 'The Wasp.'"

Sept. 1862 — "This Institution commenced its second session under the supervision of Prof. Braley on the 11th ult. according to announcement. The school opened with prospects more flattering than any former session. At the present time, (close of 2d week) the school numbers 45 students, and quite a number of the neighborhood scholars are yet detained at home on account of harvesting, threshing, etc., but still some are coming in almost daily. Quite a number from a distance are already in, and a number of others are expected soon. We anticipate there will be a full school."

Dec. 1862 — "Thanks to young ladies of Union Academy for replenishing children's wardrobes. Thanks for a load of wheat, flour, fruit, etc., Pork collected in neighborhood and delivered to his barn. Urges delinquent subscribers to pay up."

Sept. 1, 1863 — "We are authorized and requested by Mr. John H. Braley, to announce to the patrons and students of Union Academy that the next session will commence on the first Monday (7th) day of Sept. Students are desired as far as practicable, to be in attendance at the commencement." "Mr. King, who was expected to take charge of the Institution, has not arrived and will not, probably before October; therefore Mr. Braley will take charge of the school in person, at least, until his arrival."

Sept. 15, 1863 — "The stock holders are doing some essential repairs to the building, and seem to be determined that nothing shall be wanting on their part to make the school worthy of an increased degree of patronage."

The following is excerpted from an article in *The Valley Pioneer Centennial Edition*, September, 3, 1958:

"Union Academy"

Oct. 19, 1859 the cornerstone of the Union Academy was laid, under the auspices of the Contra Costa Educational Association. Trustees were: John M. Jones, Silas Stone and Robert Love. The Rev. David Mc Clure, PH.D., was first placed in charge. He was followed by Prof. J. H. Braley, and he by the Rev. Mr. King, under whose administration it was destroyed by fire and never rebuilt. The school had a short life and died a natural death; it was too far in advance of the times and wants of the communities then residing in the beautiful San Ramon Valley. (wooden sign at El Portal standing.)

Professor J. D. Smith, an esteemed California teacher, felt more strongly about the Union Academy. Johnny Smith, son of "Scotch" Smith, lived near Danville in his boyhood. He rode the early race horses to victory, receiving orations at patriotic celebrations, and noted for posterity that the Rev. Mc Clure was the best teacher he ever had.

In his reminiscences the professor recalled that the Academy had a basement, two stories, and was built on a three acre site. The basement had dining rooms and the kitchen. First floor was the school with two hallways, one for girls and one for boys, and a combined office and music room. Sleeping rooms for boarding students were on the second floor. The piano in the music room was the first many of the children had ever seen, it was said. [author: questionable as many homes of the day had organs and pianos and music was greatly encouraged.]

All the teaching was done by the Rev. Mc Clure. Not only was he ahead of his time but he was also courageous. In an era when men were excommunicated from his church for the mere playing of a violin in private, the Rev. Mc Clure gave parties (RA) for his students and played the violin for their amusement. These parties were held monthly, opened and closed with prayer, with cake and song and dancing in between. Ten o'clock was the closing hour.

One of Johnny's stories gives an even better insight into the calibre of this early teacher. Johnny, for whom the path of learning was never smooth, rode bareback from his home to the Academy. Each day, as he neared the school, a lively young lady from one of Danville's first families would lift her long skirts enough to scare the horse. Johnny's Scotch blood boiled so high that he planned revenge. He chose a faithful nag with steady nerves and equipped her with blinders. Unheeding, the young lady raised her skirts. When the nag did not shy she was so surprised she did not notice that Johnny was throwing his riata. He caught her firmly round her pretty neck, but did not draw it too tightly. In a loud voice she promised quick revenge.

Not a lass to trifle with, the next morning Johnny's name was called. In the office the Reverend confronted the boy with a letter from the girl's family. "This," he said, "is a serious offense."

Not long after this Johnny's parents both died before they could make their fortune in California. Bright youngsters were a premium, even in the eighteen sixties and Johnny was offered a scholarship at another school. Johnny, however, preferred the quiet offer made by the Rev. McClure, then head of the California Military Academy.

The following, including recollections of Maevis Wood, educator, is also excerpted from *The Valley Pioneer Centennial Edition:*

In the good "old Golden Rule Days" all of the schools that made up the Danville union were one-room schools with no electric light and plumbing. They were heated by pot-bellied wood or coal stoves. Children pumped water from a well in the schoolyard and used their hands for a cup. A trough was commonplace for watering the horses. Students rode horseback, drove a horse and wagon, or walked to school as the children came long distances, and no transportation was provided. Each of the schools also had horse sheds.

The schoolyards were small which provided a limited playing area. A ball game was always in the neighbor's pastures. Playground equipment such as is used today was unknown. Most of the schools had to close in the rainy season for the mud on the roads.

The school rooms were large with fastened down seats in a variety of sizes. Children did not start school until they were nearly eight, but families were large and most of them wanted to come to school, accounting for the unbelievable enrollments of 60 to 70 students. At the end of each term, closing exercises were always enjoyed by everyone as the school was the community center and entertainment was few and far between so that everyone always came.

At the turn of the century the Valley had six elementary schools, but the closest secondary school was Mount Diablo High in Concord, built in 1906. The local Union Academy had served as the Valley's only advanced school from 1860 to 1868. With the growing population of the Valley and by popular vote of Alamo, Danville, San Ramon, Green Valley and Sycamore districts, a high school was established in Danville in 1910 and given its valley namesake: San Ramon Valley Union High School. The first high school board included early pioneers: John Baldwin, William R. Meese, Charles J. Wood, David Bell and W. E. Stewart.

As the high school continued to grow during its first three years, another teacher was added to the faculty, bringing the total to three, and it was necessary to find larger quarters. In 1913 the school moved into the vacant store building belonging to Mrs. Lillian Close at the corner of Diablo Road and Front Street. The upstairs portion of the building also served as the Oddfellow's Hall.

Increasing growth forced the high school to look for a permanent location. In 1916 the district purchased ten acres of land from Robert McAdoo and the following year San Ramon Valley Union High School moved to its present site. The original structure was a two-story building, located where the present music building now stands [1958]. First year attendance in 1918 was 48 students and a faculty of four.

"When I arrived in Danville in 1929," says Mrs. George (Maevis) Wood, "I thought it was the loveliest high school building I had ever seen. It was built around a court in the style of the California missions. At the time it had an enrollment of 125. Students came from the same area as they do today [1958] and some from as far as Lafayette. Children from that area all rode the Sacramento Northern Electric train to Walnut Creek, changed to a bus and rode to the front of the high school building." The home economics building was under construction and Mrs. Wood had been employed to teach in it. There were nine teachers. There was a shop and a commercial department and all were ranked well by the University. There was a small library at the end of the study hall. There was a tennis court and a football field and a lot of school spirit, according to Mrs. Wood.

A shop building was added in 1936 and the old gymnasium in 1939, built under the old Works Progress Administration (WPA). The gym was constructed at a cost of only $30,000. At today's prices it would run close to $200,000. [author: remember this is 1958!]

The old classroom building was declared unsafe in 1949 and a $250,000 bond issue was passed in 1950 to erect the present modern one-story main wing. The final two wings were added in 1951, the music building in 1953 and the swimming pool in 1953. This last year [1958] saw the completion of the new $400,000 boys' gymnasium, as well as the new football and baseball fields.

In 1957 the high school district purchased the eight room Danville Elementary school next door (now Community Center) to meet its enrollment increase. The classrooms will be used in the fall of 1958.

In its 48-year history San Ramon Valley High School has grown from a makeshift cottage with 30 students and two teachers in 1910 to a school plant valued at $1,500,000 of 35 acres, complete with athletic and shop facilities and pool, with more than 700 pupils and a faculty of 40, today [1958].

The newly built $600,000 Montair School on Linda Mesa Drive will replace the Danville Elementary school, which had outgrown its classrooms with over 350 students. The four classrooms of the recently completed $155,000 St. Isidore's School also will be put into use by the Danville Union School District for the coming year.

As of 1957-58 attendance for Danville's three elementary schools totaled 1,594 students, with Green Valley school heading the list with 723, Charlotte Wood with 482, and Danville with 390 students. The high school, which draws from San Ramon and Alamo as well as Danville, [author: let's not forget Diablo too] revealed 725 students for 1957-58.

Although adequate for the time being, what of Danville's future educational growth? Already plans are being made by both the high school and elementary school districts to meet the present and predicted growth in the area.

According to Dr. Roger J. Schulte (RA), high school superintendent and principal, a survey recently completed by the Contra Costa County Planning Department indicates that the future population of the San Ramon Valley Union high school district will support three high schools, one each for the Danville, Alamo and San Ramon areas. Enrollment predictions for the high school in the next five years [to 1963] based upon students now in the district's elementary schools, not any population increase, reveal the following for 1958-59, 794 and 1959-60, 864.

Enrollment Statistics, 1865-66

In 1865-1866 the County Superintendent of Schools showed the San Ramon Valley enrollment to be: Alamo 46, Green Valley 24, San Ramon 36, Sycamore Valley 16, and Tassajara 9, total of 131 students.

Early School

A schoolhouse had been built a mile from the town site in 1858, but was moved into town (Danville) in 1870 to replace a grammar school, erected in 1865, which had burned. The county school was used until 1895, when a new one was built on the same site. A new school, old Danville Grammar School, was erected on the edge of Danville in 1922.

News Items

June 1934 — for the second consecutive year a San Ramon Valley boy won the pentathon at UC, Berkeley—1933 Lee Ferreira of San Ramon and 1934 Ted Main of Alamo.

Jan. 1956 — operation of *all* Contra Costa Schools in 1955 reached a cost of $26 million.

SAN RAMON SCHOOL

First settled in 1850, San Ramon did not establish a school until 1867 when the old schoolhouse fronting on Highway 21 was built. Albert J. Young, one of the Valley's pioneer educators, was the first to teach there from 1867 to 1871. The two-room school, with its thirteen-foot high ceilings, was used for eighty-three years, the longest service of any school in the Valley. It was replaced by a three-room school on Crow Canyon Road in 1950. Mrs. Ray Gans, teacher and principal for thirteen years, was the last to teach in the old building, which was torn down in 1960.

San Ramon School, built in 1867, was used for eighty-three years, the longest service of any school in the San Ramon Valley. It was a two-room building with thirteen-foot high ceilings. (Photo by Les Sipes, Oakland Tribune, 1948)

HIGHLAND SCHOOL

Another early school was the Highland School near the county line on Highland Road. (There was also an Alcosta School at one time.) The Highland School was erected in 1926 by Thomas Carneal, wealthy land owner in the Tassajara Valley. He wanted an up-to-date school building for the children of that isolated area. He set aside an ample tract of land for playgrounds and had a fine concrete building erected and equipped with the latest fixtures and furniture and also an automatic player piano.

The entire investment amounted to $13,000, which he donated to the district. Carneal also added a modern radio-receiving set to keep the students alerted to world happenings.

Mrs. George (Maevis) Wood, a valley educator for over twenty years, taught at Highland School from 1944 to 1948, when the school lapsed due to too few students.

I was told the dividing line for Sycamore and Tassajara School Districts was the lane going into the Maxcy-Coats home. The west side was for Sycamore School District and the east side of the lane was Tassajara District.

The Danville Grammar School on Front Street, present site of San Ramon Chapel Mortuary.

TEACHER HAZEL ARTHUR
(Mrs. Edward Wiester)

The following notes are excerpted from talks given by Hazel Wiester for the Mariners Group of Danville Presbyterian Church, September 1974, the Congregational Church in 1975, and at Monte Vista High School, February 14, 1977. I have her consent to share them with you.

In August 1911, Hazel Arthur came to Danville. Trustees had asked the Normal School (now San Jose State College) to choose a teacher with qualifications similar to a previous teacher they had liked. She left San Jose about 8:30 A.M. on the Southern Pacific train for Oakland Mole. Spent several hours layover. Took another train north around the Bay and Carquinez Strait to Avon and up the Valley to Danville, arriving about six o'clock, with no baggage! Her trunk was lost in transit. She was met by the chairman of the board of trustees and taken to Mrs. Lillian Close's (Dr. Wilson Close's grandmother) to board. The house was a charming white cottage set in a grove of walnut trees on the corner of Hartz Avenue and Diablo Road. A high school teacher, Maude Cornwall, one of the three teachers, also boarded there.

The next day she went to the Presbyterian Church with Mrs. Close and saw her school for the first time on Front Street (present site of San Ramon Valley Mortuary). The church was a quaint New England type with tall steeple which was a landmark and could be seen all around. Her future mother-in-law was the organist (later followed by the talented Sarah Young who played for many years).

The schoolhouse, where the mortuary now stands, had eight and one-half grades, sixty-four children. Her salary was $80 per month. The weather was very hot that first day and she was in her traveling clothes. Open windows were the air-conditioning, no screens, flies unbearable. Drinking water came from a bucket and no indoor plumbing. Heat in winter was a pot-bellied stove. At the entrance to the building was a good-sized library. The janitor was a seventh grader, Perry Wing, a rosy-cheeked boy who walked down from near the top of Montair, only a muddy trail, road was not even gravel. Teachers were royally entertained by the residents. Card playing was popular—Five Hundred and Whist.

Mrs. Close made ice cream, a rare treat, and she invited Ed Wiester to share it. That was Hazel's

151

first meeting with her future husband. His brown hound dog used to sleep on the porch under her window, to the amusement of the town's people.

At the end of the first month, a second teacher was hired, as it was illegal to have more than forty-five pupils to one teacher. Marion Birrell, a former Berkeley teacher, was hired. She taught the first four grades. On weekends a carpenter worked at putting in a partition; it was slow going and made teaching difficult. By Christmas Marion couldn't take it any longer and a classmate from San Jose took over her grades. She was Lydia Hey who later became principal and was there for several years until she joined the Oakland Department in order to live with her family.

In those days, the teachers made their own recreation, mostly walking. The railroad track was a good place as it was neither dusty or muddy.

There was dancing at San Ramon Hall on Old Crow Canyon Road (across from Franco's former Villa San Ramon). The orchestra most in demand came from Livermore. Always a hearty supper— fried chicken, potato salad, cakes and pies and coffee, made in a wash boiler, the grounds put in a cloth salt bag, and the coffee brought to a boil on a wood stove.

School programs were expected. One Christmas the gas lights (carbide) went out. The trustee, Mr. McCiel, went home for some and the "show went on!" After Christmas, courtship with Ed Wiester was common knowledge. He bought a Durant car which was exciting. He had flowers (always different kinds in season) shipped from San Francisco by a friend. When school was out they were engaged, and there was a wedding in November 1912. They lived in the Danville Hotel (see Chapter Seven, *Places*) until their home was built. They lived in that house on San Ramon Boulevard one mile south of town for fifty years. After her marriage she substituted occasionally, and soon the one-room school began to disappear.

They could see clear across the valley—open fields, wide open spaces, and great stillness— especially at night; few cars. There was the howling of the coyotes—hooting of the owl and many deer, quail, etc. Walnut orchards began to be planted. Hazel Wiester also remembers in those good ole days!—Lawrence's Meat wagon, the vegetable wagon from Pleasanton, ice wagon twice a week in summer driven by Russell Stow from Walnut Creek. Milk 5¢ per quart, bread 5¢ per loaf, lamb chops 5¢. The town was mostly on Front Street in 1911. The formalness of dress,

hats, gloves, veils. They went to Oakland and San Francisco for Light Opera and theatre.

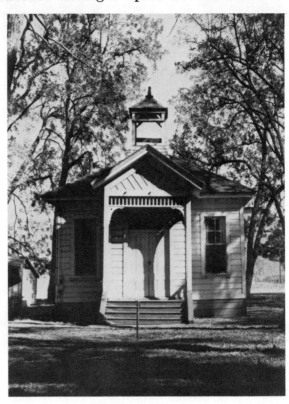

Tassajara School, built in 1888, is still standing.

TASSAJARA SCHOOL

The following is excerpted from a talk by Mrs. Grace (Sampson) Corbett, given to the Contra Costa Historical Society meeting at the Danville Hotel, May 14, 1970. I have her permission to use any or all of it.

"My Days in Lovely Tassajara in 1919"
I had graduated May 1917 from San Francisco State Normal, a teacher's training school exclusively. Educators regarded it highly and graduates were usually preferred to fill vacancies. It is now quite a famous institution with Dr. S. I. Hayakawa at the helm.

I was selected to teach a one-room school of eight grades in north Marin County, at Marshall on Tomales Bay, a large dairy community. Our nation was deeply involved as World War I had drawn us into fray in April. I taught there a year and a half. The Armistice was signed on Nov. 11, 1918. As the war ended, the flu epidemic of 1918 struck in both Europe and the U.S.A. It ravaged the populace like the reports of the black death of the Middle Ages. Teachers in Oakland and elsewhere were sick and dying. It was a time of hysteria. I left Marin County and went to Oakland to offer my services. The dean at S.F. State suggested I go out to Tassajara where the teacher had departed.

The next morning on Lincoln's birthday, Feb. 12,

I was on a train bound for Pleasanton, the nearest Southern Pacific depot to Tassajara. Mr. John Rasmussen, clerk of the school board, met me in his Model T Ford. We drove out into the countryside. The fields and hills were green and beautiful. I began to love it then and there!

I boarded at the Peterson home, at the junction of what is now Finley Road and Camino Tassajara. I walked up the road to view the little schoolhouse. How picturesque it appeared, like a jewel in a park-like setting surrounded by huge black walnut trees. I learned those trees were planted by the school children when the building was new in about 1879. [author: not 1879; this, the second Tassajara School was built in 1888.]

Feb. 13, 1919, I opened the school to 25 or 30 pupils, grades first to eighth. I often recall it was like a circus parade going down the road, as they left each day homeward bound. Their transportation was varied: horseback, carts, buggies and buckboards. The jolly, laughing group always seemed happy. In the short time I had been there, I was in love with it all.

There are three events which stand out in my memory. One, the delightful horseback ride to the summit of Mount Diablo. We left on a beautiful sunny morning on March 16, at ten. There was a blanket of snow on the mountain. Reached the summit about two o'clock. Cooked coffee with melted snow. Delicious!

Surveyed surroundings—what a tremendous view! Reached home about 10:30 p.m. No problems.

Two, was the excitement of the boys in uniform returning from war. That war was what was believed to be "The War to end all Wars." The 363rd Regiment of the 91st division, which trained at Fort Lewis in Washington, was acclaimed as San Francisco's own. April in 1919 they were greeted wildly as they marched up Market St. from the Ferry Bldg. in S.F. Two years later I met one of those returned veterans and he later became my husband. He had also served in the 363rd Regiment as had the Byer boy from Tassajara. In Peter Byer's memory the American Legion Post in Livermore bears his name.

Third, was the death of the aged Mrs. Phoebe Apperson Hearst of Pleasanton, mother of William Randolph Hearst, the newspaper king. She was a great lady. Her Spanish style castle on the hill linked with the range of larger hills overlooked the town of Pleasanton and the whole Amador Valley. She had been widowed many years. Her husband, George Hearst, had been U.S. Senator from California, in the days of Leland Stanford and other notables sometime before the turn of the century. Mrs. Hearst used her wealth in a benevolent way, giving many gifts and bequests to education fields, including the University of California. She was a co-founder of the P-TA, now national. After a time, her heirs, five grandsons, sold

Students at Tassajara School in about 1887. Back row, left to right: Mamie Fergoda, Lizzie Koch, Wilson Finley, Ella Coats, Ernest McPherson, Nina McPherson, Richard Williams (teacher), Ella Drennan, Edward Williams, Phoebe Bowles, Mary Finley, Clarence McPherson, Bertha Hanna, Rose Davina. Center row, left to right: Elsie McPherson, Louise Finley, Jennie Coats, Abbie Finley, May Coats, Mary Davina, Augusta Koch, Lucy Finley, Ella Fergoda. Front row, left to right: Frank Davina, Chester Johnston, Tony Olivera, Manuel Antone, John Kroeger, John Madeiros, Wille Hanna, Charlie Hanna and Alfred Podva. (Courtesy Vivian Coats Edmonston)

the huge estate. It became a Dude Ranch for visitors for several years [author: I remember it well in the thirties; we used to visit it often.] It is now Castlewood Country Club. My son, Bill Corbett, is the head golf pro at the club. His uncle was Harold Sampson, a famous pro in the early days of golf. The famous castle burned on a hot night in the summer of 1969. A new clubhouse is under construction. [1970] The community of Tassajara is equidistant of eight or nine miles from Danville or Pleasanton.

Mrs. Victor Edward (Grace Sampson) Corbett, now widowed, returned to the Tassajara Valley July 3, 1974 and makes her home on Old School Road, just behind the Tassajara School. In 1953 her son-in-law and daughter, Robert T. and Victoria "Vicky" Wright, moved to Diablo Acres in Danville from Oakland, then after three years in the Los Angeles area, returned to Danville on Liberta Court. In 1970 they built a new home with acreage, and named Old School Road.

The original Tassajara School was built by Albert Galatin Wilkes on his land on the left side of the road on Finley Road, near the Alberg home and the Tassajara post office. It was built in 1865. Sabra Simpson Bright from Danville was one of the first teachers.

The second Tassajara School (building still standing) was built in 1888. Some of the teachers were: Richard Williams, 1887 (see photo); Miss Evelyn Stetson, 1890; Miss Ellen Riley, Margaret Bowles (sister to Phoebe Bowles who married Bethel Coats), Will McPherson, Cora Boone from San Ramon, Jennie Boswill, a Jones (not of the Alamo family) related to Lill Drennan. In about 1900 there were two teachers at one time. They were Maude Merritt and Minnie Harris. In about 1912-13 there was a Miss Denyke.

Some of the students in about 1878 were Bethel, Ella, and Russell Coats; Belle, Mary, Mattie, Tillie and Wilson Finley; Edgar Harris; Caroline Joseph; Annie Martin; Effie, Emma, Ernest and Willie McPherson; Ed, Lizzie and Richard Williams.

The following was run as an item in my by-lined column, "I Cover Alamo and Miscellany," in the *Valley Pioneer*, dated July 13, 1966.

"Chart of Progress of
San Ramon Valley Union High School"
(1921 to 1927)
(Taken from the *Valley Kernel '27*, SRVUHS Yearbook of 1927, Statistics by Paul C. Bickel, Faculty Advisor.)
1921-22: Total enrollment 49, number of graduates 9, number of teachers 4. Music Dept. organized.

Established free student transportation. Third *Valley Kernel* (yearbook) published.
1922-23: Total enrollment 64, number of graduates 7; faculty increased to 5. Interior of school renovated and varnished. Sewing added to curriculum.
1923-24: Total enrollment 89, number of graduates 15, faculty increased to 6. Shop built and equipped with benches and hand tools. Full time janitor employed.
1924-25: Total enrollment 89, number of graduates 15, number of teachers 6. Built gas generator house, installed girls' lockers and showers, added auto mechanics to curriculum, competitive vaudeville substituted for old Freshmen Reception, organized Honor Scholarship Society, patrons established Citizenship Scholarship Prizes, published fourth *Valley Kernel*.
1925-26: Total enrollment 99, number of graduates 22, faculty increased to 7. New study hall built and equipped, table saw purchased for shop, shop boys built parking shed, showers installed for basketball boys in Fraternal Hall, purchased new Schmer piano, installed new typewriters and mimeograph in commercial dept., organized girls' club, auto mechanics boys "created" Ford truck No. E 12-749, fifth *Valley Kernel* published.

San Ramon Valley Union High School. It was built in 1917 and this photograph was taken in 1925. Note the orchards on both sides, the wall, and the lighted towers at the entrance. Las Trampas range may be seen in the background. (Courtesy Vivian Coats Edmonston)

1926-27: Total enrollment 101, number of graduates 21, number of teachers 7. Steam plant installed, band saw placed in shop, tennis court started, addition to shop built, new office built, store room built, boys partitioned off library, boys built lockers for athletic supplies, teachers' rest room furnished, sixth *Valley Kernel* published.

The following is a list of the entire student body of 140 students attending San Ramon Valley Union High School, 1927-28, taken from the *Valley Kernel of 1928*, the school's yearbook:

Directory, 1927-1928

Freshmen (33): Augusta Andersen, Elvena Armanino, Madeline Armanino, John Baldwin, Margaret Baldwin, Jean Brear, Stanley Brown, Amelia Camacho, Carmelita Guisto, Hazel Goularte, Rachel Gutzman, Melvin Hunt, Lloyd Ivory, Leo Kerkhof, L. B. Kidwell, Loraine Lawrence, Duncan Monroe, Mabel Myers, Jack Neumeister, June Neumeister, Mac Osborn, Herbert Reinstein, Laurine Saunders, Selma Schwartz, William Schoener, Dolly Sellick, Florence Sellick, Lillian Soto, John Stoddard, Samuel Thomson, Jack Wallace, Elsie Waddell, Angelina Zunino.

Sophomores (33): George Andersen, Claude Artero, Clara Camacho, George Campbell, Don Carrington, Edmonds Chandler, Everett Crosby, Elizabeth French, Alberta Gifford, Edith Gibbs, Albert Hansen, Alfred Jones, Byron Jones, Evalyn Leech, Dan Lucas, Mary Lucas, Charles Morey, Flood Morss, Fukashi Nakagawa, Aline Neergaard, Hans Oeser, Tony Oreglia, Adolph Peterson, La May Podva, Irene Saari, Alice Simas, Robert Smith, Henry Smith, Grace Spence, Leslie Stevens, Kay Tevlin, Wayne Wyman, Frank Zunino.

Juniors (27): Arvida Andersen, David Barnard, Thomas Buchanan, Madelyn Cabral, Ray Collins, Walter Elliott, Evelyn Fereira, Lucille Glass, Victor Hansen, Doris Hunt, Phebe Johnson, Alex Lucas, Ruth McKay, Ethel Rodgers, Ruth Sandkuhle, Virginia Schnoor, Henry Schutt, Kathrine Schutt, Alverta Scott, Joyce Smith, Evelyn Smith, Lorine Soto, Bernice Spence, Laurel Thomson, James Tomwye, Berring Towsley, Alice Waddell.

Seniors (14): Matilda Bettencourt, Marie Fereira, Olga Huber, Lorraine Ivory, Steve Johnson, Constance Manor, Alex MacDonald, Norman MacDonald, Louis Oeser, Edith Rutherford, Albert Smith, Harriet Smith, Leona Sollars, Lois Woodward.

Post Graduates (3): Edna Miller, Mason Smith, Fred Watson.

Soccer vs. Football

In more recent years, soccer has become a popular sport and had a revival. However, San Ramon Valley Union High School in yesteryear boasted championship soccer teams. In the fall of 1929, the class of 1930 voted to discontinue their championship soccer teams and start football. What determined that decision, in part, was that an anonymous donor from the county school district had offered to give the team football outfits.

The coach of that first football team was Laverne Brown, a graduate of San Jose. He had taken the soccer team to play the San Jose frosh for one game.

Among those playing on the football team were Claude Artero, Sam Hemme, Alfred Jones, Dan Lucas, Charley Morey, Fukashi Nakagawa, La May Podva, the Scott twins, Arlen and Arven, Bob Smith, John Stoddard and Wayne Wyman.

One unhappy incident relayed by one of the players was that on one occasion six members of the 1931 football team were injured and taken to the hospital after one game with Livermore! Those early football teams were not champions and did not gain the reputation that the former soccer teams had experienced—but then, the team did get new, free uniforms!

The Valley Kernel
1927, 1928, 1929

The sixth edition, in 1927, was "affectionately" dedicated "To our fathers and mothers who have made these four happy years possible." Seven teachers made up the faculty: Ernest Von Gruenigen (University of California), science and athletics; Paul C. Bickel (University of Chicago and University of Berlin), Principal and mathematics; John B. Thomas (Oregon Agricultural College), shop and basketball; Bertha B. Holtz, (University of California), economics, music, girls' athletics; Carmel Dilworth (University of California), English and drawing; Lottie Jane Reilly (University of California), history and Spanish; and Mrs. J. B. Thomas (Stanford University), commercial department.

The dedication of the seventh edition, in 1928, read: "To Paul Clark Bickel who for five years as our principal has so earnestly devoted himself to the upbuilding of San Ramon Valley Union High School, we affectionately dedicate this seventh edition of The Valley Kernel."

The Board of Education: Wm. E. Stewart, President; Walter M. Smith, clerk; Elmer H. Baldwin, Dr. V. J. Vecki and M. C. Anderson. Added to the faculty was Mrs. Alberta A. Rossello (University of California), Spanish and French. She replaced L. J. Reilly.

In 1929 the dedication read: "In appreciation of the good fellowship, sympathy, and understanding, we, the Senior Class of 1929, dedicate to John B. Thomas, our Principal, this eighth edition of The Valley Kernel."

The Board of Education: William E. Stewart, president; Walter M. Smith, clerk; Clarence Close, Dr. V. J. Vecki, and M. C. Anderson. There was a memorial to classmate Grace Helen Spence 1912-1928. Added to the faculty were Mr. Lee C. Noderer (San Jose State Teachers College), shop and athletics, and Miss Maevis Batchelder (Colorado State Teachers College), home economics.

The student body of San Ramon Valley Union High School in 1929.

SRVUHS Boards of Trustees

There are many things of interest to note when reviewing old copies of *The Valley Kernel*. Most of the years they were printed professionally, with merchants' advertisements defraying the expense. However, a few issues were mimeographed and one year, 1934, all the photographs were hand-pasted.

The following are Boards of Trustees for seven years: 1922, Gardner G. Goold, Edwin Dobson, Hugh Riley, Corodon Sharp and Lloyd Wood. 1926: the same board but a fifth member, Milton Smith, was added. 1931: William E. Stewart, president; Albert E. Brear, clerk; Clarence W. Close, H. J. Sandkuhle, Henry Hansen. 1933: W. E. Stewart, president, H. J. Sandkuhle, clerk; F. R. Woodard, Henry Hansen and Edgar H. Lion. 1934: Edgar H. Lion, W. R. Meese, J. H. Spence, W. E. Stewart and F. R. Woodard. 1935: J. H. Spence, president; F. R. Woodard, clerk; W. E. Stewart, W. R. Meese, and L. H. Kamp. 1936: J. H. Spence, chairman, F. R. Woodard, clerk; W. E. Stewart, W. R. Meese and L. H. Kamp.

For a time different classes put out a book called "Snickers," which contained stories, poems, lots of jokes, and articles and, I'm sure, student labor and effort.

The Valley Kernel, 1922
End of the Trail Edition

In Memoriam: In memory of those of our school who have passed into the Great Beyond: Gardner G. Goold, Edwin Dobson, Hugh Riley, Corodon Sharp and Lloyd Wood [you will note all had served as Trustees].

Dedication: In the Great War of Nations Lloyd Wood gave his life that there might be world peace. In honor of his noble sacrifice, and to his memory, we, the Students of the San Ramon Valley Union High School respectfully dedicate this End of the Trail Edition of "The Valley Kernel."

School Directory: Seniors: Dorothy E. Close, News Editor of *Valley Kernel* '22 and Snickers II and IV; Effie M. Collins, treasurer of Student Body '22; G. Howard Groom, Student Body President '22 and business manager of *Valley Kernel*; Alden A. Jones, Class president, manager of track team; Edward T. Peters, secretary of student body, editor of Snickers II and IV, Editor of *Valley Kernel*, Editor of Stylus I, and manager of basketball team; Frances S. Rutherford, senior play, assistant business manager, Stylus I; Henry Louis Schnoor, Secretary of senior class, athletic editor Snickers II, and Captain basketball team '22; Agnes Lorena Stone, vice-president of student body '21, highest honors for scholarship '21 and '22, assistant

editor, *Valley Kernel* '22; and Susie S. Trevitts, treasurer of student body '21 and treasurer of senior class '22, art editor, Snickers II, business manager, Stylus I, assistant business manager of *Valley Kernel*.

Juniors: Claire Andreasen, Kenneth Fry, Evelyn Groom, Shirley Harris, Homer W. Marion, Rose Peters and Elizabeth Woodward.

Sophomores: Carolyn Abrott, Charles Benton, Hazel Bauer, Bertha Bell, William Donahue, Ralph Ellis, Mamie Fereira, Eral Flautt, Charlotte Foster, Verne Gordin, Marion Harris, Faithe Johnson, Elisa Lorenzen, Thelma Oswill, Hazel Owen, Loraine Riley and Lee W. Short.

Freshmen: Joseph Alves, Myra Benton, Eldon Clark, Fletcher Collins, Margaret Davis, Harold Groom, Wanda Goold, Evelyn Peters, Helen Read, Charles Silva, Leslie Thomas, Petrea Thorup, Gordon Turner, Isabel Vecki, Leland Wayne and Mabel Wells.

There were forty-nine students in total enrollment at local high school in 1922. There were four teachers: Paul C. Bickel, Dorothy P. Shaw, Mrs. Mary L. Owen and E. Virginia Ballaseyus. The teachers' and seniors' class photographs also included a baby picture for each.

Message to the High School Board 1922

To the members of the High School Board we wish to express our thanks and appreciation for their part in furnishing us the facilities for our high school education. Serving upon the board is not an enviable task, being without financial compensation of any sort; and when mistakes—if any—are made, criticism is widespread and abundant. But upon the members of the board devolves, by law, the responsibility of maintaining the school. And to these men who have so well and faithfully discharged their duties the gratitude of the community is certainly due. [author: merits repeating, don't you agree?]

Alumni

Alumni in 1922: Lyman Labaree, '13, now lives in Illinois; Alice Bell, '14, is Mrs. Hewlett and lives in Oakland; Ora Bell, '14, now Mrs. Callaghan, lives in Dixon; Viola Lynch, '14, teaches school in Richmond; Ruth Weinhauer, '14, is a telephone operator at Mount Diablo Park Club; Astrid Olsson, '14, is teaching school in Berkeley; Jane Kendricks works in the office of an Oakland firm; Frederiche Humburg, '15, now Mrs. Richard F. Jackson, lives in Alamo; Bernice Nunes, '15, teaches school in Hayward; Ruth Crozer, '16, is a U.C. student; Bernice Donahue, '16, is a teacher in the school at San Ramon; Florence Burris, '16, teaches in Arizona; David Boucher, '16, is convalescing after a prolonged illness; Lorenz Humburg, '16, is farming on the home place; Lloyd Williams, '16, is a Stanford University student; Lloyd Abrott, '16, is in the drapery department of the San Francisco Emporium; Ila Boucher, '17, lives in Red Bluff and is now Mrs. Wm.

Gover; Christine Andreasen, '17, is married and living in San Francisco; Raymond Andreasen is employed in Petaluma, California; Howard Wood, '17, is attending the State University; Roy Bell, '17, is working on the Arnstein Ranch; Marall Smith, '17, is an employee of the Union Oil Co.; Valdo Otto, '17, works for the Shell Oil Co. in Martinez; George Wood, '18, University of Calif.; Leo Lynch, '18, takes contracts for work with his King tractor; Catherine Stelling, '18, is a student in the University of Calif.; Philip Harris, '18, is a medical student at Stanford; Mayme Kelly, '18, holds a position with the Southern Pacific Co. in San Francisco; Claude Andreasen, '18, works for Hall & Glocher, of San Francisco; Charles Stelling, '18, is remaining at home with his parents at Gilroy; Durward Van Gorden, '18, is employed on the home ranch; Edythe Love, '18, now Mrs. Durward Van Gorden, keeps house for her husband and small son; Alberta Wiedemann, '18, is now Mrs. S. Smoot; Reuben Olsson, '18, attends the University of Calif; Braddie Petersen, '18, is considering a position with the Pacific Gas and Electric Company; Vivian Coats, '18, is studying nursing in the University Hospital, San Francisco; Georgia Burris, '19, is an employee of the Shost Auto Repair Co., Oakland; Blanche McCiel, '18, works in the State Bank, San Leandro; Eleanor Abrott, '19, is a U.C. Student; Florence Pynn, '19, now Mrs. C. L. Thomson, lives in Danville; Milton Smith, '19, is recovering from an illness; Ramona Read, '20, is working for Mr. Duff, Berkeley; Edwin Olsson, '20, is an employee of the Standard Oil Co., Oakland; Dorothy Bell, '19, works for a fur company, San Francisco; Andrew Andersen, '21, is helping his father on the ranch; Helen Baldwin, '21, is at home with her parents in Danville; Marie Bauer, '21, attends the State Normal at San Francisco; Grace Donahue, '21, is a student of San Jose Normal; Waldo Wood, '21, is now at home with his parents; Evelyn Woodward, '21, is now teaching school at Isleton; John Ogden, '21, is working for Mr. Humburg in Alamo; Loubelle Morss, '21, attends Art School in Berkeley.

1922 Senior Class History
by Susie Trevitts, '22

In the fall of 1918 our class, consisting of fourteen Freshmen, entered the San Ramon Valley Union High School, then under the supervision of Mrs. Galvin.

As there was an epidemic of influenza during our first year, there were very few activities. We were so quiet and good that we were not initiated until one afternoon in the last week of school. We thought we were sufficiently grown up, so we did not mind the ill treatment.

The main event of our first year was the Senior Dance, held at the San Ramon Hall, where the Freshies remained as wall flowers, casting their opties upon the upper classmen. It was then and there that we, as a

whole, decided to treat the Freshmen differently, and I think we have lived up to our vow.

Before the end of the year, Thelma Scott, Marian Harris, Stanley Lawrence, and Henry Lorenzen dropped out. But our Sophomore year brought Thelma and Henry back and an addition of three more, namely: Lorena Morrison, Edna Turk, and Fay Hawkins. A great episode of our Sophomore year was the enjoyable musical, in which all took a prominent part. We had the honor of giving the 1919 Freshmen a reception held shortly after school began. Another activity was the Sophomore Rush. We tried our best, but, sorry to say, we were defeated.

It was during this year, too, that we demonstrated to the public our wonderful dramatic ability—Mary Garden had nothing on us when it came to being emotional. "Our Career" brought a big house, and gave us an opportunity to stand before an audience and forget our bashful Freshman days.

The 1920 May Picnic came off with a bang! Alden Jones, our class president, took his place at the head of the parade as one of the many attractions. Our Junior year brought more bad luck, for Thelma and Henry did not return. We lost the three new ones of our Sophomore year and Kirke Schnoor also dropped out. Loren Wyatt was the only new one to join us and we lost him before long.

Last and not least we gave a relishing banquet to the Seniors. Judging by appearances, it proved to agree with them perfectly. In all, we believe we have been a very successful class—in quality if not in quantity; from fifteen members, we have dwindled down to nine. Edward Peters, our literary genius and editor, with Agnes Stone, his versatile collaborator, who, by the way, has the highest scholarship standing in the school, have found it convenient and interesting to work together for a common good. Dorothy and Effie have become so inseparable during their four years that to find one it is only necessary to call the other. Louis Schnoor has gained a reputation as a basketball star, and in forgetting his violin. We have a fine Student Body President (Howard Groom) this year, one who has taken the welfare of the Student Body to heart, and has taken his official position with interest and dignity. We hope that the next President will follow in Howard's footsteps. And we also hope that some one will follow in Frances Rutherford's and Susie Trevitts' footsteps—always smiling and happy. That is an heritage that I should like to leave with the other classes—to see the bright side of life.

Our four years have passed quickly and joyfully. Now that we are leaving, we are both sorrowful and happy—sad because we must leave the associations of our school life—happy because we have been prepared for the bigger, broader things in life. The memories of our school days will remain with us forever. We hope that we shall prove worthy of our

158

diplomas and show that our education and opportunities were not given us in vain. (S.T.'22.) [Susie Trevitts is Alden Jones' cousin.]

SRVUHS Early Graduates

The following was taken from a booklet with the title "Class of 1918, San Ramon Valley High School—Reunion—May 18, at 1 o'clock at the high school." No year given. My deductions find this reunion to have been after 1955. Permission to use was granted me by Mr. and Mrs. Travis M. Boone, San Ramon.

Roll Call

Faculty: Mrs. Elma V. Galvin, Principal, English, Latin and American History; Miss Maude Cornwall, history and mathematics 1910-1914; Miss M. Virginia Stuart, Spanish, chemistry and physics; Mrs. A. G. Leeson, drawing; Miss Anna Morgan, mathematics and drawing; Miss Dora Lucas, Latin, Spanish, and commerical courses; Miss Hilda F. Webb, physics, chemistry and sewing.

Roster With Addresses

Graduated Before 1918: 1914: Ora Bell Callaghan (Mrs. Dennis) Dixon; Viola Lynch in Arabia; Alice Bell Hewlett (Mrs. Dennis), Oakland; Astrid Olsson Humburg (Mrs. L. A.), Alamo; Ruth Weinhauer Leonard (Mrs. Harry), Concord, Calif.

1915: Friederiche Humburg Jackson, Alamo; Bernice Nunes Vezzani, Oakland; Henry Anderson (deceased); Edward Anderson.

1916: Lloyd Williams (deceased); Lloyd Abrott, Saratoga; David Boucher (deceased); Lorenz Humburg (deceased); Florence Burris Resenburger (Mrs. Vincent), Phoenix, Ariz.; Bernice Donahue Leavy (Mrs. J. J.), Berkeley; Ruth Crozer Giddings (Mrs. Max), Alamo; Valdo Otto (deceased).

1917: Ila Boucher Grover (Mrs. Charles), Cottonwood; Raymond Andreasen, San Leandro; Christine Andreasen Luchinger, Vallejo; Marie Coakley Eggert (Mrs. Henry), San Francisco; Marral Smith, Daly City; Hazel Clausen, Oakland; Undine Horton Anderson (Mrs. Henry); Howard Wood, Berkeley; Roy Bell, Dixon, all California.

Class of 1918: Claude Andreasen, Montair Dr., Danville; Vivian Coats Edmonston (Mrs. Charles N.), San Francisco; Durward Van Gorden (deceased); Philip Harris, Love Lane, Danville; Mayme Kelly Wigle, El Cerrito; Edythe Love Wallis (Mrs. C.), Clear Lake Park, Lake County; Reuben Olsson, Lafayette; Catherine Stelling Chappell (Mrs. Jerome), Gilroy; Braddick Peterson, Walnut Creek; Charles Stelling, San Jose; Alberta Wiedemann Smoot (Mrs. Sam), Petaluma; George Wood, Tassajara Rd., Danville; Leo Lynch (deceased).

Juniors 1918: Travis M. Boone, 19953 San Ramon Road, Hayward; Georgia Burris Andreasen (Mrs. Claude), Montair Dr., Danville; Blanche McCiel Sur-

gart (Mrs. C. A.), San Francisco; Florence Pynn Thompson (Mrs. Clifford), Walnut Creek; Christina Rutherford (deceased); Arthur Peters, Hayward; Milton Smith (deceased); Burdette Gray, Layfayette, all California.

Sophomores 1918: Eleanor Abrott Harris (Mrs. T.), Berkeley; Elise Fereira Valentine, Walnut Creek; Rowland Gass, Texas; Ellsworth Martinelli, Colfax; Edwin Olsson, Danville; Ramona Read Abrott (Mrs. Lloyd), Saratoga; Anna Smith Wiley (Mrs. Thomas N.), Los Angeles; Harold O. Riley, Crystal Bay, Nevada; Lorraine Young (deceased); John Ogden, Layfayette; Blanche Eastland; Hermina Ogden Price (Mrs. Frank), Chico.

Freshmen 1918: Andrew Anderson, Tassajara Rd., Danville; Helen Baldwin Rasmussen (Mrs. H. C.), Concord; Marie Bauer, Paso Robles; Irene Gibbons; Grace Donahue Austin, Quincy; Mathilda Jorgensen Kessel (Mrs. A.), San Jose; Stanley Laurence, San Leandro; Loubelle Morss Bangs (Mrs. Alfred), Cathedral City; Marian Martinelli Weaver, Modesto; Irene Sueyres (deceased); Waldo Wood, Piedmont; Evelyn Woodward (deceased); Loren Wyatt; Ruth Turner, Hemme Ave., Alamo; Paul Ogden, Lafayette.

SAN RAMON VALLEY UNIFIED SCHOOL DISTRICT

My thanks to Leslie Thomas for the use of the Facilities Plan 1976-1980, prepared by the Department of Facilities Planning, SRVUSD. Committee members giving their time and effort on this study were James Graham, Preston Hunter, Mrs. Susanna Schlendorf and Mrs. Mickey Townsend.

Prior to Unification there were two Alamo elementary schools, three Danville elementary schools, and one and one-half intermediate; San Ramon had one elementary and there was only one high school.

After Unification, as of June 1970, there were eight elementary schools, two and one-half intermediate, and two high schools. There were three separate communities prior to unification. They were and are all rural and unincorporated.

Average Daily Attendance
1960-1972

1960-61 - 4215		1966-67 -	6600
1961-62 - 4393		1967-68 -	7260
1962-63 - 4645		1968-69 -	8210
1963-64 - 5051		1969-70 -	8686
1964-65 - 5545		1970-71 -	9163.46
1965-66 - 6038		1971-72 -	10,138.06

An Enrollment Comparison, from 1969-76, shows: 1969 - 8,495; 1970 - 9,207; 1971 - 10,212; 1972 - 11,000; 1973 - 11,555; 1974 - 11,932; 1975 - 12,315; 1976 - 12,650.

	Grade Level	Number of Students Over/Under Capacity		
		K-6	7-8	9-12
	Student Capacity	7044	2468	1450
HIGH RANGE	9/1977	422 over	95 under	163 under
	9/1978	1275 over	57 under	222 over
	9/1979	2356 over	61 over	378 over
	9/1980	3019 over	222 over	411 over
MEDIUM RANGE	9/1977	232 over	138 under	217 under
	9/1978	744 over	178 under	70 over
	9/1979	1370 over	162 under	95 over
	9/1980	1881 over	37 under	83 over
LOW RANGE	9/1977	232 over	138 under	217 under
	9/1978	577 over	215 under	22 over
	9/1979	1036 over	239 under	1 under
	9/1980	1410 over	143 under	52 under

The enrollment projections incorporating the expected 5,747 new students were made by using the District enrollment for September 21, 1976, which was 12,650. A projected enrollment of 16,189 students for September of 1980 shows a net gain of 3,539 new students by that date.

Enrollment September 21, 1976 in the district was 12,650. Projected enrollments, based on active housing developments, are: for September 1977, 14,426; September 1978, 15,702; September 1979, 17,058; September 1980, 17,913.

The above includes 5,747 K-12 students and a 5% growth per year in kindergarten distributed as follows:

Growth from New Building During:	Elementary 66%	Intermediate 15%	High School 19%	Total
1976/77	1,214	276	349	1.839
1977/78	910	207	262	1,379
1978/79	1,024	233	295	1,552
1979/80	645	146	186	977

160

School	Active Developments				Students Generated by Developments		
	SFR	Duets	Cond.	Total	K-6	7-8	9-12
Alamo	17			20	13		
Rancho Romero	66			77	51		
Montair	346			401	265		
Vista Grande	299	103	44	415	273		
Stone Valley	430			499	329		
Green Valley	524			608	401		
John Baldwin	323			375	247		
Greenbrook	12			14	9		
Twin Creeks	566	574	888	1183	781		
Neil Armstrong	935			1085	716		
Walt Disney	791		54	933	615		
Country Club	104			121	80		
Total					3780		
Los Cerros				2283		342	
Charlotte Wood				790		119	
Pine Valley				2139		321	
Stone Valley				519		78	
Total						860	
California High				2139			406
Monte Vista High				1542			293
San Ramon High				2050			390
Total							1039

Serving on the San Ramon Valley Unified School Board in 1977 are Edward E. Best and Jane Upp, both of Alamo. Three new trustees elected Tuesday, March 8, 1977 and taking over their duties as of April 1, 1977 are Don Sledge, Greg McCoy and Ron Harris, all of Danville. They will serve a four-year term. There was only a 20.2 per cent voter turnout of the 26,222 registered voters in the San Ramon Valley area. At the Alamo precinct where I served as Judge election officer, we had 750 ballots and used only 142! Voter apathy again. An update item: Ron Harris resigned in July 1977 when he was transferred to Dallas, Texas.

At a special meeting called April 5, 1977 officers elected were: Edward Best, president; Ronald Harris, vice-president; and Jane Upp, clerk. Supt. Allan Petersdorf was appointed secretary for the board. The Board decided to meet at 7:30 P.M. on Mondays twice a month in the Education Center, 699 Old Orchard Drive, Danville.

Year-round schools, a long-discussed possibility for the San Ramon Valley Unified School District, may become a reality. A pilot program for elementary schools was agreed upon by Board members. Year-round schools have been discussed as one solution to overcrowding, since the San Ramon Valley is one of the fastest growing school districts in the state.

It was estimated the program would cost 3.98 per cent of the district's operating budget, or $1,794,530, during the next year. In one version of the year-round school students are in class for forty-five days and on vacation for fifteen days. Vacation time would occur in four different months, rather than in summer only. Each student would attend school 175 days a year, the same as on a nine-month schedule. A 1976 study shows that initially year-round schools would save capital costs. Funds would not have to be spent on new buildings. There is a May 31, 1977 bond election scheduled. (Update: It was heavily defeated, 7,026 "no" votes to 3,540 "yes."

161

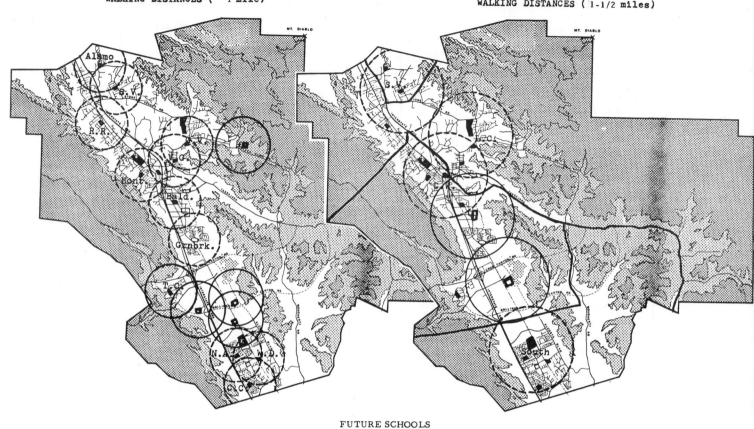

ELEMENTARY SCHOOLS
WALKING DISTANCES (1 mile)

INTERMEDIATE SCHOOLS
ATTENDANCE AREAS AND
WALKING DISTANCES (1-1/2 miles)

FUTURE SCHOOLS
1976-1980

HIGH SCHOOLS
ATTENDANCE AREAS AND
WALKING DISTANCES (2 miles)

162

Chapter Nine

Alamo

BENSON RANCH

Many hundreds of acres on the hillside of upper North Avenue (now Las Trampas Road) were once owned by a Mr. Benson, a very corpulent man (good candidate for Weight Watchers, by today's standards). There was no automobile available and he was too large to ride horseback, so he surveyed his vast acreage from a cart drawn by two large horses. For many years the paths that were made by his much-traveled cart were visible to hikers when they walked the Las Trampas range.

Sometime before the turn of the century, Mr. Benson built a large three-story home on the hillside and a smaller house just below, and at least two barns, away and detached from the houses and other necessary out buildings of the day, and those that struck his fancy.

John Louis Morss and his wife Isabelle and daughter Loubelle moved into the home following the San Francisco earthquake. (See story of Morss family later in this chapter.)

COLONEL WILLIAM LINCOLN WHITE

In about 1913 Colonel William Lincoln White and his wife, Inga, moved into the larger of the original Benson homes. They remodeled it and installed inside plumbing. Colonel White thought it appropriate to rename North Avenue Las Trampas Road, and did so. Leland Stanford White, the colonel's brother, and a Mr. Peck, a brother-in-law, lived in the smaller house.

Colonel White had started the *Walnut Creek Courier Journal* on June 1, 1911, and was its owner/editor. It later was named *Courier Journal*[1] and was distributed to and read by all of Central Contra Costa County. It was said that under Colonel White it was the "fighting backbone" that transformed Walnut Creek's Main Street

from a mudhole. Later it was managed by Harry Silver.

Tony Linhares (deceased) worked for Colonel White before World War I. When he and Bertha (Bell) Linhares (RA) were first married in 1922 they lived in the smaller house. Tony rented the 800 acres of hillside property and ran cattle there.

In the early 1920s the Whites moved to New York for a time and rented their home to Captain Meyers, whose wife was a Dunfee. The Whites later returned to Alamo, and Colonel White passed away. In time, Inga was remarried to Edward T. Lesure, known as "Ned." Mr. Lesure was a bridge contractor and worked on the Caldecott Tunnel (RA) and other smaller bridges. The bridge in Pleasanton near Castlewood Country Club was one of his. Years later Mrs. Lesure sold thirty acres adjoining the Timme property to a Reverend Finch who subsequently sold the property (Lesures later moved to Muir Lane, Alamo. Both are now deceased.) About 1955 Mrs. Lesure sold the knoll to Phillip Fay (RA) of Alamo. The following year he purchased nine acres of the lower flat property and the next year sixty-five more acres, including both houses. For years he rented the houses and also rented horse pasture land. In 1974 Fay sold a portion to a Mr. Snyder of Midland, Michigan. He was with Dow Chemical. It was thought he might build on the apple orchard. However, his plans were changed.

Attorney William D. McCann and his wife, Barbara, and children, purchased the old three-story home in 1974. He had it restored and remodeled and the family moved in in 1976. Their contractor estimated that the building had been restored at least seven times. The smaller home below, which had been used over the years by residents, hired help, caretakers, and as a gate house, has been dynamited and is gone. The acreage surrounding the home is now known as "Hide Park."

At the time reconstruction of the old three-story Benson home commenced in April of 1976, the structure had been almost destroyed. One of the interior foundation walls had been removed to accommodate a passage for a large Saint Bernard owned by one of the rental tenants. When the wall was demolished, the stones were cast down the hill into the poison oak. Many of them were covered with earth and had to be dug up and placed back in the wall. Several cases of poison oak were experienced. During reconstruction the house was physically lifted off the ground three separate times to bolster the foundation. The main fireplace in the living room had to be reconstructed, as many of the key bricks had been taken out and thrown down the hill. The old balustrade and staircase had broken down, and had to be entirely replaced with hand-hewn spokes. The exterior portico on the west side was completely broken down, and several of the large twelve-by-twelve fluted redwood columns had been stolen. Half a mile of electrical conduit was used in rewiring the house. Forty-eight cases of caulking were used to seal the house before it was painted by Rainbow Painters, Nevada.

Since Mr. Benson was a man of great proportions he required a bathtub of inordinate size. One story says the fountain found outside of the lower story was his personal bathtub. It was made of brick, with a small iron railing set in the brick. In the restoration of the fountain, it was found that cement had been poured over the brick and the iron railing.

The current owner was shown a San Francisco paper, dated 1856, found between the redwood studs of the living room. Unfortunately, it was removed by a former tenant. The fireplace ash dumps sandwiched between the massive boulders which compose the fireplace of the house were installed at the time the huge stone fireplace was built. The ash dumps were constructed by the Montague Co., located at 301 Market Street, San Francisco. The 1870 directory of San Francisco businesses shows that particular company in business at that time, but by 1890 the company was no longer listed.

Two architects experienced in the art of Victorian reconstruction noted that the exterior portico on the west side of the house appears to have been constructed in about 1890. The portico is rococo in nature, with plaster castings underneath the supports and on the corinthian mantle above the western door of the house. This portico was added to the western section of the house after its original construction. During the reconstruction of the second story veranda, many of the old nails holding floorboards were removed. These nails were hand-forged, and typical of nails used in constructing California residences in the mid-nineteenth century. Nails found in the exterior portico are a machine-made variety.

MORSS FAMILY

The following is taken from personal recollections of Loubelle Morss Bangs, who resides in Cathedral City, California, and her brother Flood Morss of Alamo. I have taken excerpts from their material with their complete approval.

John Louis Morss was born in Stockton, California, November 28, 1863, the oldest of ten children. The family moved near Cambria, California when he was quite young. He later worked in the Salinas Valley on the King Ranch, which is now King City. About 1898 John Morss went to Happy Valley (Lafayette), accompanied by Mr. King, who had purchased a small ranch there. Mr. King also owned a grocery store in Oakland.

John Morss met Isabelle Christina Flood, who was born June 21, 1878, the third youngest of eight children. Her family came from Dumdrum, Ireland, near Dublin, to California in 1883-84, first settling in Martinez, then Stege (San Pablo), and later Piedmont. They bought a ranch in Upper Happy Valley where they lived out their lives. The ranch was known as the Flood Ranch.

John Louis Morss was married September 12, 1900 to Isabelle Christina Flood, and he went to work for J. H. T. Watkins on a cattle ranch leased from the Water Co., in Bollinger Canyon, San Ramon. A daughter, Ramona Loubelle, was born August 14, 1901, at the ranch. She was named Ramona after San Ramon and Loubelle, a combination of Louis and Isabelle.

The town of San Ramon at that time had one small grocery store with a post office and a grammar school on the corner going to Haywards (now Hayward). Mr. Watkins had his business office in San Francisco, a large home in Oakland, and a big home in Maine. His time was divided between the east and west coasts. His hobby was raising registered Hereford cattle without horns, Polled Hereford and other cattle.

John Morss reported to Mr. Watkins at the San Francisco office two or three times a year about the cattle business. On these trips he would take his family. His route would be the road which went through neighboring ranches from San Ramon, over the hills to Moraga through the Trelute Ranch, came out behind Saint Mary's College, and went through the Redwoods and over the hill into Oakland. They would leave early in the morning. He would leave his wife and daughter with a sister at the Pat Medau home (a son, Alvin Medau of Lafayette, is now deceased), then he would take the train to San Francisco.

Loubelle remembers one day, when she was a little girl of probably six or seven, when a fancy buckboard wagon with two horses drove into their yard with four people in it, driven by Mr. Benson. He had driven from Alamo on the roads he had built through his ranch, circling the whole ranch from his home and barns. She also remembers the 1906 earthquake which occured early in the morning. Her father was milking the cows in the barn, her mother was feeding the cats and dogs, and she was sitting in the kitchen warming her feet in the oven. All of a sudden everything shook! They ran outside and stood under a tree. Later they drove to Oakland, as her father had to go to San Francisco on business. They stayed overnight and, from a vacant lot across the street from an aunt's home in Oakland, they watched San Francisco burning.

Shortly after that they moved into the large three-story Benson home in the hills up Las Trampas Road. Following is Loubelle's description of the house:

The Benson home was built into the side of a hill which was dug out to fit the house. The first floor they dug into the side of the hill and built out of sandstone with a large dining room, with a large restaurant size stove across one end and a formal pantry plus another which set well back into the hill for a cooler. There was also a large room for wood storage, a bedroom and entrance with French windows, and a porch on two sides. The stairway leading to the second story went out the dining room. The second floor contained a very large living room over the dining room below, with a very large fireplace plus a wing of two bedrooms and a bathroom with bathtub and wash basin only. There was a room for logs for the smaller fireplace over the lower wood room, plus a front stairway out of the living room to the third floor. There was also a back stairway. The third floor was all bedrooms with an outside entrance onto the driveway. Each floor opened out to a beautiful terraced garden, with heavenly roses which climbed up to the rooftop. From the dining room you went out around a circular fishpond to a path that led around the hill to a formal toilet (outside) with sections for men and women.

When the Morss family moved into the Benson home, following Mr. Benson's heart attack and death, it was all quite new and in excellent condition. The barn had sections for horses, cows, carriage, and hay, and all was painted red. There was a very large aviary with many sections, which housed quail and many other birds. On the flat land below the big house was a large heated hothouse. Everything was in perfect order and fine condition. The surviving Benson family members retained the third floor for their use when they came to the country. The only way to heat the house was with fireplace heat on each floor, with one chimney for all. The kitchen stove furnished hot water.

Loubelle entered Alamo Grammar School, with its one teacher, Miss Ida Hall (RA). She rode her pony to school. Among her schoolmates were Roy Bell, Lorenz Humburg, Amelia and Manuel Ventura, and Alden Jones. While they resided at the Benson Ranch, Mr. Watkins interested Mr. Morss in buying the 400-acre ranch adjoining, between the Benson and Jones ranches.

In about 1910, while living on the Benson Ranch, her father bought his first automobile, a one-seater with a rumble seat and no windshield, called E.M.F. ("every morning fix'em!"). Later he purchased a newer car with two seats.

A son, Flood Morss, was born in the Benson house on March 23, 1912, delivered by the same Danville doctor who attended his mother when his sister was born (must have been Dr. Reimer). Their telephone (RA) was on an eight-party line with neighboring families, each with its own number of rings. Viola (Scott) Root (RA) was the operator and she connected them with long distance and would even take messages.

About 1913 the Morss family moved to Lafayette to the Blum Ranch in Briones Valley on Bear Creek at Bear Creek Falls. It was a 5,000-acre ranch which Mr. Watkins leased from the Oakland Water Company. Loubelle entered the Lafayette Grammar School and had a male teacher who had taught her mother in Piedmont. The school was later divided into two rooms and she had a lady teacher. She graduated from Lafayette school in about 1917. She rode five miles horseback to school daily. Among her schoolmates were the McNeils and Cliff Thompson and his sisters. Their home in wet winters was closed in

Left, the Alamo Post Office at Las Trampas Road and Danville Highway, facing south to Danville, in about 1912. Below, same spot from opposite direction.

and their only means for getting out was by horseback. They picked up their groceries and mail in Lafayette weekly, by buckboard and horses.

Loubelle remembers that in those early days her father drove cattle into Oakland to the slaughter house. They would leave late afternoon with the herd and go as far as behind the Claremont Hotel (the route is now Fish Ranch Road), hold the cattle overnight, and at the crack of dawn drive them down Ashby Avenue in Berkeley clear to the waterfront, to the Grayson Owen Slaughter House. All their cattle were grass fed.

In the summer of 1917 Mr. Morss built a two-story house at the end of Las Trampas Road. (That house burned down in 1935 and was rebuilt as a one-story house, which still stands.) Flood walked to Alamo Grammar School and his sister commuted on the train. She was in the first freshman class in the new high school building. Her classmates were Helen Baldwin, Waldo Wood, Dorothy Close, Evelyn Woodward (deceased), Andrew Anderson and the Olsson boys. She graduated in June 1921. She graduated from California School of Arts and Crafts and earned her teacher's certificate. She worked as a designer for Pacific Embroidery Company in San Francisco. While there she met Walter Adam Groshong, whom she married December 25, 1925. They later moved to the ranch in Briones Valley and lived there until he passed away from an injury on November 2, 1928. Loubelle returned to the family home in Alamo, where she lived until she married Joseph Albert Sturm on June 1, 1929. They moved to Lincoln Avenue in Walnut Creek. Her husband had a music studio. He taught and

played for parties and dances. (My husband took piano from him and still has his first practice book.)

John Morss passed away on August 8, 1932, three months before his sixty-ninth birthday, "with his boots on!" As an old cattleman he rode his horse every day on his ranch[3]. His wife died on August 18, 1937 at the age of fifty-eight. She had continued to operate the ranch up to her death. Loubelle entered Don Lux School of Hairdressing about 1933. She opened Loubelle Beauty Shop in the Sturm Building on Main Street in Walnut Creek in 1934. On April 24, 1938 Joe Sturm suffered a heart attack and died.

On July 3, 1943 Loubelle married Alfred Darwin Bangs in Oakland. In 1945 she sold her shop and they moved to Santa Monica, where they bought and managed a motel for about two years. He had major surgery and they went to Palm Springs for him to recuperate. They lived in Santa Monica for a time and then built a home in Cathedral City and moved to the desert to live in 1955. Both earned licenses as real estate salesmen and brokers, and worked in real estate in Palm Desert. Alfred Darwin Bangs died on March 3, 1965 of a heart attack.

Flood Morss served overseas in the 16th Batallion of the Seabees for over three years. On

February 28, 1945 he married Evalyn Laura Murray in Oakland and they lived in Alamo. She died of cancer in 1976. She was the daughter of William H. and Myrtle Murray of Webb Lane, Walnut Creek. Both parents survive her.

Neither of the Morss offspring had children. Loubelle lives in a mobile home in Rancho Mirage, near Palm Springs. Flood sold his Ridgewood Road home in February 1977, and will be building a new home back on Las Trampas Road property. His architect is Lambert Wille of Danville.

Mr. Benson traveled Europe often. A Mediterranean candelabra from the Holy Land and an old wrought iron kerosene lamp and liquor cabinet from the Benson home are still possessions of Flood and Loubelle. They also have the handwritten deed to the Alamo ranch.

TIMME

At the upper south end of Las Trampas Road toward the hills is a private road called Lark Lane. Abigail (Mrs. E. G.) Timme told me in June 1976, when I visited her lovely home, that their road was named Lark for one of their female Doberman dogs. Lark, the dog, would sit in the lane below the home and guard the area.

Mr. and Mrs. Ernst G. Timme came to Contra Costa County from Chicago, and fell in love with the Valley, especially the lovely Las Trampas range to the west. In June of 1935 they were fortunate to purchase from Mrs. Inga White 17.08 acres at the end of what is now Lark Lane, then nothing but a cow path with cattle-loading facilities at the gate.

The purchase completed, the Timmes returned to Chicago where Mr. Timme was connected with the Continental Casualty Company and Continental Assurance Company as Secretary. It took some time to arrange things to leave the companies. They began to build on their new property in late 1936, and the home was completed late in 1937 and named "Magnolia Hill." The Timmes immediately became community-minded and joined the Diablo Country Club, participating in its activities. Mrs. Timme was elected president of the Diablo Garden Club (RA) in 1939 and served a two-year term. She is now an Honorary member of this active group.

In 1954 Mr. Timme was not well and they went to Florida to visit old Chicago friends. They became interested in the small town of Clermont, bought some property there, and built a small home where they spent their winters. Mr. Timme

passed away in 1957 in Clermont, Florida. Mrs. Timme maintains the home in Florida and divides her time between the two homes.

WOODLYN ROAD
Woodward - Linder

Woodlyn Road, north of Las Trampas Road, was named for two families sometime in 1948, when Kenneth J. and Helen Linder bought one acre from the Reverend Charles F. Woodward (deceased). They built their home and an adjoining smaller house for her parents, A. Fisher and Jessie (deceased) Compton. The Linder home was sold in November 1964, when the Linders moved to Rossmoor and were originals there and still remain. Mr. Compton was ninety-five years old on February 26, 1977, and resides in a rest home. The R. Radigonda family are current residents of the Linder home.

The following is from the personal recollections of Mrs. E. W. (Elizabeth "Betty" Woodward) Work, who resides at 144 Woodlyn Road.

The Reverend Charles F. Woodward grew up in Idaho and met his future wife, Elizabeth Glunz[4], while he was studying at San Anselmo Theological Seminary. She was a native Californian, born in San Francisco. The Woodwards had three daughters, Evelyn (deceased), Elizabeth, and Lois, who graduated from UC, Berkeley and made her home there.

During the years that the Reverend Woodward was pastor of the Danville Presbyterian Church (1908-13), he came to have a strong feeling for the San Ramon Valley, with its beauty and ideal climate. He purchased six acres of land at one hundred dollars per acre. This was down in "the orchard," as the Alamo area was sometimes called because of its extensive planting in prune trees.

In 1913 the family left Danville and moved to Kelseyville in Lake County, for two interesting years. Elizabeth remembers climbing Mt. Konocti barefoot with her father. All the youngsters in Kelseyville went barefoot, to her mother's considerable consternation. The boys were barefoot year-round; the girls put on shoes and stockings in the winter.

When the Woodward family returned to Alamo in 1915 there were two other families living up Las Trampas Road, Mr. and Mrs. Daniel Wilmore, who built the two-story house still standing at 1527 Las Trampas, and the Crozer family, who built the large two-story house up near the hills. Mr. Wilmore later built another house on what is now Via Lucia. The original house was sold to the

Shearer brothers, George, Ed and David. Their orchard extended from the railroad tracks to Patricia Lane[5]. (Some of it is now Via Serena subdivision.)

It was a rural area at that time. From their two Jersey cows, "Pet" and "Blossom," the Woodwards churned their own butter and delivered milk to the Crozers. They had a brooder house for baby chicks and sold eggs commercially. Coyotes howled in the hills every night. When they ventured down from the Las Trampas hills to see if any chickens were available, the shepherd dog, "Tippy," dutifully barked to announce their presence. In the spring when the chickens were let out, they would feast on the green cover crop in the orchard. "Tippy" herded them as if they were sheep and guided them back to their enclosures at night. They also had a large black pig named "Joe," who had a portable and movable pen. When he finished one patch of morning glory, he was able to shove the pen to the next green spot. "Joe" particularly enjoyed ripe Bartlett pears. Like most country families, the Woodwards had cats, and were deeply attached to their animals.

Close to their house was a "family orchard" of apples, peaches, cherries, plums, figs and quince, and also berries and grapes. They exchanged cherries for the Shearer's apricots. Once a year they went to the Love's Ranch at the end of Love Lane in Danville for a five gallon can of honey.

In the twenties, Colonel White was living in the large house in the hills at the end of Las Trampas Road. Elizabeth never saw him in person, but his large car went up and down the road almost daily. He wanted to plant palm trees along Las Trampas Road, but the local residents did not cooperate and were not enthusiastic. In time, pear trees replaced the prunes. Later the pears were being lost to an uncontrollable blight and were removed and walnut trees were planted. They were successful and gradually replaced the dying fruit trees until there was a beautiful walnut grove.

In the early twenties, what was known as a "Jap Camp" was established on Las Trampas Road. Its structure was close to what now would be known as a "commune." It had a large enclosed bath house, where a fire was built under the tub to heat the bath water. A friend named Tamiko Okomoto used to come down to visit. She taught Elizabeth to tat. The Japanese managed the pear sheds. By the mid-twenties the Alamo Grammar School was almost fifty percent Japanese.

At intervals during these years large droves of cattle were herded down Las Trampas Road from their grazing grounds in the hills.

All three Woodward girls graduated from the Alamo Grammar School and San Ramon Valley Union High School. Elizabeth graduated in 1923; there were seven in the class. An electric train, known as the "Toonerville Trolley (RA)," was transportation to high school in Danville. The motorman and conductor were very protective of their young passengers. When the rains were heavy, water in the creek became a swift, high current. The banks of the stream at the end of the Las Trampas Road had eroded and it was necessary to build a trestle to bridge the gap. When the water was extremely high, the conductor would ask the students to dismount. He and the motorman would take the trolley over the somewhat shaky trestle; when it was safely on the other side, the students clambered aboard again.

Elizabeth left for college at UC, Berkeley in 1923, and spent summers working at Camp Curry in Yosemite Valley. She married in 1928 and lived in Medford, Oregon from 1929-1946, where their three children, Beverly, Robert and Lewis were born. In 1946 they returned to Alamo to the original family property. The Work children attended San Ramon Valley High School.

R. Fuller Keys started coming to Alamo when he was about ten years old. The home on the west side of Woodlyn Road was built in about 1933, to be used for a summer home and for weekends. R. F. Keys and his wife, Zeta, sold the two-plus acreage and the home in September 1976 to eYvonne Williams of Pittsburg, who has done extensive remodeling to the structure which was in bad shape from vandals when she bought it. She moved in with her children, Brian, Lynn, Heather and Todd.

CROZER

The two-story Crozer home on La Colina, off Las Trampas Road, in Alamo, was built in 1913 for Enoch L. and Georgie Crozer of Alameda. Edward Sims, who studied under Bernard Maybeck of Berkeley, was the builder. The Crozer children were Hannah, Miriam, Enoch and Ruth. Adopted twin sisters were Esther and Sarah Lee. Ruth attended San Ramon Valley Union High School and graduated in 1915. She also attended UC, Berkeley. Enoch died several years ago of a heart attack following a fire at the home.

The senior Crozers ran the Sunday School held in the Alamo School until Mrs. Crozer's death in 1928. Their daughter Ruth played the organ and Enoch the cornet. Many Alamo children attended faithfully each Sunday (including my hubby Alfred). The Crozers gave an annual Sunday School picnic, which included all family members, at Pine Canyon. The children went by wagon and also had hay rides. Mr. Crozer and his daughter Ruth later took some of the children to Sunday School in Danville, after Mrs. Crozer's death. He died in 1936.

Ruth was a vocational nurse and worked at Alta Bates Hospital in Berkeley until her retirement. She married Max Giddings of Berkeley. At one time he worked at the toll gate at Mount Diablo entrance. They lived at "Sequoia Grande," (as they named the Crozer home, named for the tree which is still on the property), into their eighties. She died in October 1975 and he died of a stroke in 1976.

The home and one and one-half acres were sold in an estate sale[6] to Mr. and Mrs. Arthur N. (Merrill) Beebe, Jr. of Alamo, in June of 1976. They have saved the basic structure, and will remodel and restore it to its original state, using the old house plans and making additions of their own as needed. Their contractor is Arnold Wexler of Oakland. They have a daughter Leslie, born January 11, 1965 and a son, David Charles Arthur, born on St. Patrick's Day in 1977. He made his early arrival at John Muir Memorial Hospital in Walnut Creek, weighing in at five pounds and one ounce[7], and was named for his grandfather, father, and uncle. The Beebes sold a half-acre parcel to her aunt and uncle, Mr. and Mrs. Richard (Alice) Walsh of Saratoga, who will be building a new home there.

Martinez records show that Enoch Wisner Crozer sold a parcel of land to Waine M. Forss, September 8, 1943, recorded October 14, 1943.

MAURER FAMILY

Donald Dee Maurer and his wife, Bessie May (Kelly) Maurer, moved to Alamo from Walnut Creek, in July 1929. Their children were a daughter, Vivian, and three sons, Firl, Dale (deceased) and Duane. Bessie May's mother, Mary (Mrs. William) Kelly, nee Mullvaney, lived across the creek from the Maurer family for years.

Donald Maurer designed and built the suspension bridge which crosses the creek to the present Gertz property from La Serena Avenue. He was a machinist at Hall-Scott Motor Company in Berkeley for twenty-seven years. In 1929 he built a large two-story wooden home where the family lived while he and sons Firl and Dale built the stone house. It was built of rock and cement with walls one foot thick. This then became the family home until it was removed when Freeway 680 came to Alamo.

1. Vivian was born in Lima, Ohio, the same city where her father was born. Her mother, Bessie May Kelly, was born in Brewster, Kansas, where she met her husband. In 1918 the family came to California, to a little town called Las Juntas. Vivian's brother Firl was born in Berkeley just before the family moved to Walnut Creek. Vivian attended a one-room schoolhouse in Saranap. Her first teacher was a Miss Dewing. She then attended school in Walnut Creek, before the family moved to Alamo. Then the children attended Alamo Grammar School and Danville Grammar School, and Vivian graduated from San Ramon Valley Union High School in 1936. There were forty graduates that year—the largest class ever! She moved to San Francisco, where she did secretarial work and wrote for some "throwaway" newspapers. She moved to Hollywood and was secretary in a radio publicity office. She was married in 1941 to Jack Woods and moved to Fort MacArthur in San Pedro when he went into the Army. In 1947 they moved to Las Vegas, where they remain. They had two children. Jack is retired from his insurance business. Vivian is involved with writing about art, selling her own art works as well as others', and working with local cultural organizations in Las Vegas, Nevada, as well as in the Capistrano area. She was in Alamo to visit family members the first of May, and returned south to set up the Elks Helldorado Western Art Show for May 7, 1977.

2. Firl Maurer graduated from San Ramon Valley High School, class of 1938. He was on the football team and held records in cross-country. At one time he worked at the Sunset Nursery for Herman Sandkuhle. He is now with Richmond Beverage. During World War II he was in the Navy, from November 1941 to October 1947. While stationed in Australia he met (Janet) Nettie Shields, daughter of John and Mary Shields of Perth, West Australia. She arrived in the United States in 1947 and they were married May 4, 1947 in Reno, Nevada. They have three sons, John, Dan, and David. After they were married they built their own home themselves beside the other

Maurer stone house on the hillside across from La Serena Avenue. The blocks they used were twenty-five pounds of rock and cement. This house, too, was demolished when the freeway went through. The roadway up the hillside and an oak and pine tree still remain. Firl and Nettie Maurer now make their home on Ardith Drive in Alamo. She is active in SPAY and does volunteer work.

Their son John, born September 6, 1948, attended local schools and graduated from San Ramon Valley High School in 1966. He was in the Marine Corps for four years and married Melissa Mattingly of Danville. They had a daughter Jennifer, now nine years old, and later divorced. John married Laurie Pullman in 1974 and they have a daughter, Leah, four months old. They live in Hudesville, Humboldt County, and John works at Pacific Lumber in Scotia.

Son Dan was born June 14, 1951. After graduation from San Ramon Valley High School, he worked at the Hound Dog in Danville while attending Diablo Valley College. He is now at San Francisco State working toward his teacher's credential in speech and English.

Son David was born June 28, 1958, graduated from Del Amigo High School in 1976, and is a musician.

3. Dale Maurer was killed by a hit-and-run driver near Hayward at the beginning of World War II.

4. Duane Maurer lives at Capay, near Woodland, California.

Donald Dee Mauer, the father, lived on Diablo Road and now lives across the street at Tamarack Manor in Danville.

RICH - VALENTINE

James and Elizabeth Rich came to California in an ox-drawn covered wagon. At one point they were with the ill-fated Donner party (RA). James Rich settled in the vicinity of Watsonville. He lived to be 100 years old. Their son Cass was born almost immediately after they arrived from their six-month-long, arduous journey.

Cass and Laura Rich had a son, James L. Rich. As a young man he settled in Oakland and started his building career. He pioneered many of Oakland's better districts. Today all of his houses and buildings remain standing in good condition, showing the excellence of his workmanship.

He and his wife Gwendolyn, who died in 1961, had two daughters, Laura, named for her grandmother, and Anne. During the war the family lived in the very sparsely developed Berkeley Highlands. Mr. Rich learned from a friend that the Harrison place in Alamo was for sale. When he retired in 1943 he and his wife and daugther Anne (Laura had married) moved to Alamo on a six-acre parcel. There was the main house, a smaller house in the rear, an apartment in the tank house, where Mr. Harrison's brother Wilfred lived for several years. Wilfred Harrison was responsible for planting many of the walnut trees in the area in about 1913.

The Rich family arrived in Alamo before any change had come to the beautiful valley. In back of them was a huge prune orchard, which in 1948 was developed by Marchant and Lawrie as Camille Park (RA) subdivision, and Camille Court (RA) was born. There were few houses on Camille Avenue (RA). The only near neighbors on Danville Boulevard were the Pangborns, Medlyns (RA), and Waynes (RA).

Harold C. Valentine was on the front lines during World War II. He was an instrument specialist in the Air Corps. He had graduated from Curtis Wright and it was his duty to keep the planes flying. He started with the African Invasion, was on the much-bombed isle of Malta, in Italy and in France, until V.J. Day, when he came home. Harold C. Valentine and Anne G. Rich were married on August 13, 1945 in Oakland. The atom bomb was dropped while they were on their honeymoon, or he would have had to go on to Japan.

He had served his country from April 14, 1941 to August 28, 1945. His father passed away three days after his return from active service. This terminated any idea of their going into business together as they had planned. He took the first available job and was meter reader for the Coast Counties Gas Company. His territory was Orinda, Moraga, Lafayette, Walnut Creek, Alamo and Danville. He read every meter himself, plus the butane tanks! Later he went to work for Contra Costa County and progressed, taking an early retirement in order to enjoy their home and the area.

Anne was combination secretary, bookkeeper and salesperson for the *Walnut Kernel* (RA), county-wide newspaper, from 1945 to 1950. (Author's note: I arrived as a columnist on that paper in May of 1953 (RA).)

In the meantime James L. Rich, though retired, kept active by building on his own property as well as for others. He took the contract for the demolition of the first high school in Danville. The one now standing was built in its place. About 1960 some of the Rich property was sold to the Walter Xavier family. Mr. Rich is ninety years old and is in the rest home in Danville.

TURNER

Herbert and Mary (Burroughs) Turner and their two children, Ruth N. and Gordon B., moved to Alamo in 1917. The Turners had purchased 6.54 acres from Hugo and Elizabeth Herzer, part of which later became Barbee Lane.

There was a house at the end of what is now Barbee Lane, built by a Dr. Webster (or Webber) around 1910, on the present site of Number 45, the Mandalou house. In the record of the sale by the Herzers to the Turners, the property is described as "an area of six and fifty-four hundredths (6.54) acres of land and being a portion of lot No. 3 of what is known as the Hemme subdivision of the Ford Tract in the Rancho San Ramon."

Mrs. Herbert Turner contracted with Travis Boone of San Ramon to harvest the walnuts, remove the pear trees, and plant more walnut trees. The Edward White family purchased six acres from Mrs. Turner in 1956, built their home on the cul-de-sac, and named the street Barbee Lane for their elder daughter Barbara. The old two-story seven-room house was torn down when the Whites built their house in 1956-57. They lived in the old house while their new home was being built by John Osmundson. He developed the street by building some speculative homes and selling lots.

Miss Ruth N. Turner has one-half acre which faces Hemme Avenue. Her home was designed by George Simonds of Hayward and built by Roy Collins in 1951. She is a retired librarian of the Contra Costa County Library system, and remains as the original owner-resident.

Attorney Gordon B. Turner, with offices in Martinez (Turner & Huguet), and his wife, Dorothy, live in Ygnacio Valley. Their two sons are Lieutenant Colonel John A. Turner, currently assigned to Fort Sill, Oklahoma, and Dr. Stephen G. Turner, ophthalmologist with offices in San Leandro.

There are now eleven homes, including Miss Turner's house which faces Hemme Avenue, on the original 6.54 acres. Except for the Turner, Ferrando, Clottu, and Brumfield houses, all others have changed ownerships.

MACKAY

The adjoining ten acres to the west, now Rancho-Romero School, was once owned by Mrs. Hattie Mackay. She and her husband used it as a summer and weekend home. He died in the 1920s. Before her death in 1960, Mrs. Mackay sold the ten acres to Henry Jones of Oakland, who sold it almost immediately to the school district for a handsome profit.

WESTMINSTER RETREAT

The old house on the hill at the end of Hemme Avenue, now the Westminster Retreat, was built early in the century by a Professor Stratton. He was its first occupant. His daughter, Cornelia Stratton Parker, and her husband, Carleton Parker, economist and author, lived there for a period of time.

Progression of ownership is: Dr. Clark, the Kriedts, Andersons, and Forrest "Duke" and Betty Engelhart, who sold the property to Westminster Retreat.

BARBEE LANE

*Indicates original owners who still live on Barbee Lane.

Number 43, the former Edward White home, was later purchased by Alamo realtor Lee Grabel and his wife Helen. They sold to George and Ruth (deceased 1973) Palsulich and their daughter Geraldine, known as "Geri," in 1966. Geri is a teacher in the San Ramon Valley Unified School District.

Number 18. John and Tessie Ferrando* bought their home in May 1958 while it was being constructed by builder Francis T. Finigan. They did some of the finishing themselves. Their son, Gary, and daughter, Loree, attended local schools and graduated from San Ramon Valley High School. Gary married Joyce Fagliano and they have a son, Greg, born January 29, 1969. Loree went to the "old" Alamo Grammar School on Danville highway a short time before Rancho-Romero School was completed. She married Mark Mc-Candalles and they live in Walnut Creek.

Number 27. Robert W. and Lorraine Clottu* and son, Robert, known as Robby, had their home custom-built by Richard Sorley while they lived in Lafayette, and moved in on June 7, 1958. They came to Contra Costa County from Stockton. Lorraine was one of the first teachers hired for Montair School and taught eleven years. Robby attended local schools and graduated from San Ramon Valley High School June 1964 and from San Jose State. He married Cindy Claraty of Walnut Creek (her grandmother is Cora Root Daley). They have a son, Brian Robert, born July 29, 1976, and live in Fresno. Lorraine's mother, Mrs. Belle McAlpin, lived on Barbee Lane for nine and one-half years, and is now a resident of Walnut Creek Convalescent Hospital. The Clottus have been active in community affairs over the years.

Number 42. Edgar C. and Elizabeth Brumfield* moved in on September 12, 1959. Theirs was the last house built on the street. The builder was Jack Metez of Danville. Their daughter, Norma, was attending College of the Pacific and graduated June 1960. She later worked at Wells Fargo Bank in Walnut Creek. Their sons, Richard and Edgar, were ten and twelve years old and attended local schools and graduated from San Ramon Valley High School. A grandson, Ronald James, son of Richard, now lives with his grandparents during the daytime and attends Rancho-Romero School. Ed Brumfield is a realtor in San Leandro.

Number 45. Nick and Mary Mandalou, daughter, Silvia, and sons, Paul and Nick, Jr., bought their home from a pilot named Fred Paris and moved in 1961. Silvia lives in San Francisco. Nick Mandalou lives in Florida. Paul graduated from San Ramon Valley High School in June 1977 and Nick, Jr. will graduate in June 1978.

Number 34. James E. and Hilda Phebus bought their home from Mrs. Jean Ahlers (her husband was deceased) in 1961. It was built by John Osmundson. Their two children, Mike and Kathy, went to the local schools. Mike is married to Susan Cartwright of Marysville and they have a son, Grant, born March 25, 1977. Kathy married Tom Neadeau of Mokelumne in the gold country. They have a daughter, Monica, born June 19, 1975.

Number 19. Raymond J. and Phyllis Marta bought their home from Lee Bridges, August 17, 1963. Realtor Lee Grabel handled the transaction. Ray's mother, Mary, came to live with them after she was widowed. The Martas have four daughters, Marianne, Michelle, Denise and Darcelle. All attended local schools. Marianne attends California State University at Hayward, majoring in English and art. She will graduate in 1978. Michelle attends San Francisco State College, and will also graduate in June 1978. She majors in art and and psychology. Denise graduated from the local high school in June 1977 and Darcelle will graduate in June 1978. Ray Marta has been with the *Oakland Tribune* for many years, as Graphics Art Director. The family moved to Alamo from Hayward.

Number 10. John A. and Frances Anderson and their two daughters, Betty Jo (deceased 1966) and Mary, moved to Alamo, July 10, 1965. They bought their home from the Richard Brazeals. (He was a retired Navy man and she a teacher.) Realtor Ed Brumfield handled the transaction. Mary Anderson graduated from San Ramon Valley High School. She worked in Walnut Creek and now works and lives in San Francisco.

Number 26. Fred J. and Bernice Warren bought their home on July 1, 1966 from David and Ruth Neisch, who had two sons and two daughters. The original owners were the Stahle family. The Warrens have a married son and daughter. Fred is retired.

TAGG

John "Jack" A. Tagg, son of George and Myra Tagg of Walnut Creek, married Beatrice "Bea" Sweet, daughter of Eugene and Bee Sweet of Walnut Creek. Both sets of parents celebrated fifty years of married life recently.

Jack attended Pleasant Hill Grammar School, Acalanes High School, St. Mary's College and Cal Dental School. Bea attended Piedmont High School and Stanford University. They met in Hawaii and were married in Las Vegas, Nevada, October 24, 1951.

A son, Scott, was born November 24, 1954 at Peralta Hospital in Oakland. He attended Dorris-Eaton School, Rancho-Romero, St. Isidore's and De La Salle High School. He is now in San Luis Obispo at Cal Poly. In 1971 he earned his Eagle Scout award in Alamo Troop #213. Daughter Terryl was born July 25, 1958, on her mother's birthday, at the same hospital in Oakland, four months after the family moved to Barbee Lane in Alamo. She attended Dorris-Eaton, Rancho-Romero, St. Isidore's and San Ramon Valley High School, and is now at St. Mary's College.

Jack started dental practice at the Alamo-Medical-Dental Building in March of 1958. He bought his office from Dr. D. S. Harris in 1963. The Tagg family has lived on Barbee Lane the longest, arriving in March 1958. They bought their home from George and Nita Stewart, who had lived there only about six months. The Stewarts moved to La Jolla, where they duplicated their Alamo home. They recently moved again, to San Diego. They visited Alamo and their former neighbors on Barbee Lane in April 1977.

Bea Tagg taught kindergarten in 1959-60 at Rancho-Romero School when John Waugh was superintendent. He had been her physics teacher at Piedmont High School. Clarence Hockett was the principal. In 1962 she retired but continues to substitute. She is a member of the Women's Auxiliary of Contra Costa Dental Society; a member of Jasmine Branch of Children's Hospital, and was chairman in 1962; and a member of Tioga Guild of John Muir Memorial Hospital. She is also a member of A.A.U.W. and Spinsters and Dames. During the 1960s she modeled at many fashion shows for the above groups. (I met the Taggs in 1959 when Bea and I were both members of Tioga Guild.)

Jack has been interested in music as long as he can remember. When he was a youngster his mother told him he could have a horse when he earned enough money by practicing the piano. It still amuses Jack to remember her putting coins in his "horse box." Jack's interest in music led him to create his own dance band while in college. He currently plays the sax with the San Ramon Rehearsal Jazz Band. He did get a horse, but not until 1968, when he purchased "Sweet Rosie," a thoroughbred mare, from Cindy Jackson of Alamo.

The horse opened new adventures for the Tagg family. One horse was not enough for four people who enjoyed riding. "Prince Binary," "Piccadilly Paddy," and "Abbey Road" arrived so the Tagg family could ride and show together. A four-horse trailer was purchased in 1970 when the family joined the Los Altos Hunt Club, and they participate as a family. In 1974, Terryl Tagg's conformation hunter, "Merry Monarch," won the Pacific Coast Hunter Associations' Championship. Terryl has many medals for her riding ability. On March 13, 1977, at the Pebble Beach Winter Show, the Tagg family won five silver cups.

BISSET
Las Quebradas Lane
(What it Means and How it Got its Name!)

Arthur H. Bisset was born and raised in Chico, California. He met Louise Stroever through her second cousin and his uncle, who were dating. They arranged a blind date in July 1939. Art and Louise were married in September of 1942. His father, Arthur, Sr., was born in Gridley and his mother was originally from Minnesota.

Lou and Marie Stroever, Louise's parents, were both born and raised in Oroville. However, they met following World War I in New Jersey, where they married. Louise was born in Engelwood, New Jersey. They moved back to California when she was two years old.

After World War II, following Art's discharge from the Army Air Corps, the young Bissets began to look for property in Contra Costa County. In June of 1948, they found it in Alamo. Together with her parents and an aunt and uncle, Art and Grace Clements, they purchased thirty-two acres off Miranda Avenue, from Byrne Powell. The real estate transaction was done by Al Ingalls of Highland Realty.

Of the original thirty-two acres, sixteen are now a part of the Round Hill Heights development, nine belong to John and Barbara Elliott, Mrs. Stroever has three acres with a small cottage, and the Bissets have approximately four acres.

Las Quebradas Lane did not exist. There was only a gravel drive that led back to Powell's residence and the home owned by the Ed Marshalls. Mr. Stroever, Art Clements and Art Bisset built one mile of road to where they planned for their homes to be. Joe Moura, who at the time was with Boucher, Moura and Whitten, cut the pads for the homes.

Art was with Transocean Airlines as a flight engineer, so on his days off he built their home. It took two years to complete. The entire exterior and roof are hand-sawed. They did not get electricity for power tools until everything was done but the interior finishing. The Bisset family moved in in 1951 from Piedmont. They had no phone service for one year. When it arrived it was the old crank model on an eight-party line. Their telephone ring was three short, two long and one short.

Art Clements, Louise's uncle, was a retired mining engineer. Las Quebradas was named for a gold mine in Columbia, South America, that he had operated. It means "breaks in the hills," and aptly described the upper part where they lived. He planned to build a "tamped earth home"— similar to adobe. Instead of formed bricks, the adobe was tamped down between boards which were then raised as the adobe dried, until a complete wall was formed. Such walls are about sixteen inches thick. In this manner he completed a guest house and garage. He found the process too slow and built the main house himself of standard frame construction. He was seventy years old when he started the project. Louise's dad built their own guest cottage and they spent every weekend there until his death in 1960.

Louise recalls that neighbors were few in those days. On Miranda Avenue, they first knew Vernon and Pat Buls, who were living in a little cabin they built (present site of Stone Valley School). They made their own adobe bricks for their future home. Before building the adobe, they built a frame house on the corner of Miranda Avenue and Miranda Court. They built their swimming pool from scratch, as well as the two homes. Other neighbors were the Philip Haultains, still on the corner of Stone Valley Road and Miranda Avenue; the M. L. (Zoe) Gilloglys, whose son Lee cut grass along the road for his goats; Al and Vi Meyer, who raised squabs (their home is now owned by the Al Pepi family); the William Fischer family where the Dale Landes now live; and the Bolla family. Further up Miranda were Manuel and Amelia Rose, Leona and Hank Hoffman, the Badgleys, "Meps" and Dorothy Morcom, Alex and Myrtie Hollbrook, and O. E. and Louise Cook (both deceased). Al and Martha Mougin (both deceased) were on Bunce Meadow Lane. Then Warren and Val Almquist moved from Diablo and built a home across from the Mougins. Bob and Sunny Read bought acreage and built on what is now Erselia Trail. The next family to move to Las Quebradas Lane, other than the Powell, Marshall, and Bisset families, were Ed and Myrtle "Jim" Thomas, who moved into Marshalls' home.

Art and Louise Bisset had three children. Steven was born in June 1948, after they purchased the Alamo property. Denise was born in October 1949 and Jo Anne in December 1957. They all attended local schools. The older two spent one year at the old Alamo School then graduated from Stone Valley School and San Ramon Valley High School. Jo Anne attended the new Alamo School and graduated from Stone Valley and Monte Vista. Denise is married to Gene Dolan and they have a son, Devon, born July 1974. A second baby is due in July 1977. Denise teaches at Alamo School; Gene works in Livermore. They make their home in Danville. Steve attended Diablo Valley College and after his discharge from four years in the Air Force worked for Western Electric until they closed. He chose to remain in California and went to work for Intel in Livermore. He lives in the cottage of his grandmother. Jo Anne lives at home, attends Diablo Valley College and works part time in San Ramon.

BARNARD

Alleron L. and Flora Robinson Barnard moved to Alamo in 1914, having purchased ten acres on Danville Boulevard, which they made into a beautiful place. He worked for the Maples Publishing firm in San Francisco and came home weekends on the Oakland-Antioch trolley. Their son, David (former owner of the East Bay Opticians of Concord, now retired in Pismo Beach), and daughters, Marian and Doris, attended the two-room Alamo School. Twins named Jean and June were born in 1923 and caused some excitement in the community.

In 1927 the house burned to the ground and all the good people of Alamo helped the family and took them in. They built a new home and the Alamo Women's Club bought a chair for it. Doris, now Mrs. Joseph C. Bragdon, still has the chair. She taught school for a while and her husband is an art professor at Hartnell College. They now live in Salinas.

My husband, Al Jones, went to high school with David Barnard and calls him "Happy," which was his nickname then. He tells of how surprised he was following the fire, to go home and find no home there!

1. The newspaper we know today as the *Contra Costa Times*, with a circulation of 90,000, was originally the *Courier Journal*. On Friday, January 7, 1977, an historical survey by the *Times* indicated *that* edition to be the 159th issue to be published in the 66th year of publication since June 1, 1911. That day's page one read "Vol. 66 No. 159." The *Times* is owned by Dean S. Lesher, president and publisher, and is published five times a week in the Times Building, 2640 Shadelands Drive, Walnut Creek, by East Bay Newspapers, Inc. The paper receives many awards annually.

2. Inga White Lesure had a niece who was married to Hugh Bennett (RA), who was secretary of the Greater San Ramon Valley Chamber of Commerce (RA).

3. Loubelle says she rode horseback until she was thirty-six years old. When too young to manage a horse, she rode seated on a pillow behind her mother. Flood took up riding seriously after his father's death and learned to rope and show horses statewide.

4. Beverly (Work), her husband, Gordon Williams, one daughter and three sons make their home in Pacific Grove. In 1973, the Williamses and two younger sons toured Europe. They tracked down Elizabeth Glunz' family and visited Hausen-ob-Verena in Ger-

many. They found it to be very rural, and after many junction turns, arrived there late one morning. Gordon exchanged words with a stubby little man in a peaked hat and green knee socks and his name, would you believe, was Glunz! In a matter of a few minutes they were surrounded by farm wives in well-washed print dresses over old sweaters, and wearing rubber boots, as the magic name "Christian Glunz" went up and down the street. The Williamses tried to explain in German that their Christian Glunz had departed 110 years before and settled in San Francisco, so nobody could be expected to remember him! The name San Francisco brought forth a tiny old lady clutching a letter written in English and mailed from Denver, which she had received two months previously. Gordon translated it with much spitz, sputters, and body language. The bad news told of a sad death. All the housewives stood about patiently muttering "ya, ya!" "Cousin" Glunz rescued them and took them to the city hall, where the mayor himself, dressed handsomely in a suit, got out the village census records.

The family tree shows that the great-grandmother of Elizabeth Work was Elizabeth Huller. They shared not only given names, but also July 13 birthdays, 96 years apart!

5. Patricia Lane was named by Jerry (deceased) and Ruth Hersam for their daughter. Linhares Lane was named by the Water Company when the line went in, for Tony and Bertha Linhares, who lived there. Melvin and Alice Hunt had built a home there years ago. Alvern Court was named for my husband, Al Jones, a realtor, and Vern Ryan, a contractor. They developed the two acres which they had purchased from a Mr. Gibbs. Four custom built homes went in on that street.

6. Our son, Gary, and his wife, Pat, also bid on this property.

7. This "rings a bell" for me, as our son, Gary, was also a "premie." He weighed four pounds and nine ounces at birth and we took him home when he weighed five pounds and one ounce.

A. J. Young Home

Danville's "Toonerville Trolley" ran from 1914 to 1924. The car was built in 1873.

Chapter Ten

Danville (Alamo Oaks)

"REMEMBER WHEN"

Remember the expression, "everyone wants to get into the act?" How true, and how fortunate that is for people like me trying to preserve the past. Volunteered information, which has often been stored away for long periods of time and then rediscovered, helps immensely with research. On Good Friday 1977 I received photocopies of news stories twenty-five years old. The newspaper was the *Valley Pioneer*, which used a covered wagon as its logo on every issue with the following legal statement: "Published every Thursday at Danville, California, by T. Eugene Haney and Margaret L. Haney, Publishers, and William E. Haigwood, Editor. Circulation to: Danville - Alamo - Diablo - San Ramon - and Tassajara." (This is the San Ramon Valley area as we know it today.) The articles were published in the spring of 1950, written in a series and based on interviews with oldtime residents of the valley by Raymond Van Tassell, former Alamo resident and Danville businessman. I received them in the mail from Reno, Nevada from his youngest son, Pieter, who was born in Alamo. I have his permission to share them with you. Number four in the series was an interview with Mrs. Ina Boone Root, whom he refers to as "Grandma Root," a direct descendant of Daniel Boone. With a sketch of "Residence of Joel H. Boone, Danville, California," starts the story:

Grandma Root's father was a direct descendant of Daniel Boone, the leader of many of the parties of early pioneers who came through the Cumberland Gap from the Colony of Virginia to the "wilderness" of "Kaintuck." He was Joel H. Boone, born in Missouri, and he first settled on Putah Creek when he reached California in 1852. Later he moved to Danville and married Sophie Love, who had attended Union Academy, an early school of higher education, which was formerly located where the highway crosses the boundary between Alamo and Danville. They were married in the Alamo Presbyterian church, which is no longer standing.

They first lived in a small house built under the big oak tree on the present Scott place across the street from the P-X market [presently Diablo State Bank, 355 North Hartz Avenue, Danville]. This was the house in which Mrs. Root was born, Oct. 3, 1873. Later Mr. Boone built the "new" house.

On Nov. 5, 1891, Grandma married June James Root, who came to California from Connecticut and lived on the R. O. Baldwin ranch and they lived in the "new" house (in 1950 home called "Scott house") where three sons, James, Austin and Harold, and a daughter, Cora, who is now Mrs. H. H. Daley of Pittsburg, were born. All of the boys are active Danville businessmen and make their home here. Many of us recall the celebration of the Roots' golden wedding anniversary when they were guests on the bride and groom program in Los Angeles. Grandma Root, who was widowed Jan. 25, 1948, has 18 grandchildren and five great-grandchildren and drives her own car as she goes about visiting them.

Mrs. Root says the Red Barn was built about 1857 by Abraham Burney Hoag, a distant relative of hers, and that it was operated by him as a plumbing shop and hardware store. She remembers some mighty wet winters when the wooden sidewalks of Danville were all washed away as were the bridges over San Ramon Creek at Mt. Diablo Street and on Front Street by the Village Theatre. Water stood as much as a foot deep where the Danville Warehouse and bunkers and the railroad tracks are now, and all the townsite was a sea of mud for weeks.

In the early days she started out before sun-up in a horse and buggy to drive over the Fish Ranch road to Oakland to take her music lessons and the round trip took all day. Quite a change from then to now [1950] when we whisk into Oakland through the tunnel in 45 minutes if we are not in a hurry—less if we step on it.

(See Boone genealogy in Chapter Two, *Early Pioneers*, and Root Families in Chapter Three, *Other Pioneers and Longtime Residents*.)

Number Five in this series by Raymond Van Tassell had the caption, "Remember When," with a photo of Danville's "Toonerville Trolley" and comments:

Here is the famous old coach-of-all-work that wended its erratic way from Saranap to Diablo through Danville's main street back in the '20s. Many oldtimers remember the gay fun reporters on Oakland and San Francisco papers had with their stories about Danville's "Toonerville Trolley" and quite a few remember the old vehicle itself. Mrs. Harriet McNeil of Danville, violin teacher and accomplished musician, is a daughter of the "skipper," Bill French, who herded the single piece of rolling stock over the line in its heyday. She says: "When it was raining we used to have to put up our umbrellas inside the car, when we rode, because of the leaks in the roof. We never knew when we started if the trip would land us in Saranap in time to make Oakland connections, or when we would back all the way into Danville again because of trolley-line trouble or track obstructions." My dad used to tell other people that the car was hinged in the middle to let it go around the curves, but once when I asked him if that was the truth he said, "No honey, it just looks snakelike because it's covered this d--- crooked track for so many years that it's got the habit of bending in the middle!"

The line was called the S.F.S.R.R. which meant San Francisco Sacramento Railroad. It was a "step-child" of the Sacramento Short Line. The "trolley car" was built originally in 1873 as a baggage car for the old Central Pacific R.R. Half the car was used as a combination smoker, baggage, freight, express and milk department, while the rest was coach. It had tiny windows that rattled incessantly, a little stove in one corner around which the commuters huddled on winter mornings to exchange country gossip, and under the seats were assorted picks and shovels to be used in case of landslides or washouts.

Bill French, the 210-pound "skipper," was a Democrat and in election years relations between the front end of the car and the back end, presided over by Republican conductor-baggageman Frank Flautt, became rather strained. In fact, when the rains washed a cut down over the track the skipper would stop the car and call out: "Republicans, man the shovels!" Then he would sit calmly in one of the coach chairs and puff away at his pipe until Frank and the "Republicans" had cleared the track.

He was said to be very superstitious and would never make a trip with 13 fares aboard. If he was flush he would ring up an extra fare, otherwise someone had to get off. This was particularly bad in the last few years of the run because there were just 13 regular commuters and unless someone brought a guest home for the night the passengers and the skipper would spend 15 or 20 minutes matching coins to see who was

either going to pay an extra fare or walk, before the trip would commence.

During the early years of its run, it was before the Memorial (Veteran's) Hall was built and the National Ice Cream factory was where Xavier's store is now. Joe Regello was operating a saloon in the Red Barn and the corner where Acree's store came later was a drug store. The tracks of the line went along the east side of the present highway through Alamo and continued through the center of Danville's main street to the south end of town where it crossed the Danville Gardens subdivision and went over a bridge back of the site of the new Charlotte E. Wood school to Diablo.

The railroad commission terminated the line in 1923 (some references say 1924) amid loud protests of residents of San Ramon Valley and the hilarious jibes of the city press, who lapsed into very bad verse in their glee: "Out of the roundhouse at dim break of day, The Toonerville Trolley starts on its way; Down through each San Ramon village and farm, The squeak of its wheels is a first-class alarm. Taking on milk, gossips, handgrips and freight, It often arrives just a day or two late; It goes clackety-click and clickety-clack, Over to Saranap and all the way back. It paddles in winter when waters are high, It wades through the dust when the summer is dry; It has ten miles of roadway, ten curves and a knot—But it's all the darned railroad the folks there have got." And from the high school kids a yell that went: "Clickety-clack! Clickety-clack! Over the roadbed and down the track; Save all the rivets, Keep all the nails—We'll get where we're going If we stay on the rail. Rah! Toonerville Trolley. Rah! Rah! Rah!"

Number Six in the series also used the caption "Remember When" and it was about Bethel Sims Coats, who was eighty-two in 1950, having been born April 16, 1868 in the first house on the Highland Road where it turns off the Tassajara.

The house is no longer standing but the present home is just a short way up the road and Mr. Coats drives into Danville in his own car every few days and every Sunday as he has done regularly during most of his 82 years.

"When I was a lad," said Mr. Coats, "my grandfather, Wilson Coats, and my father, Felix Coats, with some neighbors, went on a hunt after a grizzly bear that had been killing stock over toward Danville. The dogs cornered the bear and my granddad was the only hunter near the dogs. He went to the spot and the bear, surrounded by a bunch of dogs, was at bay in a small gulch. When the bear saw grandpa coming he charged the dogs, killing three of them, and grandpa unable to shoot for fear of hitting the dogs, was knocked down by a blow from the grizzly's paw that nearly scalped him. When he came to, the bear was gone, but he was later killed and was said to have weighed over 500 pounds."

Mr. Coats' earliest recollection of Danville was when he was about ten years old and he remembers seeing elk and antelope along the road. There was a store run by a Mr. M. Cohen and another known as Conway's on the main corners of the village (Front and Diablo now). He also recalls a plumbing or hardware store run by a Mr. Hoag which was up the road from these stores (now the Red Barn). At about the present site of the Flournoy place there was a Cambellite church and a cemetery near what we now call Bret Harte corners (official name given by the Contra Costa County Historical Society to the little three-cornered park at the junction of Tassajara Road and Mt. Diablo Blvd.)

Mr. Coats attended the Tassajara school for ten years. His first teacher was Albert Young. He pointed out the location on what is now part of the Blackhawk Ranch were Bret Harte once conducted a school.

In 1849 Mr. Coats' father, Felix Coats, came by pack train from Calaway County, Missouri, to Placerville, California, the scene of the gold diggin's. In 1852 a Miss Leona Doggett made the trip from Arkansas to Oregon on horseback at the age of eleven. The Doggetts later moved to the San Ramon Valley where Leona and Felix Coats were married about 1859, having three boys and four girls, our subject being the

youngest boy. Meanwhile, the Coats grandparents, Wilson Coats and his wife, Mary (Polly) Philips, came to Tassajara in 1853 and bought a section of land from a man named Martin. Bethel Coats married Phoebe Bowles on Dec. 30, 1891, at Tassajara, and they have three daughters.

Mr. Coats is remarkably vigorous and hearty, his 82 years sitting lightly on his shoulders and we newcomers to the valley congratulate and salute this charming couple of oldtimers.

See Coats Families, Chapter Two, *Early Pioneers.*)

ALAMO OAKS

Alamo Oaks, out Stone Valley Road, Alamo-Danville, is on the cusp of Alamo and Danville. In early history this 160-acre piece was a part of the town of Alamo, which, it is said, extended at one time to the foot of Mount Diablo. However, as time went on, it became Danville and so remained.

It was said to be the first subdivision in the general area. The 160-acre Smith Ranch was cut up into small farms of two to ten acres, with natural horse setups. It was named Alamo Oaks, because of the many beautiful oak trees growing there as nature had planted them. Many still remain. This early sub-division was developed

Smith Ranch. Place homesteaded by Peter Macauley June 10, 1871. Sold to Lawrence Smith July 17, 1871, it is now Alamo Oaks, Danville.

179

by Byington and Fagan Realtors of Alamo, in 1934.

SMITH RANCH

The Smith Ranch is located at 199 Oak Road, Alamo Oaks, Danville. Legal county records tell us that the progression of the ownership of the Smith Ranch is as follows:

1. On June 10, 1871, Peter and Anne Macauley homesteaded 160 acres, (¼ section.) (Book #1 of Patents, page 275, recorded July 17, 1871.)

2. Sold by Macauley July 17, 1871 to Lawrence Smith.

3. Deeded by Lawrence to Hannah Smith 1906.

4. Probated July 24, 1913 to five Smiths: John, Edward, Emily, William H., and Mary Kay.

5. John Smith deeded to Helena E. Smith on Nov. 14, 1925, recorded Dec. 3, 1925.

6. William Smith to Edward Smith, July 23, 1928.

7. June 14, 1934, Frank Byington and Fagan bought at probate sale from Edward, Helena, Mary K., Emily Smith.

8. Fagan conveyed his interest to Frank Byington 1936.

9. Frank Byington sold to Delahaye, 1938.

10. Delahaye to Wellman, date uncertain, Wellman bought 3½ acres.

11. Wellman sold to Foulds (Howard and Jean).

12. Foulds sold to Phillis 1947.

13. Phillis sold to Gordon (Hugh and Mimi).

14. Hugh Gordon sold to Wesley and Lois Sizoo, Sept. 1958, and they are the current owners.

SIZOO FAMILY

Wesley Sizoo, a native of Illinois, married Lois Amundson, a native of Oregon, on February 3, 1950 in San Francisco. He had just graduated from the University of Minnesota Law School, in December 1949. They had always wanted to live in California, she, after visiting with an aunt in Menlo Park and he after serving in the Marine Corps during the war. Prior to moving to Alamo Oaks in 1958 they lived in Marin County for seven years. They selected Alamo Oaks as it was the closest settlement to town that allowed horses. Their daughter, Marilyn "Marm," owned a horse there for seven years. She attended local schools from second grade on and graduated with the first class from Monte Vista in 1969. She graduated from UC, Berkeley in 1974.

Marilyn married Samil "Sam" Beret in 1974 at Tahoe. They were married by a longtime family friend, Superior Court Judge Bruce Sumner of Santa Ana. They have a daughter, Sarah, born May 15, 1975 and a son Jon, born November 18, 1976, and live in Charleston, West Virginia. Sam

has his Ph.D. from UC, Berkeley in chemical engineering and works for Union Carbide.

John Sizoo started kindergarten at Green Valley School when they moved to "the Oaks" and graduated from Monte Vista High School in 1971. He lives in Oakland, where he works part time and attends college part time.

The Sizoo family has always enjoyed living in Alamo Oaks because of its animal orientation, the privacy of two acres, and the space for a vegetable garden and many trees. The day I was given a tour of the old Smith farmhouse, which has been remodeled and added to over the years, most extensively by the Sizoos, I was met in the driveway by "Sweetheart," a seven-year-old old-fashioned full-sized poodle. Taking over the inside of the charming home was "Ben," the calico-colored cross-eyed cat, named for Ben Turpin.

Wes served on the Danville Elementary School Board for two years and then served two years on the newly unified SRVUSD. He is currently on the County Democratic Central Committee, which he was elected to in 1976. He is a past president of the SRV Democratic Club. His legal offices are in the Wells Fargo Building in Oakland.

Lois was active in P-TAs while the children were in school. She is a past president and served five years as a director and secretary of Mary Doyle unit of MDTC, has been secretary since 1974 to the Eugene O'Neill Foundation, and currently is on the Board of Directors of Tao House. Lois took her nurses training in Tacoma, Washington (my birth state).

The former Smith bunkhouse on Smith Road near the corner of Oak had been remodeled over the years and also added to. It was the former home of Ray and Harriet McCoy (both deceased) for a time.

MISS RICKE

Miss Maurine Ricke bought the home at 153 Smith Road, in 1937 when it was under construction. She moved in December 10, 1937, and will soon celebrate forty years in Alamo Oaks. She has the longest continuous residence there.

Prior to her move to Alamo Oaks she had been teaching nursing in Denver, Colorado and had spent some time in southern California. She took a position as Assistant Director of Nurses at St. Francis Hospital in San Francisco, to which she commuted daily, getting up at five in the morning, for at least six months. She retired from Providence Hospital as an instructor in January 1965, then gave a registered nurses' refresher course at Diablo Valley College for nine years.

There were only four families living in Alamo Oaks that first winter. The Smiths on Oak Road, Mr. and Mrs. Alvar Kahnberg and family at 175 Cross Road (the Gordon E. and Margery Wogan home for the past fifteen years), the family in the "Swiss Chalet" off Marks Road, and Miss Marks, for whom Marks Road was named. Miss Marks came out for weekends and later moved out permanently. For years, early residents had their own wells for water and only electricity, until gas was piped up later.

Other early residents were the twins, Elsie and Kay Fores (both deceased), on Cross Road. (Named for Walter Cross (RA), the landlord of the developers, Byington and Fagan Realtors.) Elsie was a schoolteacher and Kay a nurse. One twin always wore earrings so they could be told apart. Later the Kaiser family moved into the Fores home. Em and Andy Rankin (both deceased) commuted from Berkeley for years to their "summer home." Another early resident was Mabel Balenseifer (deceased), who lived where the Kimballs now live. Frank (deceased) and Ethel Beckley*, with her sister Maybelle Van, who was called "Aunt Mamie" (deceased), lived on Smith Road. Frank worked for the Pullman Company in Richmond. Ethel Beckley lives in a mobile home in Santa Rosa.

Miss Ricke was in charge of organizing the clinic and hospital at Kaiser Hospital, Walnut Creek, before the building was built. The early Clinic was in the old grey building at the back, the former Newell home.

In 1957 she invented a counting device for drugs. Sleeping pills and all pain pills must be counted. Her counter is called Narcoti counter. It is plastic and in four sizes. It is quick, and the pills can be counted without being touched. She also invented the chart back (holder) for patients' charts. It is a plastic holder with spring lock and opening, and facilitates easy action so one doesn't need a "third arm." They are manufactured in colors of blue (Miss Ricke's favorite color), green and tan. Another invention was the foot board to extend beds for different patient sizes and for their comfort. It helps keep feet in an upright position.

On the afternoon in January when I called for our interview, she was wearing the medallion for "excellence in nursing" given to her in 1975 from District 9 of the California Nurses Association, so

inscribed. She is very proud of this medal, and rightly so—she deserves it!

Miss Ricke has taught nursing for forty years and is still at it. She also does insurance medical examination forms.

Her pet, "Blackie," appropriately named for his coloring, a fox terrier and chihuahua, has been cared for affectionately for four years. During the war she took up her hobby of wood carving. Many lovely pieces are on display in her home. There are other interesting antiques, along with her Ben Franklin stove that truly operates (and well), and her collection of dark blue glass art pieces. Her view is lovely and in the early spring her flower bed, surrounded by the circular driveway, is a mass of golden yellow jonquils. Though the Alamo Oaks area is quite built up and more developing is going on, as I left I had to stop my car to wait for a handsome rooster followed by three hens to cross the road in front of me.

"FOLDED HILLS FARM" - "OAKHILL FARM"
313 Cross Road, Alamo Oaks, Danville

Mr. and Mrs. Otto Druge purchased ten acres on Cross Road, Alamo Oaks, Danville and in about 1937 they built a very substantial Spanish-style home, using imported tile from Mexico. They built a large rock fireplace with petrified wood from a ranch in the mountains near Roseville. The home included a walk-in freezer which was kept well-stocked. Otto Druge planted almond and walnut trees and put in a swimming pool so its water could irrigate the orchards. There were also a covered pool cabana, several stables and a caretaker's cottage. Otto and his brother Dan operated a valve manufacturing plant out 29th Avenue, back of the old Montgomery Ward store near San Leandro. Cecil and Sybil Cole were owners during and after World

---

*Frank and Ethel (Parrish) Beckley (she was born in Grimes, Iowa) bought their Alamo Oaks property in 1936 from Byington Realty. Built a home and moved in about 1937 from Richmond, California. Mrs. Beckley remembers her husband took the car to his job with the Pullman Company in Richmond and most of the ladies in "the Oaks" at that time worked and were away from their homes. She was very lonesome but worked with her chickens and garden. Their children were married, but they took care of their granddaughter Aileane Johnson (now married and living in Richmond), who attended Alamo School for a while. Ethel Beckley now lives in a mobile home in Santa Rosa.

Patio area with flagstone and rock fireplace is now a large family room. This photo was taken in 1953.

Living room, showing imported tile archway which was later removed. Photo taken August 9, 1953.

War II. (Both are now deceased.) Later, Lloyd and Leila Wise, Pontiac-Oldsmobile auto dealers with businesses in Berkeley and Fruitvale (Oakland), bought the house and property.

Next owners were Stanley and Jane Friden (RA) and their four sons, Kim, Sandy, Charles and William, who purchased this property in the late summer of 1954. I was told that they bought this property with the blessings of the Wises, as they had watched Stan ride horseback over the hills of Friden property which adjoined Wise property and had become friends "over-the-fence."

The Fridens appropriately named the property "Folded Hills Farms," suggested by Charles Sayers, Alamo's famous wood carver. He said when looking out from the rear patio area the hills seemed to fold upon each other. The bookcases on either side of the livingroom fireplace were handmade and scribed to fit the stone by Charles Sayers. The Fridens did some remodeling to enlarge the bathrooms and pool area and removed the two tiled archways. They moved in December 15, 1954, after they had lived in Diablo for five years, and Alamo prior to that. The home was "built like a fort," which made it difficult to remodel.

Friden property then totaled 113 acres, which included the adjoining 103 acres they had on which to run cattle. The property is now what encompasses Monte Vista High School, part of Los Cerros School (most of it was property of Dr. and Mrs. John Blemer of Blemer Road, Danville) and the Mormon Church. The Friden family resided in Alamo Oaks only eleven months, but during that time entertained extensively—hospital groups, Diablo Trail Riders, and P-TA spring and summer parties. The home was well-used and loved.

In the summer of 1955, Stan Friden purchased the ranch at Fort Jones, in Scott Valley in Siskiyou County, which they named "Cloud Rim Ranch." They decided they did not need two ranches, so sold the 113-acre "Folded Hills Farm" to Charles and Doris Curtiss, their daughter, Penny, and son, Cameron, of Crest Avenue, south Walnut Creek. The Curtiss family took possession in December 1955. The Friden family returned to Diablo in November 1955, where they lived until 1966, when they moved permanently to northern California, where they had been spending summers and weekends.

The Charles Curtiss family subdivided the

Pool area with covered cabanas, 1953.

almond orchard into four lots of five acres and sold forty-two acres for Monte Vista School. One year later it was necessary for the Fridens to repurchase the over-two-acre site for the Mormon Church as Stan was on the building committee and that was the site that was chosen above all others, for the beautiful view of Mount Diablo. The acreage between the high school and church was purchased by Frank Couper. The forty-acre piece was sold to R-7 Park District.

The Curtisses rebuilt the swimming pool (inside the original irrigation pool). Charles and Doris were members of the San Ramon Valley Horsemen, and their children, Penny and Cam, were both members of the Danville Junior Horsemen. They raised quarter horses while at "Folded Hills Farm."

Charles Curtiss owned Curtiss Industries in Hayward. They manufactured furnaces and air coolers. The business and the factory property have been sold.

Curtiss sold the five acres on which the home and buildings stand, plus four acres of pasture land, to Fortney H. "Pete" Stark and his wife, Elinor (Brumbder) Stark, who was from Madison, Wisconsin. When the Curtiss family left Alamo Oaks they spent the next nine months in a rented home in Stone Valley Estates and then moved to "Rock Creek Ranch" in Klamath Falls, Oregon, where they have a cow-calf operation of commercial cattle and registered Black Angus. I have corresponded with them there.

The Stark family, including four children, moved in on September 1, 1964 and did extensive remodeling to enlarge the house, which they renamed "Oakhill Farm." Endy*, as she is known, ran a Gourmet Cooking School on the premises. "Pete" Stark became a member of Congress January 1973, representing the then 8th District of California. For a time it included part of Alamo. The area was redistricted and is now in the 9th District. The Starks divorced and put the property up for sale in 1973. It did not sell, so they divided it into two properties.

Slade and Barbara Hulbert, with their children Scott, seven, and Carol, six, purchased three acres, which included the home and pool area. The sale contract included the two Stark dogs, "Ginger," age thirteen, and "Belle," five. The Hulberts moved in September 5, 1975. They have since moved to Greenbrook, Danville.

Dan and Ginny Moody bought the remaining

183

five acres, including the caretaker's house and the "working half," on October 15, 1975. They had lived in the Diablo area five years and prior to that in Venezuela. They have three children, Sarah, born November 6, 1965, John, born November 8, 1967, and Simone, born July 11, 1970. All are interested in 4-H work. The Moodys are in the process of remodeling and adding to their home. Included in the outbuildings are seven barns, one brood mare stall, and a thirty-ton barn. There are extensive plans for their large riding ring and facilities. I was shown around most of the layout during the day I spent at "Oakhill Farm" in February 1977.

Ginny is a native of New Zealand and has a delightful accent. She loves "the Oaks," as the rolling hills with sheep remind her of her homeland. Only the fiords are missing! Dan is a native of Georgia and flew in a Navy research program in a DC-3 plane from Rhode Island in 1963-65 to the Antarctic with New Zealand the headquarters. The rescue missions, and taking scientists as passengers into virgin mountain lands, were treacherous. They had to "puddle hop" and allot their fuel very wisely. There is a mountain in the Antarctic named for him, Mount Moody.

Thomas E. and Roberta (Marling) Morris bought the three acres with the house and pool from the Hulberts on April 5, 1976 and moved in on July 17, 1976. Two days later their number four son, Andrew, was born. They had lived for seventeen years in the Los Angeles area prior to that. Tom is a native of Kenilworth, Illinois and Roberta of Madison, Wisconsin. Their four sons are Patrick Marling, born December 11, 1959, Edward Robert "Ned," March 11, 1963, Christopher Bowen, September 25, 1974 (named for the Bowen who founded the Republican party), and Andrew Newcomb, born July 19, 1976, their bicentennial baby. He is the namesake of the early settler who bought Martha's Vineyard and area from the Indians in the early 1600s. Newcomb is the parternal family name being handed down. Tom Morris is a vice-president underwriter of municipal bonds for Goldman, Sachs and Company.

On February 17, 1977 I was the guest of "Berta" Morris for a delightful luncheon with sherry served to the six of us on the spacious outside porch. It was a beautiful spring day for an interview—such a gorgeous view. Present were Roberta's parents, Robert Newcomb and Dorothy Marling of Madison, Wisconsin who had been visiting since mid-December, and their other daughter, Dorothy Aikins, of San Rafael. As I was given the "royal tour" I noted that their large hallway is hung with a family photo gallery, updated for all members. They can always remember how long they've lived in their Alamo Oaks home by son Andrew's age. It was a delightful visit—I hope to return.

FOULDS

It was while visiting Ray and Nancy Coover in Alamo Oaks that Howard B.* and Jean Foulds learned that the adjoining vacant knoll was for sale. The seven-plus acres, with seven pine trees, was the personal property of Frank Byington, and the deal was made through Byington and Fagan Realty sometime in 1943-44, for quite a bit less than $4,000. Jean Foulds' comment at the time was, "another piece of goat land!" Following the war, they began to build the lower floor of the Alamo Oaks home. Howard's father, Lester, and Jean laid the 2,200 bricks, built the forms for the concrete walls from three-by-eight surplus twenty to twenty-eight-foot-long timbers from Kaiser Shipyard #3, for the sum of $30 per thousand plus $30 to haul them. The truck could not get up the hill, so the lumber was unloaded at the base and Lester Foulds chained two timbers at a time to the rear of the old Dodge, which Jean drove to drag them up the hill.

In about March of 1946 they excavated and built on the very peak of the knoll. Howard drew the plans, obtained the necessary permits, and did the wiring and plumbing. Jean did the painting. Lester did the carpentry. Later they added one large room on the second level, Japanese-style. It had a Japanese garden on the rear deck and the entrance was over a small cement goldfish pond. During construction, water for the mortar was hauled up in a barrel from the Coovers', as the Foulds well had no pump. Howard was commuting to his job in San Francisco and worked on the construction only on

*From a January 2, 1977 *San Francisco Sunday Examiner/Chronicle*, "Ear on Washington" column I quote: "What on earth's happend to Rep. Pete Stark's ex-wife, millionairess Endy Stark, everyone keeps saying. Endy, remember, had that super cooking school right here in D.C.—she's blissfully happy. She's cook in a Buddhist monastery outside S.F. She gets up at the absolute crack of 5 a.m. and pitches right into wok or whatever (all vegetarian, natch.)"

weekends. The house was livable by mid-September 1946. Foulds quit his San Francisco job, sold the Mill Valley home, and moved out to Alamo Oaks.

There was no piped gas or water. They used propane and private wells and erected a windmill—truly pioneering! In due time, gas came in, they motored the well, later electrified, and still later drilled another 208-foot-deep Jacuzzied well, used for several years along with a couple of redwood water tanks. Several years after they moved in, the water began to be a problem, so the Alamo Oaks Improvement Club appointed a water committee to investigate securing California Water Service. Howard Foulds was its chairman. Hearings were held and much volunteer time was given to the project. The California Water put up a tank and the tranmission line to the area at their expense. Twenty thousand dollars had to be put up for additional footage not covered by the 100-foot allowance, and the line was installed in about 1956. Refunds were made as others connected. When East Bay Municipal (EBMUD) took over, further refunds were received through the San Ramon Valley County Water District. Foulds was one of the original committeemen on EBMUD and later served as one of the original five directors. He held this position until their move to the Downieville area in 1965.

The Alamo Oaks Improvement Club was very active. Someone wanted to start a "youth project" to raise chickens. It turned out to involve some 4,000 chickens! After the threat of lawsuits, it ceased. Alamo Oaks has always been a "horse area," with two acres being the minimum for a lot from the beginning of the development, later changed to one acre by deed restrictions.

Howard Foulds was in the real estate business in Hawaii from 1935 to 1937. When he gave up his position in San Francisco in 1946, he reentered the real estate business, as a salesman with Byington and Fagan in Alamo, agents for Danville Estates. Four individuals put up the money to purchase the Fred Houston walnut acreage and hill lands in the west, known as Danville Highlands.

While Foulds was with the Alamo realty company, he became involved in constructing a service station in Alamo. It was not expected to do well, as these were hard times in the Valley, but it prospered for the distributor and Foulds sold the surplus land to the Alamo Motel (RA). He then went to Lafayette, where he rented an old surplus building from the Division of Highways, the old Sun Valley Lumber Building. The Acalanes Center office was wiped out when the freeway was reconstructed for Rapid Transit in 1967.

In 1948-49 the Foulds purchased the original Alamo Oaks Smith ranch house, a large two-story house at the intersection of Smith and Oaks Roads. They intended to remodel it, but a fellow realtor happened to take a client through an open window and the house was sold immediately, to the Phillis family. After about two years they sold it to Hugh and Mimi Gordon. Gordon was a pilot with Pan American Airlines. The Foulds ended up with all the building materials on hand. However, Betty Ross wanted to sell her small house from the rear lot of the Stone property on Stone Valley Road, so Foulds moved it to the northwest corner of their seven acres and added to it. This is one of several homes on the original acreage, as it had been subdivided years before. One house was built for Jean's uncle, Mr. A. L. Scott, who was then eighty-six years old. He moved there from an old shack on the Norris ranch. He was ninety-four when he passed away, a more-than-thirty-year resident of the Walnut Creek-Alamo-Danville area. Mr. Scott was president of the State Fair Board for several years and an influence with Judge Shields in the development of the then State College at Davis, many years ago.

In 1951 Foulds purchased five acres on the main highway between Lafayette and Walnut Creek at the easterly connection of Old Tunnel Road, known as "electronic mountain." He still owns this undeveloped property. Howard Foulds admits he's experienced several "follies" in his day—and some weird real estate transactions. "The hard ones I get—others get the easy ones!" he related.

In 1957 he was involved with moving houses off the state-acquired right-of-way. He remembers earlier days in Alamo Oaks when their neighbors, the Coovers, had animals for home use, calves, pigs, sheep and ducks. Foulds often helped with the butchering as his family had done in Idaho years ago.

In 1965 they sold their Alamo Oaks home to a Chinese family from St. Helena, and moved to Downieville, where they again built another home from scratch. They employed carpenters to do some work from Foulds' plans, and did all the other work themselves. The Foulds are now apartment dwellers in Concord, having sold their Downieville home and winter condominium in Auburn in mid-1975.

Howard B. Foulds is a great-grandnephew of Captain John Sutter, who was his mother's uncle.

WEISEND

James M. Weisend, born June 26, 1912, and Florence Engel, born September 25, 1910, both in Ohio, were married there in April 1943. They arrived in Contra Costa County with her two children and bought a home in Concord in 1943. In August 1945 they bought a 1.8-acre lot in Alamo Oaks. It was owned by a Mr. Buchanan. The real estate transaction was through Byington and Fagan Realty of Alamo.

They spent all weekends there for three years, commuting from Concord to work on the house that Jim, a builder, had designed. He poured all the foundations with a small electric cement mixer, bringing water from Concord in a large drum in their car. Later a Mr. Fasching drilled their well. When the basement area was finished they sold their Concord home and moved into the basement on September 25, 1949 with their four children. There was no gas. They used a wood stove for heat and to warm water for dishes and baths. They were modern day pioneers working toward their goal of owning their own home. With the exception of the bedrooms the house was completed by February 1950. By early 1956 Jim had completed the bedroom wing; this was a part time project. It was a red letter day when they moved their beds upstairs from the basement. (There are still gold stars on the basement walls, rewards for the children for belonging to the "clean plate club.")

1. Nancy E. Weisend, born March 12, 1937 in Cleveland, Ohio, was in the seventh grade when they moved to Danville and attended the old Danville grammar school (now Community Center). She graduated from San Ramon Valley High School in 1955, then spent two years at Diablo Valley College and received her teacher's credential from Sacramento State. She taught in Sacramento and met Francis N. Pittman. They were married in August 1960 in the old St. Isidore's Church. (See Chapter Seven, *Places.*) They live in Danville and have five children. Annie Marie is a sophomore at Carondelet High School in Concord. Jim, fourteen, Mary, thirteen, Beth, eight and Kathy, seven, all attend St. Isidore's School in Danville. Nancy teaches summer school and does some tutoring. Frank is with Southern Pacific

in San Francisco in the communications department.

2. Thomas Harry Weisend was born May 12, 1940 in Cleveland, Ohio, and also attended the old Danville Grammar School. He graduated from San Ramon Valley High School in 1958 and attended Diablo Valley College. He had a cabinet shop in Danville for many years. He has two sons, Tom, age thirteen, and Ricky, eleven.

3. Robert Michael Weisend, born September 22, 1944 in Martinez, California, attended the old Danville Grammar School, then the new Green Valley school. His class planted the trees across the back. He graduated from Charlotte Wood and from San Ramon Valley High School in 1962. He graduated from Diablo Valley and San Jose State Colleges, and was married in San Jose to Cynthia Sellers. They have two children, Jennifer, seven, and Nicholas, five. For six years they lived in Alamo in the Byington house across from the Alamo Women's Clubhouse. Bob is a third generation carpenter and just finished designing and building a new home in Boulder Creek, California.

4. Mary Margaret Weisend, born September 20, 1946 in Martinez, went to kindergarten at the Danville Grange Hall until the Green Valley kindergarten was finished. She graduated from Charlotte Wood school, and from San Ramon Valley High School in 1964. She attended Diablo Valley and San Jose State Colleges and graduated in 1968. She married K. Richard Nourse of Walnut Creek in the new St. Isidore's Church on April 6, 1968. They spent eighteen months in Germany while he was in the army. They live in Sierra City, California, in an old Victorian home they remodeled. They have one daughter, Katy, age three, and a new baby, Benjamin. Mary does substitute teaching in the Downieville Schools and Rich has an insurance and real estate agency in Sierra City.

James Weisend was construction supervisor for Newhall-Scott and Scott-Ball Construction Companies for sixteen and one-half years, and built many homes in the county. Among them were Camille Woods in Alamo, Hillsdale in Pleasant Hill, and Scottsdale and San Marco subdivisions in Walnut Creek.

Florence says Alamo Oaks hasn't changed as much as other areas in San Ramon Valley due to the one-acre restrictions. There are more homes now but the area still has the same peaceful country atmosphere which first attracted them, and of course it still has the lovely view of Mount Diablo. The Weisends' first neighbors were Mr. and Mrs. Chaplin and family, who sold to Miss Anderson of Oakland, who rented the house for many years until Doug Offenhorst bought it. He lived there several years, did some remodeling and sold it to Mr. and Mrs. Ken Whipple and children, Kelly and Peter. The Whipples have made additions and remodeled. Those living in "the Oaks" when they came were: Miss Maurine Ricke, Ruth and Harold Martin, Edna Keyes, Celestine Vincent, Mr. and Mrs. Rankin, Madge and Charles Johnson, Jean and Howard Foulds, Hugh and Mimi Gordon, Mr. and Mrs. Wolf, Gil and Nina Fitch, Albert and Cordelia Williams, Phyllis and Reid Spahr, Mae and Don Duffield, Anne and Woody Carr, Mrs. Agrella, Nancy and Ray Coover, the Charles Mitchells, Jack and Ardith Steger, the Taylor family, Mr. and Mrs. Malvey, Kisa Roades, the George Sankos, Barbara Burr, the Carl Bayley family, and the Georges on the other side of them.

GEORGE

Francis X. and Doris George bought 1.28 acres in 1958 on Smith Road, from Alice Abell. The real estate transaction was handled by Benny Barton. In January 1962 they moved from Oakland into their new home, built by Francis T. Finigan (RA).

Their son, Brian Frederick (named after his great-grandfather), married Carolyn Camozzi, daughter of Bob and Freda Camozzi of Sonora Avenue, Danville. They have two daughters, Catherine Kay, born July 18, 1968, and Amy, born September 19, 1969. They make make their home in Palo Alto.

Their daughter, Melinda Kay (named for her two grandmothers), is married to Andrew Frederick Nance. They have two sons, Christopher Frederick, born July 13, 1968, and Michael Andrew, born April 9, 1970. They have lived in San Ramon, Oak Creek, one of the first subdivisions there by Gentry.

TAYLOR

Richard H. (died September 16, 1961) and Marion "Mickey" Taylor and two daughters Dolores Ann, born September 16, 1943, and Patricia Lee, born April 10, 1945, moved to Alamo Oaks from Lafayette in February 1955. The purchase of their new home was transacted by "Buz" Glines of Alamo. In addition to domestic pets, they had livestock of chickens, ducks, turkeys, a lamb and a goat.

Their daughters attended Danville schools and graduated from San Ramon Valley High School. After graduation in 1961, Dolores spent one year studying in Bourdeaux, France. She graduated from UC, Davis as an honor student. She taught as a teacher's aide at UC, Davis in 1966, and received her master's in French from Davis in 1967. She taught for three years at Continuation School in Los Angeles, and now lives in southern California with daughter Robyn, born December 18, 1970. Taylors sold their Smith Road home to the E. C. Van Bibber family in 1963.

"Realtor of the Year" award was presented to Al Jones on January 12, 1977 at Boundary Oak Restaurant in Walnut Creek. His wife Virgie (author of this book) beams on! (Contra Costa Times photo)

Pat was a pompon girl and graduated from San Ramon Valley High School in June 1963 (same class with our son Gary). In 1965 she graduated from Diablo Valley College, where she was head pompon girl, Homecoming Queen and honor student. She was also Miss Pleasant Hill in 1965. That same year she married Roger McCosker, son of Mr. and Mrs. John McCosker of Orinda. On July 14, 1966 a son Brett was born to them in Santa Clara Kaiser Hospital. They divorced and she returned to school in 1975, and was an honor student at Heald College. In 1975, upon graduation, she was hired by Healds as admissions secretary in Walnut Creek, and in 1976 as admissions representative in Hayward.

Pat was married to A. Garrett "Gary" Jones, son of Al* "Fritz" and Virgie* Jones of Alamo, on Saturday, June 12, 1976 (exactly thirteen years to the day from their graduation together from SRVHS). Their wedding was at the Fern Grotto, up the Wailua River, on the island of Kauai, Hawaii. A traditional Lei ceremony was performed by the Reverend David M. Kalama.

Witnesses were Robert J. and Kathryn E. Nohr of San Ramon. Gary, Pat and Brett rent a home at the Geldermann Ranch in San Ramon. Gary has a daughter, Jennifer Jones (July 28, 1971) who lives with her mother Mrs. Elaine Aragon Roan** in San Ramon. Gary is an Account Executive with Shearson Hayden Stone Inc. in Walnut Creek. Pat is with the San Ramon Valley Unified School District. Her mother, "Mickey" Taylor, lives in Alameda and works in Oakland.

----

*Al "Fritz" Jones was 1972 president of the Contra Costa Board of Realtors, 1974 Regional vice-president of District 5, and recipient of the Realtor of the Year Award, presented January 12, 1977. He is now an Associate Broker with Olson and Associates in Danville—same location, address and phones as the former

Jones-MacDonald Realty. And as for me, as you can see, I am still writing!

**Elaine Aragon Jones married Larry C. "Bud" Roan of San Ramon, June 25, 1977. She is the daughter of Del and Florence Aragon of Fremont, California, and teaches at Walt Disney School in San Ramon.

David Glass Home

L. Styles

188

Chapter Eleven

Diablo

Long before the days of the forty-niner, the land which is now the site of the Diablo Country Club was part of a Spanish Rancho. The climate and natural beauty made this area popular for social and recreational activities.

In the 1870s Peter Cook procured 10,000 acres from Britton and Ray, the original owners, and established the historic Cook Ranch, later known as the Oakwood Park Stock Farms. The area became famous due to his race track with fine horses and the casino and mansion he built. Other stables were added later, thoroughbred horses were raised, and Diablo had its own Epsom or Churchill Downs. Dixie Fremery, longtime resident, recollects when her father had a string of eleven racing horses. Many New York financiers came to Diablo to get away from the hot summers of the "Big City."

The Mount Diablo Country Club had its inception during a real estate development. During the 1910s Robert Burgess, Sr. acquired part of the former Cook Ranch. He planned many beautiful sites for summer homes. He transformed the Cook mansion into an "Inn" and constructed a road to the top of Mount Diablo for visitors. The project was widely publicized and promoted.

The Mount Diablo Country Club was organized as a private club in 1916. The property contained more than 600 acres in its natural beautiful rural surroundings, with many majestic oak trees, many of which still remain. It was incorporated in 1919, as a non-profit corporation. It drew a large membership from bay area families of culture, refinement and means.

Gas rationing and other World War II emergencies brought the activities of the Mount Diablo Country Club to a halt. The U.S. Navy occupied the club facilities for government use from 1942 to 1946.

In 1948 Lawrence Curtola purchased the historic site from Diablo Properties Inc. He rehabilitated the golf course and other recreational facilities and made many general improvements. Before the end of 1948 former members and other interested persons negotiated with Curtola to work out a system for a new non-profit club. The result was that the members acquired the 160-acre site and improvements.

Curtola converted the original clubhouse which was at the base of the hill at the turn of the road, where the Diablo Clubhouse later was built, into his own private residence.

Traditionally, Diablo has been an outstanding place for suburban living and enjoyment for the entire family. Many of those earlier homes have had "face lifts," rooms, heat and additional plumbing added to bring them up to the standards of today. When they were originally built they were used primarily during the warm summer months, as so many of the older homes in the San Ramon Valley had been used.

The golf course is still the favorite of many. Swimming pools, tennis courts and horse stables are available. The Chalet provides excellent accommodations for members and their guests. In 1957, the forty-first year of the club, it had 450 proprietary members and 100 social members.

The following information was compiled by Mrs. Charles G. Goold and Miss Charlotte E. Wood, appointed as the Committee on History and Landmarks for Contra Costa County, year unknown. I have edited it slightly, and made some additions.

DIABLO

By some research, it is said, the community known as Diablo started as early as the 1850s when Britton and Ray, San Francisco lithographers, owned a portion of the area. They sold to

This ornate old barn was used for the fine blooded horses of the Cook estate. From 1907 to 1948 it housed the Diablo Post Office, then was torn down by Lawrence Curtola. He gave the cupola to Ben and Sue Reed.

Urial Huntington, who became a partner of Marco B. "Mark" Ivory, who arrived in California (Contra Costa County) in October of 1858.

The property later came into the possession of W. W. Cameron, who married Alice Marsh, the daughter of John Marsh, Contra Costa County pioneer. Cameron later sold to a Mr. Miller, secretary of the Southern Pacific Railroad and then Diablo was known as Railroad Ranch.

An inn was built by a later owner, a General David C. Colton, also affiliated with Southern Pacific. When he died, his son-in-law, Dan Cook of San Francisco, bought the property from the estate. Cook built a large dairy, several barns, a race track, billiard hall and reservoir. He imported prize winning cattle and the finest race horses. His sudden death ended his dreams of more extensive improvements. Then the property was acquired by his brother, Seth Cook. The acreage was 5,000 acres but was increased by the acquisition of nearly all the small farms in Green Valley. The property then became known as Cook Farm.

After Seth's death, his niece, Mrs. Louise Boyd of San Rafael, inherited the acreage and changed the name to Oakwood Park Stock Farm.

Robert N. Burgess, Sr. purchased it from the Boyds and began the subdividing which resulted in Diablo, named for the mountain.

The following was printed in the *Walnut Kernel* of August 1957:

Robert N. Burgess, Sr. was a most noted real estate developer of central Contra Costa County in the early 20th century.

He started in 1906 as a building contractor in San Francisco and erected several commercial buildings after the earthquake and fire. Later he developed a fine residential subdivision in Oakland. About 1910 he was interested in another development in Moraga.

In 1913 Burgess acquired part of the famous Cook Ranch at Diablo and started a real estate development of beautiful homesites for summer dwelling. He constructed a toll road to the top of Mount Diablo and transformed the old Cook Mansion into an inn for tourists. During WWI he operated a shipyard at Bay Point (now Port Chicago) and developed a residential tract nearby.

He developed the old Homestead Ranch in Walnut Creek into Lakewood Estates. Burgess Sr. retired and his son Robert N. "Bob" Burgess, Jr. took over after returning from WWII service. As a general contractor he too built many fine homes throughout Contra Costa County and was a resident of Diablo as his family had been. His homes were featured in the Parade of Homes in Holbrook Heights in Concord and also Moraga.

BURGESS FAMILIES

Robert Noble Burgess was born February 10, 1878, and died January 22, 1965. He was married on July 20, 1909 to Anne Webster Fish, who was born January 26, 1886, died March 10, 1953. Their children were Robert Noble Burgess, Jr., born May 13, 1910 at Berkeley, California; Frances Webster Burgess (Mrs. John S. Enright), born June 22, 1914 at Berkeley; Suzanne Fish Burgess (Mrs. Edward L. Soule, Jr.), born May 11, 1917, at Diablo, Nancie Webster Burgess (Mrs. George Shaw), born February 19, 1919, at Diablo; and Polly Holcomb Burgess (Mrs. Thomas H. Carroll), born July 19, 1921, at Walnut Creek.

The Burgess family lived in Lakewood, which is now a part of Walnut Creek. It was started in the mid-1930s. The home up near the lake which burned was the residence of Dr. A. J. Smith, a friend of the Burgess family. The Burgess residence was below the swimming pool in the canyon below the dam.

Diablo, which was known at the time as the Oakwood Park Stock Farm, was purchased in 1913 by Robert N. Burgess, Sr., from Mrs. Boyd, who inherited the property from Seth and Dan Cook, who were her uncles. When the property was owned by the Cook family, it was known as the Cook or Railroad Ranch. Mr. Burgess purchased adjoining property as well, a total of about 13,000 acres, which included the property for the two roads up the mountain (Mount Diablo).

The following is taken from a talk on the Diablo area given by Robert N. Burgess, Jr. I have his permission to share with you.

My first remembrance of Diablo was coming out with my parents and staying at the old Cook residence. This building later became the Club House, and now is the residence of Larry and Betty Curtola and family. This building had a large porch around three sides where friends and members of the club would congregate.

In 1913 my parents decided to move to Diablo. We spent the first year living in a cottage on the main road entering Diablo, while our home was under construction. This cottage was later sold to the Fageol family, the builders of Fageol cars and trucks. In 1914 we moved into our new home on Calle Arroyo, were we lived about nine years.

About the same time the Chalet was built, containing twenty units for renting to club members when they wished to stay over in Diablo. This building has now been converted into apartments for permanent residents. The Chalet was connected with the Club House by a covered pedestrian bridge which reached from the arcade on the creek side to the second floor of the Club House. This enabled the members staying in the Chalet to walk from the Chalet to the Club House without going around by road.

The Oakland Antioch and Eastern Railroad built a line from Saranap, near Walnut Creek, up the San Ramon Valley to Danville, then to Diablo. This line, as I remember, ended a couple of hundred yards across from the entrance to the Club House. A commuter train which connected with the ferry to San Francisco was run for the convenience of those Diablo residents who worked in Oakland or San Francisco. There were three or four daily trains to Diablo. About the same time a line was run up Ygnacio Valley to Walwood to connect with the north entrance to Mount Diablo Scenic Boulevard.

The Mount Diablo Boulevard was started from Diablo Lake and built to the summit of Mount Diablo. Then from a point three miles down from the summit, another road was built to North Gate above Ygnacio Valley. The construction was done with a steam shovel, which was called overcast work. The General Superintendent was J. N. Curtis and the steam shovel was operated by a man named McCune. I met Mr. McCune when Boulder Dam was under construction; he showed me the engraved watch which my father gave him after the road up Mount Diablo was completed. The road from Diablo followed a new route, and was a great improvement over the old road which went to the old hotel which used to be near the summit. There

were even plans which were not carried out to build a third road from Marsh Creek to the Summit. My favorite entertainment at that time was to get a ride up the mountain so I could watch the operation of the steam shovel.

William Randolph Hearst became interested in the Diablo development about 1914 or 1915. Part of his contribution was in the form of national advertising in Hearst publications. There were many newspaper articles about automobile races which were held from Oakland to the top of Mount Diablo. The winners were awarded trophy cups. Some of the cars which were contenders were Kissel Kars, Mercer, Owen Magnetic, Briscoe, Chandler, Marion Handly, Maxwell, Stearns-Knight, King, and Haynes. Hearst even spoke of building a home on Mount Diablo similar to his mother's home in Pleasanton.

Sales were handled by R. N. Burgess Company in San Francisco and Oakland, and by Robert Marsh and Company in Los Angeles. There was a very elaborate advertising program with newspaper and magazine ads and articles. Special trains would be run on Sunday to bring out prospects. The Diablo development was called Mount Diablo Villa Homes. This included Oakwood Park Stock Farm with other properties added which totaled about 13,000 acres. One small part, about 1200 acres, was sold to Ansel Easton from Hillsboro, which became the start of what is now called the Blackhawk Ranch. The Blackhawk name came from the place Easton had in Hillsboro, where he raised blue-blooded stock. Many homes were built in Diablo, some as summer residences, and some as permanent homes. Among those early summer and permanent homes were: Mr. and Mrs. William Letts Oliver, Mr. and Mrs. Herbert Hall, Dr. and Mrs. Charles L. Morey, Mr. and Mrs. Ed. Bull, Mr. and Mrs. Johns, Mr. and Mrs. Al. Cooper, Mr. and Mrs. Benton, Mr. and Mrs. Abe Leach, and Dr. and Mrs. Love.

A golf course was completed, tennis courts, and a provision for trap shooting. Diablo Lake was improved for fishing, boating and swimming. Dressing rooms, a dock and floats were constructed. One of the barns was equipped with riding horses and ponies which could be rented. Another barn was converted into the Red Horse Tavern, where people could stay overnight. A sewer system was built which served most of Diablo. This system had a leach field in the Old Stock Farm Race Track. This was a mile track complete with starter boxes and judges' stand. Gum trees, some of which are still standing, circled the outside of the track.

The first school I attended was Green Valley, which at that time was a one-room structure located on the top of a knoll off Green Valley Road where the Turner residence is standing. This school, which had no inside plumbing, contained eight rows of seats, one for each grade. For the third grade I commuted by train to

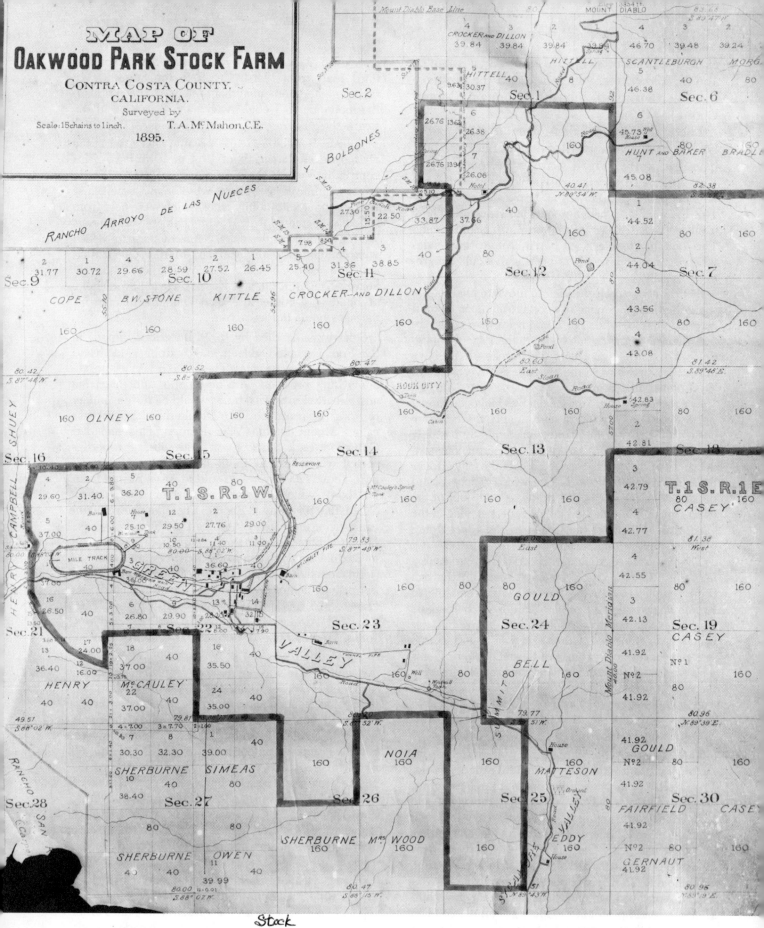

Map of Oakwood Park State Farm. To the left is the mile race track. This is now the vicinity of
Diablo Hacienda subdivision. (Note misspelling of the Goold family name.)

192

Danville, as the Green Valley School due to poor condition was condemned and had to be replaced.

During the depression which followed World War I, sales fell off. Due to other pressures Hearst withdrew from the project. My father sold our home in Diablo and we moved to Homestead Ranch in Walnut Creek.

When Bob Burgess and his wife Elizabeth moved to Diablo in May of 1953, it was to the old family home which was built by his parents. The following is a list of some of the people who lived in Diablo at that time: Mr. and Mrs. Harold Smith, Mr. and Mrs. Sam Abbott, Mr. and Mrs. Stan Friden, Mr. and Mrs. Charles Morey, Mr. and Mrs. Larry Curtola, Mr. and Mrs. Malcolm Gompertz, Mr. and Mrs. William Owsely, Mr. and Mrs. Jack Imrie, Mr. and Mrs. Joe Hendricks, Mr. and Mrs. Lloyd Rossi, Mr. and Mrs. Chet Eschen, Mr. and Mrs. Don F. White, Mrs. Fran Betts Keane and Gerrit Keane, Mr. and Mrs. Al Stott, Mr. and Mrs. Gibson, and Mr. and Mrs. George Pacini. Those on this list who still remain as residents of Diablo are: Smith, Owsely, Imrie, White and Pacini. Some of those on the list still live in Contra Costa County or the state of California, and some have passed on and are gone forever.

DIABLO COUNTRY CLUB

Originally created as a stock farm in the 1870s by the railroad kings of the day, Diablo Country Club was established as a golf and country club in 1917. A branch of the Oakland Antioch and Eastern electric line brought members from Oakland and San Francisco directly to the original clubhouse which was set in a lovely wooded grove.

It is still one of the most historic and beautiful country clubs in Northern California, set in a charming natural atmosphere, and popular for that reason. The club facilities include an historic but modernized clubhouse in the early California Colonial style. It contains men's locker room and grill, ladies' locker room, office, dining facilities, and a large ballroom. There is a pro shop and the historic Chalet.

The terrace dining room serves excellent dinners twice per week plus a number of special events. There is a large ballroom with an orchestra stand for the regular club dances and parties held throughout the year.

The golf course is nestled among the folded hills at the base of 3,849-foot-high Mount Diablo. There are exciting and varied golf programs for members, including tournaments for men, ladies, mixed and juniors. Some of the events are President's Cup, famous Gold Putter Invitational, Qualifying NCGA, V.I.P. tournament, and several inter-club meets. Mixed golf functions, several followed by dinner-dancing, are Grandma and Grandpa, Mr. and Mrs. Tourney, father/son/ daughter, mixed invitational, Italian Day, and Mr. and Mrs. Turkey Shoot.

Oakwood Stock Farm race track in 1914. Since 1962 it has been the Diablo Hacienda subdivision, St. Timothy's Episcopal Church, including Fairway Drive (well defined by outline of eucalyptus trees. Mt. Diablo in background.

The tennis program, with five championship courts, is available for members year-round. The swimming pool offers relaxation and competing meets and is open all summer. The social calendar includes member dinner-dancing monthly, the traditional Easter Egg Hunt*, Luau, Christmas and New Year's Eve parties, and others.

Aerial view taken by Oakland Tribune *showing the Mount Diablo Country Club and chalets (built about 1914) and surrounding area. Photo taken about 1926.*

Original Diablo Country Club, built about 1858 (some say as early as 1853). The Square Room was called "the Casino" and is now the main bar. It was the carriage house.

There are 410 regular members (this membership includes golf), and 100 associate members (includes tennis). Current club manager is Norman Oliver, who has been there since August 1976. Past presidents have been Larry Curtola, Herb Hall, R. D. Fish, W. K. Van Bokkelen, Joe Hendricks, Lester Foley, Allen Hart, Jack Herzig, Bailey Justice, DeWitt Krueger, John Enright, William Houston, Louis Schrepel. Robert Foley, Hal Morgan, Jack Pingree, Justin Knowlton, Arthur Brunckhorst, William Shipley, Rett Turner, Spencer Archer, Henry Steinbach, Frank Schmitt, George Padis, and Clifford L. Gant. The current president is Fred Bennett.

On Sunday, April 10, 1977, the Easter Egg Hunt at Diablo Country Club had a white furry customed "Mrs. Peter Rabbit," who was Sue Davis, wife of Ralph Scott Davis III of Hayward and daughter of Fred and Phyllis Alexanderson of Diablo. 1977 marked the 30th annual Easter Egg Hunt. Two hundred youngsters between the ages of three and nine searched for the 600 dyed eggs and the traditional chocolate and gold-foiled Diablo Egg. The committee claimed that it was the first time a female bunny had participated in the fun family day. I can recall many different starting times for this egg hunt over the years—in 1977 it was at 3:30 in the afternoon.

Diablo Country Club, possibly the oldest country club in the entire East Bay, recently went through about $500,000 in remodeling and face-lifting. The interior was redecorated and they say has retained its Victorian styling. However, when I last visited it, during the Christmas season in 1976, I truly missed the flocked red wall paper which had been in the cocktail lounge, and some other features as well. The main ballroom had been divided into two areas, a small dancing room area and a large main dining room. Somehow I liked the old Club as it was, but times do change. (I have the same opinion of Castlewood Country Club, which I adored as it used to be.)

194

FREMEREY

Dixie S. Fremerey is world-traveled and has lived in several countries, but the day she was born, one mid-June, she cancelled a trip to England for her parents. Dr. and Mrs. Eugene (Josephine Scott) Arlington, were readying to board the steamer at New York harbor for England, when Dixie decided to surprise them two months before schedule and be born in America. Her mother had wished the baby to be born in her native England, but apparently Dixie had other ideas. Her father had referred to her as "the little dickens," so the name Dixie came naturally.

Her father was with the National Health Service and was dispatched to all parts of the world as emergencies arose. Her mother passed away before Dixie was a full year old, and Dixie continued to travel with her dad as his duties called him. Much of her education was by tutor and in different countries.

Dixie discovered California in 1910 when her father purchased 200 acres in Contra Costa County in what is now Moraga. It included the old Riley Ranch, with house and barn. Part of the ranch is now Lake Chabot. Dixie remembers fishing in the creek and catching trout. After their trips this ranch would be home base. In those days, Moraga had no telephone service in the Canyon. Curriers would be sent with messages. She remembers they didn't ever use house keys, as everything was very safe and they had a caretaker, ranch foreman and crew. They raised race horses and grain, barley and mostly wheat.

As a young girl Dixie rode horseback all over the area, including the San Ramon Valley. "Wide open spaces—you could shoot a cannon down the Valley," she recollected. After her father was killed in South America during a native uprising, when she was only about sixteen, she started out on her own.

She acquired a lot by a loan default in San Francisco, at Seacliff. Eventually after a few years, she sold the lot and made a nice profit and bought two more pieces of property in the Richmond District of San Francisco, and did some speculative building. She then ventured into the Norton District of Oakland (now Redwood Heights). In order to negotiate loans she decided to get her real estate license, and in the forties got her broker's license. At that time she wanted to buy three to ten acres around San Ramon Valley. It was then that the Frick Ranch

in Diablo was being cut up. Barney Gilbert and Jack Redding of Forbrag Realtors worked on the deal. Dixie bought three acres which were in walnut orchards and later added another three and one-half acres.

She met Arnold L. Fremerey of Oregon in San Leandro. He opened a real estate business there in April 1950, and she became his partner. They are charter members of the Southern Alameda Real Estate Board. In July 1951 she purchased a home in upper Cameo Acres and moved into it on March 1, 1952. It seemed she had more furniture than house. She recalls that Wayne Bailey, formerly of Leona Court, Alamo, would say, "There's so many places to sit, there's no place to stand!"

She and Arnold Fremerey were married February 4, 1952, in Santa Barbara, California. They bought a small building in Hayward and had it moved across from the old P-X Market (present site of Diablo State Bank) in Danville. They had that business for five years before they moved to Alamo. In Alamo their real estate business was at the corner of Stone Valley Road and Danville Highway, in the small building that at one time was the Alamo post office. (Present site of Pedretti and Son, a small motor and sharpening and repairs business.) They were there seventeen years.

In 1955 they decided to build on the Blackhawk Road property on what used to be County Road 20. That was one of the flood years, but by August 1956 they moved into the 3,150-square-foot home, built to accommodate all the furniture. They have remained there.

In 1957-58 they planted 105 paradox hybrid walnut trees (F-1) instead of California black. The paradox hybrid F-1 are impervious to the black line disease that has destroyed so many walnut trees over the years in Contra Costa County.

Dixie has a son, Victor E. Sloman, born in San Francisco and educated at the U.C. School of Engineering. He designed and installed the electrical X-ray panel at Oak Knoll Hospital. He was with Tracer Laboratories in Berkeley, then went east, where he has been for ten years. He is married to Eleanora Leroy of Leroy, New York. They live in Mendham, New Jersey, and have two sons, Richard and Chris. Richard is married to Gayle Hugo, granddaughter of the writer Victor Hugo. They have a son Dylan, born June 2, 1975, and another offspring due in April 1977.

Chris Sloman is unmarried and presently in Europe. His home is in San Diego, California.

Dixie is still a member of the Contra Costa County Board of Realtors, though presently inactive. She is a member, and several times past-master of, the Danville Grange #85 (which was organized in October 1873), and is present master, and five times past-master of the Contra Costa County Pomona Grange #45. She was appointed to five county chairmanships by the California State Grange for "GAP" (Grange Action Program), which is legislative. She is a member of the Contra Costa County Farm Bureau Women, a twenty-four-year member of Danville Women's Club, member of Valley Action Forum and Community Center Guild, member of Advisory Committee, San Ramon Valley Unified School District, and a member of the Mariners Club.

Arnold L. Fremerey was born in Oregon, between Turner and Salem. He came to California in 1936. He traveled as a manufacturer's representative for an electronics firm, frequently passing through the San Ramon Valley and Walnut Creek. He entered real estate in 1946, for J. A. Clemenson, Oakland, after serving as Deck Engineer for the Merchant Marine, 1942-43. He dropped real estate in 1965 and became an insurance broker. Currently he has an office in Dublin, California. He was a fifteen-year member of the Board of Directors for the Contra Costa County Farm Bureau. He is an officer of the Contra Costa County Pomona Grange and the Danville Grange, and a member of the Mariners Club. He enjoys pruning the walnut trees and has often said that the San Ramon Valley is "as close to Heaven" as he expects to get.

The following two items were written by two students of San Ramon Valley Union High School and printed in the 1927 and 1929 *Walnut Kernel* yearbooks.

MOUNT DIABLO'S MENAGERIE
by Mason Smith, '27 Senior

In the Spring our little valley is one of the most beautiful in the State, but when as Summer comes with its scorching sun, the green fields are burnt to a yellow-brown, the small streams dry up, and even the trees seem to lose some of the freshness which they display before the sun plays its havoc.

Old Mount Diablo has watched over our valley for hundreds of centuries. Its massive peak can be seen from anywhere on the campus of our small but rapidly growing school. In every season of the year the old mountain presents an ever-changing panorama. Upon its rugged top and sloping sides are numerous stone images of animals which Mother Nature has carved. In fact, there are so many they may easily be called Mount Diablo's Menagerie.

The rock most often visited by sightseers is that of the turtle or the tortoise. This stone shows a striking resemblance to the real creature of the lakes and ponds. Its head is pointed directly toward the Golden Gate, and it will only be a few million years until the turtle goes swimming and enjoys the environment which Nature intended it to have. For scientists say that the mountain is moving westward at the slow but remarkable rate of three inches per year.

Besides the turtle, the mountain offers stone bears, lions, tigers, and even birds. But not all the animals on the mountain are made of stone, for there are deer, coyotes, foxes, and even an occasional mountain lion is reported to have been seen upon the slopes of the mountain.

MOUNT DIABLO BEACON
by Eleanor McDonald, '29 Freshman

The Mount Diablo Beacon, when night begins to fall,
Shines out upon the darkness as a splendid guide to all.
Just as the North Star guides all those who sail the seas—
This beacon guides all those who fly away above the trees.
It spreads its rays o'er San Joaquin and Sacramento blue,
And over seven counties and Mount Tamalpais, too.

Chapter Twelve

San Ramon

CATTLEMEN IN SAN RAMON VALLEY

In 1860 American cattle growers in the San Ramon Valley with established brands were listed as: Alamo: F. A. Bonnard, S. A. Carpenter, W. C. Chapman, E. H. Cox, Golder Field, A. Ford, James Foster, David Glass, B. Hall, Austin Hammitt, Joel Harlan, W. Hays, August Hemme, V. Huntington, John M. Jones, M. B. Mitchell, Samual Wolff & Company, D. P. Smith, Albert Ward Stone, Silas Stone. Danville: Robert O. Baldwin, J. Flippin, Thomas Flournoy, J. L. Larake, John Smith, D. L. Spencer, J. Sterne.

Problems for the cattlemen over the years have included 1852, 1862, and 1871, floods; 1887, range fires at Diablo; 1922, a 2,000-acre fire on Mount Diablo; and 1924, hoof and mouth disease.

San Ramon Valley's stockmen in the 1930s and 1940s were Robert C. Force of Blackhawk Ranch and Charles J. Wood of Tassajara Valley. In the fifties Blackhawk Ranch and Fred C. Wiedemann were the valley's largest cattlemen. Other stockmen at the time were Jerry Bettencourt, Herbert Elworthy, the Hansens, Leo Lynch, George C. Wood. Sheep were raised by Bishop Ranch and George C. Wood.

In 1850-51, Leo Norris, William Lynch, and Joel Harlan were the first farmers. In 1852, Robert O. Baldwin and William Meese came. Other early farmers were James and Wellington Boone, William Cox, Harrison Finley, Thomas Flournoy, David Glass, August Hemme, Charles and Nathaniel Howard, Frederick Humburg, Robert Love, George McCamley, Francis Matteson, Levi Alexander Maxcy, David Sherburne, D. P. Smith, Bruce Stone, and Charles Wood.

In 1858 there were 23,170 acres of cultivated land in Contra Costa County. Of those, 16,870 acres were in wheat and 6,300 in barley.

THOMAS BENTON BISHOP

Thomas Benton Bishop, California pioneer, was an outstanding corporation attorney in San Francisco during the 1880s and 1890s, a member of the law firm of Garber, Boalt & Bishop, later Bishop & Wheeler. About 1895 he completed purchase of Norris League of old San Ramon Rancho in Contra Costa County, some 3,000 acres. The property was one and one-half miles square, between Norris Canyon on the west and the Southern Pacific Railway on the east.

T. B. Bishop passed away in 1906, leaving four sons: James Hall, Thomas Porter, and twins Edward Francis and Francis Edward. The sons carried on with the huge enterprises of Thomas B. Bishop Company, following in their father's footsteps. At first the ranch raised about 400 head of cattle and livestock. About 1909 a walnut orchard was planted. It later became one of the largest producers in the county. In 1911 a pear orchard was started, which later developed into what was referred to as the largest single block of Bartlett pears in the world. During the 1910s the Shropshire purebred sheep operation gained acclaim for prize winners in the state and nation. Peaches, prunes, grapes, tomatoes and hog raising also were added.

Improvements consisted of headquarters with superintendent's house, office, machine shops, dehydrator building, foreman's house, commissary and tool sheds, bunkhouse, large warehouse, and shipping shed on the spur of the Southern Pacific tracks on the eastern boundary.

James H. Bishop, attorney, was president of the Thomas Bishop Company from 1906 to 1946 and spent much time at the Contra Costa County property in San Ramon. Thomas P. Bishop, attorney, spent most of his time in charge of the

In front of Olsson's horseshoeing and general blacksmithing shop, left to right: Edwin, Rueben, (unknown), Andrew, Oscar Olsson, Fred Wiedemann, McIvor. Circa 1910. This is the present site of Villa San Ramon. (Courtesy San Ramon Valley Historical Society)

business interests in central California and South America. Edward F. Bishop had as his main interest the raising of purebred sheep at San Ramon. Francis E. Bishop managed the Mexico and Santa Barbara holdings and became head of the company after James Bishop's death.

In 1904 Frank Rutherford (see Chapter Three, *Other Pioneers and Longtime Residents,* Rutherford Family) was superintendent of the Bishop Ranch. He had owned and operated ranch properties in the Santa Barbara area. During the early days, there were many problems and hardships to overcome in getting the undeveloped ranch into shape for production. Rutherford served as ranch boss for forty years, because of his wonderful accomplishments. He retired in 1944. During his lifetime he was a highly respected county leader, well known for his ranching knowledge and orchard development. He made the Bishop Ranch one of the finest and best producers in Contra Costa County and the state as well. Mrs. Florence Roy, his daughter, served as superintendent's secretary and bookkeeper.

Rutherford's son-in-law, Verne T. Andreasen, was superintendent from 1944-55. Robert Sealy Livermore arrived in the fall of 1955.

The following is taken from a tape recorded for my use by Bob Livermore while he was en route to a ranch in Lake County. I have done minor editings.

Bob Livermore arrived the fall of 1955 during walnut harvest. He was in his twenties and a bachelor. He took over the big house and for a time slept in the office. He was not readily accepted by the "old-timers" there, who looked upon him as "a young whippersnapper"—and college educated to boot! In the mess hall which continued for about twelve years, when he would attempt to sit down, he would be told: "You can't sit there, that's Joe's place (or Tom's, or Dick's, or Harry's)." With each move he soon discovered most places were taken. So Bob moved into the kitchen and ate his meals there.

Bob Livermore married Jean Everett July 7, 1956. They were the surprised honorees of an old-fashioned farmers' shivaree! Fred and Charlotte Wiedemann asked the newlyweds if they could come down to dinner, which the young bride and groom thought rather strange. But trying to be hospitable in their new surroundings, they said okay and Jean went to some trouble preparing a chicken dinner for them. Then the people began to arrive, all 200 of them (some they had never seen before or since!), bringing food and many desserts—also gifts of homemade preserves, jams, jellies, and normal household necessities, like toilet paper, etc. They also brought a live orchestra and there was fun, merriment and dancing until the very wee hours. Fantastic!

By 1956 the new superintendent had not proven himself. He had read about a new product called OMPA (O.M.P.A.), a spray for walnuts to rid pesty aphids. The university testing had proven excellent. It was a year of lots of aphids. Bob gambled and sprayed the entire ranch with the new material. It was a very good year for walnuts—no aphids—biggest crop and best quality, so Bob turned out to be quite a hero and was accepted. Mostly luck, he says.

When he first arrived there were quite a few tractors on the ranch. The oldtimers were: Harry Steinmetz as shop foreman, a great old guy, George Rose, Al and Francis O'Shay, and, of course, "some characters!" Bob did manage to make friends with them, but it wasn't easy since he was half and sometimes more than a third

their ages. Bob says when he arrived the Bishop Ranch was not really in good financial shape, and they were looking for a sale of the ranch. It was sold to a man in Chicago named Robert Crown, who paid cash for it. Bob continued to run the ranch for the Crowns until 1971-72 when it was sold to Western Electric.

Some history of the Bishop ranch as noted by Bob Livermore: The 300 acres of ranch area mostly to the east of Highway #680 were all in pears, the largest block of pears in the world! Each row of trees was over an acre long. When Bob arrived their system of irrigation was by furrows, without much water. Bob found some old abandoned pipe on the ranch. He cut the ends off and made sprinklers and was able to get water to the entire pear orchard.

Blacksmith shop in Old San Ramon was on present site of Franco's Restaurant, formerly Villa San Ramon. The old blacksmith building was razed in 1955. The business had had several owners, including Olsson and Son and later a Mr. Fry. One story goes that he was told that there was gold in San Ramon Creek at the rear of the building, so he spent lots of time digging in the building and on one occasion almost disappeared in his own excavation.

San Ramon Hall was a community center, built on property donated for that purpose. Many great dances were held there, and later it was used as a playhouse. (I remember Howard Wiedemann and my husband, Al Jones, and others did "A Solid Gold Cadillac" there. Morgan's Masonry Supplies, San Ramon, is now on the site.

He tells the story of Adeline Yargee, a Crete Indian, who worked in the mess hall for about ten years, and never missed a meal. Her husband was a large Indian Chief who had struck oil on part of his tribal lands. He would sit around the ranch saying, "I got plenty of money." He had a lot of tribal medicines and weird little bows and arrows for ceremonial purposes. One time when Jean Livermore was about to have a baby, he brought her a bottle of awful looking stuff and told her to drink it. Of course she didn't. Adeline was a nice person and really very nice to Bob. After she left the ranch she was killed in an automobile accident.

Another story told to Bob by George Rose: There always were lots of horses used for the ranch work. The first change was a large steam tractor with huge wheels. The steam boiler had a great loud whistle. When discing along out in the fields, if the coyotes came down (which they did) the fellow running the tractor would blow the whistle. Back at the ranch the cook would release the greyhounds who would come tearing out in the direction of the whistle and run down the coyotes. The greyhounds would kill the coyotes and then they were able to raise sheep.

Ranch foremen were Al O'Shay, and two brothers, Carlos and J. D. Walker from Arkansas,

very nice fellows. Francis O'Shay later became the captain of the San Ramon Fire Department.

Bob and Jean Livermore have four children, Caroline, who is nineteen, Lauren, who is seventeen, and the twins Rob and Sara, who are fifteen. The Livermores bought the Harold Frazier home on Danville Boulevard, and are residents of Danville.

Western Electric had planned a huge home development for the ranch, and, through the expertise of Dan Coleman and Associates, certain densities in specific portions of the property were clearly defined. But eventually, with the passing of time, they gave up the entire project. The former Bishop Ranch is now Shapell Industries and will be developed into homesites.

Podva Home

200

Chapter Thirteen

Potpourri

IMPORTANT NEWS BRIEFS
Over Almost One Hundred Years

The following short news clips are taken from 1858 through 1954 newspaper articles. Highlights in news of the day, they were taken from several newspapers but mostly from the *Walnut Kernel*.

September 18, 1858—There is no law laid down in the statutes of Contra Costa County regarding hogs running-at-large in the county.

September 18, 1858—A slight earthquake shock was felt in the county Sunday evening about 8 o'clock.

September 18, 1858—Through mail to Memphis and St. Louis starts from San Francisco at one o'clock tomorrow morning. It is calculated by the contractor that it will get through in 25 days. Preparations have been made to transport promptly any number of passengers that may offer, or any amount of mail matter. One hundred miles per day is the distance to be traveled, which, if the stages are able to perform, will cut the time considerably under 25 days.

December 1875— The new church in Danville rapidly nearing completion, the Reverend Symington, pastor.

1880s—An advertisement in a county newspaper in the late 1880s offered for rent 230 acres of "rich soil, nearly all under cultivation, divided into five fields, living water and all," at $2 per acre by J. A. Shuey, Danville, California.

January 6, 1883—The snow-storm on Sunday was a surprise and a novelty, although it was general throughout the bay counties, where snow is seldom experienced. There fell at least five inches in the county, and east of Mount Diablo it amounted to a foot.

June 9, 1883—First direct shipment from Danville to Grangers' warehouse at Port Costa, made by R. O. Baldwin, 150 tons of wheat.

June 9, 1883—E. W. Hiller starts ice route through Pacheco, Walnut Creek, Alamo and Danville.

January 1884—The year 1883 was ushered out by a remarkable snowstorm; New Year's Day 1884, was mild and pleasant.

February 2, 1884—Rainfall to date, 6.12 inches. Everybody is smiling this week on account of the rain. The farmers and merchants are all happy. Up to Friday noon of this week 3.36 inches of rain had fallen.

June 6, 1885—The thermometer reached 100 degrees in the shade Friday May 29, at Alamo.

January 1, 1886—13.83 inches of rainfall to date. Farmers in the county are anxiously waiting for the ground to dry enough to plow.

February 13, 1886—Contra Costa County is destined to become a Paradise of vineyards and orchards, of which Ygnacio and Diablo Valleys will be the central portion.

April 3, 1886—The fare from San Francisco to Stockton is 10¢ via the river boats.

July 17, 1886—The losses sustained from extensive grain fires in Sycamore Valley were: Charles Wood, $2000; David Sherburne, $300; J. D. Smith $100; John Camp, $250; also damage to pastures of Wood and Sherburne.

June 4, 1887—Express offices were opened by Wells Fargo & Company, at John Conway's Store in Danville and H. C. Hurst's store in San Ramon.

September 10, 1887—The boom has struck Danville! Two real estate offices have opened and several old residents have sold out!

January 7, 1888—Michael Cohen, formerly of Danville, has opened a store in the Martinez Hotel Building, Martinez, county seat.

1888—In the minutes of an early missionary society meeting held in Danville 13 women present, offering was 35¢.

January 11, 1889—The past few days the weather has been intensely cold. Thermometers went down to 14 degrees, the coldest since 1854. Ice over an inch thick has been taken out of troughs and all puddles are frozen over. Water pipes burst and plumbers were in great demand.

October 9, 1889—The first rainfall of the season was phenomenal! 1.50 inches fell during Monday. This is considered remarkable for the first rain.

May 17, 1890—The Alamo bridge is completed on the Green Valley Road.

December 10, 1890—Work on the San Ramon Branch railway is progressing very satisfactorily.

April 25, 1891—Railroad graders have passed Danville and track laying is under full swing.

April 29, 1891—At the Monday session of the Board of Supervisors, Charles Wood of Danville was appointed public administrator to fill the vacancy caused by the passing of Mr. Scammon.

May 30, 1891—Four locomotives at Danville at one time impart a lively appearance to the neighborhood.

January 28, 1892—The fine warehouse of J. A. Shuey at Danville was totally destroyed by fire Tuesday night. Contents were 4,000 tons of hay in storage. Building and contents were well insured.

September 29, 1894—The thermometer ranged between 105 and 110 degrees in the shade for the closing days of the week.

March 30, 1895—The Mountain House on Mount Diablo closed due to lack of patronage.

July 13, 1912—A crew of 50 workmen, with tools arrived at Danville Wedensday night to begin work on the new road to the summit of Mount Diablo, starting at Oakwood Park Stock Farm (Diablo Country Club). The work has been started by the R. N. Burgess Company. Over 150 cars of rock and gravel has been ordered and will be delivered over the Southern Pacific Railroad.

August 1931—Little highway work to be done in county.

September 1931—Civic bodies start move to keep unsightly buildings off San Ramon Valley Hwy.

November 1931—Women in crowded beauty parlors almost went into hysterics when power failed for two hours.

December 1931—The Chamber of Commerce elects directors for 1932: Fred Wiedemann, San Ramon, and Edgar Lion, Alamo.

Fiscal year 1931-32—Real estate boom starting in San Ramon Valley and Lafayette -- a new law raises speed limit from 40 to 45 mph -- trying to eliminate dangerous curve at south end of Hartz Avenue in Danville -- Chamber of Commerce dinner at Diablo Country Club to celebrate state taking over Broadway Tunnel -- F. J. Reilly to teach music in Danville schools -- Danville Grange fetes 50-year members: Mrs. Jeanette Bunce, Alamo, and Miss Charlotte "Lottie" Wood, Danville. -- Macadam strip removed from center of Danville - San Ramon Road.

April 1933—McMarr Market advertises: coffee 17¢ pound, 3 cans of peaches 25¢, milk 4¢ per can, fresh peas 5¢ lb., spring lamb 13¢ lb. -- Mr. and Mrs. A. J. Young of Danville die a few days after their 65th wedding anniversary.

May 1933—Danville revives May Day Fete.

August 1933—Danville Fire District is only one in state without a tax this year. Commissioners are Ed Wiester and Roger Podva. Mrs. Ruby Podva beat Marcia Eddy, Pat Parkey and R. Elwanger to succeed Mrs. Emma Dodge as postmaster.

September 1933—San Ramon Valley observes NRA Day with a Big Parade and Mass Meeting.

October 1933—Alamo parents defy school trustee ban by sending children to Danville and Walnut Creek schools -- CCC Camp starts on Mount Diablo.

January 1934—Walnut Creek has more real estate dealers than any other town in Contra Costa County except Richmond, and yet none of them belong to the Contra Costa Real Estate Board, says the organization's new President, "Cappy" Ricks, Martinez.

October 1934—At suggestion of DAR, County Superintendent of Schools, B. O. Wilson, orders all schools to open each morning with pledge to the flag.

November 1934—Milk goes up to 11¢ per quart. - Brewers price war lowers beer from $1.80 to $1.20 per case on small bottles.

January 1935—Emery Smith of Alamo, pastmaster of Danville Grange, after criticizing Bay Bridge proponents because they have not considered 50,000 commuters, is named by Oakland as a consulting engineer on the span!

February 1935—The Insurance Society being formed in San Ramon Valley to furnish gifts to members who get wedding invitation. -- Also in formation, Widowers' & Bachelors' Protective Society, next year being leap year.

March 1935—John Adford, Walnut Creek barber, asks permission to be first to cross bay bridge.

June 1935—Chairman Charles Wood reports to Danville Grange on campaign to eradicate star thistle in Valley. -- Courts decide 45 mph speed limit.

July 1935—Business Women ask Chamber of Commerce and City Council to hold Walnut Festival this fall.

November 1935—Mount Diablo CCC Camp reopened with 75 Veterans.

August 1936—First Walnut Festival a success. Lasted 3 days, with Legion '49 camp, 3 parades, "eruption of Diablo," 2 dances, carnival. Sunday parade was led by Elmer Cameron who rode at the head of grape festival years ago (1911).

November 1936—San Ramon Valley ministerial association has a 6-day preaching mission.

December 1936—Southern Contra Costa County farmers organize soil conservation district.

Septembr 1938—Johnny Walker, Mount Diablo's oldest living native son, heads third annual Walnut Festival parade.

April 1939—William Timm of Walnut Creek and Associates reopen old coal mines on Diablo.

August 1939—Mount Diablo becoming radio center -- Museum to be enlarged too.

October 1939—Selling stock in Tassajara oil corp.

June 1940—Walnut Creek population now 550.

July 1940—William Stewart re-elected and Horace Van Gorden succeeds Claude Andreasen, not a candidate, San Ramon Valley High School trustees.

October 1940—Men between 21 and 35 years register for draft. A total of 3909 in Walnut Creek and San Ramon Valley.

January 1941—First contingent of 31 South Contra Costa County draftees got to Camp Ord for training.

September 1941—With the European market gone, because of the war, the government is buying nearly all the California prunes this season, says Grower J. B. Near.

November 1941—Wynne Newell house, south of Main Street bridge Walnut Creek to be made into art center (present site of Kaiser Hospital, W. C.).

February 1942—131 enemy aliens swarm Post Office to register, mostly Japanese.

May 1942—Sugar rationing starts with householders registering at schools.

July 1942—Fourth of July fireworks banned, account of war.

September 1942—No Walnut Festival this year - First blood bank in Walnut Creek.

November 1942—South Contra Costa County entertain 100 navy men at Thanksgiving home dinners.

January 1943—Cattle rustlers getting busy - 4 arrested so far in San Ramon-Livermore area.

March 1943—Promoting victory gardens, the Chamber of Commerce seeks cheaper water.

July 1943—Haircuts going up. Sign on door of John Bednary's Shop: "Come in and let us give you an estimate!"

July 1943—All the male residents of Contra Costa County were threatening to let their hair grow back in July 1943, when the barbers raised haircuts to $1.00 effective July 19, 1943. (Author: Now in modern times (1977) the going rate for a man's haircut is minimum $4.50 and upward with specialized styling, permanents, tinting, bleaching, straightening, blower cuts, etc. and more available.)

September 1943—Canneries shorthanded, can't take all pears offered.

October 1943—Plan trunk sewer for South Contra Costa County.

March 1944—Letter postage goes from 2¢ to 3¢ (author - 33 years later up to 13¢).

August 1944—Many "Oakies" and other mid-westerners who came to California in another "Gold Rush" (high wartime wages) return home.

April 1945—San Ramon Valley women inviting for Sunday dinner soldiers from nearby training camps.

September 1945—Move on for needed hospital.

May 1946—Lumber dealers report insufficient material for veterans' houses.

February 1947—A. J. Geldermann of San Ramon, new president of Contra Costa Real Estate Board.

April 1947—Bank of America moved to new Main St. building with new manager Anton Cvietusa of Alamo.

November 1947—County Health Dept. assigns inspector to Walnut Creek and San Ramon Valley.

January 1948—Greyhound and Southern Pacific send questionnaires to commuters to learn what the customers want.

October 1948—Emil Hagstrom of Diablo drives prize winning team at Walnut Festival.

January 1949—Headed by President R. Biggs, San Ramon Valley Improvement Club voices objection to widening highway because it will ruin its beauty.

April 1949—Gretchen Green, two and one-half, wins Kernel baby contest.

July 1949—Pears down to $40 a ton, a third of last year, many growers won't pick.

August 1949—Southern Contra Costa County has 78 of county's 120 polio cases. Health Officer Blum asks support for Danville sewer bonds.

September 1949—Still bulging at seams, county schools start fall term. Over 300 children on double session.

October 1949—Harvesting the county's biggest walnut crop.

December 1949—Danville citizens group asks to study pupils' report cards to learn what type of education is desired by parents.

December 1949—Planning Commission says every fence in Walnut Creek is illegal.

February 1950—Governor Earl Warren guest of honor at county's 100th anniversary dinner at Diablo Country Club. John Baldwin, Danville, in charge of 75th anniversary of Danville Presbyterian Church.

November 1950—Not enough crime in Walnut Creek to warrant a city jail; prisoners will continue to be taken to county jail at Martinez.

November 1951—A score of stores open in new Broadway Shopping Center in Walnut Creek, "Fastest growing city in the world!"

March 1952—Auto insurance rates high in Contra Costa County because of poor roads.

August 1952—Danville leads county in sky watching.

December 1952—California Newspaper Publishers Assoc. announces *Walnut Kernel* newspaper has third biggest weekly subscription list in state. (Author: I worked for them as a by-lined columnist from May 28, 1953 until April 18, 1958.)

January 1953—Prosperous year predicted for Contra Costa County, and especially for Walnut Creek.

May 1953—Banker Larry Davitt of Alamo, new president of Walnut Creek Lions Club, Elliott Mauzy president of Rotary.

August 1953—State to ask bids for six-lane Tunnel road job.

October 1953—Walnut Festival attended by 60,000.

November 1953—Rezoning in Danville to permit million dollar shopping center.

December 1953—A. J. Geldermann, San Ramon, picked for 1954 president of Danville Chamber of Commerce.

January 1954—Almonds in bloom and four inches of snow on Mount Diablo.

February 1954—Flood control district forms Walnut Creek watershed district from Suisun Bay to San Ramon on south, Charles Hill on west.

January 1956—The operation of Contra Costa schools in 1955 cost $26 million.

RECOLLECTIONS OF ISABELLE (CROSBY) McGEEHON

By now you know how much I appreciate interviews with those who have experienced the happenings. After reading my book *Remembering Alamo...and Other Things Along the Way*, Isabelle (Mrs. James C.) McGeehon of Oakvale Road, Walnut Creek, sent me a letter of appreciation on April 29, 1976. It contained her recollections of much about which I wrote, as well as the information that she had been a resident at her present address for the past sixty-four years. Her maiden name was Crosby and she was born and lived on a ranch near Livermore named "Mulfontes," a Latin word meaning "many springs." The home is still standing. Her father was William Crosby, who came to San Francisco in 1869 from Bangor, Maine.

Isabelle was a close and dear friend of Bessie Drury, a member of the Harlan Clan. She recalls having two encounters with Elisha Harlan. Bess spoke of "Uncle Lisha" and "Aunt Minervie." Possibly in 1914, her husband and small son Jim and she (Isabelle) were returning home to Walnut Creek, after Thanksgiving with her father and two sisters, Mary and Elizabeth, at the family homestead in the Livermore hinterlands. They were met by a man on a bay horse. He trotted by and compared notes, and told them the history of El Nido. Some years later, he and Albert Glass came up their hill to buy some kale plants and a clutch of eggs from the Barred rock hens. Mr. Glass explained his cane by saying he had an "ossified knee" which had cost him a mint of money. His cane was a staff with realistic wooden serpents twined around it. While he pulled plants he threw the cane to the ground. For a split second Isabelle says she recoiled as it looked so like the real thing. This of course amused the two elderly gentlemen.

Her recollections of Friederiche (Humburg) Jackson were many. One was of a time when a group met at the Jackson's Alamo home. Since

Above, an eighty-year-old photograph of the Bunce family, Martha Jeannette (Stone) and Edward Augustus Bunce and their daughters, Martha and Olivette.

Top left, Martha at age two. Left, Olivette at age two.

Her youngest sister was just out of grade school. Another sister was not well, and Isabelle had a bit of residue from typhoid, so they had a teacher at home that fall who was studying to receive her MA at UC, and was taking advantage of a leave to earn some money. Friederiche and Isabelle were good friends and belonged to the same DAR Chapter. Friederiche hostessed a large benefit card party at her Alamo home and was often hostess for regular chapter meetings.

She says of Olivette, who was a bit older, how she mistakenly called her Martha Mougin's niece. Martha corrected her sharply for the error, since Olivette was Martha's older sister by one and one-half years! A few days after Olivette's death, Isabelle met Martha in the bank and told her of it. She knew the Stows well, and remembered that Martha's daughter, Evelyn, married Bill Stow, son of the Rufus Stows of Walnut Creek.

She also recollects a relative, Florence Beck, formerly of Livermore, whose family moved to Berkeley, where Madison Beck married one of

there was time, they chatted pleasantly of many things and enjoyed the view out the windows. They spoke of Martha (Bunce) Mougin and her sister Olivette McMillan. In about 1905 Olivette and Isabelle were students at Berkeley High School together. The principal was Morris James, and it was then shortly before he married Juliet. Isabelle entered school in August 1904 and left in the spring of 1907 with a case of typhoid fever!

the three Inman sisters. He became an insurance man after disposing of his interest in the George Beck & Company grocery firm. A few doors up the street from that store was the Livermore Commercial Company, owned by the brothers-in-law married to the two Inman sisters. Later they moved to Fulton Street in Berkeley. Florence has a younger sister, Genevieve.

She remembered when she and Bess Drury visited the old Silas Stone Home for the last time before it was demolished and torn down in 1954. As they chatted on the front porch two sisters strolled by—Lilias, married to Elmer Short, and Betty Ross. The Shorts lived in Livermore. Dan, a tall, thin, blonde man, was a relative. He worked for the Crosbys in Livermore in 1908, the summer "the new house" was built on the knoll. He was a reliable and frugal man who could be counted on to return sober from town. He never needed to draw advance pay.

Isabelle told that some years later Bess visited another of her cousins, Carmen Geldermann, who was living in a smaller house she had built on the property after renovating El Nido to the tune of several thousand, including an elegant staircase, according to Bess. Zylpha Bernal Beck, about to be ninety-four, still lives in Livermore. They drove a team of perfectly matched bay ponies owned by the Bernals. Isabelle recalls how well broken they were.

She knew where Tal Thorne lived on Stone Valley Road, Alamo, and saw him in and around Walnut Creek with his horses and wagon.

She also knew Hilda (Mrs. E. B. Bradley), mother of Cecile (Mrs. La May) Podva of Danville.

Isabelle remembers the loss of O. W. Peterson of Alamo, as she served on the board of the Mount Diablo chapter of the American Red Cross. She remembers teas at Mrs. Ewell's at Seven Hills Ranch, Walnut Creek. Sumner Crosby was the father of one of her cousins. She refers to Everett Sumner Crosby as "Pony," a nickname he received when attending Piedmont High School before coming to Alamo and San Ramon Union High School. Their line of the Crosby family coincides up to Nathan. Her father was William Crosby of Maine.

She mentioned that she knows Bertha (Bell) Linhares and knew her first when she was in the Walnut Creek post office. Years later, when renting the Alamo Women's Clubhouse, she was surprised to see her again when she picked up the key.

Joe Lawrence, who ran the Butcher Shop in Danville, she remembers came from Half Moon Bay. The father was in the meat business first.

Nancy Reagan accepting an autographed copy of Remembering Alamo... and Other Things Along the Way *for Governor Ronald Reagan, at a reception at Round Hill Country Club, Alamo, on Monday, May 10, 1976. On May 25, 1976 I received a letter from Ronald Reagan with comments: "...enjoyed...and will make a special place for it [the book] in Nancy's and my library....Also enjoyed the pictures you included of me."*
(Photo by Linda Johnson of the Valley Pioneer)

After their move to Walnut Creek, the father would drop by the butcher shop to check how they were running the business.

(Author's note: I'd say she read my book well. And it is nice to make her a part of this one.)

Isabelle's two married granddaughters have stayed rather close to the old homestead. One is building down the Valley of San Ramon and the other is the mother of an adorable five-year-old. They live in Mission San Jose.

Epilogue

The author's family, to whom this book is dedicated: A. Garrett "Gary" Jones, the son; Bertha Morris Boggini, the mother; Alfred Bensen Jones, the husband; and Jennifer Nicole Jones, the granddaughter, age five years and nine months. Photo taken on Easter Sunday, April 10, 1977.

To further update and conclude—now that Volume Two of *Historical Persons and Places in San Ramon Valley* has ended, I wish to thank all those who cooperated and participated. It had to be a team effort. A complete credits list would be almost another book.

But I do want to give special thanks to Bertha (Bell) Linhares of Alamo, to whom, when in question or doubt regarding Alamo, I could always turn; and Hazel (Arthur) Wiester, who did the same for me of Danville; and Vivian (Coats) Edmonston of San Francisco, who volunteered much information and help on early-day Danville.

And again, last, but by no means least, my appreciation and love to my mother, Bertha (Morris) Boggini, to whom I have continued to proofread aloud every Sunday my endeavors and labors in writing of the week, for her approval and acceptance and continued encouragement.

Once again, I will use my former newspaper column sign-off—OK? 'til next time?

Virgie Jones
May 1977

Index

Boone, Sarah (Morgan)(Mrs. Squire), 39, 40
Boone, Sarah (Uppey)(Mrs. George II), 39
Boone, Sophie (Love)(Mrs. Joel Haden), 68,177
Boone, Squire, 39,40
Boone, Squire, 40
Boone, Susanna, 40
Boone, Susanna, 39
Boone, Travis Moore "Bud," 39,41,89, 159,171
Boone, Wellington T., 40,197
Boone, William, 39
Boone, William, 40
Booth, Dr. Fred, 7,122
Booth, Governor, 16
Booth, Teresa (Mrs. Fred), 7
Borges, S. P., 15,131
Borghini, Mrs. Stella (Marengo), 124
Borlandelli, C. P., 125
Borlandelli, Mrs. Mary (Marengo), 124
Borst & Giddens, Ventura, 139
Boswill, Jennie, 154
Botelho, Mr. & Mrs. Antone Silva, 121, 125
Botts, Ennetta, 85
Boucher, David, 143,146,157,159
Boucher, Ila, 143,157
Boucher, Josiah, 121,146
Boucher, Moura and Whitten, 173
Bowen, Helen Carver, 66
Bowersmith, Adele (Alexander)(Mrs. John E.), 49
Bowersmith, John A., 49
Bowersmith, John E., 49
Bowersmith, Jane V. (Tuttle)(Mrs. John A.), 49
Bowles, Margaret, 154
Bowles, Phoebe, 153,154
Bowman, J., 30,31
Box, Dr. Ina A., 6
Boyd, Mrs. Louise, 190
Boydston, Margaret, 85
B.P.O.E., 39
Bradley, Edward, 53,58
Bradley, Hilda (Mrs. Edward B.), 53,58, 206
Bradshaw, Rev. T. R., 120
Bragdon, Doris (Barnard)(Mrs. Joseph C.), 174
Bradgon, Prof. Joseph C., 174
Braley, Prof. (A.B.) John H., 145,147,148
Braley, Miss Lizzie, 147
Brandes, Joan, 87,95,96
Brass Door Restaurant, San Ramon, 93, 96,98,102
Brazeals, Richard, 172
Brazil, Rose, 122
"Breaks in the Hills," 173
Brear, Albert Edward, 45,46,157
"Brear-Brae," 45,46
Brear, Frederick, 45
Brear, Frederick Gillette, 44,45,46,120
Brear, Grace Marie (Gillette)(Mrs. A. E.), 45,46
Brear, James Frederick, 44
Brear, Jean, 155
Brear, Linda Marie, 44,45
Brear, Mary Frances (Lax), 44,120
Brear, Maud, 45
Brear, Nellie, 45
Brear, Samual Scott, 46
Brear, Sarah (Herbert)(Mrs. Frederick), 45
Brear, Shirley (Kamp)(Mrs. F. G.), 44,45
Brear, William, 45
Breed, Horace, 32
Breidenbach, Florence Susan (Rutherford)(Mrs. R. W.), 76
Breidenbach, Lauren Ann, 76
Breidenbach, Prof. R. W., 76
Breidenbach, Wendy Lynn, 76
Bresnan, Rev. Patrick, 123
Bret Harte Park, 88,179

Breuner, Rosellen, 101
Breven, 30,31
Brevensville, 30
Brewer, Mrs. Arthur, 97
Brewer, Thalia, 137,138
Bridges, Lee, 172
Brigaw, A., 31
Briggs, Rev. Samuel, 120
Brigham Young University, 80
Bright, Sabra Simpson, 154
Brink, Leigh Mervyn, 48
Brink, Lucille (Mrs. Leigh M.), 48
Brink, Mr., 48
Brink, Thomas, 48
Brink, Timothy, 48
Britton and Ray, 189
Broadway Tunnel, 51,202
Brock, Dora, 14
Brose, Dorothy Leiz, 99
Broussard, Mary Stewart, 99
Brown, 31
Brown, Alma, 86,101
Brown, Denise Jay (Wing)(Mrs. Gary), 55
Brown, Dyke, 138
Brown, Elam, 9,15
Brown, Freda, 51
Brown, Gary, 55
Brown, Jennifer, 71
Brown, June, 94
Brown, Laverne, 155
Brown, Mrs. Leslie K. Ward (Fereira), 70, 71
Brown, Manual, 130
Brown, Patricia, 87
Brown, Rev. Roy, O.F.M., 123
Brown, Stanley, 155
Brown, Sybil, 15
Brownlee, Don, 120
Brubaker, Isabelle Spencer, 16,100
Brugger, Joe, 120
Brumfield, Edgar, 172
Brumfield, Edgar C. "Ed," 171,172
Brumfield, Elizabeth (Mrs. Edgar C.), 172
Brumfield, Norma, 172
Brumfield, Richard, 172
Brumfield, Ronald James, 172
Brunckhorst, Arthur, 194
Bryant, Dr. H. C., 18
Buchanan, Mr., 186
Buchanan, Thomas, 155
Buckley, Roy, 45
Buckner, Robert, 86
Budde, Lillie M., 94
Budge, A. G., 142
Buena Vista Youth Ranch, 100
Bull, Mr. & Mrs. Ed., 191
Buls, Pat, 174
Buls, Vernon, 174
Bunce, Edward Augustus, 85,205
Bunce, (Martha) Jeannette (Stone)(Mrs. E. A.), 202,205
Burdick, A. M., 121
Burford, Chris, 87
Burgess, Anne Webster Fish (Mrs. R. N., Sr.), 190
Burgess, Cecil, 61
Burgess, Charles, 61
Burgess, Frances, 61
Burgess, Elizabeth (Mrs. R. N., Jr.), 193
Burgess, Rev. J. C., 120
Burgess, Robert Noble, Sr., 77,189,190
Burgess, Robert N. "Bob," Jr., 190,191, 193
Burgess, Susan (Yager)(Mrs. Charles), 61
Burk, Dr. Raymond V., 6
Burling, Miss Helen, 92
Burner, Irma, 94
Burpee, Mary (Sherburne)(Mrs. W. S.), 64
Burpee, Winfield S., 15,64,74
Burr, Barbara, 187
Burris, Florence, 143,157
Burris, Georgia, 158

Burton, Arthur, 15,131
Bush, Bob, 87
Bushey, Marion (Mrs. A. H.), 87
Bushman, Libby, 87
Butter, Mrs. John, 89
Buttner, Jake, 31
Byer, Peter, 153
Byington, Charles T., 105
Byington, Frank J., 104,105,180,184,186
Byington and Fagan Realty of Alamo, 104,105,180,181,184,185,186
Cabral, Anthony B. "Tony," 93,102
Cabral, Duana (Elliott), 75
Cabral, Madelyn, 155
Cabral, Mike, 75
Cache Creek Bank, 76
Cady, Teresa, 107
Cain, Mrs. Forrest, 89
Caldecott Tunnel, 163
Caldwell, Dave, 31
Calhoun, Darlene (Hawkinson)(Mrs. Richard), 109,110
Calhoun, Superior Court Judge Richard, 96,110
California Arts Council, 137
California Federation of Women's Clubs, 87,100
California High School, 86
California Military Academy, 149
California Newspaper Publishers Association, 204
California Nurses Association, 181
California Patron & Agriculturist (newspaper), 24
Cal-Poly, San Luis Obispo, 104
California Presbytery of the Cumberland Presbyterian Church, 118
California Real Estate Association, 39
California School of Arts & Crafts, 166
California State Division of AAUW, 98
California State Real Estate Commission, 39
California State University at Hayward, 103,104,172
California Water Service, 51,185
Callaghan, Ora (Bell)(Mrs. Dennis), 157, 159
Callaghan, Phyllis Fitz, 99
Callaway, Flanders, 40
Callaway, Jemima (Boone)(Mrs. Flanders), 40
Call-Bulletin (newspaper), 130
Camacho, Amelia, 155
Camacho, Clara, 155
Cameo Acres, 5,117,195
Cameron, Alice (Marsh)(Mrs. W. W.), 190
Cameron, Angus, 146
Cameron, Elmer, 203
Cameron, Rev. John M., 120
Cameron, W. W., 190
Camille Park Subdivision, 170
Camille Woods, 186
Camozzi, Bob, 187
Camozzi, Freda, 187
Camp, John, 31,201
Campbell, Almina (Woodard)(Mrs. Robert), 47
Campbell, George, 155
Campbell, Gladys, 62
Campbell, Isla, 62
Campbell, Harry, 138
Campbell High School, San Jose, 108
Campbell, Jack, 62
Campbell, Minerva (Labaree)(Mrs. Jack), 62
Campbell, Mr. & Mrs., 54
Campbell, Robert, 47,50
Capers, Gina, 87
Capling, Donald, 96
CARE, 93,100
Carefree Travel Service, 98
Carey, Mrs. Clara, 14
Carey, Daniel Thorpe, 55
Carey, Elmer W., 55

217

Jones, Alfred "Fritz," 3,28,102,116,135, 142,155,166,169,174,175,187,188,199, 207
Jones, Bryon, 155
Jones, Candace, 10
Jones, George, 30
Jones, Gregory Alden, 120
Jones, Henry, 171
Jones, James Cass, 15,79,131.135
Jones, Jennifer Nicole, 125,188,207
Jones, John M., 6,9,10,12,57,81,90,118, 143,144,145,148,197
Jones, John R., 49
Jones, Josephine, 10
Jones, Marilyn, 120,137
Jones, Mary Ann (Smith) "Grandma Jones" (Mrs. John M.), 10,12,37,57,118, 119,143,144
Jones, Melvin, 93
Jones, Nathaniel, 6,9
Jones, Patricia Lee (Taylor) (Mrs. A. Garrett), 175,187,188
Jones' Pets: "Blondie," "Mitzie," "Sparky," 110
Jones, Roscoe, Jr., 120
Jones, Sarah Jane, 10
Jones, Viola (Lynch) (Mrs. John R.) 47,49
Jorgensen, Helene Marie (Thorup) (Mrs. Nils Jorgen), 43,44
Jorgensen, Marjorie, 44
Jorgensen, Nils Jorgen, 43,44
Joseph, Caroline, 154
Joseph, Ruth M., 94
Jossey, Mary Jane, 98
Judd family, 91
Julliard School of Music, New York, 45
Julian, Clara, 108
Julian, Joe, 108
Junior 4-H Auction, 125
Justice, Bailey, 194
Juul Residence, 122

Kahnberg, Mr. & Mrs. Alvar, 181
Kaiser family 181
Kaiser Hospital, Walnut Creek, 181,203
Kalama, Rev. David M., 188
Kalmanir, Tom, 104
Kamp, Andrew, 45
Kamp, Bill, 45
Kamp, Carl, 45
Kamp, Carolyn, 45
Kamp, Ed, 45
Kamp, Hans, 45
Kamp, Hans Nicholsen, 45
Kamp, Honsina (Lausten) (Mrs. Hans Nicholsen), 45
Kamp, Ida, 45
Kamp, (Julia) Anita (Mrs. Louis Hansen), 43,44,45
Kamp, Karl (Kamp) (Mrs. Grayson), 45
Kamp, Louis, 45
Kamp, Louis Hansen, 43,44,45,157
Kamp, Mame, 45
Kamp, Margaret, 45
Kamp, Maria, 45
Kamp, Minnie, 45
Kamp, Paul, 44
Kamp, Regina (Kelly), 44
Kamp, Robert Hayden, 44
Kamp, Robert, Jr., 44
Kamp, William "Bill," 45
Kane, Gerald, 48
Kane, Pat (Brink) (Mrs. Gerald), 48
"Kansas," 25
Kantrowitz, David N., 57
Kantrowitz, Elaine, 57
Kantrowitz, Kathryn A. (Close) (Mrs. Samuel B.), 56,57
Kantrowitz, Laurel Elaine (Matteson), 57
Kantrowitz, Richard Lance, 57
Kantrowitz, Samantha, 57
Kantrowitz, Samuel B., 57,90
Kaplan, Al, 31
Kaplan, Ann M. (Wiedemann) (Mrs. Al), 31

Kaplan, Christine, 31
Kaplan, Freda, 31,32
Kaplan, Hazel, 31,32
Karling, Carl, 32
Karlo, Mr. & Mrs. Leo H., 79
Katzer, Grace, 98
Katzer, Melvin, 120
Kauder, Rose Nell "Boots," 86
Kaufmann, Joan, 87
Kay, Beatrice, 109
Keane, Mrs. Fran. Betts, 193
Keane, Gerrit, 193
Keith, John, 10
Kjellejian, Laura, 140
Keefe, Richard, 93
Kelleway, Mrs. Fred T., 97
Kelley, Arline, 87
Kelley, Dorothea (Torrey) (Mrs. Harold), 92
Kelley, Virgil, 121
Kellogg, Abby Ann (Tubbs) (Mrs. Sheldon, 106
Kellogg, Sheldon, 106
Kelly, Helen, 138
Kelly, Mary (Mullvaney) (Mrs. Wm.), 169
Kelly, Mayme Belle, 146,158
Kelly, Nik, 87
Kelly Ranch, 74
Kelsey's, 64
Kendall, Anne Marie (Wille) (Mrs. William K.), 45
Kendall, Karleen Louise, 45
Kendall, Katheryn, 45
Kendall, Kay Marie, 45
Kendall property, 104,145
Kendall, William Kenneth, 45
Kendricks, Jane, 143,157
Kennedy, Pres. John F., 123
Kennedy, Marjorie, 98
Kenny, James, 6
Kerley, Angel, 95
Kerhof, Leo, 155
Kermit, Mark L., 3,4
Kerns, Barbara, 92
Kerns, Leslie H. "Les," 133
Kerr, Emma V. (McPherson) (Mrs. James), 52
Kerr, James J., 52,120
Kessel, Mathilda (Jorgensen) (Mrs. A.), 159
Ketsdever, William J., 97,132
Keyes, Miss Edna, 187
Keys, R. Fuller, 168
Keys, Zeta (Mrs. R. F.), 168
Kidwell, L. B., 155
Kihlken, Lorine R., 94
Kimball Company, 4
Kimball, Gloria (Mrs. C. B.), 96
Kimballs, the, 181
King, John, 11
King, Mr., 147,148,164
King Ranch, 109,164
King, Richard, 96
King, Rev. Robert, 145
King, Samuel D. Esquire, 118
Kinney, William, 101,102
Kirkcrest Road, 72
Kirtland, Narcissis (Tucker) (Mrs. Thomas), 52
Kirtland, Thomas, 52
Kitamure, Dr., 111
Kiwanis Club of San Ramon Valley, 96. 97
Knibbe, Kathy, 110,111,112
Knibbe, Marion, 112
Knibbe, Paul, 112
Knowlton, Justin, 194
Knox Road, 117
Koch, Augusta, 156
Koch, Lizzie, 156
Kovatch, Martha, 93
Kriedts, the, 171
Kristick, David, 53
Kristick, David Michael, 53
Kristick, Kevin Randolph, 53

Kristick, Paula, 53
Kroeger, John, 156
Krueger, De Witt, 194
Krusi, Rev. Carlisle H., 139
Krusi, George S., 139
Krusi, Harriet (Hume) (Mrs. Leroy F.), 139
Krusi, Leroy F., 139
Krusi, Leroy H., 139
Kurtz, Jean, 95
Kuss, Carola Rose (Mueller) (Mrs. Peter Nicholas), 71
Kuss, Edward, 71
Kuss, Miss Mabel E., 71,72
Kuss, Peter Nicholas, 71,72
Kuss Ranch, 71,72,73
Kuss Road, 72
Kyle, Merry, 87

Labaree, Adel, 62
Labaree, Alice (Linekin) (Mrs. John), 62
Labaree, Alma, 62
Labaree, Amy (Balch) (Mrs. Wm.), 62
Labaree, Anna, 62
Labaree, Annette (Stevens) (Mrs. Milton), 62
Labaree, Edna, 62
Labaree, Elsie, 62
Labaree, Eugene, 62
Labaree, Hubbard, 62
Labaree, Isabella, 62
Labaree, Jennie, 62
Labaree, John, 62
Labaree, (John) Lyman, 62,146,157
Labaree, Dr. John Lyman, 31
Labaree, Joseph, 62
Labaree, Margaret, 62
Labaree, Marion, 62
Labaree, Milton S., 11,62
Labaree, Minnie (Hemme), 62
Labaree, Olivia, 62
Labaree, Sarah, 62
Labaree, Sarah Minerva (Cox) (Mrs. John L.), 62
Labaree, William, 62
Lacey's Arabian Center, 123,125
Lacey, Murrel, 125
Lacey, Randi, 125
"La Cueva" (cave), 91
Lafayette Grammar School, 165
Laird, Mildred (Barry) (Mrs. Clyde), 51
Lake Merritt, 71,117
Lakewood Estates, Walnut Creek, 190
Lambert, Laura Beck, 99
Lande, Rev. Henry J., 123
Landes, Dale, 174
Landis, Emma (Hack) (Mrs. George), 52
Landis, George, 52
Langan, George Washington, 13,14
Langan, Luella Dora (Mendenhall) (Mrs. G. W.), 13
Langdon, Judge William H., 31
Langlais, Eleanor Bertha (Wiester) Jantzen Neel (Mrs. Rodney), 78
Langlais, Rodney, 78
Langridge, Olive, 87
Lanier, Sydney, 40
Larake, J. L., 197
Las Juntas Chapter of Toastmasters, 102
Las Palmas, 58
"La Tierra de la Contra Costa," 90
Latimer, Henry and Emmrietta, 9
Laughlin, Abbie Joseph (Finley) (Mrs. Grant A.), 67
Laughlin, Grant Alexander, 67
Laurel Camp No. 7276 R.N. of A., 85
Laurence, Annie, 50
Laurence, Bill, 50
Laurence, George, 50
Laurence, Isabel, 50
Laurence, Jessie, 50
Laurence, Joe, 50
Laurence, Josie, 50
Laurence, Manuel, 50
Laurence, Marian, 50

Osborn, Mary Ellen, 80
Osborn, Michael, 80
Osborn, Michelle, 80
Osborn, Myrtle (McNally)(Mrs. I. M.), 79,80
Osborn, Nancy, 80
Osborn, Patricia (Anderson)(Mrs. Mac D.), 80
Osborn, Paul, 80
Osborn, Russell, 80
Osborn, Ruth, 80
Osborn, Sherry (Gessel)(Mrs. David), 80
Osborn, Shirley (Newell)(Mrs. James), 80
Osborn Spraying Service, 80
Osborn, Steven, 80
O'Shaughnessy, Rev. Thomas, 123
O'Shay, Al, 199,200
O'Shay, Francis, 199,200
Osmundson, John, 171,172
Oswill, Charles Emmett "Tunne," 53
Oswill, Claudeen, 53
Oswill, Donald Cameron "Gint," 53
Oswill, Donnalee, 53
Oswill, Dorothy, 53
Oswill, Edna (Mathison)(Mrs. Geo. McCamley), 53
Oswill, Ethel (Oakes)(Mrs. Wm. D.), 53
Oswill, Eva (Turk)(Mrs. Donald Cameron), 53
Oswill, Evelyn, 53
Oswill, Fern, 53
Oswill, George McCamley, 53
Oswill, Georgeann, 53
Oswill, Gurdon, 53
Oswill, John, 31,52
Oswill, Kenneth, 53
Oswill, Margaret (Sorum)(Mrs. Warren W.), 53
Oswill, Marie (Borba)(Mrs. Chas. Emmett), 53
Oswill, Mary Ann (Hack)(Mrs. John), 52
Oswill, Minnie (Lafranz)(Mrs. Richard C.), 53
Oswill, Richard Cathcart, 53
Oswill, Thelma, 157
Oswill, Warren W., 53
Oswill, William, 53
Oswill, William Daniel, 53
Oswill, William Daniel, Jr., 53
Otto Home, 74,91
Otto, Kirk, 96
Otto, Valdo P., 143,146,158,159
Outhouse, the, 98
Owen, Hazel, 157
Owen, Mrs. Mary L., 157
Owsley, Mr. & Mrs. William, 193

Pacheco, Antone V., 125
Pacheco, Rafael Soto de, 89
Pacheco, Salvio, 7
Pacific Coast Hunter Association Championship, 173
"Pacific Cumberland Presbyter" (newspaper), 120,121,147
Pacific Embroidery Company, San Francisco, 166
Pacific Telephone Company, 80
Pacini, Mr. & Mrs. George, 193
Padis, George, 194
Page, Harold, 99
Page, Mary, 99
Palace Hotel, San Francisco, 37,57,71, 74,79
Palermo, Darla, 62
Palermo, Darlene (Page)(Mrs. Paul), 62
Palermo, Paula, 62
Palermo, Paul Cornelius, 61,62
Palermo, Perry, 62
Palermo, Ruth (Yager) Smith, 60,61
Palsulich, George, 171
Palsulich, Geraldine "Geri," 171
Palsulich, Ruth, 171
Pan American Airlines, 185
Pancoast, Abagail (Boone), 39

Pangborns, 170
Parade, 110
Paris, Fred, 172
Parker, Carleton, 171
Parker, Clarice, 94
Parker, Cornelia (Stratton)(Mrs. Carleton), 171
Parker, Lee, 11
Parkey, Pat, 202
Parkhurst, Elaine, 87
Parrish, Bess (Mrs. Larry), 101
Parrish, Joseph W. F., 93
Parsons, G. M., 32
Parsons, Jack, 74
Parsons, John, 128
Parsons, Kay, 74
Parsons Lane, 74
Pascoe, Clara, 66
Pascoe, Henry Lee, 66
Pascoe, Jeptha, 65
Pascoe, Lee, 65
Pascoe, Lester, 66
Pascoe, Lucy Ann Lulu (Wilkes)(Mrs. Lee), 65,66
Pasquale, Martha, 140
Pasquale, Nita, 38
"Patch the Pony," 100
P. A. Thorup Boot & Shoe Manufacturing Shop, 43
Patton, Gen. George S., 75
Paul, Susan (Sue), 86
Paulson, O. D., 120
Paul, Susan (Sue), 86
Payne, John, 25
Payne, William, 25
Peal, L. G., 64
Pearce, Ruberta, 38
Pearson, Abner, 65
Pearson, Arlene, 98
Pearson, Dr. Joseph, 6,7,16
Pearson, Sarah J. (Mrs. Joseph), 7,16
Pebble Beach Winter Show, 173
Peck, Mr. 163
Pedersen, Egon A., 5,114
Pedretti and Son, 195
Pember, Lyle, 120
Penn, William, 78
Pennington, Hannah (Boone), 40
Pennsylvania Assembly, State Convention, 40
Pennsylvania Historical Magazine, 39
Pentacostal Church, 130
Pepi, Al & family, 174
Pereira, M. E., Jr., 93
Perkins, Annie (Norris), 46,47
Perkins, Bill, 31
Perkins, D., 31
Perlowin, Hilda, 138
Peters, Arthur, 159
Peters, Edward T., 157,158
Peters, Evelyn, 157
Peters, Mary V., 86
Peters, Rose, 157
Peters, Sherm, 96
Petersdorf, Supt. Allan, 161
Petersen, Alton, 66,83
Petersen, Annie Catherine, 83
Petersen, Ane Margrethe (Thorup)(Mrs. Anton), 42,43
Petersen, Anton, 42
Petersen Associates, 130
Petersen, Eva (Pascoe), 66
Petersen, William, 49
Peter Thorup Shoe Shop, 42
Peterson, Adolph, 155
Peterson, Braddick T., 77,146,158,159
Peterson, Carrie (Trevitts), 77
Peterson, Chancey, 50
Peterson, Eliza P. (Shaw)(Mrs. John C.), 50
Peterson, Ella, 50
Peterson, G. Howard, 133,134,135,142
Peterson, Imogene (Mrs. O. W.), 105
Peterson, John C., 50
Peterson, Marion (Mrs. G. Howard), 133, 135,142

Peterson, O. W., 206
Peterson, Peter A., 83
Peterson Ranch, 91,132
Peterson Tractor, San Leandro, 133
Pettigrew, Honey, 86,87
Peyret, Betty Joan Peterson Lawton, 44
Peyret, Dorothy Edna (Smith)(Mrs. Joseph Gene II), 42,44,58
Peyret, Douglas Gene, 44
Peyret, Joseph Gene II, 44
Peyret, Joseph Gene III, 44
Peyret, Melinda Sue, 44
Peyret, Olive May (Hugi)(Mrs. Joseph Gene III), 44
Peyret, Roger Lee, 44
Phebus, Grant, 172
Phebus, Hilda (Mrs. James E.), 172
Phebus, James E., 172
Phebus, Mike, 172
Phebus, Susan (Cartwright)(Mrs. Mike), 172
"Phelena," 64
Philips, Jerry, 30
Phillips, Dorothy, 130
Phillips Petroleum Company, 139
Phillips, Shirley, 98
Phillis, 180,185
Phinney, Dellrose I., 94
Physicians and Surgeons, San Francisco, 129
Pickford, Mary, 130
Piedmont High School, 108,172,173,206
Pike, Fern (Osborn)(Mrs. George), 79,80
Pike, George, 80
Pike, George, Jr., 80
Pike, Ross, 80
Pingree, Jack, 194
Pittman, Anne Marie, 186
Pittman, Beth, 186
Pittman, Francis N., 186
Pittman, Jim, 186
Pittman, Kathy, 186
Pittman, Nancy E. (Weisend)(Mrs. F. N.), 186
Pitts, Charles M., 96
Pittsburg Blind Center, 93
Pizanis, Sadie, 101
Plum, Frank, 87
Plum, Vera, 87
Plunkett, Rev. Father Henry, 122,123
Podva, Adolphus Godfrey "Adolph," 53, 58
Podva, Adolphus LaMay, 52,53,155
Podva, Alfred McPherson, 53
Podva, Cecile (Bradley)(Mrs. A. L.), 52, 53,206
Podva, David, 53
Podva, David (son), 53
Podva, Deneice, 53
Podva, Diane (Cottrell)(Mrs. David), 53
Podva, Dolf, 53
Podva, Doreene, 53
Podva, Holly, 53
Podva, Janice (Timmons)(Mrs. Dolf), 53
Podva, Jessleen, 53
Podva Lane, 58
Podva, Margaret (Neilsen)(Mrs. Roger Oswill), 53
Podva, Mary Alma (McPherson)(Mrs. Adolph G.), 52,53,58,120
Podva, Mina, 53
Podva, Robert Randolph, 53,122
Podva, Roger, 53
Podva, Roger, 53
Podva, Roger LaMay, 53,79,202
Podva, Roger Oswill "Boo," 53
Podva, Ruby May (Oswill) "Tokie" (Mrs. Roger LaMay), 53,58,81,82,202
Pointer, Bonnie (Johnson)(Mrs. Jim), 78
Pointer, Jennifer, 78
Pointer, Rob, 78
Polk, Herbert, 120
Polk, Mrs. Herbert, 89
Polsley, Nancy (Mrs. Bill), 101
Pond, Nancy, 140

223

225

St. Paul's Catholic Church, San Pablo, 103
St. Perpetua's, Lafayette, 122
St. Raymond, 29
St. Timothy's Episcopal Church, 95,96, 101,117,193
Starkey, George, 31
Starkweather, Dick, 120
"Starlighters," the, 103
Star of the Sea Parochial School, San Francisco, 123
State Department of Parks and Recreation, 114
State Fair Board, 185
State Grangers' Association, 12
State Historical Resources Commission, 114
State Park Dept., 137
Statler, Samuel E., Jr., 96
Steak and Ale Restaurant, Danville, 94
Steele, Dwight, 138
Steger, Ardith (Osborn)(Mrs. Jack), 79, 80,187
Steger, Cynthia, 80
Steger, John C. (Jack), 80,93,187
Steger John, Jr. "Jay," 80
Stegman, David M., 97
Steinbach, Henry, 194
Steinhart Aquarium, San Francisco, 107
Steinmetz, August, 77
Steinmetz, Daisy (Rutherford)(Mrs. Henry H.), 76
Steinmetz, Florence (Trevitts)(Mrs. August), 77
Steinmetz, George E., 76
Steinmetz, Henry H., 76,199
Steinmetz, Henry H., Jr. "Hank," 76
Stelling, Catharine Louise, 146,158
Stelling, Charles Edward, 146,158,159
Stelling Property, 76
Stephens, Bud, 87
Sterling, Lord, 15
Sterne, J., 197
Stetson, Miss Evelyn, 154
Stevens, Audrey, 61
Stevens, Bertha, 61
Stevens, Charles O., 62
Stevens, Elmer, 61
Stevens, Leslie, 155
Stevens, Marguerite (Yager)(Mrs. Elmer), 60,61
Stevick, Alice M., 94
Stewart, George, 172
Steward, Harry C., 93
Stewart, Mary, 94
Stewart, Nita (Mrs. George), 172
Stewart, William E., 120,121,146,149,155, 157,203
Stieger, Evelyn, 87
Stieger, Paul, 87
Stillwell, Charles W., 85
Stillwell, Lou L., 85
Stitch and Time Yardage Shop, 78
Stock, Mrs. William E., 97
Stockton, Gertrud, 130
Stoddard, Alda, 51
Stoddard, John, 155
Stoddard Place, 72
Stolp, Addie Elmina (Harlan)(Mrs. Fred A.), 33,38
Stolp, Fred A., 33
Stone, A. L., 125
Stone, Abijah, 10
Stone, Agnes Lorena, 157,158
Stone, Albert Edward, 58
Stone, Col. Albert Ward, 9,10,11,197
Stone, Miss Alice, 45
Stone, Almas C., 11
Stone, Almas E., 10
Stone, Amos, 10
Stone, Bruce W., 10,85,197
Stone, Celestia Jenette, 10
Stone, Delia D., 10
Stone, Ebenezer, 10
Stone, Edward Albert, 58

Stone, Eleanor Thirza, 10
Stone, Elias, 10
Stone, Elizabeth, 10
Stone, Esther A., 10
Stone, Esther Almira, 10
Stone, Esther M., 11
Stone, George M., 10
Stone, Hannah, 10
Stone, Hannah, 10
Stone, Hannah Stratton, 10
Stone, Helen M., 10
"Stone House" (John Marsh's Home), 63, 80
Stone, Hugh B., 11
Stone, James, 73
Stone, Janet, 98
Stone, John, 10
Stone, John (son), 10
Stone, John B., 10
Stone, Lucia May, 58
Stone, Lucinda, 10
Stone, Lydia (Mrs. B. W.), 85
Stone, Lysander, 10
Stone, Mark S., 11
Stone, Martha Elizabeth, 58
Stone, Martha (Smith), 10
Stone, Matilda (Bird), 10
Stone, Millicent, 10
Stone, Myrtle M., 58
Stone, Neil, 135
Stone, Sally, 10
Stone, Sarah Jenette, 11
Stone, Squire Silas, 9,10,104,141,145,148 197,206
Stone, Susanna Ward, 10
Stone, Thirza, 10
Stone Valley School, 86,104,174
Stone, Welcome G., 10
Stone, William E., 11
Stone, William Z. "Willie" "Pap," 10,11, 58,85,91,117
Stonebreaker, Betty, 105
Stott, Mr. & Mrs. Al, 193
Stott, Mrs. Ethel, 84
Stover, Jacob, 39
Stover, Sarah (Boone)(Mrs. Jacob), 39
Stow, Bill, 205
Stow, Chadbourne, 146
Stow, Evelyn, 205
Stow, J. M., 4,125
Stow, Rufus, 205
Stow, Russell, 146,152
Straight, Frank, 85
Strange, Harry, 30
Stratton, Elias, 10
Stratton, Millicent (Frost), 10
Stratton, Prof., 171
Stroever, Lou, 173
Stroever, Marie, 173
Strong, Sharon Foster, 99
Strout, Wilmar, 132
Strutton, Bernice (Smith), 61,62
Strutton, Kathleen Ruth, 62
Strutton, Michael, 62
Strutton, Patrick, 62
Strutton, William Harmon, 62
Stuart, Miss M. Virginia, 143,159
Stuchell, Rev. John E., 120
Sturm Building, Walnut Creek, 166
Sturm, Joseph Albert, 166
Styles, Jimmy, 130
Sueyres, Irene, 159
Sullivan, Ellen, 72
Sullivan, John Graham, 72,120
Sumner, Barbara (Mrs. Charles), 101
Sumner, Judge Bruce, 180
Sun Valley Lumber Building, 185
Sunny Glen Center, San Ramon, 100
Sunny Read Realtor, 130
Sunset Nursery Company, 88,104,119, 169
"Sunshine Camp," 88
Supriano, James, 81
Supriano, Mrs. Yvette (Morris), 81

Surgart, Blanche (McCiel)(Mrs. C. A.), 159
Sussman, Angie, 140
Sussman, Joan, 87
Sutter, Capt. John, 186
Sutters Fort, 37,46
Swartz, Alice, 85
Swedberg, Marge, 87
Sweet, Bee (Mrs. Eugene), 172
Sweet, Eugene, 172
Swigers, David, 99
Sycamore Grammar School, 17,18,19,20, 21,22,24
Sycamore School District, 150
Symington, Rev. R. S., D.D., 119,120
Szybolski, Mollie (Mrs. Steven), 87

Taber, J. D., 9
Tacconi, Del, 101
Tagg, Beatrice "Bea" (Sweet)(Mrs. John A.), 172,173
Tagg Family Horses: "Sweet Rosie," "Prince Binary," "Piccadilly Paddy," "Abbey Road," "Merry Monarch," 173
Tagg, George, 172
Tagg, Dr. John A. "Jack," 172,173
Tagg, Myra, 172
Tagg, Scott, 172
Tagg, Terryl, 172,173
Takahashi, Dr., 111
Talaska, Chad, 53
Talaska, Gordon, 53
Talaska, Jonie Lee (Podva)(Mrs. Gordon), 53
Taliman, Ann (Lincoln)(Mrs. William), 39
Taliman, Benjamin, 39
Taliman, Dinah (Boone)(Mrs. Benjamin), 39
Taliman, William, 39
Tamalpais, Blythedale, Cascade Canyons, 92,196
Tamarack Manor, 16,98,170
Tantan and Stockholm, 106
Tao House, 72,89,135,136,137,138,180
Tarpley, Dolores, 49
Tarpley, John, 49
Tarpley, Lilas (Podva)(Mrs. William), 49
Tarpley, Naomi J. (Lynch)(Mrs. John), 49
Tarpley, William, 49
Tassajara Post Office, 82,83,154
Tassajara School, 15,152,154,179
Tassajara School District, 150
Taylor family, 187
Taylor, Dolores Ann, 187
Taylor, Marion "Mickey" (Mrs. R. H.), 187,188
Taylor, Norma, 138
Taylor, Richard H., 187
Taylor, Sandy, 87
Teed, Elizabeth Brown, 99
Tefft, Helen (Mrs. Stanley W.), 93,95,96
Temple, Fr. David, O.F.M., 141
Tennessee, 107
Tennis, Laura, 93
Terry, Rev. William Earl, 120
Tervelling, A. C., 30
Tevlin, Kay, 155
Thiessen, Brian D., 93
Thomas B. Bishop Company, 197
Thomas, Ed, 87,174
Thomas, Edith E., 94
Thomas, John B., 155
Thomas, Mrs. John B., 155
Thomas, Leslie, 159
Thomas, Leslie, 157
Thomas, Myrtle "Jim" (Mrs. Ed.), 174
Thompson, Bill, 124
Thompson, Cliff, 165
Thompson, Don, 124
Thompson Floor Company, Danville, 128

227

The San Ramon Valley Union High School yearbooks carried paid advertisements such as these. The first iss